THE QUEEN'S WARDS

William Cecil, Lord Burghley
Master of the Wards, 1561-1598

THE
QUEEN'S WARDS

Wardship and Marriage under Elizabeth I

by

JOEL HURSTFIELD

Department of History, University College London

with corrections by the author

FRANK CASS : LONDON

Published 1973 in Great Britain by
FRANK CASS AND COMPANY LIMITED
67 Great Russell Street, London WC1B 3BT

and in United States of America by
FRANK CASS AND COMPANY LIMITED
c/o International Scholarly Book Services, Inc.
P.O. Box 4347, Portland, Oregon 97208

Copyright © 1958, 1973 Joel Hurstfield

First edition   1958
Second edition   1973

ISBN 0 7146 2953 7

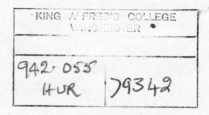
Printed in Great Britain by
Fletcher & Son Ltd, Norwich

TO
My Mother

Contents

	Page
Preface	xi
Introduction: Feudalism Declining	xiii

PART I: *The Revival of Royal Wardship*

Chapter
1. Feudalism Resurgent	3
2. Resistance	18

PART II: *Procedure*

3. Discovering a Wardship	33
4. Suitors for Wards	58
5. The Grant of a Ward	81
6. Private Wardship	96

PART III: *Wardship and Society*

7. Guardians and Wards	111
8. Marriage	130
9. Coming of Age	157
10. Corruption	181

PART IV: *The Rule of the Cecils*

11. Offices and Office Holders	221
12. Lord Burghley as Guardian	241
13. Lord Burghley as Master	260
14. The Vacant Mastership	283
15. Sir Robert Cecil	297

PART V: *Conclusion*

16. Wardship and the Government of England	329
Index	353

Illustrations

William Cecil, 1st Lord Burghley   *Frontispiece*
    By kind permission of Earl Beauchamp

                                                           Facing page

The Court of Wards and Liveries in Session   92
    By kind permission of the Duke of Richmond and Gordon

Sir William Paulet, 1st Marquess of Winchester   244
    By kind permission of the Society of Antiquaries

Robert Cecil, 1st Earl of Salisbury   245
    By kind permission of the Marquess of Salisbury

NOTE

To avoid confusion between father and son I have, save for exceptional reasons, referred throughout the book to William Cecil by his later title of Lord Burghley and to his son, Robert, as Cecil.

As many of the manuscripts used in writing this book are in the Public Record Office, the initials P.R.O. are not inserted before each reference. In all other cases, the title of the collection is given before the reference to the individual manuscript.

Preface

I BEGAN collecting material for this book a number of years ago and then set it on one side to write a volume on government policy during the Second World War. When I began again to think about wardship and marriage in the sixteenth century I found that my approach had been much changed by the experience of living under, and writing about, modern government controls. I have no particular use for historical parallels: they obscure at least as much as they reveal. But writing about the events of recent history thrusts forward new questions about the society of an earlier age; and some of these questions I have tried to answer.

This book is, therefore, not a study of the organisation of the Court of Wards: for that the reader is referred to Mr. H. E. Bell's valuable account of it. What I have examined is, first, the origins, as well as the personal and social consequences, of the revival of feudal wardship and marriage; and secondly, its effects upon government. In the concluding section, I have said something about the crucial struggle for power within the government circle of the late Elizabethan period, as reflected in the feudal context. In my story, William Cecil, Lord Burghley, and Robert Cecil his son, inevitably play a large part; and the profound contrast between the political conservatism of the father and the vigorous, imaginative approach of the son provides the central theme of these chapters. It is not possible here to explore it in its widest implications, but I propose in due course to write a full-scale biography of Robert Cecil as a minister of Elizabeth I and James I.

Anyone writing in London on Tudor history does so under a heavy debt of gratitude. My greatest is to Sir John Neale: master, colleague, friend. It was he who first suggested the subject to me and, as usual, was prodigal with his help, ending with a scholarly reading of the whole book in typescript.

Second only to this is my debt to his famous Tudor seminar—that commonwealth of students and scholars still flourishing on the free commerce of knowledge and ideas. My gratitude to individual members of it is acknowledged elsewhere in this book. Dr. G. R. Elton, Dr. E. Kerridge, Mr. Lawrence Stone, Professor R. H. Tawney and Professor H. R. Trevor-Roper all helped with material or comment on particular points; while three of my colleagues, Professor A. Cobban, Professor R. A. Humphreys and Miss Margaret Skerl, read critically sections of the book.

The Marquess of Salisbury generously made accessible to me his superb collection of manuscripts at Hatfield House, and gave permission also to reproduce his portrait of Robert Cecil. To Earl Beauchamp I owe the portrait of Lord Burghley, to the Society of Antiquaries that of the Marquess of Winchester, and to the Duke of Richmond and Gordon the picture of the Court of Wards in session. Mr. C. K. Adams, Director of the National Portrait Gallery, gave me most helpful advice about the illustrations.

To the officials of the Public Record Office, the British Museum, the Bodleian Library and the Institute of Historical Research I owe much for a variety of kindnesses; and Mrs. Audrey Munro has placed one more historian in her debt by her patient and skilful typing.

It is an admirable custom among historians to pay tribute to their wives for their help (and forbearance) while their books were being written. It may perhaps be understood that, if I have in any way succeeded in presenting a balanced view of an aspect of Tudor marriage, I thereby acknowledge another debt as well.

University College, London   J. H.
December 1957

The re-issue of this book has enabled me to enter corrections very kindly sent me by readers, as well as to add references to other works which have appeared since it was first published.

J.H.   1972

INTRODUCTION

Feudalism Declining

A READER of the books and sermons which were pouring from the presses in the sixteenth and early seventeenth centuries is struck by the vehement criticism of the current attitude to marriage. 'There was never such marrying in England as is now' was a typical outburst from Hugh Latimer in his sermon before Edward VI in 1549. 'O merciful God!' cried Henry Brinklow, a pamphleteer, 'what innumerable inconveniences come by selling of wards for marriage, for lucre of goods and lands.' To Sir Nicholas Bacon, minister of the young Elizabeth I, the treatment of wardship and marriage was 'a thing hitherto preposterously proceeding'; and, as the reign wore on, bitterness grew in intensity. Meanwhile, foreigners coming to this country rubbed their eyes to see the prevailing marriage customs and frankly said that no one but the phlegmatic English would tolerate them for one moment.

In the next reign the eminent lawyer and judge Sir Edward Coke (quoting Leviticus) would sternly warn the oppressors of the fatherless and the widows; Shakespeare would have some tart observations to make on the subject of marriage in *All's Well that Ends Well*; while a lesser playwright of his day, George Wilkins, earns at least a momentary rescue from oblivion because he devoted a whole play (otherwise of no merit whatsoever) to *The Miseries of Enforced Marriage*.

The institution of marriage, and the welfare of children, mirror—in every age—the social climate and institutions which surround them. If, for any reason, the social institutions are distorted, then the laws and bonds of marriage will tighten or loosen in response to the pressures they meet. Unfortunately, about the history of marriage in this country we know at present very little; and such documents as survive are often unrewarding and ambiguous. But it so happens that one aspect of it, the royal right of feudal marriage, was caught up in the politics and economics of the age and, as a result, led to the establishment of a special department of state to deal with it. This, in turn, threw up a vast, rich and diverse collection of material which casts a vivid, if narrow, shaft of light upon the Elizabethan way of life. It is with the nature and consequences of feudal marriage that this book is primarily concerned; but to the Elizabethans it was wholly bound up with their lives, liberty and property. For they were beginning to ask themselves whether they were free to live and work and marry as they pleased or were still governed by the harsh—and unyielding—feudal customs of the past. Within that context feudal marriage will be considered, but in the process we at once encounter a vigorous and profound conflict of opinion as to whether Tudor Englishmen were free at all.

In his delightful contemporary description of Elizabethan England the Reverend William Harrison pays high tribute to the liberty of Englishmen. He reminds us that 'by the especial grace of God and bounty of our princes . . . if any come hither from other realms, so soon as they set foot on land, they become so free in condition as their masters'. This was no isolated tribute to the English love of liberty. The diplomat Sir Thomas Smith, writing his description of the Commonwealth of England, in the 1560s while he was *en poste* in France, had described in no less glowing terms the freedom of the land. Perhaps distance lent enchantment to his view; but he had no doubt about the progress made by his fellow countrymen. Feudalism, a form of society which still flourished over a great part of Europe, involved, as he tells us, the use of bondmen. They were of two kinds: slaves bound in their person, by which he means slaves in the fullest sense of the word; and secondly villeins bound to the soil, men enjoying certain rights but rigidly governed by the unfree conditions under which they held their land. 'And of the first,' he goes on, 'I never knew any in the realm in my time; of the second so few there be that it is not almost worth the speaking.' They are famous passages and, with this and other evidence before them, it is not surprising that historians have tended to see the ending of feudalism more or less keep pace with the waning of the Middle Ages. Englishmen, at least, seemed with the passing centuries to move forward from an unfree to a free world. By the Tudor period, it would appear, the substance had gone out of feudalism though some of its shadows remained.[1]

But an English exile or a foreigner sometimes saw things with very different eyes. For example, Cardinal Allen, leader of Catholic Englishmen abroad, and the Spaniard, Count Olivares, were engaged, in about the year 1588, in drawing up a programme of reform which the victorious Armada should carry out, once the English navy and defences had been broken. They referred in the strongest possible terms to the manner in which Queen Elizabeth was exploiting her feudal rights, including her rights of marriage (which they regarded simply as a grossly inhuman method of taxation), and declared that 'it would be a most glorious way for a new prince to solemnize his entry if he were to abolish this evil tax'. They were not alone in their opinions. From the capital itself there came evidence to support them. 'Grave abuses have crept in,' wrote the Venetian Ambassador in London in his description of the feudal revenues in the early years of the next century, 'and the subjects cry aloud to heaven.' They 'do all they can to avoid such an inheritance, which brings a plague and ruin upon their estates!'[2]

How is this discrepancy in the opinions of Englishmen and foreigners to be explained? Did Englishmen live in freedom or were their lives darkened and distorted by the evils of decadent feudal institutions? Sir Thomas Smith, who so vigorously trumpets the liberty of England, himself provides the clue. If we read on in his *Commonwealth*, we find, after his tribute to the economic and social freedom of Englishmen, this remarkable sentence: 'No

---

[1] William Harrison, *The Description of England*, 1577, ed. Furnivall (1877), ii, 134; Sir Thomas Smith, *De Republica Anglorum*, ed. Alston (1906), p. 131.

[2] *Letters and Memorials of William, Cardinal Allen*, ed. T. F. Knox (1882), p. cvii; *Venet. Cal.*, 1603–7, p. 507.

man holdeth land simply free in England, but he or she that holdeth the crown of England : all others hold their land in fee'— that is to say as a tenant of somebody else. For outright ownership —in the modern sense—is quite unknown. Smith is in fact telling us that feudal bondage is virtually extinct, yet, in one and the same chapter, he says that no one holds his lands freely and all hold by some tenure of a superior lord, 'and he again of an higher lord, till it come to the Prince'. Here is a contradiction; but it is more apparent than real.

For the whole issue turns upon whether sixteenth-century England was or was not a feudal realm. This is not mere technical antiquarianism. The stigmata of long-forgotten tenures are to be seen on English society and politics from that day until this, and on the very constitution under which we live. The tenures also provided the framework for wardship and marriage, for these royal rights could derive only from the way in which a tenant held his land from the crown or some other lord. So, because of the importance of feudal marriage in Elizabethan society, we must attempt a brief definition of our terms.

Feudalism, like socialism and capitalism, is not an exact and scientific expression. There are almost as many definitions of these forms of society as there are writers about them. Although it is the fashion to speak of the capitalist system, the socialist system, the feudal system, the very use of the word system begs the question. It is most unlikely that the loose, diverse, many-sided relationships of medieval England could for one moment have seemed to contemporaries to bear any resemblance to what has since been described as a feudal system. Indeed, people only began to examine feudalism as a concept when the forms of feudalism were outliving its practices. Before that, only technical studies had appeared. Lawyers such as Glanville in the twelfth century and Bracton in the thirteenth had been writing about the feudal processes while they were still living elements in their daily life. But the discussions of feudalism as a system, as a conception of politics, society and law came later. It belonged to the problems of a different age.

Certainly, by the second half of the fifteenth century feudalism was acquiring an almost scientific meaning which might have puzzled the administrators of feudalism in its heyday. From now onwards there was a continuous stream of analysis and commentary on feudal institutions. Statesmen, lawyers, historians were searching for the basic principles underlying the inherited institutions of Tudor and Stuart England. If some of their history was fanciful—and the farther they got from origins, the greater rein they gave to their imagination—they were at least trying to analyse the framework of their society.

With the acerbities of their debate we are not here concerned; but it is evident from their writings that many of the virtues of feudalism—as of so many other social institutions—lay in the eye of the beholder. We shall see elsewhere in this volume some examples of a debate which has lasted over the centuries and can still, in favourable circumstances, awaken old battles amongst modern historians. For there are innumerable ways of defining feudalism though none can do justice to its complexity. In this context we must be content with a brief definition which, if it blurs the innumerable distinctions within the whole, at least makes a bid to grasp at its essence.

Feudalism, one may say, is the name given by lawyers and historians to a form of society based on land tenure, the relationship between a man and his overlord. In other words, economic life, politics, social customs and laws derived from the conditions under which a man held his land. The characteristic unit of administration was the manor. The Norman official of the eleventh century believed—or pretended to believe—that there was *nulle terre sans seigneur*—no land without a lord, for the Conqueror's men after 1066 could not imagine anyone possessing land without at the same time owing service to some lord. But—in theory at least—a man's lord held the land in turn from some overlord. So the chain went on, with the king holding the last link. The final stage was with God: for the king held his land from no man.

This concept bridged the five centuries between William the

Conqueror's civil servant and the Tudor Sir Thomas Smith, although in their hearts both Norman and Tudor must have known that the general theory was in practice riddled with exceptions. The manner of settling a particular man's tenure—of determining from whom he held the land and under what conditions—was to summon a local jury who, from their knowledge and the communal memory, would declare what the tenure was. But local juries knew also a thing or two about how to ameliorate harsh theory with neighbourly practice.

A man's title to land depended, then, upon the kind of service he owed for it. Until quite recently, it was the practice to speak of the whole feudal community as though it were divided roughly into three classes. The first group, it was said, held their land in return for prayer: *oratores*—men who prayed. But the service which the church rendered the state came to have a far wider meaning than this. Crown and baron and merchant had made grants and bequests to the church, in return for which the church had usually—though not always—served them well. Administration, education, the welfare services and much more were given by bishop and abbot, friar and priest, in the medieval centuries before the welfare church began to give up its duties to what would in time become the welfare state.

The second group held their land in return for agricultural service—so many days' labour in the fields of their lord. They were the *laboratores*—the men who worked; and this relationship between peasant and lord was the essence of feudalism.

Finally, there were those who held in return for military service —*bellatores*, wagers of war—men who had sworn to fight so many days in the field for the lord from whom they held their land. If for this purpose their overlord was the king, they held by a military tenure *in capite*—in chief.

This method of class-division is now somewhat discredited. It is quite clear that there were not simply these three classes in the medieval world: those who prayed, laboured, or fought. Trader, wage labourer, industralist cannot be fitted into these groupings. Rigid theory was constantly being stretched into elastic practice.

Yet it was still the case that, over a large part of England, tenure dominated the economic, political and social life of the community. Feudal custom had the last word.

No less important, writers in the sixteenth and seventeenth centuries, when they tried to explain—or explain away—feudal wardship and marriage, believed them to have originated in this somewhat unhistoric division of society. In many ways they were wrong; but their opposition to—or defence of—feudal marriage was governed by this vision of the past. So one must, at least for the time being, think of feudal society as they thought of it.

For to them it seemed that two of these three principal classes had passed, or were passing, out of the feudal order. First the churchmen. The land held by the church remained in its possession until the Reformation. Then, by a series of confiscatory acts, unparalleled until our own day, the laity resumed ownership of the pious gifts it had made over the centuries. Monasteries, chantry lands, gild endowments, all these during the 1540s, the crucial decade of Tudor history, passed from the church to the state. Only the bishops' lands remained, to tempt for a long time the zeal and the avarice of the reformers. The English Reformation was a turning point in our economic and feudal history no less than in our religious history. The *oratores* dropped out of the feudal scheme. The results may or may not have been socially catastrophic: the process by which the change was accomplished is simple enough to follow.

Less simple to understand is what was happening to the laymen —villeins, cottars, and the rest—who held their land in return for their labour. These men, it is well known, enjoyed varying degrees of liberty and prosperity. Some were substantial farmers; others scraped a wretched existence from the reluctant soil. Many of them bore the marks of their servitude in their daily lives; they could not leave the manor, change their work, marry their children, without the consent of their lord. About the varying fortunes of the manorial community in the late medieval centuries a whole discordant literature has grown up and many questions still remain unsolved.

In the view of some historians, the Black Death of the fourteenth century, the series of visitations which may have wiped out a third of the population of Europe, finally made clear that the old feudal relationship was no longer viable. The population fell, labour was scarce. We who live in one of those rare intervals in modern history when full employment prevails can at least sense how at such times the traditional social relations can be dissolved. With labour at a premium it could often dictate the terms of its labour—which might include freedom. Not the Black Death alone but population changes in the fourteenth and fifteenth centuries, which we still do not wholly understand, spelt the end of agricultural feudalism.

To other historians this is a false and over-simplified picture. The Black Death, they admit, shook the social and economic framework of the medieval manor but, not long after the disease had run its course, medieval life reverted to its traditional forms, at least for a time. This controversy is as yet unresolved. What is less in dispute, however, is that in England, by the fifteenth century, the older manorial tenure was changing its shape and name. For one reason or another labour was short; and the descendant of the medieval villein was often escaping from the manor of his birth to the welcoming and more favourable conditions of another manor or to the growing textile industries of both the town and the countryside. But many stayed in the place of their birth on new conditions, which meant that they often bought their personal freedom, though some measure of economic bondage remained. In other words, a man might convert his relationship from a villein tenure, under which he held by service, to a copyhold tenure under which he held by rent. He became a copyholder, a curious term which meant simply that he had a copy of the entry on the manorial court roll which recorded the change in his status. In theory the relationship between a villein and his lord remained in force; in effect it was becoming the relationship between a tenant and his landlord. The villein was well on the way to becoming a leaseholder, if he was not already there. One day he might become a Tudor yeoman.

But villeinage was not yet extinct; and this gave rise to a curious practice in Elizabethan England. If we examine the backs of the Tudor patent rolls, where commissions of appointment are inscribed, we find a number of commissions specifically authorising certain courtiers and others to 'manumit' bondmen, that is, sell them their liberty. We notice also the relatively high price sometimes charged for their freedom, as much as a third part of their lands. These commissions may perhaps be used as a commentary upon a righteous, if ambiguous, passage of Sir Thomas Smith when he tells us that Englishmen hate feudalism and seek to end it, because it conflicts with their Christian conscience. This extraordinary situation takes on the element of farce when we find that Sir Henry Lee obtained such a commission, in the seventeenth year of Elizabeth I, in which it was stated that he could compulsorily enfranchise bondmen. Anyone who refused his manumission, that is to say, who refused to buy his freedom, was to have his land seized. The device is, of course, transparent. Bondage had lost its agricultural, and probably its social, significance; but it had gained an irrelevant monetary significance. When, in 1586, Lord Stafford was seeking to reclaim the then Mayor of Bristol as an escaped villein, still in bondage to the manor, it is unlikely that Stafford hoped for much in the way of agricultural labour from this prosperous city businessman. But, on the other hand, he might be compelled to buy his liberty—at the appropriate price. In other words bondage was by now, as one historian puts it, 'a pretext for extortion'. In effect the high-sounding manumission of bondmen was merely one of a number of minor rackets flourishing in Tudor England.[1]

The manumission of bondmen was not a game that they played solely on the royal estates. It was going on all over England and was attractive to king and lord alike. For a bondman set free must sacrifice part of his property to gain his freedom.

By the middle of the sixteenth century perhaps not more than

---

[1] I. S. Leadam, 'The Last Days of Bondage in England' (*L.Q.R.*, ix, 348–65); E. P. Cheyney, 'The Disappearance of English Serfdom' (*E.H.R.*, xv, 20–37); A. Savine, 'Bondmen under the Tudors' (*T.R. Hist. S.*, 2nd. ser., xvii, 235–89).

one per cent. of Englishmen were bondmen, and even these were on the road to freedom. Bondage still had a nuisance value, and a monetary value, but very little else. At first sight one might almost say that the practices and profits of feudalism were rapidly becoming a thing of the past. If land had been held only by ecclesiastical service or in return for labour, this judgement would be sound; and one brief chapter would here suffice to record the demise of medieval feudalism. But, as we have seen, throughout the Middle Ages land had also been held in return for military service, which itself involved a whole series of consequential feudal dues. This story was far from over. Military feudalism was changing its shape and content, but it had remarkable powers of recovery. Under the Tudors it was once again to reach deeply into the society and politics of the age. Upon it they would erect a system of feudal marriage which would arouse the astonishment of Europe.

I

THE REVIVAL OF
ROYAL WARDSHIP

When this bill came first amongst the Commons, Lord! how the ignorant persons were grieved and how shamefully they spake of the bill!

Hall's *Chronicle*,
referring to the wardship bill of 1532

I

Feudalism Resurgent

I T may be that, before even the first Norman landed in England, military feudalism, tenure by knight-service as it was called, was leaving its mark upon the countryside. Whether the Normans found something upon which they built, or transplanted alien institutions upon English soil, has long been hotly debated by medieval historians; but the dust and heat of that controversy need not delay us here. What is beyond doubt is that the Normans and their successors granted out large tracts of land in return for military service. In turn the great barons, the tenants-in-chief of the crown, transmitted on like conditions their military obligations to their own tenants. With the grant of the land, held by knight-service, went the obligation of the tenant to serve his lord for forty days in the field.

But in an age of war and plague and sudden death it frequently happened that the tenant died leaving as heir a child, who was manifestly unable to render the appropriate military service. What was the lord to do but take back the land temporarily and use it, if he wished, to obtain military service from someone else? That was what was meant by the expression that the land had passed into wardship. And with the land went the child. The lord could reasonably claim that he should control the upbringing of the minor in order to ensure efficient and loyal service when he came of age. In the language of the time, the lord obtained the wardship of the body. If the heir were female, the lord went further and claimed the right of consent to her choice of husband; otherwise, if she married without regard to her lord's interests, she might choose a husband who was either incapable of performing the necessary services or, for other reasons, *persona ingrata* to the lord. He might indeed wage war on the man who was now his lord. Wardship of the 'body' and the 'land' we know to have existed in Norman times. Sir Edward Coke, writing in the seventeenth century, asserted indeed that they could be traced back to the time of Alfred the Great; but Coke was a better lawyer than historian, and medieval scholars of today are generally reluctant to accompany him all that way.[1]

From 1066 onwards there is a gradual, and sometimes imperceptible, expansion of the authority of the lord over minor heirs. In the time of their origin the feudal incidents rested securely upon the mutual obligations, between lord and tenant, which gave them birth. But soon they began to lose their original character as a means of protecting the legitimate interests of the lord. They came to be looked upon as a considerable, if irregular, source of revenue. An impoverished baron or king—for that matter any baron or king—might tear the feudal customs out of their context, if there was money to be made in the process. So they extended their reach and tightened their grasp. Less than fifty years after the Norman conquest the crown was already being challenged on account of the extension of its demands in these matters. By the second half of the twelfth century, the overlord's logical right of *consent* had become the *control* of the marriage of minor heirs if female; that is, he now had the right to choose husbands for them. Within two generations it appeared that the lord enjoyed in principle the same powers over male as over female heirs. By now, in effect, the right of wardship had extended to the wardship *and marriage* in the fullest sense of the term. The logical right to withhold consent had by the middle of the thirteenth century become the less defensible right to *choose* whom the ward should marry.[2]

Worse was to follow. If the overlord possessed these rights, then he was fully at liberty to dispose of them if he wished—at a

---

1 Coke, *First Instit.*, ii, sect. 103.
2 Bracton, *De Legibus*, ii, c. 38.

price. That is precisely what he did. And since the crown was the chief overlord in the realm, its opportunities for joining in the business were greater than any man's. So by a gradual, but by no means unconscious, process the feudal incidents had ceased to be military safeguards and had become articles of trade. As early as the reign of Henry I, in the first half of the twelfth century, there is evidence that the king was selling wardships and marriages. In Henry II's reign these sales were increasing. By the reign of John, at the beginning of the thirteenth century, 'when few other articles were being bought and sold on a large scale' the selling of wardships had developed into a veritable 'speculative traffic'. By the middle of the century the sales of wardships were frequent and the revenue considerable. The lords and, *par excellence*, the king, were exercising their right of wardship not primarily to maintain the feudal contract and safeguard their military strength, but to increase their revenue.[1]

By now, indeed, wardship and marriage were 'valuable proprietary rights. They were chattels which could be sold, which could be bequeathed, which would pass to the guardian's executors and administrators.' Their principal value lay in the fact that they were 'welcome but temporary windfalls'. In short, these feudal dues were already, in effect, a tax: a land tax which was distorted, anachronistic, irregular and inefficient, but a land tax *faute de mieux*.[2]

At this stage, then, feudal wardship had lost for ever its chief moral justification. So it became possible to offer some very odd arguments in its defence. Thus, the Speaker of the House of Commons, in a debate in 1404, averred that 'the king had wardships of all lands of the nobility, and these wardships and customs were granted originally to cover the cost of wars, so that the country might not be subject to taxation'.[3] Bad history but sound economics! Meanwhile the crown was stretching its rights to the full. Already in 1215 the complaints against their misuse

1 F. M. Stenton, *The First Century of English Feudalism* (Oxford, 1932), p. 219; Pollock and Maitland, *History of English Law* (Cambridge, 1911), ii, 117.

2 W. S. Holdsworth, *History of English Law* (1923), iii, 64; F. M. Powicke, *King Henry III and the Lord Edward* (Oxford, 1947), i, 105.

3 Quoted in J. H. Wylie, *History of England under Henry IV* (1884), i, 407.

were sufficiently vigorous to claim separate clauses in Magna Carta. But in spite of the increasingly extensive demands of the crown, there was no great outburst against feudal wardship during the medieval period. Later, amongst historians, the solitary voice of Freeman spoke of the evils of wardship that weighed heavily upon the baronage. Most other historians rejected this view: 'To speak of the English lords as groaning under the burdens of wardship and marriage is hardly permissible; we do not hear their groans.'[1] Even so, Magna Carta—which has become so much bound up with our national liberties, but which began life in defence of the class interests of the baronage—sought in vain to call a halt to the expanding demands of the king in wardship and marriage. But if tenants-in-chief were at all acquiescent when faced with these feudal claims, it must be remembered that the barons enjoyed, in relation to their own tenants, rights similar to those exercised by the king over them. Part of what the barons lost on the swings as tenants, they gained on the roundabouts as lords. This single fact, more than anything else, may have enabled feudal wardship to survive for centuries after it had outlived its original usefulness. But while the barons as a class made profits in their capacity of lords and losses in their capacity of tenants-in-chief,.the king was the supreme gainer by these incidents: the heavy burden of wardship could not fall upon him because he held his land from no earthly being.

But if the day should ever come when the barons' profits were reduced almost to vanishing point, while the royal rights survived both to mulct and to mock them, then the whole situation would change. Change it did. If only one acre were held of the crown by knight-service in chief, the lengthening arm of his officials reached out to take the feudal dues, in most cases quite regardless of other men's claims. This was 'prerogative wardship' and, like the prerogative itself, it yielded to no man. So, in practice, the barons' profits from feudal wardship dwindled while the king's grew at their expense. We must bear in mind this shifting balance as between the king and the other lords when we try to

[1] Pollock and Maitland, *op. cit.*, i, 324.

account for the increasing hostility to feudal wardship which the sixteenth and seventeenth centuries were to witness.[1]

Meanwhile, during the later Middle Ages, as society became less feudal in content, wardship in its new and distorted form had travelled far from its original and inherent purposes. It had become simply a means of making money: no more but no less. Time had shown up the feudal claims for the anachronisms they were; but they were a long way from extinction. Administrative weakness, it is true, had often limited the royal profits. Civil war had broken the continuity of feudal claims. Widespread concealment—practised from generation to generation—had corroded this great revenue source. But it needed only a parsimonious despot, and a few tortuous-minded and industrious lawyers, to resurrect some of the boldest claims of the crown and to seize the opportunity to which some of his predecessors had pointed the way.

That is exactly what happened at the beginning of the sixteenth century. On the morrow of his victory at Bosworth Field, the first of the Tudors took good measure of what his feudal rights could be made to yield. In politics he was essentially anti-feudal and set about completing the destruction of the political and economic powers of his aristocratic tenants-in-chief. But the feudal *incidents*, by contrast, still had a useful role to play.

So Henry VII set to work reviving and perpetuating his feudal rights. The searching out of 'concealed' wardships was going on in the first year of his rule, and the efforts of Empson, Dudley, and his other ministers cast a wide net over the country. When in 1503 Henry VII appointed Sir John Hussey to take charge of the royal wardships, it was a characteristic way of serving notice that his feudal claims were something to be reckoned with. Here is the story of the manumission of bondmen, which we told in the Introduction, re-enacted on a grander scale. An antiquated and moribund institution was called back to life for a totally irrelevant purpose: revenue.[2]

---

[1] *Statutes of the Realm*, i, 106, 226.
[2] Cf. W. C. Richardson, *Tudor Chamber Administration, 1485–1547* (Baton Rouge, 1952), pp. 166–75, 192–214.

In 1504 a curious measure on the part of the king gave the broadest hint of what he had in mind. He approached the House of Commons, as he was entitled to, for two feudal 'aids': one was *pour fille marier* and the other *pour faire fils chevalier*. These were the well-known contributions that a king might ask from his vassals towards the cost of marrying his eldest daughter and knighting his eldest son. The king of course needed money, and parliament on this occasion appears to have been willing to grant it. Yet it was an odd way to go about the business. His daughter, it is true, was about to marry the king of Scotland but his eldest son had been knighted fifteen years before and had been dead for two years![1]

What was behind this strange transaction? The ceremonial knighting of a prince had, of course, little to do with Henry's manoeuvre. First he wanted money. But more important than the money that he hoped to get was the official record of the land tenures; for the grant of these aids had to be accompanied by a statement of the lands his tenants held of him in chief. Here was a magnificent opportunity to obtain an up-to-date register of his tenants-in-chief, a record which would repay earnest study by a succession of impoverished kings in search of wardships, marriages, and other feudal dues. The Commons saw through the transparent device. They resisted the feudal aid and obliged the king 'in recompense and satisfaction' to accept £40,000 instead. They frankly gave as their reason that they wanted to be spared 'the great unquietness for the search, and non-knowledge of their several tenures'. They preferred to leave all that in a decent obscurity. So although the king's feudal officials would go on searching out the feudal tenures, they would do so without the help of his loyal Commons.

The death of Henry VII in 1509, and the accession of a young and popular king, offered the illusory prospect of a decline in these charges. 'All England is in ecstasies,' wrote a delighted English peer, 'extortion is put down. Liberty is the order of the day.' The principal instruments of his father's feudal policy,

---

[1] *Prerogativa Regis*, ed. S. E. Thorne (1949), pp. xx–xxi.

Empson and Dudley, were broken by Henry VIII; and one of his first statutes aimed at ensuring that over-zealous officials should moderate their zeal and make up for it with their honesty. Another statute ordered redress for those who had been the victims of false statements establishing a feudal tenure. A few years later it was enacted that a special exemption from the claims of royal wardship should be given to the heirs of men killed in the wars. In this, at least, the capricious and impecunious king kept his word, or his ministers kept it for him. In the last year of the reign, Elizabeth Basforth lost her husband fighting for his king in Scotland; and her debt to the Court of Wards amounting to £48. 6s. 3d. was cancelled by royal warrant.[1]

But it was only the excesses of the former policy which were attacked. The efforts to organise and increase the income from wardship continued unabated and gathered momentum in the second half of the reign. An act of 1512 confirmed the existing financial arrangements for collecting certain revenues, including the feudal profits, and the searching out of concealed wardships continued unchecked.[2] New and important officials appeared on the scene. There was from now on an unbroken succession of masters of wards; and their local officials, the feodaries in the shires, were implementing the orders they received from the office of wards at Westminster as well as transmitting to London their detailed surveys of land. The records of this period moreover are part of a continuous series which underwent no fundamental change with the formal establishment of the Court of Wards in the last years of the reign. The year 1540, when the Court was erected, saw no notable breach in the records of the Office of Wards and a good deal of its procedure remained unchanged.

But why, it may be asked, was it necessary to establish a Court of Wards at all? The explanation is to be found in the crucial developments of the years 1535-40, for in these years the dissolution of the monasteries suddenly opened up the feudal prospects of the crown in a startling and unexpected manner.

---

[1] E. Erbach, *Tudor Artists* (1954), p. 4; I Hen. VIII, cc. 8, 12; 3 Hen. VIII, c.4; *L.P.*, xxi, pt. i, p. 475.   [2] 3 Hen. VIII, c.23.

It used to be believed that Henry VIII in his supreme folly either gave away, or sold at ridiculously low rates, the monastic lands he seized during the last stages of his Reformation. It used also to be believed that, in his supreme wisdom, Henry enriched the English landed and commercial classes with this stolen property so that they would become a vested interest in the new order, eager to sustain and safeguard the Reformation to which they were now committed. We do not give much nowadays for this legend which makes Henry's monastic policy either too foolish or too clever by half. The truth seems much simpler than that.

The unassuageable appetites of war, diplomacy, administration and extravagance drained the royal exchequer. At the same time, the unwillingness of the House of Commons to satisfy more than fractionally the royal demand for money forced Henry to seek the highest price for the great mass of land which had now come his way. Courtiers, officials and others did sometimes benefit from the mercurial generosity of a hard-headed king; and more than one great and enclosed estate of today recalls the spasmodic bounty of Henry Tudor. But gifts were the exception, not the general rule. There was only one brief period, during the minority of Edward VI, in the middle of the sixteenth century, when a corrupt court-circle reaped a golden harvest at the expense of a weak boy, sick unto death. But, under Henry VIII, for the overwhelming majority of sales, each acre of land was surveyed, valued, and recorded before being disposed of.

The official valuation tended to be lower than the market price, and lower than the price at which the land was subsequently re-sold; but it was as high as the traditional methods of estimation would allow. No less important, there were other charges to which the purchaser became liable. He was normally obliged to pay an annual rent and, more important still, in the vast majority of cases the recipient was required to hold his lands by knight-service of the crown. Here was a bold and cunning step; and a costly one from the point of view of the purchasers. Knight-service meant little or nothing now except wardship and marriage; in this, and in this alone, lay the reason for fastening an old tenure to a modern land transaction. If we accept the estimate that Henry VIII sold church lands to the value of £90,000 a year, a significant increase in the revenue from wardship could be anticipated.[1] The day came when the landed classes awoke to the predicament to which their eager purchases had brought them; and they began to offer resistance to the crown's policy. But they could not undo the damage that had already been done. The officials selling on behalf of the crown might well have uttered the warning: *caveat emptor!*

It was, of course, quite fantastic to call up a Norman system of government for so totally irrelevant a purpose as the sale of monastic lands, nearly five centuries after the Norman army had taken England by force. But here was an opportunity not to be missed. Tudor ministers were faced with a tough financial problem which grew more grave each day. They could not afford to trouble their minds with the fact that monastic lands had nothing to do with knight-service and that knight-service had nothing to do with the military conditions of Tudor England. They took a notion which lay to hand and made of it something rich and strange: especially rich. The unwilling knights of Tudor England had nothing in common with the knights in armour of the Norman hosts. But their sons and grandsons would have to twist and turn to escape from the heavy charges of wardship and marriage. So the dire necessities of a needy and extravagant king imposed this disguised rental—in human welfare as well as money —upon the third and fourth generation of those who had seized monastic lands. There is almost an Old Testament concept of retribution in the way the descendants of Henry VIII inflicted suffering upon the descendants of those who had bought up the confiscated lands of the church.

All this formed part of a larger problem. The king's rights— and not least his financial rights—must be upheld, revived, extended, defined. In spite of his continually having to sell land to meet current expenditure, he was still the greatest landlord in the realm. And to be a landlord was to be a feudal lord. But the full

[1] H. A. L. Fisher, *The Political History of England, 1485-1547* (1919), p. 500.

measure of his feudal rights was, naturally enough, difficult to discover and establish. For example, it was notorious that tenants bought and sold land in such a way as to disguise both its ownership and its tenure. Sometimes the land passed from hand to hand until the name of its lord and the tenure by knight-service had passed beyond the memory of man. Now the king struck hard at these practices. A statute of 1536 required all land transfers, within six months of their being completed, to be enrolled in a court of record at Westminster or at the county sessions. By these means the crown intended at least to keep itself informed of changes in tenancy, whether collusive or not. The measure was reinforced by a statute of 1543 under which false transfers, designed to defraud the king of his feudal dues, were declared invalid. But of far greater importance than these enactments were the Statute of Uses of 1536, the Statute of Wills of 1540, and the statute establishing the Court of Wards, passed in the same year.[1]

With the Statute of Uses we come upon one of the most important—and most obscure—enactments in English history. It enjoys amongst sixteenth-century historians the same unenviable position that the Schleswig-Holstein question occupies amongst historians of the nineteenth. For it has darkened counsel during the four centuries which have elapsed since its passage. Yet it has served many changing purposes, some of them very far from the intention of its first architect. *His* purpose was simple enough. Henry VIII wanted to destroy the innumerable trusts which were being fabricated for no other reason than to deprive him of his feudal profits. These profits, as we have seen, were mainly inheritance taxes. They could therefore only arise when the tenant died and left behind him an heir to take over the lands. Clearly, then, if the tenant did not die the profits could not arise. But life is short—and it was a good deal shorter in the Tudor period than today, especially for those who took up politics as a career. Yet, if the tenant could not hope for immortality, there was available a device to create the illusion of immortality. In short, if he trans-

[1] 27 Hen. VIII, c. 16; 34 and 35 Hen. VIII, c. 20; 27 Hen. VIII, c. 10; 32 Hen. VIII, cc. 1, 46.

ferred his land to a corporation of people—executed a *use* as it was called—and if this corporation could perpetuate its life by replacing dead members, then the inheritance dues might never fall to the king. For the corporate heir never died. Since also the trust undertook to give back the full enjoyment of the land to the tenant, and his heirs and successors, then they had all the benefits of land-holding without the feudal dues which kept it company.[1]

Against these growing practices Henry VIII was bound to strike hard. He must somehow force the man who was the owner, in fact though not in theory, to assume the full responsibility of his lands. Clearly, he saw that such a step would encounter bitter resistance from the landed classes as well as from the lawyers, whose services in fabricating complicated conveyances to *use* were no doubt well remunerated. In 1529 Henry VIII tried to cancel the effect of the *use*. The landowning classes were solidly against him and he failed. In 1532 he tried again. In that year he sought once more, by act of parliament, to fasten upon his tenants their feudal responsibilities, tried to break through the barrier of the *use* behind which they were sheltered in comfort and obscurity. The purpose of the bill they clearly recognised: the 'wardships bill' they called it. And they fought it tooth and nail. 'When this bill came first among the Commons,' wrote the chronicler Hall, 'Lord! how the ignorant persons were grieved and how shamefully they spake of the bill.'[2]

So Henry perforce used pressure and concession in his dealings with the Commons, and finally he succeeded in dividing the forces against him. By one means or another—promise and threat—he was able to force the Statute of Uses through parliament in 1536. In the same year he proposed to safeguard the fruits of his victory by the statute requiring the enrolment of land transfers, which we have already noted.[3]

As the law now stood the victory was complete. The king had re-established his feudal claims and had, at least in theory,

1 Cf. Holdsworth, *op. cit.*, iv, 407-80.
2 E. Hall, *Chronicle* (1809 ed.), p. 785.
3 F. W. Maitland, *Equity* (Cambridge, 1936), pp. 34-42; Holdsworth, *op. cit.*, iv, 450-61. See also E. W. Ives, 'The genesis of the Statute of Uses', (*E. H. R.* cccxxv, 673-697).

destroyed the power of his tenants to evade any part of the dues accruing to him by conveying their land—in theory—away from their heirs. The stifling effect of this legislation, particularly at a time when such vast areas of monastic land were about to be sold and re-sold, showed what a tremendous victory he had won.

The hostility to the extreme powers now vested by the statute in the crown was widespread. For example, hatred of it won it a place amongst the grievances of those who took part in the Pilgrimage of Grace in 1536. But the king struck again: this time with the full weight of his military power. Then, after the legal victory, embodied in the statute, and the military victory against the rebels, the government was able to lighten the burdens imposed by the measure of 1536. The Statute of Wills of 1540 restored to those who did not hold by military service the right to dispose of all their land as they thought fit; those who held by knight-service were allowed freely to dispose of two-thirds of their lands—that is, convey them out of wardship—but one-third had to descend to the legal heir. In the case of a minor, therefore, only one-third of the land might pass into wardship, not the whole estate.[1]

Here were notable concessions; but the king's powers were still extensive. Hence we find that lawyers were already at work upon various schemes for evading the effect of the Statute of Uses. In 1540, a 'remembrance' prepared for the king drew attention to the loss of wardships 'by means of wills'. But although the reform was not watertight, the king had reasserted his legal powers by the statute of 1536 and had overcome some of the consequences of the conveyances of use. The Statute of Wills went part of the way towards establishing a free market in land. But as long as tenure by knight-service remained, this amount of freedom was not enough. Meanwhile the concession of 1540 coincided with the erection of the Court of Wards to exercise a full surveillance over the king's feudal rights.[2]

Thus economic and legal developments during the preceding

---

[1] 32 Hen. VIII, c. 1.
[2] *L.P.*, xv, no. 439; see also no. 1028.

five years revealed to the government both the need and the occasion to erect an institution capable of taking full advantage of the opportunities now at hand. It was clearly doubtful whether such machinery as existed in the Exchequer and the Office of Wards could sustain the increased burden of work or was possessed of sufficient power and prestige to carry the king's claim through the realm. The medieval Exchequer had amazing powers of survival and it was long to outlast the Tudors, but it was notoriously defective in handling modern financial problems. The Mastership of the Wards had itself been created at the beginning of the sixteenth century so that the crown's control of this important source of revenue might be immediate and more effective. Henry VII and Henry VIII had tried somehow or other to short-circuit the activities of the Exchequer by the creation of new financial and legal organs. In particular, during the 1530s the augmented powers of the crown in ecclesiastical matters brought in their train important financial responsibilities which could only be assumed through the media of special departments. As part of this process of administrative specialisation the functions of the Master of the Wards were taken over by the Court of Wards, established by statute in 1540.[1]

This general programme of modernising existing institutions, and the anticipated rise in the revenue from wards, would alone have justified the establishment of a special court. But apart from all this, the manifest weakness of the Office of Wards not unexpectedly stimulated Henry's minister, Thomas Cromwell, to formulate what proved to be the final administrative reform of his career.

During the last years of his life, when he stood at the crest of his power, he was, as the king's leading official, intimately concerned with stretching the crown revenues to meet its rapidly mounting expenditure. He was connected with the dissolution of the monasteries and the Statute of Uses. He was no less closely connected with plans for reforming the Office of Wards; and a number of his 'remembrances' during this period were concerned

[1] 32 Hen. VIII, c. 46.

with wards and related matters. He was convinced that the existing machinery stood badly in need of reform and was leading to severe losses to the crown. It was a sound judgement, and he was not alone in his opinion.[1]

So the Court of Wards was called into being to serve a number of purposes. It was needed, in the first place, because the economic and social changes arising from the dissolution of the monasteries brought in their train the prospect of a considerable increase in the feudal dues, if only the official organisation proved equal to the opportunities. It was created also to raise the stature of the Master and his officials and to make possible the concentration of power in one office and in the person of one minister. Hitherto the Office of Wards had lacked both the prestige and the information to discover and lay claim to the full number of wardships and other feudal payments which had fallen due to the crown. The steep rise in the number of wardships after 1540 is a further proof of the original deficiencies in administration. In addition, the act was designed to make the Master a judge no less than an administrator, and thereby to end the diffusion of legal authority by which the trial of causes was submitted to various commissions of law officers and other servants of the crown. After 1540 the Master, aided by his own law officer, the Attorney of the Wards, and with the help of judges where necessary, was ready to deal more directly and authoritatively with the evasions, collusions and concealments which were taking so heavy a toll from the crown revenues. In all these aspects, also, the creation of the Court of Wards formed part of the remarkable administrative revolution of which Thomas Cromwell was the pivot.[2]

But, above all, the erection of the Court of Wards was a further confirmation of the dire economic straits in which Henry's government found itself in the closing years of his reign. It recorded the government's failure, within the existing framework

[1] B.M. Cotton MS. Tit. B. 1, ff. 159v, 477r, 478r, 493r; *L.P.*, xv, nos. 438 (2), 439; cf. also *S.P.* Hen. VIII, no. 159, ff. 47r–48r (misdated in *L.P.*, xv, no. 503); see my 'The Revival of Feudalism in Early Tudor England' (*History*, n.s. xxxvii, 142–4).

[2] For a full discussion of Thomas Cromwell's role in government reform see G. R. Elton, *The Tudor Revolution in Government* (Cambridge, 1953).

of society, to gain for itself an adequate share of the rising national income. So Henry exploited to the utmost, as needs must, the surviving feudal incidents and sought at the same time to redress the balance of economic power in his favour as against his landed classes, old and new. None the less the feudal incidents as a means of land taxation were inequitable and clumsy—and were to prove in the end insufferable. But that is another story. Meanwhile, by the act of 1540 the crown established more firmly, and openly proclaimed, its control over the main items of its feudal revenue and stood ready to tap these sources more effectively than it had done for generations. In so doing it would make feudal marriage pay a dividend greater than ever before in its long history.

2

Resistance

AFTER forty years of trial and error, the crown in 1540 knew exactly where it stood. It was fully armed with a Court of Wards and a body of skilled officials. It had asserted its rights. If a tenant of the crown died, while holding land by a so-called knight-service, then his heir, if under age, became a ward of the crown. He rarely stayed a royal ward except in name. Soon his guardianship would be sold, sometimes to his mother, more often to a complete stranger. With his guardianship would go his 'marriage'—the right to offer him a bride whom he could rarely afford to refuse, for his refusal meant that he must pay a crushing fine to his guardian. Meanwhile his land would also have passed into wardship, either to his guardian or to someone else, for them to snatch a quick profit until the ward was old enough to reclaim his own.

Feudal marriage was up for sale. This, and this alone, was the significance of the feudal revival of the early sixteenth century. It was part of the heroic efforts of the Tudors to make their monarchy financially secure. And in the vigour of his assertions, the first of the Tudors was the boldest of them all.

Yet these accessions to the financial prerogative of the crown did not represent the steady unchallenged progress to a goal. The landed classes, and the investors and speculators in land, began to get a shrewd notion of the price that they, or their children, would have to pay for resurgent feudalism: a charge upon their happiness no less than upon their wealth. Soon the landowning classes and their lawyers began to forge the weapons of resistance: and this was well known to Henry VIII. It was as an early gesture of conciliation to such resistance that he had thrown Empson and Dudley to the wolves at the beginning of his reign.

It was an empty gesture. Though there is reason to believe that, in the early years of Henry VIII's reign, administrative weakness made itself felt in the day-to-day work of the Office of Wards— a recurrent malady throughout Tudor administration—by the 1530s a new drive was on. It grew all the more vigorous under the remorseless pressure of war finance, inflation and the steeply-rising cost of government itself. Where would it all end? What satisfaction the landed classes may have derived, as they inspected their land surveys recording acre added to acre and manor to manor, must have been mingled with anxiety and bitterness as they learned of their neighbours' lands and heirs passing into the uncertainties and dangers of a feudal wardship. Anxiety bred resistance; and there is one curious episode, at the time of the dissolution of the monasteries, which shows that the landowning classes were taking stock of a dangerous situation.

When, as a young research student, I began to read inquisitions and surveys drawn up after the death of a landowner, I was struck by the large amount of land held from the crown 'as of our manor of East Greenwich'. In Yorkshire, during Elizabeth's reign, the Hastings heiresses held in this way twenty messuages of land, four cottages and a good deal of meadow, pasture and woodland, worth £11. 6s. 8d. a year. In Cheshire Alice Deane held 20s.-worth of land by this tenure. Farther south, in Northamptonshire, William Lane held land worth £17 a year of the queen as of her manor of East Greenwich; while away in the west country Thomas Prediaux held, in the same curious fashion, land worth just over £8 a year.[1]

But the manor of Greenwich was in Kent and how could men living hundreds of miles away be tenants of a Kentish manor? Who were they and how did such an extraordinary situation come about? A chance reference to this same manor in an early statute of Edward VI's reign provided a hint of the answer and a reading of the patent rolls finally pieced the story together.

[1] The feodary's surveys are to be found in Wards 5 and Wards 9, 129ff.

Behind an innocent and technical reference to a Kentish manor lurks a profound and significant story of how the English land-owning classes struck back at the reviving feudal claim of the crown.[1]

The Tudor sovereigns, like their predecessors, were from time to time acquiring portions of land through escheat or confiscation. But during the last years of Henry VIII's reign their possessions were suddenly and vastly increased through the acquisition of church lands. From 1536 the lesser monasteries were being dissolved; from 1539 the greater ones; and by the end of the reign the seizure of the college and chantry lands had begun. As we have seen, they had to be quickly put up for sale. But the purchase of monastic lands clearly brought in its train heavy charges as well as heavy risks: annual rents and, worse still, feudal tenures. For some they were too heavy. Already in 1542, we learn that not all the recipients of church lands were paying the annual rents due from them and that delinquents would be fined.[2]

Two years later, the government recognised that some of the purchasers were not able to 'maintain their poor family of the yearly issues and profits' from their land and perform the necessary services. Yet the remedy offered had nothing to do with reducing the price. Instead, the government agreed that land of relatively low value—that is, worth 40s. a year—could carry (at the discretion of the commissioners for sales) either a tenure by knight-service of the crown or a tenure in free socage or burgage, that is one which did not carry the most severe feudal burdens. The term 'socage' had a complicated and mysterious origin but, to the sixteenth-century purchaser of land, its meaning was clear enough. It was free from feudal wardship. It was immune also from most other feudal dues. But it is significant that the yearly rent was to stay. It was not the 'poverty' of the tenants which precipitated this issue, it was their hatred of feudal wardship. And the crown

[1] For a discussion of this problem see my 'The Greenwich Tenures of the Reign of Edward VI' (*Law Quart. Rev.*, 1949, lxv, 72–81). Cf. also Joyce Youings, 'The terms of the disposal of Devon Monastic Lands, 1536–58' (*E.H.R.* 1954, lxix, 18–38).

[2] 32 Hen. VIII, c. 39.

had begun its long retreat from its high ambitions, of the last half-century, to re-establish the feudal bonds.[1]

From now onwards the crown was forced step by step to enlarge the area of land it sold without the military tenure. But the buying and selling of lands was a highly technical process. Purchasers complained about 'ambiguities, questions and doubts'. How could they be sure that, long after they were dead, some zealous official might not deny their feudal immunity and claim the wardship dues? Somehow the purchasers must establish beyond any shadow of doubt that, though they held the land of the crown, they did not hold it by knight-service in chief.

It was in these middle years of the sixteenth century that a solution was found. For the king was not only king of England; he was also lord of many manors. The difference was fundamental. It was far better to hold the land from him as lord of a manor than as king; for the feudal burdens were much lighter, especially if there was no knight-service. If, then, the purchaser had to hold his land from the crown, he must somehow avoid holding it from the king *as* king. For that was what the earlier purchasers had done—and burnt their fingers in the process. In short, the purchaser must have it enshrined upon his deed of purchase that he held by socage tenure, as of some local manor. By so doing, as was confirmed by statute, he would keep his land—and his heirs— out of wardship. In response to a very real need, the royal manors up and down the country appeared on the records of sale.

At the beginning of the reign the nearest royal manor to the site of the disposed land was usually chosen; but the later years clearly reveal the increasing and widespread use of East Greenwich. For example, we find that during the first year of Edward VI's reign there were forty-four grants of land to be held by socage or other non-military tenures, of which two were to be held of East Greenwich. In the second year of his reign the total non-military grants rose to 150, of which twenty-six were to be held of East Greenwich. In the sixth year, the last complete year of Edward VI's reign, we find that there were sixty-five

[1] 35 Hen. VIII, c. 14.

non-military grants in all, of which forty-six were held of the Greenwich manor. In other words, only one in twenty of the non-military tenures created in the first year of Edward VI were Greenwich tenures; the proportion rose to three and a half in twenty in the second; by the sixth year of his reign it had reached fourteen in twenty.[1]

Various reasons have been suggested for the increasing popularity of East Greenwich. It may be because of the frequent use of the manor by Henry VIII and his successors, both as a place of residence and for the performance of official duties. In that case the commissioners might well have adopted it as the obvious source of a royal grant, especially as many official documents were issued from East Greenwich. The lawyers and clerks who arranged the enrolment of the sales at Westminster would be inclined to choose the nearest and best-known royal manor for the purpose; and of all those mentioned on the patent rolls of Edward VI, East Greenwich was undoubtedly the best known. Whatever the explanation for its original use, once it became associated in the legal mind with the socage tenure, its fame spread and it gave a feeling of security which perhaps no other manor could give.[2]

But the most important fact which is revealed by these developments arises not from the particular manor selected, but from the important change of policy applied to the sale of church lands. It is true that Edward VI's ministers continued to impose military tenures wherever possible. For example, when the king granted land in reward 'for past services' to his father or himself, he was still able to attach the incidents of knight-service to all or part of the land. This was natural enough. The crown did not in these cases need to make the arrangements attractive to the recipients; these lands were gifts, not sales. Where it was still possible, the crown therefore imposed and retained the charges of knight-service in chief. But even the recipient of a gift, a Lord Admiral Seymour, a Duke of Somerset or an Earl of Warwick could gain

---

[1] The figures in this paragraph are based on the *Calendar of Patent Rolls*, Ed. VI.
[2] E. P. Cheyney, 'The Manor of East Greenwich in the County of Kent' (*Am. Hist. Rev.*, xi, 33–4).

a socage tenure: so heavily lay the hand of corruption upon a weak king. But, above all, the use of the manor of East Greenwich, and the socage tenure identified with it, shows that the crown was being compelled under financial pressure to abandon its original system of establishing wardship tenures. The crown wanted to sell the lands quickly because it needed money. It wanted also to establish a tenure which would bring in valuable revenues, albeit intermittently, over a period of time. But these two objects were incompatible. The use of the socage tenure was a sign that the crown had decided to take the cash in hand.[1]

In the course of the century the limit up to which commissioners might establish a socage tenure was progressively raised: a clear sign that the tide was turning against the crown, for the buyers were demanding, and getting, better terms. The socage level rose from £2 to £4 per annum between 1544 and 1548. Towards the end of Mary's reign it had risen to £10. By the last years of Elizabeth's reign it reached £20. In the new century it was to be applied to vast tracts of colonial territories. Thus British settlers overseas reaped the advantages won by the purchasers of ecclesiastical lands in the middle of the sixteenth century. The introduction and extension of this tenure from the end of Henry VIII's reign marks, therefore, not 'a more businesslike treatment of crown lands', but a recognition by the crown that it must sell on better terms. It was a victory for the purchaser, not the seller. Similarly its extension to colonial settlements established not 'the closeness of legal connection between the colony and the home government', but, on the contrary, the greatest measure of freedom possible in the circumstances.[2]

The granting in Ireland and North America of large areas of land to English settlers to be held 'in free and common socage as of our manor of East Greenwich' exempted the holders from the feudal marriage which remained a burden upon Englishmen at home until the middle of the seventeenth century. It gave to

[1] C.P.R., Ed. VI, i, 33, 123, 171.
[2] Cheyney, op. cit., p. 31.

overseas settlements a freedom indispensable to their further progress. But an over-zealous reformer once tried to set the clock back. Writing in 1600 that, since the death of Henry VIII, purchasers 'desire to hold their lands in free socage as of Her Majesty's manor of East Greenwich, whereby the number of them that hold of the said manor are at this day become infinite', he went on to suggest the calling of the manorial roll and the appointment of a steward to collect the dues arising from the tenants. He wanted to turn a nominal relationship into an actual one; and the device was about as realistic as to expect a retiring Member of Parliament of today to use his Stewardship of the Chiltern Hundreds to introduce sweeping agrarian reforms in the royal manors so fleetingly in his charge. Had the project succeeded it would have made chaos of the work of two generations of lawyers resisting the expanding feudal claims of the crown, and it would have played havoc with the land market. Needless to say, the proposal was no more than a pipe-dream of a candidate for a non-existent post. Instead, the increasing use of socage tenure as of the manor of East Greenwich was a measure of the successful resistance to the establishment of wardship claims in the sixteenth century and foreshadowed the final destruction of the feudal relationship which the seventeenth century was to bring about.[1]

The story of East Greenwich is a story of successful resistance. Elsewhere resistance was met and overcome. The Pilgrimage of Grace of 1536, as we have seen, struck a blow not only for the old religion but for the old social order against the Statute of Uses, and all that that implied: but the king struck back at once, as he had done against the parliamentary opposition to his feudal schemes. Ket's rebellion in 1549 came from a different class of society and, in religion, would have been opposed to all that the 'pilgrims' stood for. But Ket's men also knew what the king's officials were doing in the counties to fasten his feudal grip upon his tenants, so among their demands they called for protection against them. They sought also for a new framework to rural society and, in their boldness, declared 'We pray that all bondmen

[1] *S.P.D.*, Eliz., cclxxvi, no. 67.

may be made free, for God made all free with his precious blood-shedding.' They too were unsuccessful.[1]

Meanwhile, pamphleteers and publicists were no more fortunate in their results, though the evidence of the evils of wardship were there for all men to see. For wards were being bought and sold, and with them went the full right to marry them according to the pleasure of the purchaser. 'There was never such marrying in England as is now!' cried Latimer in his sermon before the king in March 1549. 'I hear tell of stealing of wards to marry their children to. This is a strange kind of stealing, but it is not the wards, it is the lands they steal!' Moreover, their education seemed to be sorely neglected. 'I trow there is a Court of Wards,' he had observed in his Sermon of the Plough the previous year, 'why is there not a school for the wards as well as there is a Court for their lands?' Latimer's language seems moderate compared with the bitter outburst of Henry Brinklow in his *Complaynt of Roderyck Mors*, written a few years earlier: 'Oh merciful God, what innumerable inconveniences come by selling of wards for marriage, for lucre of goods and lands.' It led amongst other things to adultery and divorce which were, he said, clearly on the increase. 'Now God confound that wicked custom; for it is too abominable, and stinketh from the earth to heaven, it is so vile. . . . For Christ's blood sake, seek a redress for it!'[2]

Perhaps the most significant comment came from Sir Nicholas Bacon, himself Attorney of the Wards from 1547 until 1561. Viewing the activities of the Court of Wards and its guardians at such close quarters, he seems to have been driven in Mary's reign to draw up a drastic plan of reform. Echoing Latimer's sermon, or perhaps expressing an opinion held widely among reformers, he proposed to deprive guardians of the care of their wards at the age of nine so that they could be sent to a specially established school for wards. He had tried once, when Sir Francis Engelfield was Master, to get his scheme adopted, but his plan,

---

[1] S. T. Bindoff, *Ket's Rebellion, 1549* (1949), p. 12.
[2] *Sermons of Hugh Latimer*, ed. G. E. Corrie (1844), i, 169–70; *Complaynt of Roderyck Mors*, ed. J. M. Cooper (1874), p. 18.

like Latimer's, had fallen on stony ground. Now, in May 1561, a few months after his resignation as Attorney of the Wards and William Cecil, Lord Burghley's appointment as Master, Bacon was sending him his plan: 'knowing your good inclination to the thing and your place, I am in great hope of good success thereof'. Whatever Burghley's inclination, once again the scheme came to nothing.[1]

Bacon's covering letter drew attention to the irresponsible and selfish treatment to which wards were subjected, 'a thing hitherto preposterously proceeding'.

> That the proceeding hath been preposterous [the letter goes on] appeareth by this: the chief thing and most of price in wardship is the ward's mind, the next to that his body, and the last and meanest his land. Now hitherto the chief care of governance hath been had to the land, being the meanest, and the body being the better, very small, but to the mind being the best none at all, which me thinks is plainly to set the cart before the horse.

Originally, he understood, one of the purposes of feudal wardship was to enable the ward to be brought up by his lord according to the highest standards. 'Now by abuse it is come (as you know) to that, that the greater the personage is to whom the ward appertains, the less courtesy for the most part is had of the ward's bringing up.'

Bacon's anxieties had also expressed themselves in a more practical shape. In 1553 he had obtained from Queen Mary a special grant by which his own heir, should he succeed under age, would pass under the guardianship of the child's uncles, Thomas and James Bacon. This precaution is easily understandable. Bacon had been a purchaser of ecclesiastical lands which, as he well knew, often brought military tenures in their train, and, as he knew also, 'those tenures have of late days and continually do greatly increase'. If he had any doubts about this, which is unlikely, there was always a *memento mori* in the shape of Staunford's *Prerogativa*

---

[1] B.M. Add. MS. 32, 379, ff. 26r-33v. See also J. P. Collier, 'On Sir Nicholas Bacon, Lord Keeper; with Extracts from Some of his Unprinted Papers and Speeches' (*Archaeologia*, xxxvi, 339-48).

Regis, written in 1548, dedicated to Nicholas Bacon and full of the most sweeping feudal assertions on behalf of the crown. Not surprisingly, Bacon was alarmed at 'what great hurt and lack groweth to every ward particularly, yea and what to the whole commonwealth generally'. He may also have recalled that one of his predecessors as Attorney of the Wards, John Sewster, had died leaving a minor heir to the mercy of the Court of Wards. He had himself been the recipient of wardships, but what sort of guardian he made we do not know. It is clear, however, that he was genuinely anxious to introduce these overdue reforms 'as the best piece of service that ever I went about to do in the Court of Wards'. Though his ambitious project fared no better with Burghley than with Englefield, perhaps he derived some small compensation from the permission he received during the twelve months which followed to found two grammar schools, one in London (this time with Burghley's help) and the other in Suffolk. He had, long before, proposed that some of the wealth of the dissolved monastic lands should be used to establish a kind of embryonic University of London; but that vision of Bacon's was too remote from the harsh realities of Henrician England.[1]

Between the erection of the Court of Wards in 1540 and the accession of Elizabeth I in 1558, the crown had been able to build up a framework of experience and a body of skilled administrators. Latter-day feudalism was beginning to pay its profits into the royal funds. Viewed statistically the position was encouraging. The earliest account of the Receiver-General that we have, for the year 1523–4, shows a net profit from wardships of £3,134; and seven years later it had fallen slightly to £3,003. In 1536–7, shortly before the Court of Wards was established, the revenues had increased somewhat and were £3,590; but in 1542–3, with the Court of Wards beginning to get into its stride, there was a substantial rise to record: the profits now stood at £5,452. This included money received from the suing of liveries, the entry fee of the heir when he entered into possession of the land. Profits from liveries had not before 1541 been included in the wardship

[1] *C.P.R.*, Mary, i, 3; *C.P.R.*, Eliz., ii, 104, 226–7; *D.N.B.*, *sub* Bacon.

records; but it is clear that, even without them, the rise was substantial. Three years later the increase was still more impressive. Total revenue had almost doubled and now stood at £10,550.[1]

In the early years of Edward VI's reign a downward movement set in, and in his second year the net revenues were as low as £6,595. This was a sharp fall and may be explained in general by the inefficiency and corruption of minority rule and, in particular, by the activities of John Beaumont, Receiver-General of the Court of Wards, who was busily feathering his own nest at the expense of the crown. Towards the end of the reign the position was improving and in 1550-1 the revenues were as high as £14,892. In Mary's reign, after an initial fall, the profits began to climb again and, in her fourth year, stood at the record figure of £20,020. What contribution such a sum could make to the inflated costs of administration and war is a matter for discussion and we shall consider it elsewhere. Here it must suffice to say that the net revenues had gone up four or five times since the erection of the Court of Wards. The administrative reconstruction which that had entailed had amply justified itself. Manifestly, also, resistance to the Court of Wards had failed to turn back its advancing claims.[2]

What had happened to the Court of Wards during the first eighteen years of its existence? Like other Tudor institutions it betrayed marked weaknesses of policy and administration during those last years of Henry VIII's rule, as the reins of government began to slip from his hands. During the Edwardian minority its history was a chequered one, though it began to recover towards the end. Then, under Mary, it entered upon a period of reform in administration which was soon reflected in increased profits to the crown. At the time of her death in 1558 it had Sir Francis Englefield at its head, while the late Master, Sir William Paulet, was nearby at the Exchequer. In this year also, the Court

1 Wards 8.72, 73, 74, 109; Wards 9.362.
2 Wards 9.365, 367.

of Wards, in handing down its decision in Tyrell's case, had invalidated what was technically known as 'the use reserved out of an use' and thereby blocked another loophole from the feudal incidents.[1] Englefield's religion was soon to deprive him of office, but Paulet was to stay at the Treasury for many years; and, after a brief interlude under Sir Thomas Parry, the Court of Wards was to pass under the long Mastership of Burghley. What he and the new queen made of this extraordinary institution was to shape the lives of many thousands of her subjects as well as to influence profoundly the economic and constitutional history of the age.

[1] Holdsworth, *op. cit.*, iv, 472.

II

PROCEDURE

. . . Also, my masters, you shall understand that you are here appointed as judges with me upon such evidence as shall be given us. . . . It behoveth us sincerely and advisedly to work and set aside all affection and favour. . . .

From the escheator's address to the jury at the
Inquisition Post Mortem

3

Discovering a Wardship

Lᴀᴛᴇ in February 1540 two eminent officials of Henry VIII's administration were hauled before the Star Chamber and given exemplary punishment for a serious offence. Sir Humphrey Browne, a king's sergeant-at-law in the personal service of the crown, and Sir Nicholas Hare, a councillor and Speaker of the House of Commons, were deprived of their sergeanties and sent to the Tower. Their fellow conspirator, William Conisbie, Attorney of the Duchy of Lancaster, was not present at the Star Chamber but, as a fellow lawyer involved in the plot, was similarly condemned. The charge against them, to which they had confessed, was that they had aided and abetted the late Sir John Shelton to convey his land in such a manner as to evade the royal rights of wardship and other feudal dues. This was condign punishment. But here was corruption and collusion reaching up to the very council of the king; and the Lord Chancellor used the occasion to read to the assembled lawyers a homily on the subject. But remission came quickly and, by a characteristic and unconscious piece of Tudor irony, Sir Nicholas Hare was, in the same year, instructed to investigate a case of embezzlement.[1]

The government well knew that it was dealing not simply with isolated and sporadic attempts to defeat it of its lawful rights, but with what was a common occurrence throughout England. For the concealment of wardships was as old as the wardship system itself. 'I will forbear to set down either the persons

[1] B.M. Stowe 424, ff. 166v-167r; *D.N.B.*, *sub* Hare and Coningsby.

or the particular names of the land', remarked an early seventeenth-century surveyor, with a disarming show of frankness, 'for
that peradventure it may prejudice some in their tenures, who
had rather hold of mesne lords by socage tenure than of the king
in capite.' As long as the Court of Wards existed, and indeed for
generations before that, there prevailed a conspiracy of silence
among the landowning classes to 'smother their tenures', if
necessary by deliberate fraud. In such a climate informers
flourished.[1]

The fabrication of bogus transactions to frustrate the royal
title and claims exercised the creative intelligence of the highly
skilled and resourceful Elizabethan lawyers. As a result, government officials had to scour a haystack of conveyances before they
could discover the needle of the royal title. Informers, escheators,
feodaries, where it suited them, took part in the hunt. For example,
one September day in 1560, the resolute Gilbert Moreton, feodary
of Lancashire, sent 'a proclamation to the curates of Walton and
Liverpool' to be read in their pulpits and 'for the further speed
was after proclaimed at the Cross on the market day . . . which
feodary appointed and warned all men of worship, gentlemen and
freeholders, to be at the church of Liverpool upon Thursday, being
the xth day of the month of October, by ix of the clock etc. and
to bring with them such evidence as they have for the proof of the
tenures of their lands'. Those who could not be there were to be
at Wigan on the 7th October, at Ormskirk the 8th, at Sefton on
the 9th, at Childwall on the 11th or at Prescot on the 12th. This
latter-day domesday book of land tenures appears to have come
to nothing; but a reader of Lord Burghley's inward mail, now
preserved at Hatfield House, might well be pardoned if he formed
the impression that the hunting down of concealed wardships
was one of the great outdoor sports of Elizabethan England. Here
then was ample scope for private enterprise, but the problem had
to be tackled by the government itself, at the centre. By commission of inquiry, by legislation, by admonition and threat, the
government struck at the unseen and evasive enemy, whose con-

1 *The Book of John Rowe*, ed. W. H. Godfrey (Sussex Rec. Soc., xxxiv, 1928), pp. 136–7.

tortions live on in the manuscripts to confuse and trouble the historian of a later age.[1]

Concealed lands, to use a contemporary expression, meant lands held of the crown by some tenure or other, in which the link had decayed or been cut by an elusive tenant. Hence the recurrent chorus of local juries: 'of whom the land is held, and by what tenure, they say they do not know'. Until 1549, it is true, an unknown tenure could be interpreted by officials as a crown tenure; the crown was, as it were, the residuary legatee.' But in 1549, under the weak rule of Edward VI, the crown abandoned this claim and acknowledged that further inquiries must be made to establish the correct relationship.[2] More indeed was in the balance than the profits from wardship. Escheats, primer seisins, reliefs, reserved rents and other revenues lay dormant during the years of concealment. In the last months of Elizabeth's reign, Sir Robert Johnson, a correspondent of the Master of the Court of Wards, reminded him of the evils arising from the darkness which obscured so many of the crown's rights over land: 'the loss of many rents, the confounding of tenancies, the change of tenures, perverting of customs, concealing of fines'. These evils Johnson attributed to 'the cunning devices of these later times, as compared with the ancient simplicity of the overworn world'. 'Within these sixty or eighty years,' he went on, 'and chiefly forty or fifty, the witcraft of man is more and more extended to obscure ancient customs, and pervert them to private profit'. In other words, the concealments of royal rights marched in step with the expansion of royal claims. We may not be able to accept Johnson's picture of the charmed simplicity of medieval England; but his account of what was going on in his own lifetime has the authentic ring of truth.[3]

Nearly a hundred years before Johnson was writing, a commission had been set on foot, in 1505, to inquire into concealed

---

[1] *Liverpool Town Books*, ed. J. Twemlow (1918), i, 141.
[2] See my 'Corruption and Reform under Edward VI and Mary' (*E.H.R.*, lxviii, 25).
[3] S. J. Madge, *The Domesday of Crown Lands* (1938), pp. 51-2.

lands, wardships and other royal interests.[1] In 1516 there was another, this time specifically for concealed wardships. While commissions were going about their work, legislation was also playing its part in the proceedings. The General Pardon Act at the beginning of Edward VI's reign, as did subsequent pardon acts throughout the century, exempted from the royal mercy 'all ravishments and withholding of the king's wards and wards' lands and the profits of the same': otherwise a lengthy queue of landowners might have claimed what shelter the pardon could afford. In 1567, there was yet another important commission of inquiry; and in 1571 a bill against fraudulent gifts provoked a good deal of discussion in both Houses of Parliament. In 1572 we find an act on the statute book 'For the avoiding of recoveries suffered by collusion', and in 1576 a comparable enactment to cancel the effects of fraudulent conveyances by the Northern rebels who had transferred land to protect themselves against loss through their attainder. It was to be the forerunner of a similar measure in 1587, and it was to be followed shortly by another. For no less a person than a former Master of Wards, Sir Francis Englefield, dismissed by Elizabeth, had tried to shelter his estates in this way, and in 1593 to thwart him a special act was put through Parliament, in confirmation of the queen's rights. In 1596 the Privy Council itself intervened with an injunction against a group of people implicated in a fraudulent transfer of land.[1]

But measures of this kind could only scratch at the surface of a widespread abuse. 'The burden of the feudal incidents,' writes a modern historian, 'bore so heavily on tenants that the history of real property law is largely concerned with attempts to evade them.' As a result 'the law was warped beyond endurance'. Legislation was clearly not enough. It was necessary to give teeth —and eyes—to the law.[2]

For eyes the Court of Wards relied in part upon its informers. The common informer was not peculiar to feudal institutions.

---

[1] *C.P.R.*, Ed. VI, ii, 420–1, 459, 489; *L.P.*, ii, pt. 1, pp. 400, 405; 1 Ed. VI, c. 15; S. J. Madge, *op. cit.*, p. 42; *C.J.*, i, 84ff.; *S.P.D.*, Eliz., lxxxviii, nos. 14, 15, 16; 14 Eliz., c. 8; 18 Eliz., c. 4; 29 Eliz., c. 3; 35 Eliz., c. 5; *Acts of P.C.* 1596–7, (ed. Dasent) p. 369.

[2] T. F. T. Plucknett, *A Concise History of the Common Law* (1956), p. 544.

He owed his existence to the fact that the power of a Tudor government was not equal to its will, that legislation outran enforcement, that the state could not 'police' its regulations. Into this gap stepped the informer, to pester the crown with requests for authority to search out irregularities, and to plague the subject with demands for incriminating information. But informers varied a great deal in power and influence. There were, in the first place, the would-be guardians who turned informer simply on one occasion in order to pick up a desirable wardship, possibly on favourable terms. They were not informers in any professional sense and are not considered here, though we shall have more to say about them in their capacity of guardians.

Others might act as informers to help a courtier friend or to win favour in high places. 'This night being at Mr. High Sheriffs, at Babram, with many of the gentlemen of this shire,' wrote Lord North to Lord Burghley in October 1582, 'news was brought me that Sir Thomas Rivet died this morning.' This simple fact seemed open to question. 'I am persuaded that he has been dead this two days, which my Lady hath kept close, meaning to make friends to you for her daughter, whom she and her friends give out to be in her fourteenth year.' A girl aged fourteen at her father's death was out of wardship, so clearly Lady Rivet had a good deal at stake. 'But I am credibly informed that she entered into her thirteenth year at Whitsunday last.' Her age was apparently not the only important thing to bear in mind. 'She shall have a notable living. The maiden is well to be liked.' But, Lord North urged Burghley, promptitude was essential. 'Forgo not this occasion. I have known but few such fall in my time. Get her into your possession, dispute of her age after: and in the meanwhile persuade the maid. I am ready to do you any service.' But in his hope of another wardship for himself, North had to acknowledge defeat. 'I must relinquish my suit touching the elder sister because she [is] past wardship.'[1]

Many informers, however, operated on a fairly small scale, and picked up either a grant of money or a cheap wardship for

1 H.M.C. *Salis.*, xiii, 208.

their pains. 'Where by the travail of James Woodford, gentleman,' states a decree of the Court of Wards in February 1560, 'the wardship and marriage of Anthony Heveningham, the Queen's ward, concealed, hath thereby appeared and the same sold for £220, it is therefore ordered that the said James have allowance of ten pounds for his charges and travail.' We know, from another source, that the wretched Heveningham was only a week short of his twentieth birthday when his father had died in Mary's reign, and that he must have passed his twenty-first birthday when the whole thing came to light. So a commission of less than five per cent. to the informer seems at first sight a scant reward for his 'charges and travail'; but yet another source reveals that within a year or two Woodford had picked up for himself a couple of not insubstantial wardships. In the business of informing, Woodford was probably no more than a gifted amateur; and the same appears to have been true of Cuthbert Horsley who with the help of John Carr, a relative of a minor, disentangled a somewhat obscure wardship and earned between them £20 for their work. On another occasion Horsley, trading independently this time, had unearthed a concealed wardship and bought it for himself for £63. Late in Elizabeth's reign, the services of another informer, Paul Rainsforde, were rewarded posthumously with a lump sum of £94 and an annuity to his widow of £10 per annum. The cost, in terms of human happiness to his victims, it is of course impossible to determine.[1]

More powerful, and therefore more dangerous, were such men as Peter Osborne, experienced in administration and intimate in the service of Burghley. Osborne once boasted to his master that he had been busy digging out wardships concealed during the past fifteen years. No wonder in the same letter he thanked Burghley for promising that his son should have the reversion of his office of Lord Treasurer's Remembrancer, which would be the mainstay of his house, his widow and his children in the years to come.[2]

[1] Wards 9.517, f. 169r (the Clerk in error attributed to the ward, Henry, the father's name, Anthony); Wards 9.138, f. 105v; Wards 9.369, ff. 169r, 173v, 238r, 271r, 17v, 80r, 173v; Wards 9.138, f. 23r; Wards 9.388, f. 228v.
[2] H.M.C. Salis., ii, 171.

More dangerous still, because it was systematised, was the grant of authority under patent to professional informers to press on with their searches. One such patent was granted in 1575 to Henry Townshend and William Walter with a roving commission and the prospect of handsome profits; and Ralph Bosseville, the Clerk of the Wards, was instructed to give their representative, Richard Ellis, the fullest access to his official records.[1] A decade later, amidst growing public concern, a contemporary drew up a summary of the patentees' very wide powers.[2] Their authority reached back to the thirtieth year of Henry VIII's reign and forward for twenty-one years, and they were to search for concealments of

The wardship of the body and the lands.
The profit of primer seisin, not suing livery or ouster le mayne.
Fines for marriage of widows without licence.
Fines for alienation without licence.
Forfeitures of the goods and chattels of persons attainted for felony, or fleeing from felony.
The benefit of the year, day and waste of such attainders.
Arrearages of rents reserved between anno XXVII Henry VIII and XIV Regine nunc, concealed.

What would the queen get in return for all this?

—For the body of every ward one year's rent of lands in possession and half year's rent of lands in reversion [*which was the bare minimum*].
And the yearly rents of wards' lands during their nonage. [*Always undervalued.*]
And the fourth part of all compositions for the fines, forfeitures and benefits aforesaid. [*While three-quarters went to the informers.*]

Clearly, the queen, as well as her subjects, was paying a substantial price for the services of informers.

This patent was to become famous; but it was merely one of a series. Sir Edward Stafford, the diplomat, had a patent for concealed lands but he kept it for five years and then had to dispose

1 Wards 9.106, ff. 517v–521v; S.P.D. Eliz. Addenda, xxiv, no. 37.
2 B.M. Lans. 47, f. 28r.

of it to pay his debts. It went to a syndicate of men, of whom the
most outstanding was the courtier, Sir Edward Dyer, who was
to win fame as a poet and infamy for his operations under the
concealments commission. By 1586 someone not unfriendly to
Dyer was admitting that it 'hath been occasion of great dis-
quietness to the people and trouble to the country'. Besides, he
admitted, the report that a piece of land was 'concealed' brought
its price tumbling down, if indeed people could be persuaded to
touch the land at all. Dyer had been forced in 1586 to introduce
certain reforms into his procedure: for example, to let landowners
know when charges of concealment were pending against them,
to appoint as his agents only men for whose conduct he was prepared to take full responsibility, to leave the universities alone,
and to moderate his interference with cathedral churches; all
of which provides some notion of what life must have been
like under Dyer and his associates before these changes were
made.[1]

In 1593 Dyer complained that the stricter controls over his
activities were having a disastrous effect upon his whole business.
The renewal of the patent had itself required prodigious efforts.
'I was two years a suitor to Her Highness for the warrant', he told
Lord Burghley, 'and in the end by your Honour's means, with
great difficulty, the same was obtained.' But Burghley apparently
thought that the queen should have a greater share of the profits
so 'Your Lordship tied it with many straiter conditions than any
heretofore ever was.' On top of that Burghley, with his ear close
to the ground, was trying to clean up the whole procedure of
concealments. 'Your Lordship took not only my word but my
bond of £6,000 and upward, acknowledged before one of the
Barons of the Exchequer, with condition not only for the well
using of my warrant but also for the tenant in possession.' Dyer
had hoped that the patent would bring him in some money 'in
lieu of my long service to Her Highness. But as the case now is
handled, it hath, and is like, to undo me.' The patent was granted
on a five-year basis but 'I have not had fully two years and a half

[1] *Ibid*, ff. 26v-27r, 29r, 73r-78r.

execution of the same, for the first year was spent in setting down an order for my proceeding; the one half of the second year was consumed by Her Majesty's stay; and for this last year I have done nothing therein.' By now, he alleged, he was running at a loss. 'I was enforced to pay out seven several persons' interests in Sir E. Stafford's warrant before I ever received any penny profit for the same. And for £4,000, I never made but £40 and £50. And at this present am out of my purse £1,800 more than hitherto I have received.'[1]

How effective or lasting these reforms were we cannot say. In the same year that Dyer was showing how profitless a task informing could be, we find him also a successful suitor for the patent to dispense with certain statutes relating to tanning. Thirteen years later Dyer was the butt of a violent attack during a Commons debate on informers: there seemed to be no means of quenching his ardour.[2]

To judge by the informers' own versions they were engaged upon a thankless task. A correspondent of Robert Cecil's told him in 1599 that his labours in discovering a concealed wardship had brought in to the queen, amongst other things, thirty-seven tenures. But it had cost the informer £200, for which he had so far gained no return. Yet in spite of these hazards there was considerable competition in the field. We have three petitions from Sir John Norris, a famous Elizabethan soldier, for authority to search for concealed lands. A certain Nicholas Geff offered the queen £10,000 for a patent to discover concealed lands in the space of two years. No less interesting, perhaps, is the letter from a Mr. James Hudson to Sir Robert Cecil in 1602 telling him that a certain Norwich lawyer was about to offer £500 for a concealed ward. The lawyer had told Hudson that the wardship would be worth more than £2,000 and offered Hudson a partnership in the project. Hudson, however, thought it his duty to get into touch with Cecil before taking any action. An example of an informer

---

[1] B.M. Lans. 73, f. 128r. For a statement of some of Dyer's profits and losses see Lans. 165, f. 341r.

[2] *Acts of P.C.* 1592-3, pp. 357-8; *The Parliamentary Diary of Robert Bowyer, 1606-7* (ed. D. H. Willson, Minneapolis, 1931), pp. 132-4.

informing against an informer displays one more virtue of these public spirited gentlemen.[1]

There was yet another group of suitors; but they were of less importance than the professional informers in that their proposals were too ambitious or too impracticable to come to much. One of these petitioners, William Herrle, modestly asked that a post to be called 'the whole feodaryship of Wales' be bestowed upon him, an office which he was pleased to describe as 'more painful than profitable'. By means of it he proposed to remind the Welsh gentry 'that they hold *in Capite* since King Edward, of most glorious memory, the First'. Another petitioner asked Burghley to appoint him custodian of records of 'descents' and a third to be made registrar of births, deaths and marriages.[2]

Some of these projects were the harmless by-products of powerful imaginations playing upon rudimentary administration; but the practices of informers became a burning issue in Elizabethan and early Stuart parliaments. In 1566 and again in 1576 there were discussions in the Commons. The 1576 Act 'to redress disorders in common informers' sought to tighten the control over them and forbade them to compound with defendants, without leave of the court. The purpose, of course, was to stop blackmail, possibly a more lucrative source that the direct profits from informing. This act may not have achieved all that it set out to do, but it accomplished enough for it to be renewed and made permanent in 1585 because it had been 'found by experience since the making of the same act to be very necessary, beneficial and expedient for the Commonwealth'. But it was not 'beneficial' enough to spare the necessity for another 'Act concerning Informers' in 1589, which indeed was rushed through nearly all its stages in the Commons in one day.[3]

But this could not put an end to the grievances. Under James I, various grants to informers were renewed, to be accompanied by

[1] H.M.C. *Salis.*, ix, 63; xiii, 520; xiv, 195, 273; xii, 466.

[2] B.M. Lans. 18, ff. 87v–88r; H.M.C. *Salis.*, ii, 101; Lans. 43, ff. 61r–62v; Lans. 64, f. 82r.

[3] *C.J.*, i, 75–6, 111; 18 Eliz., c. 5; 27 Eliz., c. 10; 31 Eliz., c. 5; Heywood Townshend, *Four Last Parliaments of Queen Elizabeth*, p. 7.

a crescendo of criticism, which failed to gain any real measure of success. In 1606 the bill 'for the cutting of infinite suits brought against His Majesty's subjects by informers' was read a first time; but as the diarist acidly observes, 'the effect whereof is only to make playing at bowls a lawful game'. Bowls they may have legalised but informers found plenty of other outlets for their zeal. In 1617 Lord Wotton was granted a patent to recover wardships and liveries concealed since the thirtieth year of Elizabeth's reign; and the stormy Parliament of 1621 found in his and his colleagues' activities a stimulating topic for debate.[1]

It was an intractable problem; and it was not peculiar to wardship. It arose wherever the expanding economic and social controls of Tudor England rested insecurely upon a ramshackle administrative and executive machine. The passage of a new law, or the revival of an old one, brought in its train its own breed of camp-followers: informers, part-time officials, contact men, job hunters—and cranks. In the 1570s, for example, the notorious Peter Blackborow racked and harried the Wiltshire clothiers and goaded the Privy Council into putting pressure upon the local justices. In the 1620s, a time of industrial depression, a certain William Hackett roused the same county to such a white heat that the Privy Council itself summoned him to London and committed him to the gatehouse. Other informers were operating in the same promising field but, as the net tightened round them, they slipped through and left nonentities to face the music. Yet, when all is said, Tudor society paid a high price for a relatively small return. The professional informers occupy a minor place in our Court of Wards records. If they moved in unfamiliar terrain their chances of finding what they were looking for would be hampered at every stage by landowners and lawyers alike, as well as by local juries who might well proclaim ignorance where knowledge could be embarrassing to their friends or landlords. The Court of Wards owed little to informers, as such. In terms of public welfare and the political outcry, the game was hardly

---

[1] *The Parliamentary Diary of Robert Bowyer*, p. 116; *Commons Debates*, 1621 (ed. Notestein, Relph and Simpson, 1935), vii, 465 *et passim*.

worth the candle. But the professional informer was not working alone in the field.[1]

One final group to whom the work of 'informing' fell, though it was not their primary responsibility, consisted of the escheators and feodaries. The escheator dealt, as the name implies, with property or rights which had escheated, or might escheat, to the crown for lack of an heir or for other reasons. It was he who held the *inquisition post mortem* or other inquiry to establish the royal claims. But he was an amateur administrator and the post tended to circulate amongst the local gentry. As escheator, he might well, if he so pleased, discover a wardship or other casualty which had descended to the crown. But he also had the interests of his class and his friends to consider, and the Court of Wards placed little confidence in either his loyal, or his effective, service. As a result he was being elbowed out by the professional administrator, who was to prove the pivot of the Court of Wards activities in each county: the feodary.

About escheator and feodary we shall have a good deal to say in a later chapter. Undoubtedly they were important, and in the case of the feodary indispensable, servants of the crown. One example must here suffice. In October 1558, Agnes Child of Cheshire inherited from her maternal grandfather land to the annual value of £3. 6s. 8d. None of it was held by knight-service of the crown but a small portion was held by knight-service of a ward of the crown. For the time being, then, the full feudal rights of the crown came into operation; and for discovering this, Thomas Greene, feodary of Cheshire, was, three and a half years later, granted the wardship. 'It may well be presumed', an early Stuart commentator observed, 'that the diligence of feodaries and escheators, and the greediness of those that gaped after such suits, have left nothing unsifted.' 'The escheators and feodaries of these times', Lord Abergavenny's steward tells us, 'have Argus eyes, piercing into all conveyances.' That may have been so; but Richard Hurlestone, who followed Greene as feodary of Cheshire,

[1] Cf. G. D. Ramsay, *The Wiltshire Woollen Industry* (1943) and my article on county administration in *V.C.H.* Wilts., v. 101.

concealed the wardships arising from the deaths of Roger Hanley, William Forshawe, Robert Ratclyf, William Trafford, 'with many more'. Invaluable the feodaries undoubtedly were: but they too had their price.[1]

Professional informer and amateur, feodary and would-be guardian, all these joined in the hunt. How much did their combined efforts contribute in the ceaseless search for wardships? No exact calculation is possible, of course, but the heavy crop of wardships which went to strangers to the heir, and the volume of private correspondence to the Master and other officials, show that reporting the existence of a wardship was not as unrewarding a task as some correspondents would have us believe.

We may approach the problem from another angle. The clerk of the Court of Wards kept a rough calendar of the writs which were sent out to institute an *inquisition post mortem* after the death of a tenant-in-chief. These writs had for centuries been named after certain key words which they embodied. For example, the one most commonly used began: 'The Queen to her escheator in the county of . . . greeting. Because A.B. held of us in chief when he died. . . .' This phrase, in Latin, included the expression *diem clausit extremum*, and by that expression the writ was always known. But such a writ could only be used when the inquisition was held within twelve months of the death of the tenant. If more than a year had elapsed, that is if there had been some attempt at concealment, a somewhat different writ had to be used, known as *mandamus*. If we take a random year from the surviving notebook of the clerk, we find that during the fifteenth year of Elizabeth's reign there were at least sixty writs of *mandamus* issued. In other words there was a minimum of sixty cases in which concealment had either occurred or was suspected. We know also from other sources, including another rough notebook kept by the clerk, that frequently a considerable number of years elapsed between the death of the tenant and the holding of the *inquisition*. These, moreover, were merely concealments which were run to earth.

[1] Wards 9.138, f. 322v; B.M. Titus F. IV, f. 14v–15r; *The Book of John Rowe*, p. 137; H.M.C. *Salis.*, xiii, 114.

The successful concealments, naturally enough, went unrecorded. So did those in which the discoverer was bought off with a bribe. We have no measure therefore of how many heirs reached manhood without the attentions of the Court of Wards and its officials. But contemporaries believed that they were numerous.[1]

It was one thing to suspect, believe, or even know that the crown was entitled to a wardship; it was quite another to prove that such was the case. For centuries the established procedure had been by judicial inquiry, the *inquisition post mortem* presided over by the escheator with a jury empanelled by the sheriff. *Inquisitions post mortem* lasted as long as royal wardship lasted, though the government received their findings with ever diminishing confidence. For want of a better system, men clung to the ancient ways.

These inquisitions had nothing to do with discovering the *causes* of men's deaths. Then, as now, the coroner's inquest was summoned to inquire into murder, suicide or sudden death. The feudal inquest, on the other hand, was solely concerned with the tenant-in-chief by knight-service: who he was, how much land he held, its tenure and value, and the name and age of his heir. Where delay had occurred the writ of *mandamus*, as we have seen, was employed to hold an inquest; when more land had descended the writ *que plurima*; where the descent of the land was indirect and not from father to son, the writ *devenerunt*; where uncertainty existed, *melius inquirendo*. Where *prima facie* evidence of wrong findings could be bought forward, the original findings might be investigated anew by means of a *traverse*.

The jury of local men empanelled by the sheriff were not yet restricted to the mystic number of twelve. There might be sixteen or more, and their names were all entered at the top of the document stating their findings. The inquisition—or 'office' as contemporaries frequently called it—carried all the marks of an important judicial return to a royal writ; and the escheator, in his opening address to the jury, was expected to draw their attention to the solemnity of the occasion. 'Also my masters,' ran his charge

1 Wards 9.171; Wards 9.316.

to them, 'you shall understand that you are here appointed as judges with me upon such evidence as shall be given us. . . . It behoveth us sincerely and advisedly to work and set aside all affection and favour because . . . your verdict and our certificate thereof shall become a matter of record.' Their verdict once it had been sent forward could not be reversed, 'though it be wrong, without great costs and charges, which God forbid we should procure!' Here was all the panoply of an impartial and judicious quest for the truth, with all due decorum and irrespective of private and vested interests. But practice belied the theory.[1]

If the lands of the heir were thought to be worth less than £5 a year, the escheator, acting *virtute officii*—in virtue of his office and without special authority from Chancery—could hold the inquest and make his return. If the land were worth more than £5 he must wait for the appropriate writ empowering him to act. There was, however, a third system, and this was extensively used by the Elizabethan government. Reflecting its diminishing confidence in the authority and reliability of the escheator, the crown increasingly associated him with a commission of three or four men. Of this commission the feodary was invariably a member and his presence at the meeting was considered indispensable. Though the commission went out from Chancery, the structure of it was determined in the Court of Wards. Hence the pivotal role assigned to its officer, the feodary; and in London inquests, the Receiver-General, the Auditor, or the Clerk of the Court of Wards might be associated with him on the commission. Outside London, the feodary was undoubtedly its most important member. At the beginning of Elizabeth's reign, for example, the Clerk was instructed to take a bond from the escheator of Devon 'that he shall not sit during the time he shall be escheator, without the presence of the feodary'. (But this was apparently at the escheator's own request—perhaps to protect himself in some local quarrel.) In the middle of her reign, the Clerk recorded of one commission: 'This warrant was re-delivered and cancelled because the feodary, who was of the quorum, could not be in the country and a new

[1] B.M. Stowe 572, f. 17r.

warrant made.' An erring escheator who was so bold as to sit upon a commission without the presence of the feodary could speedily be taken to task.[1]

A good deal depended, then, upon the membership of the commission presiding over the inquest; and it was an important preliminary move in the struggle for a wardship to obtain the appointment to the commission of someone upon whose friendship or favour you could rely. Alternatively, it was important to oust someone favourable to the other side. As a result, the structure of the commission might simply be a compromise between two opposing groups. Amongst the loose papers used by the Clerk of the Wards when drawing up his warrants for commissions we see this compromise being worked out. For example,

The names of commissioners for Robert Lacye of Folton in the East Riding of Yorkshire:

| For Sir Henry Gall | Hugh Bethel, esquire, feodary, Walter Jobson, John Aldred. |
| For John Stanhope | Edward Stanhope, Lancelot Alford. |

The clerk had to make sure also that the balance was kept, even if the membership was altered in some way. Hence his reminder, in another context: 'If the Lord Norris go about to alter the commission, Sir John Danvers to be made privy thereto, and to have his old commissioners in the same, viz. Sir John Phettiplace and Thomas Parry.' Elsewhere in his notebook the procedure for selecting commissioners is more fully brought out. 'If any commission be required *post mortem* Thomas Cheyney armiger', wrote the clerk, 'that Mr. Attorney [of the Court of Wards] may be privy thereto for naming commissioners indifferent in the cause.' What did 'indifferent' mean? The Attorney himself provided the answer in his note of the following year: 'Let no commission or writ after the death of Thomas Cheyney esquire be awarded until both parties be made privy, viz. as well the

---

[1] For London see *Abstracts of Inquisitiones Post Mortem* for the City of London in the Tudor Period (ed. S. J. Madge, Brit. Rec. Soc., 1901), pt. ii; Wards 9.517, f. 9r; Wards 9.171, 15 Aug. 22 Eliz.

plaintiff as the defendent Anne Cheyney widow, for indifferent commissioners, day and place to be named for the execution of the same commission.' Indifferent, to a Court of Wards official, was clearly not the same as disinterested or impartial. It meant well-balanced, equally prejudiced on both sides to achieve a compromise. Justice and truth, it was hoped, would somehow emerge out of the conflict and compromise between interested parties.[1]

But sometimes even this goal—or pretence—was abandoned. 'Mr. Bosseville, my lord's pleasure is', ran an instruction on Burghley's behalf to the Clerk of the Wards, 'that a warrant be made for a commission to such persons *as this bearer shall name*[2] for the inquiry of the lunacy of the said Scott, or otherwise that a writ be directed to the escheator to inquire thereof.' But perhaps this was an act of charity, not favouritism, since the suitor was applying on behalf of the family for the guardianship of a lunatic. Less open to such an interpretation, however, is the brief observation: 'Mr. Hardy being a commissioner, you need fear no hard measure.' Who wrote it, and to whom it was sent, we do not know.[3]

Even more unmistakable is the letter from Robert Bellot, feodary of Denbighshire, to Sir Robert Cecil during his father's Mastership of the Court of Wards, 'To safeguard the queen's claim to a wardship', he wrote, 'there ought be good regard in the choice of the commissioners. Mr. Wilbram of Weddean, nor one of his friends, should be one; for that his daughter should have been married to the ward if the father had lived till morning.' 'I pray you,' wrote one of Cecil's secretaries, during his Mastership, to the Clerk of the Wards, 'send me word what writ or commission is awarded, to inquire after the death of the Lady Norris. I have order from my master to write to the escheator or commissioners, and I know neither names of the party nor of the county.'[4]

Cecil's elder brother, Thomas, likewise brought heavy guns to

---

1 *Ibid.*, Hill. 20 Eliz.; Hill. 22 Eliz.; East. 24 and 25 Eliz.
2 Author's italics.
3 *Ibid.*, East. 27 and 29 Eliz.
4 H.M.C. *Salis.*, iv, 435; x, 111.

bear upon a commissioner, a certain Richard Bagott. Writing in the summer of 1588 on behalf of 'a dear friend of mine, Mr. Fulke Greville', he asked for favourable consideration. The terms of the commission, apparently, had too many 'strict points'. Thomas had tried to persuade his father, Lord Burghley, to ameliorate them in favour of Greville. But, he confessed, 'I cannot move My Lord, my father, for redress by reason of his extreme sorrow for the present death of My lady of Oxford'— Burghley's favourite daughter, Anne. So Thomas had to fall back on Bagott for 'favour'. He did not expect that kind of service for nothing. 'I will besides thank you and do as much for you if you do anything herein for my sake.' In case this was not enough, there is a postscript: 'Good Mr. Bagott, show favour with expedition.' A few weeks later, Thomas was again writing to Bagott on the same subject: 'Let him [Greville] find favour for my sake; and, I assure you, it shall not be forgotten.' The letter ends with a friendly warning: 'I hope I shall not need any further protestation but will leave him to your favour, and judge your love to me by your proceeding in this.' Finally, there is one more postscript: 'Sir, I pray you show your favour herein to my cousin, Greville, as to one whom My Lord, my father, and I do greatly favour.' Whether Bagott did as he was told, we do not know; but greater men than he would have found it hard to say No.[1]

Yet even a commissioner devoted to his patron might prove unequal to the task. 'Good Mr. Taylor,' runs a pathetic request from an early seventeenth-century correspondent, 'this my letter shall be to let you know, and to certify the officers of the Court of Wards, that by reason of my disability in hearing, and the death of Mr. Reade, I desire to be spared as unfit for commissioner. . . . I cannot hear their answers nor the other commissioner's examinations without such loud speaking as is unfit for such a business and whereby I might do the Lady Kingsmill (that named me, not knowing of mine infirmity) great wrong, and yet no fault of mine.'[2]

[1] Appendix to Letters to Richard Bagott, Wm. Salt Library, Stafford.
[2] B.M. Add MS. 35124, f. 20r.

The difficulties of an 'indifferent' commission might be multiplied when it became involved in a feud between two noble ladies. The third and fourth Earls of Rutland died in successive years, leaving behind dowagers to dispute over the estate. Into this dispute the Court of Wards had perforce to enter, and the commission it appointed, though containing at least two members favourable to Elizabeth, Countess of Rutland, was handicapped by her at every move. 'I perceive by your letter that you are much grieved at this commission', wrote a relative to her in October 1588. He reminded her of 'the course you once resolved, which was that in all your actions you would take the advice of my brother, John Manners, and Sir George Chaworth'. They were, incidentally, members of the commission and 'they are wise and acquainted with these causes, and better able to advise you than I am'. Moreover, 'you have no great cause to mislike this commission more than the last, for Mr. Shute [the feodary of Lincolnshire], who is more curious than all the rest who are new put in, is gone to London'. To set her mind still further at rest, Burghley himself wrote to her two days later saying that he had instructed one member 'to forbear acting as one of the commissioners, as you object to him'. In spite of this and other gestures, the Lady Elizabeth proved a stumbling-block to the commission. At one stage she appears to have demanded special lawyers. The commissioners replied, with great patience, 'You cannot have any learned counsel, that be not now in the country, before the end of the term, before which time this commission will expire.' Meanwhile they needed to examine the evidences of Belvoir Castle. 'We beg you', they wrote, 'to send us the keys of the library near the chapel, of a little closet in the old great chamber and of the counting-house in Belvoir Castle.' To this she sent an unsatisfactory answer, a counter-claim for other documents in the possession of the commission (which was rejected), and the startling allegation: 'If you refuse to do this I shall think you shew small indifference to me and my son.' Again we have the expression 'indifference'. But the word had been stretched out of all recognition. The Lord Treasurer, the Lord Chief Justice, Sir Francis Walsingham, all were drawn into the dispute but, in spite of their efforts, the commission was still, during the following summer, making no headway with the Countess Elizabeth.[1]

So the case dragged on—an intolerable burden to statesmen and family alike. Yet, such was the outlook of the time that, in the midst of these controversies, one of the commissioners, Sir George Chaworth, now a sick man, wrote to the Lady Elizabeth, asking for a loan of £200 and a litter for his journey to London 'to consult the college of physicians'. In the midst of it all the Countess of Rutland found time to procure a marriage between her ward, Robert Tyrwhit, and Lady Bridget Manners, one of the queen's maids of honour, for which she earned the frankest expression of the royal displeasure.[2]

If the impartiality of the commissioners was, to say the least, open to question, the members of the jury were even more vulnerable. 'I am infinitely bound to you', wrote the Earl of Cumberland to Sir Robert Cecil in 1603, 'and for your favour to me be assured that if any friend of yours have any suit in these parts, I will find him an honest and kind jury.' That an honest jury might not be kind or a kind jury honest had, no doubt, occurred to his lordship. On one occasion Henry VIII himself had written with such effect to a jury that they, 'fearing the right by them not to be indifferently handled', could not come to a verdict. Certainly the unhappy jury was the target of allegation and criticism by the defeated party. The membership of the jury could, as in our own day, be challenged and some of its members excluded, but sometimes nothing short of a *supersedeas*—a cancellation of their verdict—and the impanelling of a new jury would satisfy a contesting party. Apart from any initial subservience, there were other pressures to be brought to bear upon the jury; hence the knowledge that a move was afoot to 'appal the jury' led a correspondent of Robert Cecil to warn him not to part with any money until the findings of an inquisition were known.[3]

1 H.M.C. *Rutland*, i, 261ff.
2 Violet A. Wilson, *Queen Elizabeth's Maids of Honour* (1922), pp. 187–98.
3 H.M.C. *Salis.*, xii, 674; iv, 298, 435; *L.P.*, v, 187.

It was possible for a discontented litigant to bring an action against a jury, and all its members might be ordered to appear in the Court of Wards 'peremptorily for the hearing of the matter between Felton and the jury'. On another occasion a plaintiff alleged that a jury 'obstinately refused to find for the queen', and sought similar redress. Someone writing to Robert Cecil went further and said that there was a conspiracy in Radnorshire to return all knight-service tenures as socage tenures. He urged that the jury be sent for, examined and punished. On the other hand one seventeenth-century critic argued that the exact opposite was happening: feodaries and escheators who could not get the verdict they sought would 'adjourn the commission from place to place, till as it were by a kind of duress they made the jury to find what they would have them'. In the same way—it was once alleged— commissioners 'utterly rejected and would not suffer any evidences to be given or showed forth for the infant'. When the verdict was reached they received it from 'the foreman of the jury, the rest of the jurors, or the most of them, not consenting but denying their assent thereunto'. [1]

A truly indifferent jury was as hard to obtain as indifferent commissioners. Sometimes it was known that a great lord, for example, the Earl of Worcester, was 'able to command most in Monmouthshire from whence the jury must come'; sometimes it was thought that the jury was simply 'hired thereunto' by the great landowners. But on one occasion a jury dared to find a verdict unfavourable to the Earl of Derby, though he had three servants empanelled on it and the other members 'such as did affect him very much'. Only the timely death of his lordship saved the opposing side from the consequences which they had been led to anticipate. What kind of a jury could a wretched sheriff be expected to assemble, torn as he was between warring factions or, more likely, himself an active partisan of one of them? 'Forasmuch as before this time there hath been much indirect dealing in the empanelling of a jury for the finding of an

---

[1] Wards 9.517, f. 58r; H.M.C. *Salis.*, x. 131, xi, 505; *Commons Debates*, 1621, ii, 101; W. West, *Symboleography* (1618), ii, 330b.

office after the death of Sir Francis Hastings knight, deceased, whereby the queen's title cannot be found nor appear', ran a message from the Court of Wards, 'we have thought good to admonish you thereof.' The sheriff was instructed 'to have circumspection and good diligence to empanel a substantial, indifferent jury for the queen, such as by no means any corruption or affection may lead'. It was easier said than done.[1]

With such commissioners and such juries it is hardly likely that *inquisitions post mortem* could be trustworthy sources for either contemporaries or historians. Key documents might be either suppressed or unobtainable. Members of the jury might be bribed, threatened or dragged through the courts so that their verdicts could be reversed. Inquisitions might be rushed through while men with interests at stake were unaware that they were going on, 'whereby many men are infinitely vexed and troubled who, if they had been called at the first, could have showed sufficient manner for their discharge'. In one case the Privy Council itself had to intervene to warn the commission that the Council was aware that the interests of one of the queen's gentlemen-pensioners were at stake. He was compelled to give daily attendance upon the queen during her progress but feared that, during his absence from the inquisition, 'some indirect course or hard measure may be offered by his adversaries, who (as we are informed) have purposely already retained all the learned counsel in that county, thereby intending by some device to frustrate the due execution of the office'. Accordingly, the commission was charged 'in Her Majesty's name (as so directed from her own mouth) to have special care that no frivolous devices nor practices be used to delay and put off the finding of the said office'. It was to be 'followed and finished with all sincerity and indifferency for all parties as to equity and justice shall appertain, without any respect of person whatsoever'.[2]

This practice—of making a false return while men whose interests were in jeopardy were out of the county—was familiar

---

[1] H.M.C. *Salis.*, viii, 263; ix, 179; iv, 522; Wards 9.231, East. 1 Eliz.
[2] B.M. Cotton MS. Tit. F. IV, f. 131; *Acts of P.C.*, 1591, p. 416.

to Tudor litigants. 'Good uncle,' wrote the Earl of Derby to Sir Robert Cecil in 1600, 'in the absence of me and my officer forth of Lancashire this last term, and upon information given and received by such as have intended the impeachment of my inheritance in my chiefest manor, namely Lathom, an office hath been sitten.' By the early seventeenth century these grievances were coming to a head and parliamentary reformers were anxious to bring such backstairs activity under control. The Court of Wards itself tried to ensure that those concerned should receive fourteen days' notice of the holding of an inquisition. It went further on numerous occasions in recommending a *traverse*, hauling a jury before the court, and even cancelling a wardship where subsequent evidence proved the jury's findings to be false. In one case the sheriff somehow drew men from the wrong county to serve on the jury. This led to other irregularities; hence for 'divers causes and exceptions' the return was nullified by decree of the Court of Wards.[1]

The procedure adopted at inquisitions and the opportunities for corruption are displayed vividly amongst the Court of Wards' pleadings of Meredith and others *v*. Rede.[2] The issue turned on a will presented at the inquisition by Rede, which the plaintiffs alleged was bogus. The effect of the will was to grant away most of the land which would otherwise have descended to the heir, who was a ward of the queen. For this reason the issue was joined in the Court of Wards. In reply the defendant declared that he showed the will and the findings of the inquisition, in draft, to the plaintiffs and their solicitor, who had indeed approved of it and contributed towards the cost of holding the inquisition. To all this the plaintiffs returned a flat denial. The will was not the deceased's last will; the defendant had used undesirable methods at the inquisition, and had by various 'sinister practices' tried to persuade the jury to approve the findings which he had drawn up for them. The inquest had started at one o'clock in the afternoon and was not finished until past midnight; and even then the jury

---

[1] H.M.C. *Salis.*, x, 17; Wards 9,104, f. 335-336v.
[2] Wards 3.3, East. 4 Eliz.

had wanted longer time, while the plaintiffs, who had seen the draft inquisition, had not yet agreed to it. Some of the jurymen had since said that they agreed that the will was *a* will of the deceased but not the *last* will.

This time it was the turn of Rede, the defendant, bluntly to contradict all these allegations. The will was undoubtedly the last will; all the alterations were sealed by the testator and each page was signed. The defendant had no personal interest in the findings of the jury and did what he was doing only because of the trust reposed in him by the deceased. No sinister practices were used with the jury as Mr. Kitchin, one of the solicitors for the plaintiff, well knew; and it must have been against Mr. Kitchin's advice that such a charge was ever put into the pleadings. Far from wishing to use undue influence with the jury, Rede said that he stood by while the plaintiffs challenged the jury. They had, moreover, put in two near kinsmen, 'which were the only stay in the matter indeed to have pleasured the defendant'; but even they agreed to the findings. Apart from this, Rede repeated, the plaintiffs' solicitor had agreed to the proposed findings and to pay a share of the costs. As for an allegation that the inquisition was held without warning, they must have been kept fully informed or how could their solicitor have managed to be present? Moreover, everything was done in public on a market day in a market town.

There our pleadings for this case come to an end, and it has not been possible to trace the final decree. What however is quite clear is that the findings returned by the jury represented the *last* stage in what might be a lengthy process of discussion between two or more interested, and opposing, parties. Their findings in fact were, as far as possible, prepared in advance and it was for the jury to pronounce, subject all the while to various pressures, upon the truth of the findings. 'For that the said books brought unto us are the drafts of the parties,' said an escheator in addressing the jury, 'let us, as it standeth us upon, thoroughly peruse and advisedly consider them.' 'And if therein any contrary part be found to be touched,' he warned them, 'we will not only hear what they can say or show for the same, but also, upon good and sufficient cause for the better proof, we will give them a further day.' 'For I trust you do consider,' he concluded, 'though it be the parties' draft, yet the offices that by you shall be found and by me certified, must be our deeds. And if it be wrong, your consciences must be therewith charged.'[1]

So much for the theory. But the documents which we are reading are essentially formal documents, their conclusions the results of compromise between opposing parties. A strong-minded escheator and sheriff, and a courageous jury, might thwart the wishes of vested interests and state the truth so far as in them lay. The chances of this were rare. A tired, hungry and browbeaten jury, and an escheator or commission subservient to a local magnate would, more probably, temper their zeal for the truth with a shrewd assessment of local circumstances. Throughout the sixteenth century and beyond, measures were before Parliament, such as 'for the returning of sufficient juries and for the better expedition of trials'. Coke, writing in the early seventeenth century, listed the various methods by which inquisitions were corrupted a hundred years before; and he laid these evils at the door of Empson and Dudley. Yet the majority of these abuses were present in inquisitions drawn up in Coke's own day. This time, however, the beneficiary was not the crown but private interest. None the less, from the crown's point of view, the inquisition had served one essential purpose. It had established whether the crown had certain feudal rights in the estates of the heir.[2]

By now solicitors had been briefed, officials and courtiers rewarded, records searched, and writs and commissions returned. The seeker after a wardship had spent many barren weeks in the legal desert and—if the verdict had fulfilled his hopes—now stood ready to enter the promised land. But when the commission's return was in the Master's hands, the petitioner was still only on the threshold. Between the discovery and the grant of a wardship stretched the lengthy and characteristic processes of a Tudor department of state.

1 B.M. Stowe 572, f. 17r.
2 27 Eliz., cc. 6 and 7; Coke, Fourth Institute, c. 35.

4

Suitors for Wards

THERE were many ways—some thoroughly disreputable—in which a candidate for a wardship might press his suit. But, however he set about it, he could not omit one important step: the presentation of a petition to the Master himself, either personally or through an intermediary. The petitions were not official documents manufactured by solicitors according to a common formula, but often intimate and personal ones. So before following the petitioner to the end of the journey, it is instructive to look at the kind of petition which found its way into Lord Burghley's office in the Court of Wards.

'Right honourable,' runs a petition of 20 March 1570 to Burghley, '. . . as I have always had occasion to think myself most bound unto you, so have I no less hope to find the promise of your goodness towards me when any occasion doth present it.' Such an occasion did indeed present itself in the shape of 'the wardship of my sister's child, the eldest son of Thomas Cooper', of Nottinghamshire. In fact Cooper was not yet dead but there was a distinct possibility that his death 'shall happen before mine which, at this instant, by the determination of physic is very likely, and by the most of them he is adjudged not to be of long continuance'. His inheritance, said the petitioner, was worth less than £100 a year; 'but I covet not Sir so much the gain herein as the furtherance and good education of my said nephew'. In other words his objects were not mercenary but charitable:

And yet, in obtaining the same, [I] shall account myself still most bound unto you and must so remain, praying to Almighty God for the good preservation and long continuance of your health and honourable estate,

> Helford, this XX of March,
> Your Honour's,
> Humbly to command to my power,
> THOMAS STANHOPE.[1]

How many hundreds of such petitions Burghley received each year we do not know; those that survive cover numerous manuscripts at the British Museum, the Public Record Office and, most of all, at Hatfield House. They came from all parts of the kingdom and from various classes of the community: courtier, administrator, friend, or relation. Amongst them we have one also from Jane Cecil, Burghley's mother, written in the year 1570. The petition is in the handwriting of a secretary but the signature is in the firm and clear hand of the old lady herself, then aged about seventy.

My hearty commendations [it begins] unto you and my lady your wife, had with the Lord's blessing and mine on you and my lady. These may be to signify unto ye that, where one William Crofts, son and heir of Thomas Crofts, late of Barwell in the county of Leicester, gent, deceased, by reason of his minority at and by your appointment is to be given and granted, that it would please you the rather at this my request to bestow the wardship of the said William on the bringer hereof, namely one John Crofts of Ketton who is uncle unto the ward, and a neighbour and poor friend of mine, one whom I may command.

Therefore I would gladly, if conveniently ye might pleasure him in this my suit and his; and I suppose he will willingly give as [much as] another will do for the same. And thus hoping that before another, for the causes aforesaid, he shall obtain (by your good means) his suit on this behalf, I leave ye to the lord, whom I beseech to bless ye with increase,

> From Stamford, the third of April, 1570,
> Your loving Mother,
> JANE CECILL.[2]

---

[1] *S.P.D.*, Eliz., lxvii, no 27.
[2] *Ibid.*, no. 41.

Lastly, from amongst many, we may consider a more formal petition:

The request of Sir John Perrot

He humbly desireth that John Vowell, Alderman of Haverford West, may have the wardship of William Warren, who is son-in-law to the said Vowell, he paying therefor as much as any other will do. The lands of the said Warren, which is descended unto him, is about ten pounds a year.[1]

These petitions have two features in common: they are from distinguished people, personally acquainted with Burghley, and they are on behalf of relatives whose principal concern, it is argued, is the welfare of the ward. In this respect, at least, these petitions belong to a small and exceptional group.

Who were the petitioners? First we may consider the servants of the Cecil household, whose personal access to their master offered prospects of a wardship here and there. Secondly, and more powerful and numerous, were the statesmen, courtiers, officials, who could put in an early and forceful bid for an important wardship either for marriage to a relative or to be disposed of at a profit. But competition could be intense and feelings bitter. There were lastly the miscellaneous petitions from those with no direct access to the queen or the Master and who had to employ the services of intermediaries, according to the familiar practices of Tudor clientage. Somewhere amongst these documents, most usually in the last group, were the petitions from the mothers of the wards, seeking at first or second hand the guardianship of their children. They took their place in the queue.

The majority of petitions forwarded to Burghley were *not* on behalf of a ward's relative and their purpose was not charitable but pecuniary. This, of course, applied especially to petitions for concealed wardships. Lord Burghley's barber, for example, a certain John Gregory, could hardly have been troubled by thwarted parental instincts when he informed his master, in July 1594, of a concealed ward whose guardian he wished to become.

[1] *Ibid.*, no. 43.

He felt, however, that a slightly sanctimonious tone was not inappropriate. Hence, because

> it hath been ever since wrongfully concealed from Her Majesty to the ill example of others and the wronging of Her Majesty's title in the same hereafter, his humble suit is therefore to your Lordship that it would please your Lordship to grant him the said wardship for the better trial of Her Majesty's title. And he will bear the charge for the trial thereof, and according to his bounden duty continually pray for your Lordship's health and prosperity long to continue.[1]

Another servant of Burghley's, Gilbert Wakering, had written two months earlier, in a similar tone with a similar request:

> May it please your Lordship, there is one Francis Jennye, in the county of Suffolk, gent., who died above a year sithence, and [it] is thought that his heir, being within age, ought to be Her Majesty's ward, which they intend to conceal. If it would please your Lordship to grant the wardship of him to your servant, Gilbert Wakering, he hopeth thereof to find a tenure for Her Majesty. And he, according to his bounden duty, shall pray for your lordship's health, in honourable happiness long to continue.[2]

Another of Burghley's servants, John Symons, had had only a short-lived success in his petition. He had previously been granted 'the wardship of [the son of] one John Gascoigne, who was then in some extremity of sickness but now, as I understand, is recovered'. He hoped, however, that he might have better fortune with another request.[3]

When Robert Cecil succeeded his father as Master of the Court of Wards, his household servants likewise hoped to pick up a few of the droppings from a great man's table. John Whyte, 'keeper of the fowl' at Theobalds, Cecil's country house, put in a claim. So did a Mr. Stileman, another servant at Theobalds, as did Richard Iveson, Cecil's porter. Mr. Benett, the footman, asked for one and got it. Thomas Browne, 'one of your Honour's

---

1 H.M.C. *Salis.*, iv, 562 (P. 632).
2 *Ibid.*, p. 524 (P. 638).
3 *Ibid.*, p. 532 (P. 1924).

stable', looked beyond his master's horses to the prospect of a
wardship in Somerset. Philip Cecil, who claimed to be a servant in
livery of the household of Cecil's kinsman, for forty years, hoped
to spend part of his old age as guardian of a ward from Hereford-
shire.[1]

In the last years of Burghley's Mastership, for which we have a
fuller collection of private documents than earlier, there had been
a steady stream of these requests from servants, feodaries, friends
and acquaintances. Under his son, Sir Robert Cecil, it became a
flood. But household servants could hope for little more than the
remains of a feast at which courtiers, high officials and the Master
himself had supped. Courtiers played a dual role in the history of
the Court of Wards, as suitors for themselves and as intermediaries for others. Of their own successful claims the official records
of the Court of Wards supply abundant evidence, but of their
original petitions only a fraction have survived. Those surviving,
however, provide some measure of the heavy pressure which a
Master had to endure. Even so, courtiers had to hasten to press
their suits lest they be forestalled. A Mr. Argol, Sir Edward Hoby
once told Cecil, was in a lingering sickness. Apparently no
petition had yet gone forward for the wardship of his heir.
Hoby was accordingly filing his claim, the news of which would,
he alleged—for some unexplained reason—lead to an improvement in Mr. Argol's health.[2]

No less a person than Lord Cobham, hearing of a man's
death, wrote the same evening to Cecil for the wardship of the
heir, adding that his haste was due to his fear of being forestalled.
The Earl of Cumberland, some years before, had obtained the
promise of a wardship from Burghley when the ward's father,
then Lord Mayor of London, lay dying. Cumberland took the
precaution, however, of seeking Cecil's help in the matter also
and added that, if his petition were successful, Cecil would share
'to his own contentment', whatever that might mean. Charles,
Lord Willoughby wrote twice to Cecil in June and October

1 *Ibid.*, ix, 222; x, 408, 464; xi, 413, 501, 506, 245.
2 *Ibid.*, xii, 517.

1601 for the wardship of his own grandchild. This appears to have led to a difference of opinion between Willoughby and the Earl of Rutland, who had plans for marrying the ward to his sister and had come into the market somewhat later. Sir Thomas Egerton, Master of the Rolls and Keeper of the Great Seal, also wrote to Cecil in 1601 for the wardship of the son of his kinsman, Sir George Maynwaringe, who was ill. Lord Morley told Cecil of a false return to an inquisition and offered, for an appropriate reward, to take steps to reverse its findings.[1]

Lord Cromwell's letter, written in March 1599, when the Mastership was vacant, had a grimmer tale to tell. His purpose was:

> To entreat the performance of his [Burghley's] promise as to the wardship of my son, if I miscarry in these wars, whereunto, after so long service, I go so smally regarded. It will not, I hope, be thought amiss if I desire that my wife and such small substance as I leave her may be protected in my absence, and that she may have the wardship of her own son if I return not with life ... that I may with better confidence hazard my life, when I know those whom I most dearly regard to be protected and remembered.[2]

Lord Cromwell survived the wars. But a different kind of disaster descended upon Sir Arthur Gorges. In a plaintive letter to Sir Robert Cecil in June 1601, he set out, with brutal frankness, his position in respect of his ward. (His reference to his daughter is in fact to his stepdaughter, who was his ward.)

> When I was to make a great benefit of my daughter's marriage, even to the value of £6,000 in present payment [that is, cash] besides other considerations, it then pleased Her Majesty to use your service and authority for the stay of my proceedings therein, to the utter undoing of me and mine. For first, I was served with an injunction either to deliver up my child upon the pretended title of Her Majesty's prerogative; or else to enter into six thousand pounds bonds not to dispose of her but by the leave of the Master and Council of

1 *Ibid.*, xii, 416; iv, 554–5; xi, 215, 406; xii, 187; xi, 193, 485–6.
2 *Ibid.*, ix, 116.

the Wards. And, after this great bond, I was so long held in suit and suspense as that my child died before I could obtain Her Majesty's bill assigned for my full and free enjoying thereof.

No wonder he went on to lament his dire poverty! 'If I had been suffered quietly to have enjoyed my own, my endeavours would have sustained me from penury.' But that was not to be and he had all his 'labours either lopped or frostbitten when the fruits thereof should have returned unto my comfort'. More successful was Lord Willoughby, who reminded Cecil in June 1601 that he had granted Willoughby before the father's death the wardship of the heir of Richard Fulstowe, his servant. The Fulstowes, Cecil was informed, had been dependants and wards of the Willoughbys for three hundred years![1]

Humfrey Plessington, who petitioned Cecil for a wardship on behalf of a mother, belonged to a totally different social class from the Willoughbys. He sent a brief petition, which is worth quoting in full. It is attractive for its direct and earthy qualities; and for these reasons we may for once abandon our practice of modernising the spelling and let Plessington speak his own language, helped only by modern print and punctuation[2]:

> Maye it please your Honour, I ame a humbele sewtor to me Lord [Burghley] for the wardshipes of Gratwicke Heires of Sussex to the ewse of the mother. But waire I heare that your Honour hath written to me Lord for tham, I ame sewer that me Lord will litte your Honour haue them and I hame glad it is me fortune to light in to your Honour's handes. For I most humbley besoche you that yow will be as good to me as you haue bene to the reste of me felowes. This with me humble dewt rembred, 12 May 1598,
>
> Yowrs Honour's Humbely Saruant,
and daly beadman,
HUMFREY PLESSINGTON.

The petitioning for wards was not solely a masculine occupation. The wives of aristocrats, courtiers and officials brought to

---

1 *Ibid.*, xi, 222, 242.
2 *Ibid.*, viii, 164 (61.15).

their part of the search a considerable measure of skill and experience. When Robert Cecil succeeded his father as Master, Anne, Lady Wentworth sought from Cecil the confirmation of her son's wardship granted by Burghley. She asked that Cecil and her uncle, Sir John Fortescue, be joined with her in the grant. Mary, Lady Cholmeley was likewise a petitioner to Cecil for her son's wardship; and Katherine, Lady Newton, anticipating the death of Robert Chamberlain of Oxfordshire, made haste to ask that his son's wardship be bestowed upon her. Anne, Lady Cobham had a more serious problem. Her daughter had married a Mr. Calverley whom she described in a masterly understatement as an 'unstaid' young man. In 1600 he was in the Fleet and his life was in danger. Should he die, Lady Cobham asked that the wardship of his brother be bestowed upon her daughter. In other words, the ward's sister-in-law would finance her widowhood by becoming his guardian. Dorothy, Lady North found herself at about this time in a worse plight. She sent two separate pleas to Cecil about the wardship of her son, whose control appeared to have passed to her husband's executors and not to herself. His marriage had been made without her consent and in virtual secrecy; the dowry, she alleged, had been taken from him. But her son sided with the executors and against his mother and pleaded for the maintenance of the *status quo*. Nor could he miss an opportunity for killing two birds with one stone. Enclosed with this opposition to his mother's request was the quite irrelevant petition that the custody of Gyles Bladwell, a lunatic, be bestowed upon George Lee Hunte, gentleman.[1]

Cecil's relatives, however distant their connection, used it to prosecute their claims. Lady Cooke sought a wardship of him, in 1602, on behalf of her husband, Sir Anthony Cooke. Mistress Anne White, another relative, openly asked for a wardship for her son-in-law, 'the greater the better for then it will bring them out of debt'; while her servant, John Barber, had fished on his own behalf in the well-stocked waters of the Court of Wards. Relatives, colleagues, noblemen, officials: from all angles the

1 *Ibid.*, ix, 215; xi, 463; x, 117, 190, 405, 410, 417.

Master was assaulted with pleas and petitions. It must suffice at this stage to select a few of the eminent names amongst the grantees of one year, the fourth of Elizabeth's reign: Sir William Cordell, Sir Walter Haddon, Sir Francis Knollys, Sir Piers Leigh, Sir Walter Mildmay, Sir William Petre, the Earl of Rutland, Sir Henry Sidney, the Bishop of Winchester, and Sir Thomas Wroth—whose son forty years later was to move in the House of Commons for an investigation into wardships as a 'burden and servitude to the subjects of this kingdom'. Yet the direct grant of a wardship was merely one of several channels through which the profits from wardship flowed to the Elizabethan ruling class.[1]

We have been considering so far only one aspect of the functions of suitors: pleading for wardships on their own behalf. Of greater importance was their role as intermediaries. There was no stereotyped system through which a candidate for a wardship was expected to operate. Any courtier, official or member of the Master's entourage could be asked to transmit a request for a wardship, sometimes at two or three stages removed; and during one period at least a Clerk of the Wards took good care to enter the name of the 'solicitor', using the word in its original sense.

We have then, in the first place, a miscellaneous group of intermediaries who for friendship, patronage or money might say a helpful word on behalf of a candidate for a wardship. Robert Cecil may have been more frequently the object of these attentions than his father, or it may be that time and lack of caution have been more kind to his surviving records. Certainly for years before his father's death Cecil had himself acted as a go-between in petitions to his father for wardships; and after his assumption of the Mastership in May 1599 this kind of correspondence continued, though the suitors were now petitioning him in his official capacity. The bombardment was soon in full swing. We have a letter from Lord Cobham to Cecil asking for a wardship for a Captain Wiatt; another from the new Lord Burghley, Cecil's elder brother; one from Dr. Richard Neile, his chaplain; one from the egregious Lady Edmunds, a family connection; and

1 *Ibid.*, xii, 490; xi, 440–1; xii, 44; x, 119; Wards 9.156; *C.J.*, i, 151.

one from what looks like a reception committee of fourteen gentlemen-pensioners on behalf of a colleague. But many other petitions were being channelled through Cecil's secretaries, working for him in his private household, not at the Court of Wards. In particular a good deal of correspondence was going through Richard Perceval and Michael Hickes.[1]

Richard Perceval was one of the many officials in Tudor England who held no high office in the state but, as confidential secretaries to a minister, stood very close to the fountain of power and wealth. In virtue of this, their correspondents were not simply men of like social standing but were drawn also from the upper ranges of government and society. These personal assistants were the ancestors of the principal private secretaries in a government department of today, whose modest place in the civil service hierarchy gives no measure of the significant role they play. They are not the permanent secretaries of their department, charged with advising the minister on the carrying out of policy but, sitting as they do in what is still described as the minister's outer office, they hold the key to the inner room and the inner councils of the minister himself. Richard Perceval and others sat in the outer office of Burghley and Cecil; and when men like Perceval, Maynard, Townshend, Skinner, Clapham and Hickes have at last yielded us their story, we shall know a good deal more about how the Tudor government went about its business.

Certainly the most eminent men thought nothing of writing modestly to the Master's secretary in furtherance of some scheme. No less a person than Sir John Popham, Lord Chief Justice, having obtained from Cecil the promise of a wardship to a suitor, sent a friendly word to Perceval asking him to further the matter. The Lord Chief Justice got a little muddled about Perceval's Christian name but it was at least an attempt to establish personal contact. Sir John Stanhope, vice-Chamberlain of the Household, similarly thought fit to make his approaches to the secretary; and the same applied to Sir James Marvin. There were of course numerous letters from the smaller fry, sometimes seeking to forestall a

[1] H.M.C. *Salis.*, x, 2; xi, 379, 359; x, 133; xi, 507.

competitor, jog the official memory, add supporting details, or give broad hints of private rewards. An active suitor might be presenting two petitions at once. 'Were it not that I am engaged in the like suit to Mr. Secretary [Sir Robert Cecil] in a matter of more moment to myself', wrote one correspondent of Perceval's, 'I would have written to him to this end.'[1]

Sometimes the petition indicates how many stages it had to pass through before it could reach the Master's table. For example, Sir John Herbert wrote to Perceval for his favour to a Mr. Glyn, who was making a suit on behalf of a Mr. Evans (with whom Herbert had some connection). Between Mr. Evans and the Master there were in effect four stages and, even by then, Mr. Evans's journey had only just begun.[2]

Amongst the secretaries of the Cecils there was one who seemed to enjoy a special position of confidence, almost of friendship, with Sir Robert Cecil. Michael Hickes was very often the principal channel through whom suitors for a wardship made their pleas; and even the great in the land spared a friendly word—and often a gift—for this astute and cynical trader in wards. To his friendship with Cecil was added the office of feodary of Essex in 1598, and his part in the distribution of wardships was now doubly significant. To him the Earl of Huntingdon wrote in December 1597: 'Mr. Hickes, I have been beholding to you for your travail and pains taken in soliciting my causes for me to my good Lord, for which I hold myself in your debt and will come out of it ere it be long.' There was a further letter from the same source in February 1598. The Earl of Nottingham's letter of October 1598 (written a few months after Hickes' appointment as feodary) sets out frankly the services for which his Lordship hoped.

> Where an inquisition is shortly to be made before you [the writer observes], after the death of my late loving and kind son-in-law, Sir Robert Southwell Kt . . . these are therefore very heartily to pray you, and the rather for my sake to show unto my daughter,

1 Ibid., x, 126; xi, 498; xii, 487; x, 108.
2 Ibid., xi, 436.

the Lady Elizabeth Southwell, his widow (for the easy values of the said lands and for her proceedings otherwise) all the favour you may. Nothing doubting of your friendship, which I will always accept very thankful, I bid you heartily farewell from the Court at White-hall this 26 October 1598.

The Earl of Cumberland sent an anxious inquiry to Hickes the day after he heard that a father's death had brought another ward-ship on the market: 'I pray you, therefore, if it be not too late, deliver my letters and further it all you may, for which you shall well find I will be very thankful.'[1]

If noblemen could write in this tone, humbler folk were also numbered amongst his correspondents, though sometimes they themselves needed an intermediary before approaching this inter-mediary! The Earl of Worcester once asked Hickes for a wardship on behalf of a servant but added that if the wardship were too small for him to deal with, would he let him know in whose hands the matter was? Hickes was not always successful. One suitor asked for his gift back when Hickes failed to live up to the occasion.[2]

For a time, he and Robert Cecil worked hand in glove. 'For the hundred pounds', Cecil once told him, 'I will find a ward to pay it—or 200 rather than fail.' Between them, in the last years of Burghley's Mastership, they were handling some dubious transactions which, if it could be shown that Burghley had cog-nizance of them, would reflect credit on neither father, nor son, nor servant. In the early months of James I's reign, when honours were falling thick and fast from the grateful king, Hickes seems to have declined a knighthood—'Good Master Hickes, that would not be Sir Michael', Cecil scoffingly wrote to him. But Hickes accepted other things under James I and his predecessor, and when the offer came a second time in 1604, he did not say No. Later, as Robert Cecil rose to high and responsible office, the warmth seemed to go out of his relationship with Hickes, perhaps one of several indications that Cecil was turning his back on the practices, and the friends, of his youth. The Earl of Salisbury,

1 B.M. Lans. 84, f. 164r; 86, f. 53r; 87, f. 41r, f. 30r; 82, f. 46r.
2 B.M. Lans. 77, f. 180r; 91, f. 145r; 107, f. 205r.

Lord Treasurer under James I, was a very different man from the Robert Cecil who had operated in the shadows of his father's greatness. Perhaps, as the friendship languished, Hickes sought comfort in the 'sentences or adages' of which by some quirk of hypocrisy or cynicism he had made a collection in his leisure hours. 'Let nothing be so esteemed of you that it make thee do against honesty or right', is the kind of advice he must have found easier to give than to accept. He also drew up a series of model answers to be given to suitors on appropriate occasions. One of of these—'Make your suit to the queen, I will do the best I can for you. If she ask my opinion, I will tell her what I think of you and your suit'—is a masterpiece of courtierlike ambiguity. This skilful and charming rogue awaits his biographer.[1]

From the petitions that we have already considered—and they are only a fraction of a larger total—it is clear that many and circuitous were the roads which led from a claimant for a wardship to the Master of the Court. A small minority indeed forged their own path direct to the queen or her Privy Council, and in so doing might by-pass, wholly or partly, the tedious and discouraging procedures, now hardening into a tradition. At the end of Mary's reign, when the Marshal of Berwick was murdered, the queen's instructions to the Privy Council set aside the usual practices and granted the wardship to the next of kin. In so doing she followed the good precedent of her father who, on one occasion, released from feudal wardship the heirs of those killed in the war against the Scots. Peregrine Bertie, Lord Willoughby, when he came to make his will in 1599, instructed his executors to spend £100 of his money on a jewel or other gift for the queen in the hope that she would grant his heir's wardship to the guardian appointed by the father. He apologised for his temerity, but the soldier-courtier, born during his parents' flight from the Marian persecution, had served his queen faithfully. His son was nineteen at his father's death and he appears to have succeeded to his barony and estates at once—an especial sign of the queen's good-

---

[1] *Original Letters*, ed. Ellis (3rd. ser.), iv, 151; B.M. Lans. 88, f. 153r; 98, ff. 217r, 215r.

will. He too grew to be a distinguished soldier and died fighting for Charles I at Edgehill.[1]

The Earl of Huntingdon, before soliciting a wardship from Burghley, *via* Hickes, approached the queen. Armed with 'Her Majesty's good liking of the same, whose princely pleasure therein I sought to know before I durst attempt to write unto my Lord', the earl felt strengthened to press on with his project. For the official processes could only rarely be avoided. Lady Wentworth's petition for the wardship of her son, though it was backed by her kinsman Sir John Fortescue, Elizabeth's tutor in the dangerous days before she came to the throne, had nevertheless to be referred to the Master of the Wards. The same thing happened when the mother of Christopher Hatton, cousin and heir of the late Lord Chancellor, applied for the wardship of her son. Over him a battle-royal raged in which the redoubtable Sir Edward Coke, the Attorney-General—who knew a valuable ward when he saw one—joined issue against her. Amidst the struggle the wretched Hatton was 'forced to live obscurely in a college in Cambridge'. The mother begged that the queen would 'accept some reasonable sum for his wardship and marriage' so that he might gain his freedom 'wherein your Majesty shall give hope and mean to continue the name in the house of your faithful servant, Sir Christopher Hatton, by your most royal Majesty advanced'. Coke maintained that his opponents were using 'indirect and sinister courses' against him while the mother expressed herself in even stronger terms to the Master of the Wards. 'I beseech you', she wrote, 'to afford me in this plunge of my hard fortunes but such favour as your noble disposed mind denies to none, that when reports of Mr. Attorney's grievance for the marriage of his ward shall come unto your ears, you will not conceive of me further than you see good proof.' For the majority of suitors the road to a wardship might be rocky, perilous and, in the early stages, unrewarding. The distant prospects, however, were usually worthy of the most arduous campaign.[2]

1 *Acts of P.C.*, 1556–8, pp. 254–5; H.M.C. *Salis.*, xiv, 194.
2 B.M. Lans. 87, f. 37r; H.M.C. *Salis.*, xii, 577; xi, 201; x, 429, 435, 443.

So much for the wards. But the Master of the Court of Wards was also the royal guardian of idiots and lunatics, so amongst his voluminous correspondence we come, here and there, upon petitions for their custody. These applications bore a formal resemblance to the petition for a wardship, but here the scope for abuse was very much more limited. In the case of an idiot—that is to say, one of simple mind who could never hope for the full development of his faculties—his land and profits remained in the crown's hands, to be disposed of at will, until the idiot died and the next heir succeeded him and reclaimed the land. In the case of a lunatic who was assumed to be only intermittently insane a near relative would often be granted the custody both of the person and the lands; but the guardian would have to render an account of his proceedings when his charge recovered his mental health. We rarely meet offers of bribes for the grant of a lunatic, nor do the petitions seem to pass through so many hands. If there was less opportunity for the skilled practitioners in the handling and transmission of petitions, there is more than one indication that not all guardians or petitioners were acting purely from altruistic motives. Gilbert Moreton asked Burghley to grant his brother the custody of an idiot who was being sold, as he said, from one to another. Miles Raynsford asked for a lunatic called William Barnes who had been kept in Bridewell for fourteen years. Robert Pamplyn, a yeoman of Her Majesty's Robes, asked for the custody of Christopher Wannesford, a lunatic, and challenged the claim of another petitioner.[1]

At the beginning of Elizabeth's reign, Burghley wrote in a considerable hurry to Sir Francis Englefield, then Master of the Wards, asking advice as to the property of lunatics. In a brief answer Englefield pointed out that the crown could gain nothing from lunatics. 'Sir, because this bearer seemeth to make haste in returning answer of his message', he wrote, 'it may like you to be advertised that . . . by the laws of this realm, the prince hath no property in any of the possessions of any lunatic.' The guardian 'amongst many other covenants, especially is bounden for the

[1] *Ibid.*, xiii, 95–6; xi, 507.

answering of the surplusage of the whole profits that shall remain
above the convenient finding [that is, upkeep] of himself, the
said lunatic, his house and family'. The remainder went to his
'heirs, executors or assigns for that it is taken that when he enjoyeth
such times as the law taketh him to be *sana mentis*, then he may
make a testament, assignment or any bargain. . . . And thus, for
haste of the messenger, I can enlarge the same no farther unto you
presently,' concluded Englefield, 'but within a day or two I will
wait on you and declare the same more at length.' That was at
the beginning of December 1558 and it was to be one of the last
official services Englefield performed.[1]

Since the crown had little to gain, it was very common for the
custody of a lunatic to go to a relative. For example, John Leyland
the younger, who held several rectories in Edward VI's reign,
was found in an inquisition before Sir Andrew Judd, Lord Mayor
and escheator of London, to be 'mad, insane, lunatic, furious,
frantic, enjoying drowsy or lucid intervals so that he cannot
manage his affairs'. The custody of the man and his property was
accordingly committed to his brother John Leyland the elder,
who was to enjoy all the profits accruing to his brother, including
the income from the rectories, and was to maintain divine service
and cure of souls, where required. If John the younger ever
recovered and reclaimed his possessions, and then became
insane again, his brother should resume the grant as originally
made.[2]

Not all relatives acted from disinterested motives. Lady Vaux,
in an unsavoury dispute with Sir Thomas Tresham, was alleged
to have had her father-in-law certified insane in order to further
her cause. More trustworthy evidence of this kind of thing came
from Lord Zouche, President of the Council in Wales, in a letter
to the Master of the Court of Wards in December 1602. One
John Aston had been found a lunatic 'by his wife's procurement'
since he was 'once sick and in that sickness raving'. His wife had
no children by him and had seen his will which bequeathed to her

[1] *S.P.D.*, Eliz., i, f. 47r.
[2] *C.P.R.*, Ed. VI, iv, 181.

less than she desired. She had accordingly procured a commission for lunacy in order to obtain all his goods, 'since which time he has been so kept as it would make a sound man lunatic'. He had escaped to Ludlow but the President had not believed his story until a member of his council, after investigation, had confirmed it. 'The man's want of money and friends,' his Lordship admitted, 'his dissolute life in loving drink and women, have many times procured as evil speeches as from a lunatic which hath given great colour to their foul device.' 'But', he concluded, 'if you will inquire into the matter you will find it a foul practice.' In contrast to this case, Alderman Robert Lee of London fought to disprove that his brother Rowland Lee was a lunatic and in the end won his point.[1]

On the other hand, James Wyne married Joan Bedell, though there were strong grounds for believing that she was an idiot. But how was he to know? In a formal interrogation by the Court of Wards, he was asked 'whether in your conscience or to your knowledge is the said Joan an idiot or natural fool, or not? And whether can the said Joan number with any discretion twenty or not? Or guide or govern a household as a woman ought? If not, what moved you to take her to your wife?' To these pointed questions, Wyne said, in the first place, that 'in his conscience he did not consider her a fool or an idiot.' As to whether she could count up to twenty or not, he blandly replied that he did not know because he had never tested her. Finally, he thought that she was able to govern a household 'as a woman ought to do'. We do not know whether she was a mental defective, or what kind of wife she made for Wyne. But there is other evidence to show that the marriage was a shady business; and the Court of Wards viewed it with the greatest suspicion.[2]

Other 'foul practices' came to light from time to time. A Mr. Richard Lowther had a lamentable tale to tell of the misfortunes which had befallen his only daughter. She had married a Thomas

[1] G. Anstruther, *Vaux of Harrowden* (1953), pp. 225–6; H.M.C. *Salis.*, xii, 507–8; xi, 242; xiv, 178.
[2] Wards 3.12, pt. 1, Wyne Deposition.

Cleyburne, a ward who, by claiming to be older than he was, obtained possession of his land and, on the advice of two wicked uncles, leased most of it to them. When, however, he realised what he had been persuaded to do he went into a 'raging frenzy' and had been put under forcible restraint by them. It was feared that the result would be either a 'settled madness or a lunacy'. Lowther's appeal therefore, addressed to Sir John Stanhope, asked for help in gaining the guardianship of his son-in-law, so that his daughter and grandchild might salvage some small benefit from what little remained of Cleyburne's possessions. The letter ends with the curious offer to share 'half the profit' with Stanhope if the suit succeeded. Whether redress was ever obtained we do not know; what we do know is that in another case the Court of Wards and the Star Chamber did take steps to remedy an abuse. A man was found by inquisition to be an idiot, but subsequently this was reversed and he was found 'very simple and foolish but not an idiot from his birth'. He was accordingly removed from the custody of Smallman, his stepfather, who had brought about the false return, and transferred to his uncle's care. Smallman was also ordered by the Court of Wards to account for £700 arrears. This he failed to do. Meanwhile the supposed idiot went to live in the country with a surgeon and manservant to look after him; but Smallman gave the doctor a bribe of £40 and the servant one of £10 and plotted with them to convey the idiot away. This with the help of four others and with 'swords, rapiers and daggers, and three pistols', they achieved by brute force. But the Court of Star Chamber came down heavily with fine and imprisonment on this combination of force and riot.[1]

The normal procedure for determining idiocy and lunacy was by a commission sitting with a jury, and this naturally gave rise to charges of false return. In one case the jury declared that a man was not an idiot, whereupon the guardian Henry Newport, 'yeoman of the queen's boiling house', challenged their finding.

[1] H.M.C. *Salis.*, xi, 515; Hawarde, *Reportes del Cases in Camera Stellata*, ed. Baildon (1894), pp. 69–70.

Cecil referred the matter to a commission who passed it back to the Court of Wards itself.[1]

But since the profits to the crown were small, in the records of the Court of Wards idiots and lunatics occupy an insignificant place. Before their responsibility had been transferred to the Court of Wards they had been in the care of Chancery, before that under the Exchequer, and before that under the baron from whom the land was held. The barons may have used their powers cruelly and scandalously, and the assumption by the crown of authority in this matter may have been to remedy a long-standing abuse. The instigator of the reform was, according to Maitland, Henry III's favourite, Robert Walrond, himself the uncle of two idiot children, his heirs. Similarly, the subsequent transfer from the Exchequer to Chancery has been held to be in recognition that the care of the mentally sick was not to be considered a source of profit but a social duty, upheld by the crown. So far as we can tell, the Court of Wards performed its inherited duties from Chancery with a reasonable regard for human welfare.[2]

The absence of serious competition for the custody of lunatics is itself some measure of the narrow limits within which the prospector and the speculator could operate. By contrast, the sharp competition for many wardships shows what rewards lay open to the skilled manipulator of court favours. 'I cannot gratify Mr. Petre's desire', the Earl of Hertford had told a correspondent at the end of Henry VIII's reign, 'having not so few as three sundry times been an earnest suitor for my friend.' In Elizabeth's reign the Earls of Pembroke and Worcester fell to disputing over a wardship which threatened to cause so terrible a quarrel, Leicester told Burghley, 'as was not in Wales this forty years'. Hence his suggestion that it should be bestowed on some 'indifferent man'. How bitter these disputes could be, Burghley must have known better than any man; but courtiers and officials in

1 H.M.C. *Salis.*, xi, 486.
2 F. W. Maitland, *Collected Papers*, ed. Fisher (1911), ii, 184–6; Holdsworth, *op. cit.*, i, 474–5.

general were submitted to a fierce onslaught by petitioners from all directions. 'I am very loath to trouble you with any suits', Walter Haddon, a Master of Requests, once wrote to Burghley, 'but that I am often times more pressed than I would.' He was appealing on behalf of a suitor who was himself forwarding the petition of a mother. Hence, 'if you have not been prevented by some other', Haddon told him, 'I trust you will be favourable to the poor mother'. 'In this wardship before you moved it,' Cecil once wrote to Hickes, 'I had been dealt with from the mother.' 'This reason', he confessed, 'is not the greatest which hath moved me and yet too great (I think in your opinion) for me to deny.' 'I vow to you,' said the harassed Master, 'the Court is absolutely full of importunity for it.'[1]

The laconic notebooks of the Court of Wards officials, in the briefest of entries, show clear evidence of competition but yield us no details of the struggle and intrigue which must have preceded the grant. At the beginning of Edward VI's reign there were two competing claimants for the wardship of William Pyrry of Dorset, whose inheritance was worth £6 per annum. As the clerk tells us, it was 'preferred by Philip Lentall, uncle to the ward, who desireth the wardship—the last day of April 1547. And since, Richard Barrow esquire desireth the same, 8 May 1547.' From another page we learn that Lentall was the successful candidate, but whether because he filed his application a week before his rival, or because of his kinship to the ward, we cannot say. A few years earlier, in Henry VIII's reign, there had been three claimants for the wardship of Christopher Hunt of Nottinghamshire:

preferred by Mr. Lee
Francis Meryng desireth preferment
Mr. Markham hath the preferment, wherewith
Mr. Lee is contented.

Mr. Meryng's views on the subject went unrecorded.[2]

[1] L.P., xxi, pt. 1, pp. 370-1; B.M. Harl. 6992, ff. 77r and v; Lans. 10, f. 12r; Lans. 88, f. 91r.
[2] Wards 9.154 (Dorset); Wards 9. 151 (Notts.).

But the official records are only summary reports of what may have been long-drawn-out struggles. For glimpses of the intervening stages we have to look to the private correspondence of the Master and others. In the last years of Burghley's Mastership, the surviving evidence shows the complex role that his son was playing. 'In respect I was the first causer of the motion unto you', wrote Thomas Blount to Sir Robert Cecil in 1593, 'and am engaged so far as my undoing upon your honourable promise, I hope I shall deserve no less than the grant of it for my money, before another, giving as much as any other.' In another case Cecil himself appears to have bought the wardship or leased the ward's lands, and competitors were anxious to purchase his rights from him.

> Mr. Handen pretendeth that he hath your Honour's grant of the lease of the lands on Saturday last [Joseph Mayne, a member of Burghley's household, wrote to Cecil], which is the thing I make most account of, though I fear that both that and the wardship of the body will scarce countervail the charge I have already and must be at. I have thought good to prevent his coming to you tomorrow by this letter, desiring you to answer him absolutely that you have passed all your interest in the lease of the lands to me.

More than one petitioner, finding himself in competition with Cecil himself, drew the obvious conclusion that Cecil would get the wardship and asked, therefore, to purchase it at second-hand.[1]

Nearly as formidable a competitor, on one occasion, was the Archbishop of Canterbury; while his brother bishop of St. David's put forward a successful claim against a client of the Countess of Warwick. A certain William Style, on the other hand, was less successful in competition with the Countess of Kildare, who seems to have obtained a personal grant from the queen in the interval between the death of Burghley and the appointment of his successor; but the unsuccessful candidate was still hoping to buy the wardship second-hand from Lady Kildare at reasonable terms. Sometimes there was competition between a stranger

---

[1] H.M.C. *Salis.*, iv, 353; vii, 223; viii, 164 (the calendar misreads 'heirs' as Heriet).

and a kinsman of the ward, sometimes between two members of the same family. But always much depended upon the resources of favour and power upon which a claimant could call. Hugh Cuffe, acting on the advice of Sir Walter Raleigh, called off his application for a wardship on the ground that Cecil, now Master, had bestowed it upon one of his household servants. But the dispirited petitioner could not resist a lament over the heavy charges and long time expended upon this suit, so that, now penniless and unable to leave the capital, he begged for some employment in Ireland or some other release from his penury. James Gerald, writing from the Tower, and, as he said, tortured with the clamours of those to whom he was indebted, begged for a wardship to help restore his fortunes.[1]

What broad trends can be detected in the flourishing and complex businesss of claiming a wardship? Clearly it was a traffic which embraced men of all classes and all professions from the personal servants of Cecil's household, or private bidders with a few pounds to speculate, to the most eminent men in church and state. In these transactions there was little room for emotion or sentiment. 'I pray that we may hear that you are Master of the Wards,' wrote John Udale to the Earl of Essex, shortly after Burghley's death, 'for then I shall hope that you will bestow a male or female upon me.' Essex did not become Master of the Wards but Robert Cecil did; and to him wrote Henry Fitzwilliam, claiming kinship—'the decayed man of his name'—and asking for a wardship or a post in the Court of Wards to help towards the maintenance of his wife and ten children in their cottage near Arundel. An eleventh child, if he proved to be a lucrative ward, could no doubt be easily squeezed into his modest home. Philippa Cotton, also alleging in the same sentence her poverty and her kinship with Cecil, petitioned likewise for a ward to redress the family fortunes. Jane Jobson on the same basis made a similar request, though she frankly admitted that she needed some ready cash to buy herself a summer gown. Thomas

[1] *Ibid.*, xiv, 154, 149; viii, 324; xi, 359; x ,118.

Alabaster, more businesslike altogether, accompanied his request for a wardship with an offer to buy cinnamon from Cecil.[1]

While such negotiations were going on, a mother's claim, however well sponsored, might easily be trampled upon. A certain Mrs. Lee sought the wardship of her son. She approached Sir Thomas Cecil, who undertook to speak to his father Lord Burghley; the Earl of Essex and the Earl of Huntingdon also promised her their aid. In the end the wardship went to Sir Thomas Gerrard. Sometimes relationship to the ward helped, but one claimant at least put it in merely as an afterthought. 'I forgot to advertise My Lord that the ward is my wife's kinsman, which may be a good motive, if it please you to remember it in your letter.' Sometimes the mother arrived late on the scene and besought the Master, who had already bestowed the wardship, to use his good offices to enable her to purchase it second-hand at a reasonable price. Robert Cecil himself during his father's Mastership had obtained what looked like being a valuable wardship and spared no effort to press his interests against those of the mother. The wardship of Edward, Lord Vaux, went first to Burghley's eldest son Thomas Cecil; and it is only later that we learn that the mother 'hath to her great costs and charges purchased the wardship and marriage of the said son'.[2]

Yet some of the most moving petitions are those from parents and, most of all, from fathers anxious to ensure that, in the event of their untimely death, the wardship should pass to someone interested in the welfare of the child. The evidence, which will be considered elsewhere, shows that the mother's prospects were, in general, not very good; and that on many occasions the machinery for granting the wardship was already in motion while the breath was still in the father's body. Yet even the successful suitor, in these early stages of presenting the petition, had still to traverse the shifting sands of Tudor administrative procedure, which might at any time swallow up his petition almost without trace.

---

[1] *Ibid.*, viii, 415; ix, 255; xi, 467, 247; xii, 645.

[2] B.M. Lans. 68, f. 29r; H.M.C. *Salis.*, viii, 31; xi, 229; iv, 292, 297–8; G. Anstruther, *Vaux of Harrowden* (1953), pp. 231–2.

5

The Grant of a Ward

SIR JULIUS CAESAR, eminent in Elizabeth's day as a lawyer and Master of Requests, and of famous memory to later generations as a collector of manuscripts, once sat down in a bitter mood to calculate his heavy charges in purchasing the wardships of his step-daughters, Alice and Mary Dent. They were wealthy young ladies and he had paid £1,000 as purchase price. But that was only one item, for throughout the negotiations his money had to flow freely to oil the Tudor administrative machine. To people whom he describes as 'solicitors and friends' he paid £150 and to the Attorney and another official £20 each. A dinner for the commissioners holding the inquisition in Southwark cost him £11. 5s. 6d. and a dinner for the jury a further £3. 6s. 8d. There were fewer commissioners than jurymen, so either the commissioners had a very good dinner or they had something to carry away with them as a memento of the occasion. Caesar also had to pay the sheriff's bailiff's servant—there was no limit to the claimants for perquisites—6s. for assembling the jury; and the servants of a Mr. Coxe and a Mr. Necton (the feodaries) received 1s. and 5s. respectively, but what they did he does not tell us. ('A clerk's clerk's clerk's escheator and hath attended and pulled off the feodary's boots', was the acid comment by an M.P. in 1604 upon this kind of thing; and he may not have been too far from the mark.) Next Caesar had to pay £2. 3s. 0d. in the Pettibag Office of Chancery when the inquisition was returned by the commissioners and a Mr. Bashford collected 6s. 8d. for a schedule of the lands. On top of that Caesar had to pay £1. 10s. 0d.

for privy seals, £1. 10s. 0d. for a statement of the value of the inheritance and £16. 13s. 4d. as part of the Court of Wards fee. Hare, the Clerk of the Wards, reduced his charge by £10. 6s. 8d. and Tooke the auditor reduced his by £2. 0s. 0d.; but Hare's clerk collected his own fee of £1 for 'engrossing the leases'. And so it went on: attorney, receiver, messenger, private lawyer, agents, feodaries, more dinners for the commissioners and jurymen. At the end Caesar calculated that he had spent £1,739. 6s. 10d. But his arithmetic was at fault. He had in fact spent 26s. more than he realised! It was borrowed money and, by the middle of 1605, when the girls were almost out of wardship, he had been charged nearly £650 in interest alone. He must have paid, fed or rewarded a minimum of fifty officials, commissioners, and jurymen.[1]

Caesar was by no means an exception. Sir Hugh Paulet spent £43. 12s. 0d. on one part of one item alone, inquisitions in Somerset, Dorset, and Wiltshire—for 'the charge of them, the commissioners, feodaries, counsellor, and of himself, his and their horses and servants'. There exists, at Hatfield, the relic of some quarrel between two guardians over a wardship they had bought. Who wrote this account of his costs we do not know, but there is little doubt as to his feelings on the subject.

The report of such charges as hath been laid out by Mr. Thomas Buskell and myself for Mr. Cholmeley's wardship as followeth, 1595.

There was offered to my Lord, as Mr. Barnard knoweth	£400
Whereof given to me	£50
And there was paid, as Mr. Barnard knoweth	£350
Whereof I paid for my part	£150
The queen's fine	£80
Whereof I paid, for my part	£40
The charges for finding of two offices and for double fees paid into the Court of Wards by reason of the death of Thomas Cholmeley, who was elder brother to William Cholmeley	£62. 15s. 0d.
Whereof I paid for my part	£31. 7s. 6d.

[1] B.M. Add. MS. 12497, ff. 423r, 427r–428r.

Allowed to the ward in exhibition, over and above
   the queen's allowance which was £6. 13s. 4d. per
   annum, between us both   £80
   Whereof I paid for my part   £40
Given in reward   £20
   Whereof I paid for my part   £10
My charges for riding with him into Norfolk to my Lady
   Browne's upon communication about the marriage of
   her daughter   £3. 10s.
The sum of the money I have laid out of my purse
   which I have forborne six years is   £283. 17s. 6d.
Not reckoning the fifty pounds it pleased my Lord to abate
   and give to me of my first offer   £50
Nor yet accounting the charges he hath made me spend in suit of
law which amounteth to £36. 13s. 4d. or better, beside the for-
bearing of my money full two years expired.

For whose benefit was this account drawn up, and who was 'my
Lord' who received £350 as a gift, more than four times the
queen's fee of £80? We do not know. All that we can say is that
this financial statement was found amongst the papers of Lord
Burghley, and all the evidence points to him.[1]

Even for more modest grants to humbler suitors the Court of
Wards could hardly relax its accustomed routine. Although on
some occasions, the promise, or the half-promise, of a wardship
might be made before the inquisition, more usually the Master
would delay his decision until the inquisition had been held, and
even later than that. The inquisition was the first crude attempt
to determine who was the heir and to estimate the value of his
inheritance. But before completing the transaction the Master
wanted not one estimate but three. As he sat pondering the price
he should charge he liked to have in his hands the *inquisition post
mortem*, the survey made subsequently by the feodary and the
'particular', or statement of the nature and value of the inheritance, prepared by the suitor for a wardship. Even so the estimates

---

1 Wards 9.104, f. 279r–280r; H.M.C. *Salis.*, v, 529 (P.2460). The addition has an error
of £9.

the master had to work upon were, as he well knew, wide of the mark.

In the majority of *inquisitions*, the feodary was a member of the commission. But this was not enough. It was still necessary for him, and for his colleagues in other counties where the ward held land, to survey and value the inheritance. Each portion of land was described and valued and, where his survey rose higher than that of the inquisition, as was frequently the case, the difference would be duly noted, as for example:

> Valor per inquisitionen per annum £25. 10s. 8d.
> per supervisionem feodari £28. 10s. 2d.
> And so increased 59s. 6d.

Some time afterwards, when all the surveys of the ward's property in the different counties had come in, they would be put together and entered in a book. Those that survive form a valuable, though neglected, source for the historian and the genealogist.[1]

However sceptical the Master might be about the estimates with which he was presented, they were of crucial importance to him in the two separate bargains which must now be struck. The first was the sale of the wardship and what that involved: custody of the child and the right of marriage. This the guardian bought outright and the patent conferring the grant clearly stated that this royal grant belonged to him, his executors and assigns. In other words it was a commodity which could be inherited, bought and sold. If the boy died and was succeeded by a male heir under age, his wardship automatically passed to the same guardian. If the new heirs were female or over age, that was another story: the speculative venture had proved a total loss. That was why wardships, with no minor heir to succeed, fetched a lower price than where there was a minor heir in prospect.[2]

But, apart from the wardship, there were also the wards' lands to be leased away, and these called for a quite separate transaction. The crown had resumed possession of the land, because the ward

---

[1] Feodaries' Surveys, 39 Eliz. (John Wombwell, Yorks.).
[2] H.M.C. *Salis.*, iv, 597.

could not render military service, and held it until the ward was of age and in a position both to serve the king and therefore reclaim his land, that is to say, to sue livery. Meanwhile the crown could let the land at an annual rent for the period of the minority. Sometimes it went to the purchaser of the wardship, sometimes to a complete stranger. There was first a 'fine' or premium to be paid by the lessee, usually half the rent of the lands, and there was the annual rental for the property. This rental was easy enough to assess: it was the same as the figure provided by the feodary's survey. Low it undoubtedly was (and that is where the lessee gained enormously), but it was as high as the current attitudes and procedures would allow. But how should the Master assess the price of the *wardship*? For that, too, he had to use as his basis the value of the inherited lands.

Of the three surveys before him, the Master invariably placed the greatest reliance upon the feodary's survey. The *inquisition post mortem* might establish that there was a wardship but the feodary's survey determined its value. Yet the valuation of the lands was only one item which the Master had in mind in settling his price. He must consider who was the next heir if the ward should die before coming of age; the health and station of the ward; the value of the lands coming to the heir 'in possession'—that is, at once—and the amount coming 'in reversion'—that is, ultimately, when some life interest in the land had expired; the possessions of the ward apart from his land. The Master had also to take into account various other intangible, or at least incalculable, considerations, before he finally set the price. No system of pricing, however delicately balanced, could allow for all these variables; and Burghley of necessity had to have some rough and ready formula upon which to work.

For a clue to the kind of formula which he used we must look, curiously enough, not only to English methods but to what was happening across St. George's Channel. Ireland had no Court of Wards and the normal practice was to establish a commission specifically charged with the selling of wards. One such commission, drawn up early in Edward VI's reign, instructed the crown agents that the selling price should be the equivalent of one year's rent if the ward were male and of two years' rent if the heir were female. This applied equally to lands 'in possession' and 'in reversion'. In other words, if the heir inherited lands worth £10 per annum the wardship and marriage should be sold for £10 if the heir were male, and £20 if female. This basis of calculation was applied also to later commissions. In England, on the other hand, when Townshend and Walter were given their commission to search out concealed wards, the values were set at one year's rent for lands in possession and one half year's rent for lands in reversion. No distinction was made between males and females.[1]

Such formulae were clearly too rough and ready for so conscientious and cautious an administrator as Burghley. Yet, though he tried to treat each case on its merits, his selling price followed fairly closely upon the annual value of the lands. A few examples, drawn from the fourth year of Elizabeth's reign, may exemplify the trend. John Smith's lands were worth £12 and his wardship was sold for £13. 6s. 8d. That of John Norton, whose lands were valued at £6. 6s. 8d., went for £6. 13s. 4d. John Vaughan's lands and wardship were put at the same figure, £16. 9s. 0d. William Armorer's wardship likewise went at the valuation of his lands, £2. Alice Collye's went at £20, £3. 10s. 0d. more than the value of her lands. On the other hand, George Cotton's lands were worth £69. 6s. 8d. but the wardship went for £53. 6s. 8d., while Nicholas Rowse's wardship went for £33. 6s. 8d., less than the annual value of his lands, put at £40 per annum. Henry Morgan's wardship, though his lands were valued at £74. 15s. 10d., went for nothing to a Mr. Clavencurry; but this was by special warrant of the queen and the matter had, in effect, been taken out of the hands of the Master.[2]

If we take the year as a whole we find that, apart from the fact that female wards were more expensive to buy than male wards, the selling price bore a direct relationship to the valuation

1 C.P.R., Ed. VI, i, 136; Wards 9.106, f. 519r; see also above p. 39.
2 Wards 9.156.

of the lands. The overwhelming majority of the wardships were, during Burghley's Mastership, sold at either less than the annual value of the lands, the equivalent of the annual value or up to one and a half times the annual value. In the fourth year of Elizabeth's reign well over eighty per cent. of the wards were disposed of at these rates. More than thirty years later, in the year 1596–7, just under eighty per cent. went at the same rates.[1]

Yet, when all is said, there was bound to be an illusory element about the whole of this pricing system. Townshend and Walter's patent laid it down that the lands should be 'rated and valued as the same lands hath been accounted, accepted and taken in value most commonly by the space of forty years before this our grant'. Rated and valued by whom? A traditional value was a difficult one to determine. The petitioner for a wardship was unlikely to set the value of the lands very high. The *inquisitions post mortem* were notoriously unrealistic in their valuations. The feodary's survey might aim higher, but custom and bribery between them would set their own limits. Aaron Rathborne, a surveyor in James I's reign, sets out in detail the procedure for holding a manorial survey; but the method of valuing lands was something, he tells us, 'which I hold not fitting here to relate'. All England, and none less than Burghley, knew upon what untrustworthy figures the Court of Wards must perforce operate but, for the time being at any rate, it kept to its accustomed ways. One day, when a young Master succeeded an old one, he might totally reject the basis upon which the Court of Wards was working and, in so doing, place the whole future of royal wardships in jeopardy. Meanwhile Burghley operated the system as he had inherited it and, within these limits, he made it work.[2]

With the angular signature of the Master upon his petition, the suitor must now resume his protracted journey from office to office in the Court of Wards before he could enjoy the fruits of his already burdensome labours. If, as was common but not invariable, he was to obtain the lease of all or some of the ward's

---

[1] See below pp. 275–6.
[2] Wards 9.106, f. 519r; E. G. R. Taylor, 'The Surveyor' (*Econ. Hist. Rev.*, xvii, 123).

lands during the minority, that too must be approved by the Master in a separate series of transactions.

The prospective guardian accordingly entered upon two quite distinct transactions: the lease of the lands upon an annual rental basis, plus an initial premium; and, secondly, the purchase of the wardship for a capital sum. Neither this sum, nor the premium on the lease, need be paid 'in hand', that is to say, in cash. They might be paid in half-yearly instalments stretching over a period of years. In these cases, which represented the overwhelming majority, a group of guarantors would enter upon 'obligations', fiduciary undertakings that the sums would be paid at the appropriate times. The 'obligation' was usually one third higher than the instalment due and was cancelled when the payment was made. There were usually three guarantors, though there might be more or less. The purchaser was often one of his own guarantors, and the others could be drawn from any class of society: country gentlemen, court officials, lawyers, London merchants. Whatever the county in which the ward or the guardian lived, we frequently find amongst the guarantors the name of a Londoner. Of 149 guarantors noted in the fourth year of Elizabeth's reign, fifty-seven were Londoners. In only twenty out of forty-nine cases analysed did no Londoner at all appear as a guarantor.

The leasing of the lands would be done by indenture; the granting of the wardship by letters patent issuing from Chancery, on the receipt of a signed bill from the Master of the Court of Wards. The indenture was a formal document which began with all the pomp and verbiage of an Elizabethan agreement, for example: 'This indenture made between the most excellent Princess and most dread sovereign Lady Elizabeth by the Grace of God, Queen of England, France and Ireland, Defender of the Faith etc. of the one party, and Peter Tichborne, gent. of the other party . . .' after which it got down to business.

Tichborne had paid £20 as a premium to the Receiver-General of the Court and was therefore put in possession of the lands listed in the indenture. But he was not in full possession of all the rights which went with the land. The indenture specifically reserved 'all advowsons, presentations, nominations, gifts of churches and spiritual promotions, woods, underwoods, wards, marriages, knights fees, reliefs, fines, heriots and any mines of metal, stone or coal rising or growing upon the said manor'. On the other hand he could draw upon the wood for 'housebote, fyrebote, hedgebote, ploughebote and cartebote' if they were needed for the estate. Tichborne, the indenture went on, was to pay an annual rent of £32, by half yearly instalments, to the feodary of Hampshire, and to pay in addition to the Receiver-General such sums as 'shall be deemed right' from the profits of the manor. (On top of this, the lessee normally had to pay the fees of bailiffs and other servants of the manor, as well as pensions, and other grants already 'reserved' out of its income.) He undertook also to allow the feodary from time to time to survey the estate and was to pay whatever extra amounts were demanded from him in view of the increased value of the land. He was to hold the manorial court, keep the land in good order and to prevent any waste of the land. He could not sell his lease without the knowledge and consent of the Master and Council of the Court of Wards.[1]

So much for the lands. The grant of the 'body' of the ward, as the contemporary documents factually describe the transaction, was by letters patent issued under the Great Seal. This was a Latin document, in the full and conventional language of these medieval charters of privilege. The patent usually granted three things: it started with an exhibition or maintenance allowance paid by the Court of Wards to the guardian during the ward's minority. This was not invariable practice, but an exhibition accompanied most grants. The guardian, secondly, received the 'custodium' of the ward, that is, the actual possession of the child, though the guardian might subsequently lodge it elsewhere. He received finally, and what was of most value to him, the *maritagium*, the right to marry the ward to whomever the guardian chose, provided that the marriage was *absque disparagatione*, without disparagement.

[1] Wards 9.116, f. 21r-23r.

The whole procedure had by Elizabeth's reign become systematised under the watchful eyes of officials and clerks whose vested interests, as the recipients of fees, were so intimately involved. But it remained true that the wards were the queen's wards and she alone could dispose of them at her will and pleasure. It had always been the prerogative of the crown to sell or grant wardships without using the Master or the machinery of the Court of Wards. In 1541 John Hastings, a ward, was granted his own wardship by direct authority of the crown and without charge, partly because of his father's service to Henry VIII, but, even so, the Master was instructed to estimate ' what the value of the same marriage is in case you had sold the same in our behalf'. Sir William Paulet duly calculated this at £20. Similarly, in Elizabeth's reign we have seen that a Mr. Clavencurry received a valuable wardship 'by warrant freely'—that is, by royal favour. Examples of these grants may be found throughout the reign; but they are isolated cases. For the majority of suitors, though they might by-pass individual officials and formalities here and there, there was in general no escape from the tortuous corridors of a Tudor administrative court.[1]

According to the statute establishing the Court of Wards, the guardian was obliged to sue his patent within four months of the bill being issued by the Court. Failure to do this meant a cancellation of the grant and, in theory, the wardship was forfeit. In fact, however, as may be seen from the Elizabethan patent rolls, the practice was for the guardian to buy from Chancery a 'release' from the forfeiture, for which he paid a fee.[2] There were, of course, other reasons for cancelling the grant, sometimes before it had reached the stage of letters patent: for example, the death of the ward before the formalities had been completed. But often the cancellation reflected an interesting, and sometimes scandalous, aspect of Elizabethan wardship. About this more will be said in the appropriate place.[3]

---

[1] Above p. 86; Wards 9.149, f. 102r.
[2] E.g. C.P.R., Eliz., ii, 24, 79.
[3] Below pp. 274-5.

We have been concerned in this chapter with the problems of procedure; and, though so much consisted in sheer formality, it would be a misjudgement of the Tudor mind to minimise its importance to either the petitioner and his lawyer or to the queen and her officials. For example, Sir Walter Raleigh once bought himself an Irish wardship, which earned him some money when he disposed of it. But it also brought him a great deal of trouble, when a minor official discovered that the grant did not have the official seal affixed to it in completion of the purchase. As a result, another man stepped in and obtained the wardship. It required nothing less than a personal letter from the queen to the Lord Deputy of Ireland to set matters right for Raleigh; but even so, the Lord Deputy was told that he might recompense the second claimant, now about to be evicted, with some other wardship or gift. This was no isolated example. Another petitioner, mistaking the name of the ward he wanted, wasted money on futile preliminaries, with the result that 'another hath stepped in before me'. The obtaining of a wardship could be as tricky as it was expensive.[1]

But there were pitfalls for the crown as well as for the suitor. At least, that was the opinion of the Clerk of the Wards, who warned Burghley, late in Elizabeth's reign, that some suitors obtain 'Your Lordship's hand to rate the schedule or particular'— that is, carry the negotiations up to the last stages of the purchase— but then 'keep back' and never apply for the Court's seal on their bill. As a result, the queen 'either loseth her fine wholly' or 'for many wardships is seldom paid her fine till the full age of the heir'. In other words no purchase-price was paid, the wardship was not granted, and the heir came of age without his wardship being sold. Was this a device by the friends of wards to save money, or to block another applicant for the wardship? Certainly, the Clerk gave an impressive list of wards who had reached full age without their wardships being sold. He could not resist the opportunity for a little inter-departmental guerrilla warfare,

---

1 Guildhall Letter Book of Queen Elizabeth, P.D. 2309, p. 227 (I am indebted to Miss M. Booth for the reference); H.M.C. *Salis.*, xii, 82–3.

so he laid part of the blame at the door of the Clerk of the Liveries.[1]

We may perhaps obtain an insight into what lay before a would-be guardian if we consider the advice as to procedure prepared during the next reign. It had not fundamentally changed from Elizabethan practices except that, by the reform of 1611, a mother or next of kin had a prior claim for the ward, if application were made within the first month of the wardship. The writer therefore cautions the petitioner that he must make sure that no such claim by a relative is before the Master. Once the initial hurdle was passed, the suitor could begin his rounds of the Court of Wards officials. First:

> You must prefer a petition to the Master and Council of the Wards showing the place where the ancestor lived, and by what tenure he held his lands; and in the prayer desire that you may be admitted to compound for the body and lease of the lands of the said ward, and that you may have a writ [to] find the office. Whereupon directions will be given that you shall have a writ and that you shall attend the Master and Council of the said Court of Wards at a certain time with a schedule and a confession of the estate of the said ward.

This was merely the first formal request for a wardship of which the Master would take cognizance without in any way committing himself. 'After you have the petition answered, you must carry the same to the king's Attorney of the said Court and he will make an order according to the aforesaid direction. When you have entered that order, go to the clerk which is appointed for the making of that warrant and he will make you a warrant thereupon. When you have the warrant you must enter into bond to find the office or to return the writ.' For the moment the suitor's work in London was over. He or his representative must now take himself off to the shires to attend the inquisition establishing the wardship.

'Then you must deliver the writ to the escheator and desire him

---

[1] Wards 9 315, f. 1r.

The Court of Wards and Liveries in Session

to appoint a day for the finding of the office; and against that day get your office drawn, and when the office is found, procure the escheator to return the same into the pettibag.' Now the suitor was back in London: 'And there you must likewise procure the same to be transcripted and then take a copy thereof with the officer's hand thereunto, and carry the said copy into the Court of Wards office, and then get the schedule drawn. And when it is done you must enter into bond to prosecute the wardship under seal, or else to return the schedule to the Clerk of the Court.' Now the suitor was once again wandering from office to office. 'Then your schedule must be carried to Mr. Attorney of the Wards and he will have the same ready at such time as you are directed to compound'—that is, to pay for the wardship. However, it was not as straightforward as that. 'But before you go to compound you must procure a certificate from the feodary to the Master and Council of the Wards touching the value of the lands.'

At this stage, then, further details were required. 'And you must likewise make a confession in writing of the value of the lands and of the personal estate. And you must likewise set down in your confession, if [whether] you be either mother, or nearest of kindred, the debts and what children are unprovided for, and what other charges the lands are subject unto. And then you may proceed to compound.'

Here the suitor could only pause to take breath. There was still much to be done. 'After the composition repair to the Clerk of the Wards and you shall have from him the schedule and also a writing called a contract. And carry them both to the Auditor's office and there get a particular to the Master of the Wards to have the same signed by him. Then bring the same to the Clerk of the Wards and he will appoint a clerk in the office to get the grant drawn ready for the seal of the Court.'

So much for the wardship; there remained the question of the ward's lands. 'When you have the draft of the lease ready, you must carry the schedule and draft of the lease in paper to the Attorney to have them signed by him and then take the said draft with you and go pay the fine of the lease at Mr. Receiver's office and take an acquittance for the payment thereof'—that is, a receipt.

'And likewise take the schedule with you and pay the value of the marriage if you be to pay it all in hand'—in cash—'or so much thereof as you are to pay in hand, and there likewise take an acquittance. Then bring back from thence the schedule and draft of the lease with the acquittances unto the Clerk of the Wards' office.' Now at last harbour was in sight. 'And they will procure you the grant of the body and lease of the land under seal of the Court. As soon as you have them under seal, take up the two bonds formerly entered into, and then enroll the lease in the Auditor's office.'

But the writer still had some words of warning about pitfalls:

'Note: if you desire days of payment for the fine of the marriage you must procure the said days of payment to be set down by the Master of the Wards when he signeth the schedule.

'Note also to take several acquittances for payment of every several sum of the fine as you have the days of payment.' [1]

Looking back over what must have seemed an endless, timeless journey, one is a little amazed that anyone could have embarked upon it at all. It required a stout heart and a well-lined purse to see the business through to the bitter end, for each step must have been accompanied by either a fee or a gift. But the hope which spurred on the wearied traveller was that these heavy charges would ultimately be met not from his own pocket but from his ward's: a chilling prospect at the start of a relationship between foster-parent and child. To us the whole procedure seems administratively prolix and backward, a monument to the conservatism and vested interests of Tudor and Stuart civil servants.

Yet perhaps we should not be too hasty in dismissing the working system of a past age. More than three centuries after this contemporary account of wardship procedure had been written, a British representative wrote home, during the dark days of the Second World War, to tell his beleaguered government of the administrative steps necessary to obtain scarce

1 B.M. Harley 1323, ff. 202r–204v.

munitions and materials to send across the Atlantic. Everyone negotiating in Washington with the United States government spoke in the highest terms of the generous and gallant aid flowing from the arsenal of democracy. But the administrative machine bore heavily on all men.

> It sets up a colossal amount of paper work [he wrote]. The contractors would have to answer thirty-nine complicated questions on the quarterly form and more than twenty questions on supplementary monthly forms. The information gained from the forms would be layered laboriously up from level to level and then back down again level by level until the allocations finally reached contractors and suppliers.[1]

Plus ça change . . .?

The historian should be impartial. For our final example we therefore go to the other side of the political world: the Soviet Union. In a lengthy memorandum, issued in 1957, Mr. Khruschchev had some frank remarks to make about the Soviet government service and its overlapping, competing and confusing departmental controls. He instanced what was happening by referring to a building project: 'In the Chelyabinsk region, for example, construction work is carried on by 182 building and assembly organisations of 25 Ministries and Departments. In Sverdlovsk region it is done by 203 building and assembly organisations of 30 Ministries and Departments, often working side by side in one district or even in one street.'[2] As a beginning of reform, he announced the dismissal of 900,000 bureaucrats; but even this seemed hardly enough. 'O what a tangled web we weave!', he cried, as he surveyed the monstrous framework of administration. There is a timelessness about his observation.

[1] Cited in my *Control of Raw Materials* (1953), p. 95.
[2] *The Times*, 4 April 1957, p. 11.

6

Private Wardship

ABOUT many of these procedures which we have been considering in the last chapter there is an abundance of evidence, much of it repetitive and some of it conflicting; and the historian, like the sixteenth-century petitioner before him, must walk warily through the labyrinths. Of this embarrassment of riches the historian would gladly sacrifice a portion, if in return he might obtain evidence in one field for which the material is tantalisingly scarce: private wardship or, as contemporaries called it, wardship of a mesne lord. Such evidence as survives of the feudal wardship of the baronage and others is scattered amongst the private and estate papers of the heirs to the great families of Tudor England and in stray references elsewhere. Such material is perforce slow to yield its secrets and sometimes a chance remark by a contemporary obscures more than it reveals. Somebody once scribbled, in the margin of the Act Book of the Dean and Chapter of Wells, 'a naughty form of the grant of a ward'; but we can only guess what shocked him. A systematic search through family archives might one day reveal that private wardship had a wider significance than we at present believe. To Ket's rebels in 1549 the evils of private wardship seem to have been sufficiently great to have earned a clause in their petition: 'We pray that no man, of what estate, degree or condition he be shall from henceforth sell the wardship of any child, but that the same child if he live to his full age shall be at his own chosen concerning his marriage, the king's wards only except.' Yet in spite of this, it is quite likely that in private wardships we have an instance where lack of evidence confirms what the legal and historical developments suggest: namely that private wardship was a waning element in Tudor society.[1]

In theory, wardship of the queen was not fundamentally different from the feudal wardship of any other person. It had about as much historic justification: no more and no less. It was a feudal right torn out of its context for a fiscal end. But time, and government policy, had wrought havoc with the feudal rights of private lords. Military tenures of a lord were a stage even farther removed from reality than military tenures of the crown. A Tudor lord, of course, would not hesitate to call upon his tenantry where his power or his property seemed in peril; but before doing so he would not read the roll to discover which of them held of him by a military tenure. Clientage—which, unlike wardship, was a true descendant of medieval feudalism—and family loyalties would bring the tenantry to arms.

A good deal of land had changed hands and now the process was being intensified. Estates had been broken up and the fragments assimilated into other units. Where, out of this mosaic of estates and tenants was a new lord, or his steward, to discover who exactly were the 'military tenants'? And if he did discover them, and discovered also that they held some lands, however negligible, of the crown by knight-service, then all his work was in vain. For prerogative wardship, continuing the work of the thirteenth-century statute *Quia Emptores*, gave the crown an over-riding title to a feudal wardship however tiny the portion which the tenant held of the crown. Yet, in spite of all this, private wardship was a tough plant, and, in the shelter of a distant lordship or a conservative estate, it could still flourish, and occasionally yield a random harvest.

Bracton had said in the thirteenth century that the king was

---

[1] H.M.C., *Dean and Chapter of Wells*, ii, 275; Bland, Brown and Tawney, *Select Documents*, p. 250. For references to private wardships I am indebted to Prof. R. H. Tawney, Dr. E. L. Hembrey, Mr. R. T. Spence and especially Dr. E. Kerridge.

entitled to the wardship and marriage of the heir and to the custody of all his lands, even though only a part was held of the crown; and in the sixteenth century the crown was in no wise prepared to abate its claim. As far as the wardship of the body and the grant of the marriage were concerned, there could be no dispute. *Prerogativa regis* ruled supreme. But as far as the lands were concerned there was room for differences of opinion; and we need not take contemporary lawyers as seriously as they took themselves. Robert Constable, for example, swimming with the royal tide, speaks at the end of the fifteenth century in the boldest terms of the king's prerogative rights. Staunford, writing in the sixteenth century, is less certain. He asks whether the crown has the wardship of the lands held by a minor of some lord other than the king: the statute does not grant it in all cases but practice has gone ahead of theory. Even at the end of Elizabeth's long reign, men were by no means sure where exactly they stood. Thomas Mackworth of Rutland held certain land by knight-service of Lord Berkeley, 'as of his manor of Melton Mowbray'. But he also held land by knight-service in chief of the queen and this he imagined sheltered him from paying a 'relief' to any other lord. But he was mistaken. The matter was brought to trial at common law and, as John Smyth of Nibley, steward and chronicler of the Berkeleys, recounts, it became a leading case. 'Upon argument both at bar and bench [it] was adjudged against Mackworth, and was the first express judgment in the law in that point as was then affirmed, whereof many students then present in court have since had the number roll.' [1]

Coke in the early seventeenth century says explicitly that 'the king shall have wardship of all the lands by his prerogative' of whomsoever held, if any portion were held by knight-service in chief. If land were held not in chief but as of an honour of the king, the rule did not apply. But prerogative wardship was in fact disputed territory, made all the more confusing by the immense

[1] Bracton, *De Legibus*, ed. Woodbine (1922), p. 253; R. Constable, *Prerogativa Regis*, ed. Thorne; Staunford, *An Exposition of the King's Prerogative* (1548), cc. 1 and 2; John Smyth of Nibley, *The Berkeley Manuscripts*, ed. Maclean (Brist. and Glouc. Arch. Soc. 1883), ii, 350.

variety of tenures and transactions which enriched the lawyer no less than they harassed his client.[1]

Yet, in spite of its all-embracing character, prerogative wardship had not wholly extinguished the wardship of other lords. Smyth of Nibley, who preserved for us the Mackworth case, had also a few examples to offer of the Lords Berkeley having wards of their own: private wards as compared with royal wards. One of Berkeley's wardships, that of Ralph Burton, the 'Lord Henry gave in the second [year] of Queen Elizabeth to Thomas Duport his servant, a prudent man'. But there the matter was not allowed to rest. This prudent man sold it to a certain Purefy who, in turn, sold it to Agarde, father of the future historian, from whom Smyth got the story. But Burton refused the bride offered him by his third guardian who brought an action against his ward at the Leicester assizes for the loss of his profit of marriage—*valor maritagii*. The unfortunate ward lost his case and the guardian recovered damages. Later, early in James I's reign, John Goldesborough, son of the late Bishop of Gloucester, was also a ward of Lord Berkeley. But someone came and seized him and took him out of the possession of his guardian. His lordship accordingly brought an action for 'ravishment of ward' at Gloucester assizes, won his case and obtained nearly £270 damages. But the lords of Berkeley were, in this respect, almost in a class by themselves. Henry, the sixth lord, went so far as to claim from his tenants an 'aid' on the knighting of his eldest son in 1610, a fantastic aping of his royal master's claim of the year before. But he had a good, or at least an urgent, cause. His state of bankruptcy was, in his own sphere, fully a match for the king's.[2]

Smyth, faithful steward of the Berkeleys, once earned a handsome reward in the shape of the private wardship of Stephen Huntley, granted by Lady Berkeley in 1632, in consideration of 'divers good causes'. Smyth seized his chance and sold his free gift—for £150. But Smyth himself clearly saw that private

1 *First Instit.*, sect. 103.
2 Smyth of Nibley, *op. cit.*, ii, 338-9, 351-2; W. B. Willcox, *Gloucestershire* (1940), p. 269, n. 3.

wardship was a wasting asset. In the second half of his reign James I sold some land which was subsequently re-sold to some of the Berkeley tenants, who accordingly became tenants not only of the Berkeleys but of the crown. This opened the door to prerogative wardship. As a result, by 1639 there had passed to the king 'seven or eight wardships, with as much loss almost to the Lord Berkeley'. This could happen though most of them 'held lands of the said lord by knight-service, having no other land held of the crown save small parcels of this . . . some scarce of one acre'. Thus could a dubious thirteenth-century statute sap the wealth of a seventeenth-century lord.[1]

Other noblemen were making occasional profits from the wardships upon their estates. In 1592 the Rutland wardships brought in £26. 13s. 4d., in 1593, £13. 6s. 8d., in 1594, £20. In 1603, when we meet wardships again amongst their accounts, they brought in £80. 3s. 4d. The Earl of Cumberland obtained £60. 6s. 8d. for a wardship in 1598. In other years he sometimes made more in this way, for example in 1621 probably as much as £136, in 1637, £400. But these were exceptional years. The Cumberland estates did not generally derive more than about £30 a year from wardships and heriots. The Earl of Pembroke also seems to have made a little profit from his private wardships; so does the Earl of Warwick from a wardship in Charles I's reign. In Clayton, Yorkshire, we have a private wardship in 1571, and one in Comberton in Worcestershire in 1578. The grant of the wardship is, in this case, interesting in that while the mother received it, her own son was protected against her in two ways: if he refused the marriage she proffered him, she was not to exact more than £3 from him as damages; if his mother re-married, the stepfather was not to force him to marry against his will, or the grant of the wardship became null and void. On the other hand, Lord Rich, under the impression that the wardship of one of his tenants belonged to him, disposed of it to the mother, only to discover that he had overlooked the prerogative wardship which had given the ward to the crown. He had the embarrassment of

[1] Birm. Ref. Lib. Fletcher Coll. no. 207; Smyth of Nibley, *op. cit.*, iii, 315.

writing to the Master, apologising, and asking him to bestow the wardship where it had in fact already been bestowed.[1]

If noblemen, here and there, were able to salvage some feudal profits before the advancing tide of the crown's prerogative, their ecclesiastical colleagues were bent on doing the same thing. In 1511 the Dean and Chapter of Wells Cathedral sold a wardship to the Dean himself for £5, which sum was to be divided amongst the resident canons. In 1553 they sold a wardship to a Mr. William Lyte for £20; but this was the 'naughty form' of a wardship and the recipient was exempted from giving any account of his guardianship. In 1572 we have another wardship and in 1593 one more.[2]

In the bishopric of Durham the position was somewhat obscure. In 1550, the venerable Cuthbert Tunstall asserted his claim to three wardships although, in the case of two of them, part of the lands were outside his area. The matter went before a commission which found in favour of the bishop and reported that

> the said bishop and all other bishops of Durham of long antiquity, without any memory of man to the contrary, have had and used to have prerogative of ward and livery . . . of all lands . . . being holden of the said bishop by knight's service. Neither the king [the report continued] nor any of his most noble progenitors, kings of this realm, have taken any rents or profits of any manors, lands or tenements which were held of the said bishop by knight's service.

Accordingly it was decreed that the bishops of Durham 'shall have, hold and enjoy the rents and profits of all the said manors, lands etc. . . . without let, interruption or demand to the contrary by the said Master and Council of the Court of Wards'. The bishopric was a county palatine, like Lancaster and Chester, enjoying peculiar immunities and privileges, holding its own *inquisitions post mortem* and, at least in part, enjoying its ancient

---

[1] H.M.C. *Rutland*, iv, 404, 5, 9, 439–40; Bolton MSS. Bks. 249, f. 15r, 176, f. 16r; P.R.O/E. 178, no. 2445; C.R. Straton, *Survey of Manors of Earl of Pembroke* (Roxburghe Club, 1909), p. 129; Ipswich Free Lib. Ref. Dept. S.1/1/76.10; A. G. Ruston and D. Witney, *Hooton Pagnell* (1934), p. 305; Worc. Rec. Off. 950/3/53; *Original Letters*, ed. Ellis (3rd. ser.), iii, 352–3.

[2] H.M.C., *Dean and Chapter of Wells*, ii, 228, 275, 292, 327.

rights. But if the land were held *of the crown* in chief, and not of the bishop or 'count palatine', then the royal rights of wardship fully applied.[1]

The bishop's immunities from prerogative wardships, along with the immunities of the Archbishop of Canterbury and of the marcher lords, had been recognised by the 'statute' *Prerogativa Regis*. Robert Cecil was fully aware of the bishop's immunity; and, ever ready during his father's lifetime to snap up a lucrative wardship, he extracted in 1594 from Matthew Hutton, then Bishop of Durham, the promise that he would 'willingly and with all his heart' bestow upon Cecil a Durham wardship which had attracted his attention. Yet there remained an element of doubt. His lordship was not sure whether, in this particular case, though the land was held *in capite* from him, he was entitled to the wardship and marriage or only to the land during the minority. Earlier in the reign, the Archbishop of Canterbury had successfully staked a claim to part of the land of the Earl of Oxford, when he was Burghley's ward.[2]

About the Duchy of Cornwall some doubt appears to have arisen. But in another county, an acre of land, worth 1s. a year, held of Philip and Mary by knight-service in their capacity of Earls of Chester, brought to the crown a wardship worth £72. 4s. 1d. The surviving profits from private wardship, where they were secure against the prerogative, were not insignificant. The Bishop of Durham was compensated to the tune of £880 a year when feudal wardship was abolished in 1660.[3]

Elsewhere the immunities gave up the unequal contest. It is unlikely that the 'liberties' of the Cinque Ports, claimed in one case, could in fact withstand the royal right of wardship. No county or city as such could claim immunity, not even the capital. It is true that London enjoyed special rights and responsibilities in respect of orphans of its citizens, for whom a special

[1] C. Sturge, *Cuthbert Tunstall* (1938), pp. 255–6; Coke, *Fourth Inst.*, c. 35; 18 Eliz., c. 13.

[2] H.M.C. *Salis.*, iv, 557; Wards 9.105, f. 145v.

[3] H.M.C. *Salis.*, xv, 264; Wards 9.138, f. 3r; G. T. Lapsley, *The County Palatine of Durham* (1924), pp. 200–1.

fund existed, but these were orphans in the ordinary sense of the word, not feudal wards. Where land was held by knight-service in chief, whether the land was in London or not made no difference; the queen's right of wardship was irresistible.

There are sundry of Her Majesty's poor subjects within the City of London [wrote George Carey to Burghley, who hold] tenements, shops, garden plats and such petty parcels and quillets of land, which be holden *in capite*, unto which tenure there is incident (as Your Honour best knoweth) ward, marriage, finding of offices, suing of liveries, licence of alienation, respites of homage, perpetual keeping of attorneys in the exchequer, with other charges.

All these, he argued, could consume more than the total profits from the small pieces of land. Hence he proposed the establishment of a commission to sell to these tenants the right to change their tenures to 'free burgage and free socage'—that is, exemption from feudal claims. The profits from the commission, he modestly proposed, should be divided into two parts, one half going to the queen, the other to himself. The scheme, he stressed, was only to help the poorer inhabitants and should not extend to lands 'above the yearly value of £10, nor to any parcel of any manor to the dismembrance of the same, nor to any part of this realm but to the city of London and three mile compass thereof'. Wardships, he admitted, would be lost to the queen but they were of little value in any case; indeed, people were giving up their lands rather than face intolerable feudal charges. He finally invited Burghley to satisfy both public and private interest: 'if this commission may be granted by Your Honour's means, you shall deserve the prayer of many poor folks, and bind me everlastingly to honour and serve your Honour'. Needless to say, no more was heard of the proposal. Like the grander projects of wardship reform of the next reign, it was out of line with the economic and constitutional setting of the crown's prerogative.[1]

Beyond the English borders, the crown officials asserted their feudal claims, though Jersey proved a hard nut to crack. By Norman custom the crown was titular guardian of all orphans in

[1] H.M.C. *Salis.*, xiv, 282; B.M. Lans. 107, ff. 116r and v.

the island; but the actual appointment of guardians was committed to the justices, who relied upon the choice made 'by those who call themselves kin, neighbours and friends of the said infants'. This custom, however, did not apply to those who held 'nobly', and, at the end of Elizabeth's reign, a dispute arose between Sir Antony Paulet, the Captain of Jersey, on the one side, and the father of a child whom Paulet claimed as a royal ward. The matter went before the Privy Council, which appointed a commission to investigate the matter. Its findings have not been traced, but it seems unlikely that a royal wardship can have been established, since it was contrary to English custom to claim a wardship while the father was still alive. The commission, however, would have to decide whether Norman custom, upon which the decision would be based, ruled differently.[1]

In the marches of Wales the feudal rights of the crown went back to medieval times, and in Wales itself, by the Elizabethan period, the crown was exercising, through the Court of Wards, the identical feudal power that was to be found in England, sometimes grafted upon a native system. For example, David Lloyd ap Evan of Cardiganshire held lands in Llechewethllwivan, Penkraige and Rhydd—this was the best that the English Clerk of the Court of Wards could make of them. Ap Evan held these lands of the queen, 'as of her principality of South Wales' by knight-service; and in the ninth year of her reign we find him a ward of the queen. Wales like England had her feodaries but the records show that they had less to do than on this side of the border. There was almost certainly less tenure by knight-service in Wales, and, where it existed, it may be that the Welsh spoke their own language and kept their own counsel. In Scotland which, of course, was not part of the queen's dominions, a comparable system to knight-service is known to have existed, sometimes described as 'ward holding'. Apparently it survived until the middle of the eighteenth century.[2]

---

[1] *C.P.R.*, Eliz. ii, 426–7; *Acts of P.C.*, 1597, p. 356, 1597–8, p. 487.
[2] W. Rees, *South Wales and the March, 1284–1415* (Oxford, 1924), pp. 44, 59, 148; Wards 9.138, f. 596v.

In Ireland things were different. A good deal of land was held by knight-service, especially as, in the early plantations, the settlers took up possession on the basis of a military tenure, sometimes for very small portions of land. Accordingly the evasion of feudal liabilities seems to have been as much an Irish as an English activity. This cannot have been unknown to crown officials, hence the recommendation by one of them 'to examine feoffments and see that they are not made to defraud the king of the custody of lands of minors'. In 1547 the Privy Council gave direct instructions to the Lord Deputy and Council of Ireland to grant a wardship to William Fitzwilliam, a Gentleman of the Privy Chamber; but from the beginning of Edward VI's reign, if not earlier, the normal practice was to establish a commission for the sale of wards. In the first of these, the commission consisted of the Lord Deputy of Ireland, the Chancellor, the Chief Justice, the Vice-Treasurer, and the Master of the Rolls of Ireland. Any three of them, of whom the Lord Deputy and the Vice-Treasurer must be two, were empowered to sell 'the custody, ward and marriage' of the minor heirs of those who died 'in the king's homage in Ireland'. With the sale were to go enough lands for 'the finding' of the heirs, what was known in England as the 'exhibition'. The price was, as we have seen, to be the equivalent of one year's rent for male heirs and two years' rent for female heirs. Of the income from Irish wardships we have no record in English sources; the revenues went to meet the costs of the government in Ireland.[1]

Yet Irish wardship was not the concern of Irish interests only. Sir Walter Raleigh bought an Irish wardship at second-hand— and sold it again. On another occasion Sir Francis Knollys bought one and ran into the acute difficulties of fighting out in Ireland a case of a disputed wardship. He was Treasurer of the Queen's Household, cousin of the queen, and therefore influential enough to obtain a Privy Council letter to the Lord Justice of Ireland. The Irish authorities were reminded that Knollys 'hath not

---

[1] *L.P.*, xii, pt. 2, p. 156; *Acts of P.C.*, 1547, p. 454; *C.P.R.*, Ed. VI, i, 135–6; H.M.C. *Salis.*, xvi, 442; Irish M.C. *Ormonde*, vi, 101. For later developments see H. F. Kearney, 'The Court of Wards and Liveries in Ireland' (*Proc. R. Irish Ac.*, lvii, 29–68).

presently anybody to prosecute the matter in the ward's behalf', and the Lord Justice was accordingly 'required to cause special heed to be given and admonish those that are appointed to deal in this matter that all indifferency be used so that, without any partial leaning, either to the one side or other, the due and upright administration of justice may take place according to equity and conscience'. Stimulated by this exhortation—or perhaps in spite of it—the justices in Ireland gave their verdict against Knollys; but there the matter was not allowed to rest. Another letter was accordingly sent to the Lord Deputy asking for a report of the proceedings and ordering him 'not to suffer the Queen's Majesty's committee'—that is, Knollys—'to be dispossessed of the ward's lands until by due order of law it shall be evicted'. This apparently brought no satisfaction, for the next step was to submit the case to two crown lawyers in England, the Attorney-General and the Solicitor-General. So the matter dragged on from 1571 to 1574 until it was finally transferred to two English judges, Wray and Manwood, who were asked to report to the Privy Council. What they reported we do not know.[1]

The long arm of the English crown could reach out into an Irish conflict over wardship. Yet it may well be that it was never powerful enough or sufficiently well informed to dig deep into the complexities and obscurities of Irish society. According to Bacon, in the early seventeenth century it was a profitless task until he reformed it. 'I received yesternight a brave account of the commission of wards in Ireland', he wrote to the future Duke of Buckingham in 1618, 'which this one year is advanced from £200 per annum to £4,000, which is twentyfold multiplied'! He could not resist a boast and a prophecy. 'This I write for two reasons. First, because I glory in it, because it was my work wholly: next, because His Majesty may take occasion by this to look better to the improvement of his wards in England in due time.' 'Improvement' meant greater income, not greater welfare. Four years later, it is true, a Court of Wards was established in Ireland; but

---

[1] Guildhall Letter Book of Queen Elizabeth, P.D. 2309, p. 227; *Acts of P.C.*, 1571-5, pp. 39-40, 157, 221, 233-4.

Bacon's role in Irish wardship was less significant than he would have us believe. It is also true that the profits from wardship in England climbed higher still. But it was a brief triumph. Three decades later, the practices and profits of wardship—Irish and English alike—were swept away for ever by the Long Parliament.[1]

1 J. Spedding, *The Letters and the Life of Francis Bacon* (1872), vi, 320-1; *Cal.S.P. Ireland*, 1615-25, p.396; V. Treadwell, 'The Irish Court of Wards under James I', (*Irish Hist. Studies*, xii, 1-27).

III

WARDSHIP AND SOCIETY

Many men do esteem this wardship by knights-service very unreasonable and unjust, and contrary to nature, that a freeman and gentleman should be bought and sold like an horse or an ox.

Sir Thomas Smith, *De Republica Anglorum*

7

Guardians and Wards

MANY of the wards with whose fortunes this book is concerned are unknown to history. The formal documents record their age, their possessions, their parentage and their guardians; but about their experiences, their emotions, their lives at home, or at school and university, our manuscripts maintain a dispassionate silence. Here and there, however, a lawsuit, a letter, or some other informal document breathes life into the official account books and schedules, and the uneasy and uncertain relations between guardians and wards can be reconstructed. Yet, if the informal document, because of its rarity and interest, is rated highly it may, as a source, present pitfalls of its own.

We may take as an example the wardship of Lord Herbert of Cherbury, who has special claims upon our attention because he has left us his autobiography. This bombastic nobleman was a teller of incredible tales, largely about his own imaginary achievements; but we know enough of his position as a ward to be able to distil some of his fact from a welter of fiction. Herbert tells us that he was a sickly child and that it was 'so long before I began to speak, that many thought I should be ever dumb'. He made up for it later on. As he grew and 'when I understood what was said by others, I did yet forbear to speak, lest I should utter something that were imperfect or impertinent'. That reticence he also overcame. He suffered punishment willingly rather than tell a lie, 'and I can affirm to all the world truly that, from my first infancy to this hour, I told not willingly anything that was false, my soul naturally having an apathy to lying and deceit'. Before he was nine he had written fifty or sixty verses in a day, but the recurrence of sickness prevented his completing his study of Welsh and other languages under a tutor in Denbighshire. He recovered and at twelve he was an undergraduate at University College, Oxford, already taking his full share in disputations and in Greek exercises.[1]

This vigorous intellectual life was interrupted by the death of his father and, immediately, as he tells us, his mother requested his uncle, Sir Francis Newport, 'to haste to London to obtain my wardship for his and her use jointly, which he obtained'. Shortly afterwards, he goes on, when he was fifteen he was betrothed and married to an heiress, six years his senior. After that he went back to Oxford, accompanied by his wife and mother, where 'I followed my book more close than ever' until he reached the age of eighteen when he left the university and divided his time between his mother's house in London and Montgomery Castle. By the time that he was twenty-one not only had he 'divers children' but 'I did, without any master or teacher, attain the knowledge of the French, Italian and Spanish languages'. In what leisure was left 'I attained also to sing my part at first sight in music, and to play on the lute with very little or almost no teaching.' Even in this his object was utilitarian—'that I might not need the company of young men, in whom I observed in those times much ill example and debauchery'. But he was anxious also to make himself, as he said, 'a citizen of the world'. So, after a spell at the court of Elizabeth I, where the queen sighed to think that he was already married, and a further spell at the court of James I, he took himself abroad where, we must conclude from his own narrative, he distinguished himself for the gallantry and debauchery for which he had had so little time during his misspent youth in Oxford, London and Wales.

We need not follow him farther in his elaborate and circumstantial account of his deeds of prowess at home and abroad or in the philosophical and moral disquisitions which interlard the history of his life. It is a wonderful story and we must take him as we find him. Yet in one particular case, his wardship, if we care

[1] *The Autobiography of Edward, Lord Herbert of Cherbury*, ed. Lee (2nd ed.), pp. 15–23, 44–8.

to test him, we find a curious omission of all the relevant facts. This important aspect of his life he dismisses in a single sentence, namely that Sir Francis Newport hurried to London to obtain his wardship. After that he goes on to discuss other things and the reader is left with the impression that Newport was his guardian. But the truth is, as we know from other sources, that Newport was *not* his guardian, for he disposed of the wardship almost at once to Sir George More, of Losely. Yet to More there is not the slightest reference throughout the autobiography.

Was Herbert unhappy with his guardian? Hardly that. The evidence provided by Herbert himself, elsewhere, is strong testimony on the opposite side. Once he sent More some Shrewsbury bread with the message, 'Measure not my love by substance of it, which is brittle, but by the form of it, which is circular' which symbolised his love; and he signed himself 'Your son that honoureth your worth'. On another occasion he began: 'Noble knight, I perceive your love placed in this our family to be as faithful in continuance as it hath been excessive in greatness.' 'Such a love', he went on, 'in these days wants an example, and is not like to be patterned.' A third letter of his began: 'Your continual remembrance of us (noble knight) though it cannot add to the opinion of your worthy love (only in respect of yourself worthy), yet it may confirm it, if there can be a confirmation, of that which is held most assured.' He ends: 'So, with the protestation of an unfeigned affection to do you any acceptable service, I rest Your adopted son in name but natural all other ways, HERBERT.' It is addressed: 'To his most honoured father, Sir George More, Knight, at Losely.'[1]

But these demonstrations of filial piety are not to be found in the autobiography; they are amongst the manuscripts at Losely. Why did Herbert suppress all appreciation of a man to whom, according to his own testimony, he stood so deeply in debt? It may be that these letters were sheer hypocrisy, coming without difficulty from a glib and sanctimonious youth. Alternatively, it may be that a man who claimed to accomplish most things on his

1 *The Losely Manuscripts*, ed. A. J. Kempe (1836), 354-9.

own initiative and unaided—including the learning of French, Italian and Spanish—could not find it in him to acknowledge a debt to a kindly and considerate guardian. Somewhere in that tortuous mind there was an explanation for this conflicting evidence, but it may be that the psychology of his megalomania will never yield its secret.

We are on different ground when we come to his guardian, Sir George More. By his own account he dealt faithfully with his ward and he supplied financial details to support his case: 'I procured his wardship (with much trouble to my brother Sir Francis Newport) beside the expense of £800 in the obtaining of it.' This was a substantial investment and once More had obtained the wardship 'whereas I might have married him without disparagement for £3,000, I did not only *not marry him for money*, as well I might have done, but with expense of almost £1,000 more, the particulars whereof are hereto annexed, procured him a marriage with not much less than £30,000'. More did this 'in sure confidence that, when by his marriage he should be enabled, he would give me good satisfaction for the value of his marriage, and all other sums thus for his good disbursed, which he performed accordingly'. So there followed an assignment to Newport by Herbert of some of the leases of his wife's lands now vested in him; and Newport in turn seems to have passed certain property on to More. These estates, More observes, heavily encumbered with debt, were a source of continual anxiety to him; and with that he joins the ranks of those who lamented over the profitless burdens which descended upon the feudal guardian.[1]

What did a ward expect from his guardian and what did a guardian expect from a ward? However mercenary a guardian's motives might be—and wardship was officially recognised as a commodity which could be bought and sold—the pecuniary element was not allowed wholly to obliterate more humane considerations. This was reflected, in the first place, in the provision by the Court of Wards of the exhibition or maintenance grant for the care of the ward. It came out of the income from the

[1] *Ibid.*, pp. 353–4.

ward's lands, now in crown possession. According to a commentator in the reign of Charles I, it was worth one-tenth the annual value of the land. But in Elizabeth's reign there was clearly no hard and fast rule. A selection from the wardships granted in the fourth year of Elizabeth's reign will show the great variety of the 'annuities' or exhibitions.[1]

The lands of Agnes Thornton of Middlesex were worth £3 per annum, the exhibition was £1. 6s. 8d. and the wardship was sold for £12. John Smith of the same county had lands worth £12, his exhibition came to £6. 13s. 4d. and the wardship was sold for £13. 6s. 8d. John Vaughan of London inherited lands worth £16. 9s. 0d., at which price his mother obtained the wardship along with an exhibition of £7. Thomas Green of Essex had lands worth £24, his wardship was sold for £25 to Mr. Caustey of the Queen's Chapel, who received also an exhibition of £20. On the other hand George Cotton of the same county had lands worth £69. 6s. 8d., but his wardship was sold to Sir Thomas Wrothe for £53. 6s. 8d. and his exhibition was only worth £12. Nicholas Rowse of Hertford had lands worth £40, his exhibition was put at £10 but his wardship was sold for £33. 6s. 8d. In Buckinghamshire, Edward Bulstrode's guardian, Robert Keilway, Surveyor of the Liveries, received an exhibition of £20 'if so much be descended'. John Battesford of Kent inherited land worth £24. 3s. 4d. His wardship went to Sir William Damsell, Receiver-General of the Court of Wards for £20, together with an exhibition of £18. William Bodleigh of Devon had lands worth £71. 14s. 3d., his wardship was sold to Sir Gavin Carew for £66. 13s. 4d., 'with the exhibition of all that shall come to the Queen's Majesty, saving 6s. 8d.' Richard Rossiter of Yorkshire had lands valued at £12. 5s.; his wardship went to Brian Boyles, for £13. 6s. 8d. with an exhibition of £6 'if so much descend and, if not, then so much as shall descend, saving 20s. by year'.

What conclusions can be drawn about the relative size of the

1 B.M. Egerton MS. 2978, f. 80r; Wards 9.156 (the wards are entered under counties).

exhibition? Clearly, though there was usually some correlation between the total value of the lands and the price at which the ward was sold, an issue which forms a central theme of a later chapter, there was not the same correlation with the amount of the exhibition. On analysis, this appears reasonable enough. When Burghley granted an exhibition he had, as we have seen, to take into consideration how much land was in fact in the queen's possession. She could claim her third part but, under the Statute of Wills of 1540, all or part of the remaining two-thirds could either be bequeathed to people other than the ward or conveyed in such a way that he was not the nominal landholder. By one way or another the money available for the exhibition might be no more than a third of the total value of his lands. Secondly, Burghley would have to take into consideration the educational and other needs of the ward. Finally, as the examples cited and others in the same volume show, a courtier or an official might be rewarded not only with a favourable price for the wardship but with a substantial exhibition as well. How he used the exhibition was left to his own conscience.

Payment of the exhibition money might be made either by the feodary locally, who in effect deducted the money from the rent paid him by the guardian, if he were in occupation of the ward's lands; or where the sums were large, payment might be by the Receiver-General of the Court of Wards in London. Sometimes the smaller wardships were granted without an exhibition, while the more valuable ones might bring increased exhibitions, as the ward grew older or as more land descended to the ward. That was for the master to decide, either at the time of granting the wardship or in answer to a petition later on.

For example, George Goring and Edward Bellingham, guardians of John Bellingham, had received an exhibition of £10 when the wardship was sold. Now, runs a decree of the Court of Wards of November 158?, 'the said John Bellingham, the ward, being of the age of sixteen years and more, is desirous to study the laws of the realm and is now preferred to an inn of a court'. For this 'the said exhibition of ten pounds by year granted by the said letters patents is not sufficient for the maintenance of the said ward in learning'. As a result, 'as well the said committees [guardians] as other the friends of the said ward have made their humble petition for further increase of exhibition in that behalf. In consideration whereof, and for the better advancement of the said ward in learning, and for that also there is descended to Her Majesty, in the right of the said ward, lands and tenements in possession amounting to the clear yearly value of thirty-two pounds', the exhibition was accordingly increased by £3. 6s. 8d. per year. It is worth observing in this connection that one of the guardians stood very close to the Master: he was George Goring, Receiver-General of the Court of Wards—and not the most trustworthy of royal officials.[1]

An increased exhibition was similarly awarded to the third Earl of Southampton, Burghley's ward and, in time, Shakespeare's patron. But the lands in the queen's hands were, in this case, alleged to be inadequate to yield an increase of exhibition. The will of the Earl's father was accordingly modified by the Court of Wards in order to divert some of the money 'to the Lord Treasurer to defray the necessary expenses and honourable maintenance of the young Earl, over and above the small annuity allowed him by the queen, as appertain to the estate and years of the young earl'. The money went to Burghley who, at this stage, was both Lord Treasurer and Master of the Court of Wards, and in power and influence nearest the queen. But it is also true that many of the lesser folk gained an addition to their exhibition where good cause was shown and the estate large enough to yield an increase.[2]

Not all the expenses were met in the shape of an exhibition. Sometimes a special allowance had to be made where a guardian had not yet been appointed or for some other reason. For example, the Usher of the Court of Wards, Marmaduke Servant,

1 Wards 9.107, f. 358r.
2 C. C. Stopes, *The Life of Henry, Third Earl of Southampton* (Cambridge, 1922), p. 26.

paid the following sums in September 1602 on behalf of Charles
Carter and his tutor:

1. Diet for nine weeks at 14s. a piece, the week: £12. 12s. 0d.
2. Ready money for two suits of apparel: £12. 12s. 7d.
3. For lodging and washing, and the attendance of
   myself and my man for nine weeks at 6s. 8d. the
   week: £3. 0s. 0d.

Total £28. 4s. 7d.

On the other hand the confusion and uncertainty which prevailed
in the Court of Wards after the death of Burghley in 1598 made
matters difficult for at least one ward. Christopher Hatton,
nephew of the late Lord Chancellor of that name, lamented to the
Earl of Essex in November 1598 about his unfortunate situation.
As Essex was strongly forecast for Burghley's successor as Master,
his lamentation had particular point. He had had no exhibition or
maintenance since the preceding summer. The last Master had
allowed him £86. 13s. 4d. a year but this was grossly inadequate
to maintain him, now that he had reached man's estate. He prayed
that the earl would use his favour with the queen to obtain for
him an increased exhibition as well as some ready cash to supply
his wants and to pay Jesus College, Cambridge, from which he
was writing, the debt he owed it. The earl's 'favour with the
queen' failed to get himself the Mastership, so Jesus College,
Cambridge may well have had to wait for its money. But we
have evidence that the Master of the Court of Wards was willing,
in normal times, to make special grants for 'necessary reparations'
to a ward's house or estate, or for other purposes.[1]

A guardian was concerned with more than the physical welfare
of his ward; he was explicitly made responsible for his ward's
education. This was a large commitment and many a guardian
fell short of the mark. But whatever charges may be made
against Lord Burghley, in the matter of education he aimed far
higher than any of his contemporaries. This we shall consider

[1] H.M.C. Salis., xii, 355; viii, 463.

when we come to examine, in full, his role in Tudor wardship. Here it must suffice to say that his household was famous throughout England as a training ground for young courtiers and statesmen, and admission to it was sought after by the best families in the land. He was always alive to the needs for the highest standards in education and, whether as Chancellor of the University of Cambridge, or Master of the Wards, he was the target for the most progressive ideas in contemporary educational theory. To him Sir Nicholas Bacon dedicated his plan for a school for wards. After a discussion which started in Burghley's room—about some runaway scholars of Eton, who had fled before the wrath of their masters 'for fear of beating'—Roger Ascham was stimulated to expound his brilliant analysis of the task of education. And Burghley himself, amidst the unrelenting burdens of high office, made time somehow to encourage and chide both university and ward along the path of a disciplined search for knowledge.[1]

Burghley set an excellent example. His son, Robert Cecil, seems to have kept up his father's interest in education and we find him, in 1602, after the manner of Burghley, advising the tutor of 'young Mr. Clifton, Her Majesty's ward', to make arrangements for him to go to Cambridge. 'I have thought good, out of the care that appertaineth to my place over all Her Majesty's wards, to advise you to take such order for his present maintenance, above Her Majesty's allowance, as shall be necessary.' To Cambridge he should go as soon as possible 'where I could also wish he were placed in St. John's College, because I am particularly acquainted that there is not any place in the university where there is a more careful master nor better government'. The Privy Council itself, during the anxious war years of the 1590s, took a special interest in the guardianship of wards; but that was merely to keep track of the Catholics and their movements overseas. Hence the Council wanted to know the names of wards or other children who had been sent out by relatives under pretence of the study of languages, or for any other reasons. The recusants

---

1 B.M. Add. MS. 32379, ff. 26r–33v; Ascham, *The Scholemaster*, ed. J. E. B. Mayor (1934), p. 62.

or evilly affected were to be hauled before the Council and their homes searched.[1]

If Burghley set a good example, it was only occasionally followed. The average guardian who by one means or another had obtained a ward had neither the interest nor the capacity to make education his primary concern. Hence what evidence we have is highly critical of their conduct. 'That the proceeding hath been preposterous', Sir Nicholas Bacon told Burghley in 1561, 'appeareth by this: the chief thing and most of price in wardship is the ward's mind, the next to that his body, and the last and meanest his land.' That was the theory, but the practice was utterly different. The buyer of a wardship, wrote Sir Thomas Smith, quoting contemporary opinion in his *De Republica Anglorum*, 'will not suffer his ward to take any great pains, either in study or any other hardness lest he should be sick and die before he hath married his daughter, sister or cousin, for whose sake he bought him: and then all the money he paid for him should be lost.' Sir Humphrey Gilbert's opinion was even more trenchant. He spoke of wards being brought up 'in idleness and lascivious pastimes, estranged from all serviceable virtues to their prince and country, obscurely drowned in education for sparing charges'. These poor standards of education were, he said, deliberate, 'of purpose to abase their minds lest, being better qualified, they should disdain to stoop to the marriage of such purchasers' daughters'.[2]

Hugh Latimer in Edward VI's reign, Nicholas Bacon in Mary's reign and again under Elizabeth, and Gilbert a decade later, all proposed the establishment of a school for wards where their educational needs could be far better satisfied than in the average private household. Their proposals came to nothing. The origin of the Court of Wards had nothing to do with contemporary educational theory and the significant and remarkable efflorescence of educational ideas which the century witnessed passed it by.[3]

If self-interest played so large a part in the kind of education a

[1] H.M.C. *Salis.*, xii, 540; H.M.C. *Rutland*, i, 318–9.
[2] *De Republica Anglorum*, ed. Alston, p. 121; Sir Humphrey Gilbert, *Queene Elizabethes Achademy* (ed. Furnivall, E.E.T.S. Extra Ser. 8), p. 1.
[3] *Sermons of Hugh Latimer*, ed. G. E. Corrie (1844), i, 69.

guardian bestowed upon his ward, the same approach marked the guardian's care of the estate. It is true that there were many warrants going out of the Court of Wards for special grants towards the upkeep of the property, preceded in important cases by a special survey made by the feodary. But the grant might be tardy and the need urgent. No less a person than the Earl of Leicester experienced difficulty in getting authority from Burghley for expenditure upon the estate of his (Leicester's) ward, Edward Verney. For the child's sake, Leicester said, he was willing to do what was necessary out of his own pocket, but meanwhile Burghley was warned that the house and lands were decaying. More serious than any failure on the part of the Court of Wards was failure on the part of the guardian, through neglect, cupidity or for other reasons. The lease of the ward's lands could, by the nature of things, be only of limited duration. His death, or his coming of age, would terminate it. Here were all the temptations to a lessee to force the land to yield a quick return. In theory the ward when he came of age, or his friends when he was still a minor, could bring an action against the guardian for the damage suffered by the property; but it is unlikely that a ward would have been tempted to call upon an already depleted estate to meet the heavy costs of a legal action. Sir Thomas Smith, who quoted some frank comments about the education of wards, had even sharper words to say about the treatment of their estates. Their inheritance, he tells us, when they came of age, consisted of 'woods decayed, old houses, stock wasted, land ploughed to the bare'.[1]

From the guardian's point of view there was much to be anticipated from a promising wardship—but promises were not always fulfilled. There might indeed be a physical struggle to obtain possession of the ward. Evan Lloyd of Denbighshire obtained the wardship of a certain Morgan Lloyd, who may or may not have been a relative. The next we hear of the ward is a letter from the ward's schoolmaster to the ward's uncle saying that the child

---

[1] *S.P.D.*, Mary, *Addenda*, vii, no. 34; B.M. Lans. 18, f. 194r; Lans. 121, f. 30r. (I quote here a MS., not the printed version of the *Republica*).

had been forcibly taken out of his possession by the guardian, Evan Lloyd. But in July 1601 the guardian protested to the Council in the Marches of Wales that he had been prevented from taking his ward into his care. This in turn was followed by a protest from the ward's uncle to the same Council that the guardian had in fact not waited for the *inquisition post mortem* to be held but had, accompanied by a gang of twelve men, armed with 'petronels and pistols', forced entry into the school and seized the ward. In the struggle to get him into the saddle, the boy had been wounded. In that state he had been carried for twenty-four miles amidst a hue and cry with the kidnappers firing at their pursuers, until the chase ended with the recapture of the child and his being lodged with a local justice. Now the uncle asked for the delivery of the child and the redress of the grievances. What the end was we do not know, but it was clearly an inauspicious beginning to a guardianship.[1]

The custody of the child, his marriage and the occupation of his lands, all these the crown sold or leased for what price it could get. But some things were not for sale. Advowsons, inherent in the property, were retained by the queen and resistance to this right was swept aside. On one occasion the queen wished to present John Underhill, Rector of Lincoln College, Oxford, and tutor to a ward, to a benefice in the diocese of Chester. She claimed that the right was hers in virtue of the wardship but, runs a letter from the Privy Council to the Bishop of Chester, 'Your Lordship (as we are informed) refuseth, upon Her Majesty's said presentation, to institute the said Mr. Underhill, because certain of Cheshire pretend title to the gift of the said benefice, by virtue of a feoffment made to them (as they allege) by Sir William Booth, father of the said ward, in his lifetime.' The Council retorted to this claim that the queen's right rested upon common law whereas 'the feoffees claim (if they have any indeed) standeth upon an extraordinary fact which (as we are informed) is first to be proved'. Meanwhile his lordship was instructed to 'cause order to be given for his institution and induction, to be given according to Her Majesty's

[1] H.M.C. *Salis.*, xiv, 181, 182, 185, 197.

said presentation, any caveat or other dealing of the feoffees to the contrary notwithstanding'. That was in 1581 and in 1589 Underhill himself became Bishop of Oxford.[1]

Other rights of this sort might be involved. In 1576 the mastership of Magdelene College, Cambridge, was vacant. The right of presentation to the office lay in the Lords Audley but in that year it had passed to a minor, Lord Thomas Howard, and, through him, to the queen. Accordingly the crown exercised the right and appointed Richard Howland, chaplain of Burghley and friend of Whitgift, to the vacant office. This Howland later became Bishop of Peterborough, where he earned the reputation of impoverishing his bishopric to gratify his patron, for which he gained a special and characteristic notice from Martin Marprelate. In 1577 Howland moved from Magdalene to St. John's, and the vacancy led to grave confusion at Magdalene. On the request of the fellows of the college, Burghley nominated Degory Nicholls, another of his chaplains. The queen, apparently without the knowledge of Burghley, nominated Henry Coppinger. Coppinger obtained the post but as the historian of the college puts it 'though he came in here by the queen's authority, yet he was so much discountenanced by the hereditary patron of the house that he was forced to quit his mastership; and by accepting that, having parted with his fellowship, to the which there was no return, was thereby turned out of all: a very hard fate upon so deserving a man'. In rapid succession, then, the college had a third master, and this time it was Burghley's nominee, Degory Nicholls. But he was soon involved in quarrels with the fellows of his college and in the cross-currents of college intrigues we must leave him.[2]

Presentations, advowsons, the right to metals on the land are examples of the prerogative which the crown would not yield. But so much else was sold that the competition for wardships was, as we have seen, acute. What kind of people bought them? In a

1 *Desiderata Curiosa*, ed. Peck (1732), bk. III, p. 32.
2 H.M.C. *Salis.*, xiii, 136, 147–9; T. Baker, *History of St. John's College, Cambridge* (Cambridge, 1869), i, 173–4.

number of cases the widow became the guardian of her son. But the proportion was not high. Of the grants made in the fourth year of Elizabeth's reign, seventy are sufficiently detailed to make possible an analysis of the recipients. Of these seventy, ten were mothers of the wards. During the year as a whole only one of the mothers, Lady Parry, widow of Sir Thomas Parry, late Master of the Wards, bought her wardship at less than the normal price. But even she had to see at least part of the lands go to a stranger. The remaining nine received no favourable treatment. Other widows, after the initial purchase of the wardship by a stranger, may have gone into the open market to buy the guardianship of their own sons at second- or third-hand. But such evidence as we have does not indicate that many transfers ultimately restored the child to its mother. Nor have we more than scanty evidence of what these transfers must have cost the mother. What we do know is that they sometimes lamented that the price asked them was beyond their reach.

At no period in the reign of Elizabeth was a very much higher proportion of the wardships granted in the first place to mothers or other relations. An uncle sometimes obtained the wardship. Sometimes the guardian, before or after obtaining the wardship, married the mother. But these were exceptions, not the general trend. When petitioning for a wardship a mother enjoyed as yet no priority as against other bidders. Under the reforms of 1611, relations were granted a month's pre-emption—for what that was worth.[1]

For the rest, the guardians were drawn from almost all classes of men, but more especially from noblemen, courtiers and royal officials. The Earl of Leicester had at least seven wards. Sir Francis Knollys had extensive interests in the business of wardship. The Earl of Bath likewise was deeply involved. The greater and the lesser officials picked their plums. The following list, drawn up by a contemporary, provides an admirable sample of the

[1] S.P.D., Jas. I, lxi, no. 6.

guardians willing and anxious to take a ward into their care. It covers the period 1594–8.[1]

A Note of Wardships granted by the late Lord Treasurer and Master of the Wards unto divers noble personages and others Her Majesty's servants within these 4 years past.

Bucks	Hawtrey	Sir John Wolley
London	Quiny	Mr. Waad, Clerk of the Council
Dorset	Samways	Sir Arthur Gorges
Bucks	Lovell	Sir John Fortescue
Cambs.	Grey	Dr. Bull of the Chapel
	Carvill	Mr. H. Seckford of the Privy Chamber
Somerset	Hedges	Mr. Herbert, Master of Requests
Suff.	Short	Hunnings of the Revels
Suff.	Mendham	Nixon of the Wardrobes
Somerset	Carrant	Beck of the Spicery
London	Branthwayt	Lord Cobham, defunct
	Best	Mr. H. Seckford of the Privy Chamber
Norfolk	Downes	Ambrose Jenny, the Queen's Footman
Wilts.	St. John	Lady Leighton
Leic.	Purefy	Mr. Beale, Clerk of the Council
Yorks	Musgrave	Sir John Stanhope
Worc.	Cavell	Carswell of the Guard
Glouc.	Raylop	Sir William Brook
	Andrews	Sir Richard Knightley
Derby	Gell	Earl of Shrewsbury
Dorset	Malyns	Mr. H. Brook, *modo* Lord Cobham
London	Butcher	Dr. Smith, the Queen's physician
Norf.	Knyvett	Lady Paget
Worc.	Washburn	Lady Digby
Surr.	Drew	Stone, the Queen's Footman, and Norton of the Cellar
Somerset	Alambridge	Kirkham of the Revels

[1] S.P.D., Eliz., cclxviii, no. 42.

Suff.	Flatman	Webber of the Privy Kitchen
Suss.	Cook	Hawkins of the Guard
	Fetherston	Sir John Stanhope
Kent	Harteys	Mattingley, the Queen's joiner
Surr.	Wilkinson	Sir Wm. Brook
	Blunt	Sir Thomas West *modo* Lord de la Ware
Derby	Babington	Damport, the Queen's Footman
Worc.	Acton	Mr. Herbert Crofts
Norf.	Cobbe	Mr. Nedeham, the Pensioner
Suff.	Seckford	Mr. H. Seckford
Beds.	Farre	Mr. H. Brook, *modo* Lord de la Ware (sic)
	White *alias* Hole	Gilbert Haines, the Queen's Servant
Essex	Covell	Burrow the Sewer
Lancs.	Westby	Mr. Poynts, Clerk of the Kitchen
Hants	Paulet	Sir Thomas West, *modo* Lord de la Ware
Derby	Talbot	Mr. Roger Manners
	Tuckevill	Mr. Michael Stanhope
Suss.	Rootes	Cranmer of the Jewel House
Kent	Hales	Sir John Stanhope
Yorks	Metcalf	Mr. Edward Stanhope
Kent	Sulyard	Sir William Brook
Kent	Baker	Lord Buckhurst
Dorset	Chevrell	Sergeant Burrell
Oxon	Parsloe	Barret, Knight of the Cellar
Lincs.	Harrison	Saye, one of the children of the Privy Chapel
Suff.	Lingwood	Lanman of the Guard
Cheshire	Lee	Starkey the Sewer
Northants	Manley	Sir William Lane, the Equerry
Somerset	West	Stone, the Queen's footman
Suff.	Smith	Mr. Smith, Clerk of the Council
Oxon	Lental	Sergeant Burrell
London	Haughton 1	Lord Buckhurst
	Fortescue	Mr. Chancellor of the Exchequer
Devon	Prest	Hill of the Guard

Denbigh	Wynne	Wynne, gentleman harbinger
	Tomson, lunatic	Lord North
Bucks	Hamden	Lady Kildare
Glouc.	Woodward	Sergeant Burrell
Yorks	Smelt	Mr. Brackenbury
London	Haughton 2	Sir John Stanhope
Beds	Sibley	Vizakerly of the Guard
Dorset	Hannam	Mr. Ferdinando of the Privy Chamber

£1000 (by report) given to Mr. Ferdinando for this

| | Pavet | Lady Burgh |
| Yorks | Vaughan | Mr. Thomas Knyvett |

When we consider this list of guardians, it is clear that, if wards or their mothers had been free to choose, they would have gained most from the household of a great nobleman. Here, with its schoolroom and its tutors, with its chapel and its country sports, its experience of estate management and its entertainment of the great in the land, a ward could expect to receive the best training in the art of living and governing which the age had to offer. In the stately homes of Wolsey, More, Leicester, Burghley, a ward could be sure of a better upbringing and education than he had ever received in his father's house, or could expect to receive from the lesser folk who were bidding to become his guardian.[1]

Yet even behind the most considerate treatment there lurked always the dominant interests of profit and revenue. The following letter, sent in 1548 from the Privy Council to the Archbishop of York, is a nice amalgam of charity and state interest:

Where it was reported that God has called to his mercy the Earl of Cumberland who had now left behind him a daughter, being the King's Majesty's ward, his Lordship [the Archbishop] was required to take order upon receipt hereof for the sending of her up hither, so as, by the conduct of some discreet gentleman of that household, two sober gentlewomen and twelve servants of that family, she might come hither by convenient and easy journeys. And if there

[1] Cf. P. V. B. Jones, *The Household of a Tudor Nobleman* (Illinois, 1917).

should not be money allotted by the officers of her late father for that purpose, if his Lordship disbursed it, he should be repaid it with thanks.

Post Script: It was yet said that the said Earl was not dead, who if [he] were not His Grace was very glad, and they required him to stay therein till he should be so, and upon assured knowledge to execute it; and in that case to cause all the evidence and those writings to be in sure custody within the house, so as till further order they might remain sealed up.

The discreet gentleman, the sober gentlewomen, the twelve servants, the convenient and easy journeys, all these are not neglected; but neither are the evidence and the writings which the crown officers will minutely examine, once they can get their hands upon them.[1]

Nor must we forget that wardships were treated in law, and in fact, as chattels which could be bought and sold and, indeed, bequeathed by will. Robert Nowell, late Attorney of the Court of Wards, remembered the Master in his will, in what he must have felt was the most appropriate fashion: 'I give and bequeath to my very good master and friend, Mr. Secretary Cecil, the wardship of younger Mr. Walgrave, with all my right and interest in the same, paying such money to the Queen's Majesty as I should.' Here, clearly enough, the ward would suffer no peril by the transfer. Equally well served was Sir Thomas Wrothe's ward, Anthony Aucher, who was left sufficient money by his guardian to pay for his own wardship and marriage; but Wrothe's ward appears also to have been his grandson, and the benefaction is understandable. What the queen's porters and grooms, clerks and stewards, feodaries and country gentlemen did with their wardships was a different matter, in terms of the welfare and prospects of the wards in their care.[2]

The story of the relationship between guardian and ward is, as we have seen, a many-sided one. Sometimes it tells of humane and

---

[1] *Acts of P.C.*, 1547–50, pp. 542–3.

[2] *The Spending of the Money of Robert Nowell*, ed. Grosart, p. xlix; P.C.C. 16 Pyckering (Wrothe): I am indebted to Miss K.M. Longley for this reference.

considerate action, worthy of any guardian in any age. Sometimes
it has all the elements of a selfish and mercenary exploitation. One
thing, however, emerges from the diverse examples we have
considered: guardianship in terms of child welfare and guardianship as a source of private profit had, in the usual run of cases,
nothing in common. Perhaps Shakespeare, through the mouth-
piece of Bertram and his mother, the Countess of Roussillon,
strikes the keynote of the feudal relationship. 'In delivering my
son from me,' says the mother, 'I bury a second husband.' 'And I,
in going madam,' Bertram replies, 'weep o'er my father's death
anew.—But I must attend His Majesty's command, to whom I
am now in ward, evermore in subjection.' But if Bertram was, as
some critics believe, Shakespeare's version of Burghley's ward, the
Earl of Oxford, then there is another side of the story; and we
shall meet him again in a different context. Yet guardianship, as
everyone in Tudor England well knew, was a means to an end:
marriage. No judgement of this system of guardianship is possible,
therefore, until we have considered the place of feudal marriage
in Tudor society.[1]

[1] *All's Well that Ends Well*, I, i.

8

Marriage

AMONGST the notebooks of the Clerk of the Court of
Wards is to be found a brief entry that, on 9 May 1562, a
certain John Clavell paid four shillings *pro maritagio sui
ipsius*. It is a formal note and it tells us simply that Clavell had to
pay 4*s*., as one of several administrative charges, in order to buy
'his own marriage', that is, to be free to marry at his will. This
kind of entry is not wholly unfamiliar. Wards did occasionally,
for one reason or another, obtain authority to 'buy their own
marriage'; in 1562 alone we have several examples. There the
matter could for the present be allowed to rest, were it not that
this entry happens to be one of about a dozen references to Clavell
scattered amongst the records of the Court of Wards. One piece
in our puzzle is missing but with the rest we can reconstruct the
problems which had faced this young man until, on 9 May 1562,
he was at last able to begin the process which was to end in the
purchase of 'his own marriage'.[1]

John Clavell was seventeen years old when his father died in
August 1558 and his mother shortly after. He was a pupil at
Winchester College and while there was boarded out with Roger
Horde of Winchester, gentleman. As it happened John Clavell fell
in love with his landlord's daughter, Thomasine Horde, and contracted himself in marriage with her. As a result, the whole
apparatus of the Court of Wards came into action against him
since, as a ward of the queen, he had no right to marry without
her authority, or, if the wardship had been sold, of his guardian.
Moreover, his uncle, himself eager for the wardship, intervened

1 Wards 9.232 (9 May, 4 Eliz.).

against his nephew. So, in the second year of the reign, the Attorney-General of the Court of Wards drew up a searching list of 'interrogatories to be ministered unto Roger Horde of Winchester in the county of Southampton, gentleman, and Thomasine Horde his daughter, on the part and behalf of our sovereign lady the Queen'. These questions may be summarised as follows:

1. How long had either of them known John Clavell?
2. Had John Clavell boarded with Horde when Clavell was a scholar of Winchester and who procured that Clavell should stay with Horde?
3. What acquaintance was there between Clavell and Thomasine Horde before he came to board and how long were they acquainted?
4. Did Roger Horde know, or was he privy to, the fact that Clavell came to the house or was in the company of Thomasine before he came to board?
5. Was matrimony contracted between them; and, if so, how long ago and who was present, or was the contract made privily between John Clavell and Thomasine Horde?
6. If any contract was made, was it in the lifetime of Clavell's father, or after his death?
7. Had John Clavell at any time before or since his father's death admitted to any such contract, and before whom?
8. By whose counsel or procurement was the contract made? Was it by Roger Horde or Agnes his wife, or was either of them privy to it?

First we have the answer which Roger Horde gave on 19 June 1560. He said that he knew John Clavell well since he had come to board with him two years before. How long his daughter had been acquainted with Clavell he could not say, but he had heard her say she knew him before he came to board. He could not say by whose procurement Clavell became his boarder; the usher of the college came and paid for his commons. He did not know that Clavell visited his house before he came to board. He had since then realised that matrimony had been contracted because he had seen the contract in writing signed by John Clavell. He believed also that it was made in about the middle of August 1558—that is, during the father's lifetime.

If that could be established then Clavell and his bride were safe because, as long as his father was alive, the Court had no jurisdiction. But when questioned about the nature of the marriage agreement, Horde admitted that only a 'privy' contract was made during the father's lifetime and a public contract subsequently. The evidence for this, however, appeared to be simply what his own daughter had told him about the contract and the witnesses.

So now it was the turn of his daughter to face the Attorney. She answered that she had known John Clavell for three years but her father had known him only for two. He had come to board with them by his own procurement. She 'had no acquaintance as in way of marriage' with Clavell until about six months before he came to live in her father's house. He had not come to her father's house before he came to board, 'but divers times to the bishop's palace, the which her father hath the keeping'. Three months before he came she had a 'privy' contract of marriage with him but after his coming they had a public contract. She mentioned the three witnesses named by her father, to whom she added a fourth, John Dorset. The 'privy' contract was made during the lifetime of Clavell's father, but not in front of witnesses. Two weeks before his father's death, John Clavell asked her to get someone to witness a new contract. She did indeed find a tiler, who was at work on a roof, and he agreed to come if asked. But, as it chanced, she did not send for him and no new contract was made. She was able to add, however, that John Dorset had told her that Clavell had told him, before his father's death, that he had contracted himself to marry her. She confirmed that neither of her parents knew of the contract at the time.[1]

That was the end of her evidence but the ordeal was not yet over. Since November 1558 she, her mother and her father had been under recognizance of £200 to appear before the Master and Council of the Court of Wards whenever required. On 18 June 1560 she had been 'enjoined in £100 to continue her appearance

[1] Wards 9.104, ff. 108r. and v; Wards 3.3 (Clavell depositions).

from day to day and not to depart until such time as she be examined before the Attorney of the Court'. That examination, as we have seen, was held shortly after. But not until November 1562 was the £200 recognizance at last cancelled, and they were free to go. By then the case, after dragging on for nearly four years, was settled, but a search for the decree of the court has proved fruitless. In spite of this, we know how the matter ended. John Clavell paid his 4s. as we have already seen. We know also that the wardship was 'sold to himself for £40'; but he paid £20 more 'because he contracted himself without licence; and the whole is £60 to be paid as in the schedule'. In other words, the court did not recognise as valid the marriage contract made in the father's lifetime but accepted the subsequent contract as binding. This was an infringement of the queen's right of wardship and, for that, Clavell paid the penalty of £20—not very heavy in this case. And now the 'wardship', the right of marriage, was his and no guardian could intervene in the matter. So John Clavell never became his uncle's ward. He was now nearly twenty-one and, as he took the road out of London with the decree in his pocket, he carried with him the full authority of the Court of Wards to marry his Thomasine, as he had promised he would when still a schoolboy in Winchester.[1]

That is all that our documents tell us of John Clavell's marriage; but it is a good deal more than we are told about most marriages of the period. Of this most important aspect of Tudor society not very much is known. We have, of course, plenty of literary references to shrews, tamed and untamed, and the relationship between the sexes, then as now, was the stock-in-trade of moralist and humorist alike. From the lawyers, also, we have plenty of references to the tenuous rights of women, and to the technical aspects of the marriage contract; while educationists were beginning to ask questions about the upbringing and education of girls. Some authors indeed felt that the emancipation of women had already gone very far. In some things, wrote Chamberlayne in the seventeenth century, 'the laws of England are above all so

---

[1] Wards 9.517, ff. 10r, 20r; Wards 9.156 (Dorset). Alas! We now know that John Clavell never married Thomasine Horde; and she became the wife of someone else. I owe this information to Mr. J. P. Ferris of the *Official History of Parliament*.

favourable to that sex, as if the women had voted at the making of them'. His contemporary, Fynes Moryson, put the whole thing even more succinctly: 'England in general is said to be the hell of horses, the purgatory of servants and the paradise of women.' But—and it needed only a percipient foreigner to point it out— 'women there are entirely in the power of their husbands, except for their lives'. In any case assertions of this sort do not carry us very far. Of marriage as a human institution and as a central element in society, our books and documents tell us all too little.[1]

This major gap in our social history, inevitable and perhaps un-bridgeable as it is, is all the more regrettable when one considers the special problem of feudal marriage, with which this chapter is concerned. The criticisms and allegations directed against both official administrator and feudal guardian turn often upon the treatment of the ward's 'marriage'. In this context there is a considerable body of evidence of selfishness, cruelty and a materialistic and pecuniary attitude to the most intimate—and most important—event in the life of the ward. Yet these attitudes can only be adequately assessed against a background of the Tudor treatment of marriage in general, that is, where questions of feudal rights were not involved. Only in this way, can one avoid being misled by the special pleading of contemporaries.

As the law stood the position was complex enough. A man's expectation of life in those days was considerably less than in ours. He knew that if at his death his heir was 'under age', the control of his marriage might well pass out of the family and be bought and sold like merchandise. Clearly, the parents would be tempted to arrange a suitable marriage while the father was still alive, however young the heir. But what was the age of consent, the age at which the marriage contract was binding on both parties? 'The age of discretion', said Coke, quoting Littleton's fifteenth-century work on tenures, 'is called the age of fourteen years; for at this age the infant, which is married within such age to a woman, may agree or disagree to such marriage.' 'The lawful age

1 E. Chamberlayne, *The Present State of England* (1669), p. 502; Fynes Moryson, *Itinerary* (1617), pt. 3, p. 53; W. B. Rye, *England as seen by Foreigners* (1865), p. 72.

to contract matrimony by the laws ecclesiastical', wrote an Elizabethan lawyer, 'is when the man is of the full age of fourteen years and the woman of twelve. If before this year any contract be made it is not to be accounted matrimony but spousation.' Until the age of consent the contract was not binding. 'Of a contract made in the minority of both parties groweth not any matrimony, except after their full years they declare a new consent, either by words or by some fact as by spontaneous cohabitation.' If only one party to the contract was under age then the other was bound by it from the moment the minor reached full age and consented. That was all very well, but if 'the party which was of full age contract with another before the party that was in a minority cometh to age, then is the former contract utterly void because there was betwixt them no matrimony but spousation'.[1]

There was ancient custom as to the law and procedure of marriage. Betrothal, contract, marriage involved technicalities of a subtle and significant kind; and if, as was said, a Tudor king spent troubled hours wrestling with his conscience over his wife's pre-contract with his deceased brother, a conscience which could only be salved by a revolution in church and state, his was merely an extreme instance of a widespread complexity. It needed, for example, two acts of Parliament within the space of a few years to deal with only one aspect of the law of pre-contract.[2]

Here is a contemporary account of a marriage, which brings out both its primitive form and its legal force. The speaker is the curate of Bridlington, in the East Riding of Yorkshire—the 'examinate', as he is called, because he was a witness in court. The groom, a certain John Eliot, sent for him one day and said:

'Sir Robert, you are welcome. Sit ye down and I will give you a pot of ale for you must ask me in the church on Sunday next.'
'With whom?' quoth this examinate.
'Marry', quoth he, 'with Margaret Clerke.'
'Well', quoth this examinate, 'but I would hear her speak.'
And thereupon John sent for her and she came forthwith, to

1 Coke, *First Inst.*, Sect. 104; B.M. Harl. 443, f. 57r.
2 32 Hen. VIII, c. 38; 2 and 3 Ed. VI, c. 23.

whom John said 'Margaret, my wife, sit you down, you are heartily welcome, for I mean to make you my wife.' And [he] kissed her and drunk to her. To whom she said 'Sir, I thank you most heartily, if so be that you be so persuaded in your heart, as you speak it.'

Who answered that he was and 'although some say that I will turn tomorrow, yet will I never turn'.

Then quoth [I] unto them: 'Join hands together in the fear of God, seeing that you are contented to be man and wife together and say this after me.—

—And he took [her] by her right hand and said unto her after [me], 'I, John take thee, Margaret, to my handfast wife, to have and to hold from this day forward, for better, for worse, for richer, for poorer, in sickness and in health, to love and to cherish till death us depart, according to God's holy ordinance, and thereto I plight thee my troth.' And so they drew hands and joined them together again . . . and immediately thereupon, he carried her from thence to his own house in Bridlington and gave her possession of his house and his kiln.

In the eyes of the law they were now man and wife. But not, unfortunately, in the eyes of John Eliot, the groom. He came forward with the allegation that he was drunk at the time of the betrothal and the whole thing was therefore invalid. The case was brought before the ecclesiastical court, to which the curate was summoned as principal witness. But for his evidence we should know nothing of the story.[1]

The marriage contract was a highly technical treaty between two parties and it required a skilled lawyer to interpret its exact nature. Judge Swinburne, who was born under Elizabeth and died under Charles I, wrote the first book on *Spousals* in the English language. It is a long and wearisome discourse, which elaborates the conditions and limitations in the marriage contract. By the time that one has reached the fourteenth 'amplication' to be followed in due course by the fourteenth 'limitation', one wonders how anyone at all in Tudor England could have been bound by a marriage contract. 'So tangled was the casuistry respecting marriage at the beginning of the sixteenth century,' writes a modern

---

[1] Cited in J. S. Purvis, *Tudor Parish Documents* (Cambridge, 1948), pp. 72-3.

authority, 'that it might be said that, for a sufficient consideration, a canonical flaw might be found in almost any marriage'.[1]

To the technicalities and obscurities surrounding the marriage contract, feudal law added technicalities of its own. The position of a male heir was, in one sense, more straightforward than that of a female. If he was under twenty-one at the time of his father's death, his land passed into the hands of the crown until he had sued livery, and his wardship and marriage were likewise at the crown's disposal. If he were already married or fully contracted in marriage, and had passed the age of consent, which was fourteen, the crown could not offer the ward an alternative marriage. (Whether, in spite of this pre-contracted marriage, the crown could still have the 'wardship' of the land was a matter of dispute.) If no such contract existed, then the ward must accept the marriage proposal made to him by the crown or guardian—or else pay the consequences.

If there was no male heir, the inheritance was divided equally amongst the daughters, irrespective of their age. Those who were over fourteen years of age at their father's death were *ipso facto* out of wardship, both as to their lands and their marriages. Those who were under fourteen were as fully in wardship as any male heir could be. But at fourteen, unlike her elder sister, who was already fourteen at the time of her father's death, a female ward did not pass out of wardship. She must wait another two years. Meanwhile, until she reached the age of fourteen she could enter into no binding contract of marriage proposed to her by her guardian; but if, when she was between the age of fourteen and sixteen, he presented a candidate to her 'and the heir female refuseth, then the lord shall hold the land until her age of one and twenty years, and further until he hath levied the value of her marriage'. If, however, she were pre-contracted in childhood to someone, she would have the right either to consent to marry him or to accept her guardian's choice. 'But if the lord

---

[1] H. Swinburne, *A Treatise of Spousals or Matrimonial Contracts* (1686), pp. 142–4; Thwing, *The Family*, p. 83, cited in C. L. Powell, *English Domestic Relations, 1487–1653* (N.Y. 1917), p. 11.

doth not tender a marriage within the two years, he shall lose the value of the marriage and content himself with the two years value [of the land].'[1]

The value of the marriage. This was the shadow which must have darkened the relationship between many wards and their guardians. It could be immensely important and we must consider it separately elsewhere in this chapter. Here before leaving the purely technical aspects of the question we may cite, as an example of the variety and obscurity of the issues arising from wardship, an observation of Littleton's:

> Note, if there be grandfather, father and son and the mother dieth, living the father of the son, and after the grandfather, which holds his land by knight's service, dieth seised, and his land descend to the son of the mother as heir to the grandfather, who is within age; in this case the lord shall have the wardship of the land but not of the body of the heir, because none shall be in ward of his body to any lord, living his father, for the father during his life shall have the marriage of his heir apparent, and not the lord. [It is otherwise] where the father dieth, living the mother, where the land holden in chivalry descends to the son on the part of the father.

And here is Coke's observation upon Littleton: 'Yet the father shall have the marriage of his daughter if she be his heir apparent; and Littleton's reason extendeth to the daughter, for that (saith he) the father shall have the wardship of his heir apparent, within which words the daughter is included, so long as she continueth heir apparent.' The theory is clear enough. No child could become the ward of someone else while his father was still alive; but this could not apply while his mother was still alive, if his father were dead. But family relationships could, amongst the landed gentry, be notoriously complex, and, on top of this, feudal tenures gave rise to even greater obscurity. Here was plenty of room for speculation by the lawyers, and we must leave them to their case-law and their precedents.[2]

In law and in practice, the feudal guardian enjoyed considerable

---

[1] Coke, *First Inst.*, Sect. 103.
[2] *Ibid.*, Sect. 114.

powers over his ward. But his authority was not limitless. When
he bought the right of marriage, it was a marriage *absque disparagatione*—without disparagement. The ward could not be married
to someone below his rank in society. The Tudor age was admittedly a time of social fluidity: a butcher's son could rise to be
Lord Chancellor and a tradesman's son to be the king's Secretary
of State. Over a larger field the rising—and declining—gentry tell
their own story; while civic and mercantile wealth was flowing
into the country to fertilise the hungry acres and impoverished
nobility with their marriage settlements. The social movement
worked both ways. 'Gentlemen disdain traffic', wrote Fynes
Moryson without concealing his disquietude, and as the result
of prodigality, rashness or sloth, 'do in this course daily sell their
patrimonies and the buyers (excepting lawyers) are for the most
part citizens and vulgar men.' Yet this flow of population and
wealth could not wash away the rock out of which Tudor society
was hewn: degree. Men had no doubt as to their own, and
other people's, station in life; and many men were born, lived and
died in the village and station of their birth.[1]

   That being so, a ward who was threatened with disparagement
—a marriage below his station—could appeal to the traditions of
the medieval centuries and to the law. What was disparagement?
Here again there were many and subtle distinctions. The laws of
England, wrote Chamberlayne, 'look upon tradesmen and chap-
men that live by buying and selling as a baser sort of people, and
. . . a ward within age may bring his action of disparagement
against his guardian, for offering any such in marriage'. But the
law was being tempered to the changing structure of trade.
'Yet in England', Chamberlayne goes on, 'as well as Italy, to
become a merchant of foreign commerce without serving an
apprentisage, hath been allowed no disparagement to a gentleman
born, especially to a younger brother.' There was, however, a
doctrine still in force, though it was as old as Magna Carta, which
made 'it a disparagement for a ward in chivalry (which was as
much as a gentleman) to be married to a burgess'. Also 'at this

[1] Moryson, *op. cit.*, pt. 3, p. 149.

day, by rule in the Court of Wards, a ward cannot be bound apprentice without petitioning the Court'. On the other hand it was more recent doctrine, put forward by an Elizabethan York Herald, that a ward could charge his guardian with disparagement for marrying him to someone not of sound religion.[1]

Coke's analytical mind saw four kinds of disparagement in marriage. The first arose from defects of mind, 'as an idiot, *non compos mentis*, a lunatic'. The second arose from defects of the blood, 'as 1. a villein, 2. burgensis, 3. the son or daughter of a person attainted of treason or felony, albeit pardoned, for the blood is corrupted. 4. a bastard. 5. an alien or the child of an alien'. The third group consisted of defects of the body, 'as first, *de membris*, having but one hand, one foot, one eye, etc.; secondly, deformity, as to look asquint, a cripple, halt, lame, decrepit, crooked, etc.; thirdly, privation, as blind, deaf, dumb, etc.; fourthly, disease horrible, as leprosy, palsy, dropsy, or such like diseases; fifthly, great and continual infirmity, as a consumption and such like; sixthly, impotency to have children in respect either of age past children or so tender years as there is too great disparity, or for natural disability or impediment, or such like; seventhly, deflowered of her virginity'. Coke had in reserve a whole catalogue of *impedimenta* to marriage but he cut his story short: 'In a word, it must be *competans maritagium absque disparagatione*.'[2]

Here and there we have examples of action for disparagment. Dorothy Devereux, daughter of the first Earl of Essex, had a runaway marriage with Sir Thomas Perrot. It was an extraordinary ceremony with the priest, dressed in his cloak, riding boots and spurs, tearing through the service at breakneck speed, while two men kept an armed guard at the church door. It aroused the queen to a fury that another of her maids of honour had been a party to a clandestine marriage; and groom, bride and the Bishop of London himself, who had granted the marriage licence, were punished for their misdemeanour. Finally the marriage was nulli-

1 Chamberlayne, *op. cit.*, pp. 491–2; B.M. Harl. 980, f. 96r; B.M. Lans. 43, f. 61r.
2 Coke, *First Inst.*, Sect. 107.

fied on the ground that it was a disparagement for the daughter of an earl to be married to someone like Perrot, though his father had risen to be Lord Deputy of Ireland. A quarrel between the Earl of Huntingdon and the dowager Countess, late in Elizabeth's reign, produced the serious allegation that a youth had been deliberately made drunk and, when in such a state, had been married to 'a horsekeeper's daughter-in-law'! Norroy King-at-Arms once went to York Minster and pulled down the heraldic arms of a ward's father. This was disparagement in another sense and brought the Attorney of the Wards into action with a petition that the King-at-Arms be called before the Court of Wards.[1]

How could a ward protect himself against disparagement? One method was by direct action against the guardian. If the relatives —the 'cousins' as contemporaries speak of them—'have cause to make lamentation or complaint amongst themselves, for the shame done to their cousin so disparaged, which in manner is a shame for them, then may the next cousin, to whom the inheritance cannot descend, enter and oust the guardian in chivalry. And if he will not, another cousin of the infant may do this, and take the issues and profits to the use of the infant.' If no relative would act in this way, then the infant himself, though under age, could enter and evict his guardian from the property. The alternative, or perhaps complementary, method open to the ward was to bring a lawsuit against his guardian. Of direct action to prevent disparagement we have a little evidence, including that of Shakespeare's Bertram who, as a nobleman, refused on the ground of disparagement the proffered marriage to a poor physician's daughter. Of lawsuits for disparagement I have been able to trace no evidence whatsoever.[2]

These possibilities offered scant protection for the ward against marriage below his dignity and station. The other possibility was for the ward to take the law into his own hands and marry whom

[1] Violet Wilson, *Queen Elizabeth's Maids of Honour* (1922), p. 151; B. M. Lans. 83,f. 671; W. West, *Symboleography* (1618), ii, 334a and b.
[2] Coke, *First Inst.*, Sect. 108; *All's Well that Ends Well*, II, iii.

he pleased, without consent of his guardian. Here a distinction must be drawn between the refusal of a marriage tendered to the ward by his guardian and the more serious offence of contracting a marriage without the lord's consent. The law on this subject had been laid down as long ago as 1236 in the Statute of Merton. 'If an heir, of what age soever he be, will not marry at the request of his lord, he shall not be compelled thereunto; but when he cometh to full age he shall give to his lord, and pay him as much as any would have given him for the marriage.' But if a ward 'marry without licence of his lord to defraud him of the marriage . . . then his lord shall hold his land beyond the term of his age, that is to say, of one and twenty years, so long that he may receive the *double* value of the marriage'. This, as we have seen, was the charge laid against John Clavell, but the Master of the Wards was merciful and Clavell escaped with a relatively light penalty.[1]

There were two ways of calculating the 'value of a marriage', according to the Statute of Merton; and the methods it laid down were still in force during our period. One was 'after the estimation of lawful men', that is, by a jury. The other was based upon the sum that 'hath been offered before, without fraud or collusion, and after as it may be proved in the king's court'. Clearly, substantial amounts of money might be involved and it would require a bold youth to cast away a considerable share of his inheritance by rejecting his guardian's proposal. Here and there stories have survived, some from suspect sources, of wards being mulcted of thousands of pounds for refusing to comply with their guardian's request. Lord Sandys said that such a refusal, when he was a ward, cost him £2,000. Burghley himself is reputed to have offered one of his grand-daughters in marriage to his ward, the Earl of Southampton. The earl declined; and rumour had it that this affront to Burghley cost Southampton £5,000. Other refusals there undoubtedly were, as we know from the official sources,

---

1 Stat. of Merton, Sects. VI and VII.

but they were few. Most wards accepted their fate—with good
or ill grace.[1]

More serious still than the flouting of the lord's right of
marriage by the ward was the violation by strangers, the ravishment of a ward. For this the penalty was two years' imprisonment
if the ward were restored unmarried but 'if he have unduly
married him, then he is to be imprisoned by the space of five years,
or else to be banished the realm'. These dangers arose not simply
in the matter of feudal marriage but even where no feudal rights
were involved. A Marian statute made it 'a Star Chamber matter
to take away maidens from the custody of their father or mother'
even though 'she be not heir, or heir apparent, or though she do
depart with her consent, and after she is 12 years of age'. The
runaway match was no light matter; and amorous—or designing
—suitors could be a constant source of alarm. There were plenty
of early equivalents for the anvil at Gretna Green. For example,
Thomas Walker and Isabella Bamford 'were married together in
a field near the town of Ashton-under-Lyne, in the night time,
by moonlight, by one Sir John Ward, clerk'. Moreover, the mere
exchange of declarations 'I take thee for my wife' and 'I take thee
for my husband', if made by persons of age and followed by an
act of union, was a full and valid marriage. All the property and
legal rights consequent upon it were identical with those resulting
from wedlock in holy church. No wonder Burghley himself
pondered over a Latin treatise, *De Clandestinis Nuptiis*; while his
apophthegm—'marry thy children in haste lest they marry themselves', derived no doubt from his acute perception of these problems, both as head of a family and Master of the Wards.[2]

Marriage, of course, was the primary objective of the feudal
guardian; and the story of more than one famous Tudor family
is interwoven with the feudal rights of wardship. In Thomas More's
household there were a number of wards—and in the love and
education he gave them More's fame rivals that of Burghley.

[1] H.M.C. *Salis.*, xiv, 94; H. Foley, *Records of the English Province of the Society of Jesus*
(1878), iv, 49; Wards 9.517, ff. 32v, 41v, 45r.

[2] B.M. Harl. 1323, ff. 187r. and v; 4 and 5 Ph. and Mary, c. 8; H.M.C. *Salis.*, xiv, 47;
Child Marriages, ed. F. J. Furnivall (E.E.T.S. orig. ser. 108), p. 140.

Cecily More, his daughter, married one of these wards, Giles Heron, son and heir of Sir John Heron, a former treasurer of the chamber. John More, a son of Sir Thomas, married Anne Cresacre, another heiress and ward in the Chancellor's household. Elsewhere we notice similar developments. Lord Sheffield became a ward of the fifteenth Earl of Oxford, whose daughter, Anne Vere, he married. The earl's grandson, the seventeenth Earl of Oxford, became a ward of Burghley, whose daughter, Anne Cecil, he married. In the next generation, it was said that Burghley hoped to arrange a match between Anne's daughter and his ward, the Earl of Southampton, but, if he did, the plans went awry. Sir Henry Spelman, the eminent lawyer to whom we owe a good deal of our knowledge about the feudal tenures, married Eleanor, daughter and co-heiress of John L'Estrange, became the guardian of his brother-in-law and went to live on his estate.[1]

Perhaps the best example of the significance of feudal wardships in noble marriages is a contemporary account of the plans and achievements of the fourth Duke of Norfolk. He married the widow of Lord Dacre of Gilsland and became the guardian of her son, the heir of Lord Dacre. This youth 'he intended to have married to his only daughter, the Lady Margaret'. But that was 'frustrated by the untimely death of the child who, about eight years old, was accidentally slain by the fall of a vaulting horse upon him at the Duke's house at Thetford'. As a result, the ward's three sisters became joint heiresses and the Duke of Norfolk 'obtained the wardship also of the daughters whom he intended to have matched with his three sons, as in effect two of them were some years after': Anne the eldest to Philip his eldest son, Earl of Surrey, and Elizabeth the youngest to Lord William Howard, his youngest son. Mary the second daughter, who was designed for Lord Thomas Howard, his second son, died before she was marriageable. The duke was 'so desirous that these intended marriages should take effect, that he caused the Earl of Surrey to be contracted to the Lady Anne as soon as she came to be com-

1 R. W. Chambers, *Thomas More* (1935), pp. 183–4; B.M. Ward, *The Seventeenth Earl of Oxford* (1928), p. 10; *D.N.B.*, *sub*. Spelman.

pletely twelve years old (age in her sufficient to assent) though the
Earl wanted at that time some months of that age'. This same
earl, the future Earl of Arundel, became, on the execution of his
father, a ward of Burghley's. There can have been few noble or
gentle families whose genealogy does not bear the inescapable
marks of one or more feudal wardships.[1]

Needless to say these marriages were not always happy ones.
The marriage between Burghley's daughter and his ward, the
Earl of Oxford, proved a notorious failure. Lady Cobham lived
to regret the marriage of her daughter to a ward who proved to
be an 'unstaid' young man. A Mr. Richard Forster married his
daughter to Mr. Neville Godden of Laborne Castle in Kent, a ward,
Godden died and left his widow penniless. Her father was reduced to taking his daughter home again and begged Robert
Cecil to give him the wardship of the next heir. Time was pressing
because in seven weeks' time the ward would come of age.[2]

Not all of these marriages were for purely mercenary reasons,
although wealth and estate could, of necessity, never be very far
from the minds of those arranging the match. In this context the
special problem of the widow's marriage is of interest, for, if
her husband had held land by knight-service in chief, her marriage
too came into the jurisdiction of the Court of Wards. As in the
case of wards, two separate issues arose: her property and her
right of marriage. Under the common law of England she was
entitled to her dower, a life interest in a third part of the estate
left by her husband; if neither marriage settlement nor will gave
her an absolute right to the property, it returned to the heir on her
death. Here the position was fairly straightforward, though it
might vary somewhat from place to place. For example, 'By the
custom of Kilmersdon in Somersetshire, the wife hath widow's
estate. And if she marry she loseth the land. But if she be found
incontinent, and come into the next court riding astride upon a
ram, and in open court acknowledge her incontinency, she shall

1 *The Lives of Philip Howard, Earl of Arundel, and of Anne Dacres, his Wife*, ed. Duke of
Norfolk (1857), pp. 172–3.
2 H.M.C. *Salis.*, x, 117; viii, 337.

not forfeit.' On the other hand, it was a general law, upheld in the Star Chamber, that 'If a woman be married to a ravisher, and after consent to the ravisher, she forfeiteth her inheritance or dower.'[1]

Provided that none of her husband's lands were held by knight-service, she was free during her widowhood to marry whom she pleased, subject always to the possible loss of all or part of her share in the estate, in cases where her husband attached certain conditions. For example, one widow was left by her husband an annual income of £17. 6s. 8d. for life on condition that she 'commence no suit at the common law against his said heirs for the dower'. Another widow was left property on condition that she should not remarry and that she should not re-convert the land to corn. But these were restrictions imposed upon her by some private arrangement and she was immune from the provisions of the feudal law. By contrast, her situation could be very different where even a fraction of the land were held by knight-service; the feudal rights of lord or crown could, in earlier centuries, be almost as onerous as those exercised against the ward.[2]

As long ago as Magna Carta the grievances of the feudal widow seem to have been acute enough to call for the promise of redress in one of its clauses. Henceforth, an assurance was given that no widow would be compelled to marry if she declined to, provided that she entered into security not to marry without the consent of the crown or lord from whom the land was held by knight-service. Licence to remain single could, in some cases, be a costly business. The Countess of Chester had paid 500 marks to King Stephen so that she might not be compelled to re-marry within five years. The Countess of Warwick paid King John £1,000, a very considerable sum in the thirteenth century, and ten palfreys that she might not be forced to marry till she pleased. The widow was not alone in paying such marital charges; the successful suitor might be called upon to make a substantial contribution to the Exchequer. Geoffrey de Mandeville paid Henry II 20,000 marks (over £13,000) that he might marry Isabel, Countess of Gloucester.

1 B.M. Harl. 980, f. 90r; Stowe 397, f. 25v.
2 Wards 9.138, f. 579r; M. W. Beresford, *The Lost Villages of England* (1954), p. 194.

Geoffrey, needless to say, anticipated not only the comforts of a wife but 'all her lands, knights fees, etc.'[1]

The royal concern with widow's marriages lasted on into the sixteenth century, sometimes in the shape of a personal intervention on behalf of a candidate for a widow's hand, sometimes in the formal, and by now fixed, charge for her licence to marry. 'It may like Your Grace to be advertised', wrote Sir Thomas More to Cardinal Wolsey, 'that the King's Highness this night going to his supper called me to him secretly and commanded me to write unto Your Grace that, whereas it hath pleased our Lord to call to his mercy Mr. Myrfyn, late alderman of London, his Grace very greatly desireth, for the special favour which he beareth toward Sir William Tyler, that the same Sir William should have the widow of the said late alderman in marriage.' The Cardinal was accordingly requested to use his 'well approved wisdom and dexterity in the achieving and bringing to good pass his virtuous and honourable appetite'. On other occasions powerful support was given to candidates for marriage. We have letters to Alice Moore, widow, in favour of Roland Hunt, Groom of the Chamber; to Mrs. Breame, widow, in favour of Mr. Man, with the support of Mr. Secretary Paget; to Mrs. Meredith of London, in favour of Mr. Birche. Mrs. Myrfyn was not necessarily a feudal widow but the other ladies almost certainly were.[2]

Yet, by the sixteenth century, the crown had abandoned its right to impose a marriage upon a feudal widow, though there were, of course, opportunities for exercising pressure upon her. Lord Burghley, to judge by his correspondence, seems to have been a matchmaker for all England; but this arose from his unique role in politics and society and was not specifically the result of his authority as Master of the Wards. On the other hand, there is no mistaking what Sir John Davis had in mind in a letter written to Sir Robert Cecil, during the latter's Mastership. 'There is nothing left', he told Cecil, 'but to repair my fortunes by

---

1 Magna Carta, clause 8; *A Relation of England*, ed. C. A. Sneyd (Camden Soc., xxxvii, 1847), p. 119.
2 *Original Letters*, ed. Ellis (1st. ser.), i, 207–8; *L.P.*, xxi, pt. 1, p. 71; pt. 2, pp. 327, 407.

some marriage. If it be agreeable to your Honour I do not know any whom I could better fancy than Mrs. Bassett, over whom your power is so much.' He asked Cecil to send her 'a few favourable lines to intimate your readiness in the gratifying her with the wardship of her daughter's lands, if for your sake she entertained my suit'. If Cecil were to make such a promise, Davis was certain that his proposal would succeed; if the grant of a wardship was too much to expect, then he asked Cecil to use whatever persuasion he could. 'If in my request I have gone beyond the limits of one that is already so deeply bound to you', the impertinent letter ends, 'I humbly beseech you to pardon me.'[1]

Persuasion remained; but not the power. In the majority of cases the arrangements for widows' marriages had been systematised under fixed charges. The licence to marry was normally granted to the widow at the rate of a third of the annual value of her dower; but if she married without a licence the fine was three times as high—that is, one year's income from her dower. In this case, however, her husband was, in addition, liable to a fine for contempt of court. The charges for a licence seem generally to have been adhered to, though one entry does show an interesting variation in that Margaret Berke was charged £10, 'in consideration she is of the age of sixty years'. By the Elizabethan period widows' marriages were of negligible significance compared with wardships; and the profits arising from this source were small.[2]

A selection from amongst numerous examples has been sufficient to show that feudal marriage brought all too often in its train opportunities for the tyrannical misuse of a guardian's authority. For the selfish exploitation of marriage in the interest of a third party there can, of course, be no defence. Early marriages, mercenary marriages, calculating marriages, arranged by guardians without regard of the wishes or interests of the children in their care, all these reduced the most sacred bond to the level of an auction mart. Yet before we take at full force the righteous indig-

---

[1] H.M.C. *Salis.*, xii, 370–1.
[2] B.M. Harl. 39, f. 195a.

nation which feudal marriage aroused amongst contemporaries and historians, it is relevant to ask whether these evils were peculiar to feudal marriage. What do contemporaries tell us about ordinary marriages in which the feudal contract was not involved?

'Some parents greatly abuse their authority,' wrote Thomas Becon, chaplain to Archbishop Cranmer, 'while they sell their children to other for to be married for worldly gain and lucre, even as the grazier selleth his oxen to the butcher to be slain, having no respect to the person, whether he be godly or ungodly, honest or unhonest, wise or foolish.' What then was the principal consideration in the parents' minds?—'If money, if riches, if the muck of the world come, let the child go!' Elsewhere, speaking of the marriages of noble families, Becon says the same thing: 'Who that will give most money shall be soonest sped.' 'Little infants in swaddling clowts', wrote Philip Stubbes in his *Anatomy of Abuses*, 'are often married by their ambitious parents and friends, when they know neither good nor evil; and this is the origin of much wickedness, and directly against the word of God, and examples of the primitive age.'[1]

The theatre, also, had an example to offer.

For look you, Sir [Sir Francis Ilford says to his young friend Scarborrow, in Wilkins's *Miseries of Enforced Marriage*], the father, according to the fashion, being sure you have a good living, and without incumbrance, comes to you thus: takes you by the hand thus: wipes his long beard thus: or turns up his mustacho thus: walks some turn or two thus, to show his comely gravity thus: and having washed his foul mouth thus: at last breaks out thus: 'Master Scarborrow, you are a young gentleman. I knew your father well. He was my worshipful good neighbour, for our demesnes lay near together. There, Sir, you and I must be of more near acquaintance.'

Then he goes forward thus: 'Sir, myself am lord of some thousand a year, a widdower (Master Scarborrow). I have a couple of young gentlewomen to my daughters. A thousand a year will do well divided among them? Ha! wilt not, Master Scarborrow?'—At

1 *The Catechism of Thomas Becon*, ed. Ayre (Parker Soc. 1844), p. 372; C. L. Powell, *op. cit.*, p. 15; Stubbes, *Anatomie of Abuses*, ed. Furnivall (New Shakespeare Soc. 1879), i, 97.

which you, out of your education, must reply thus: 'The portion will deserve them worthy husbands.' On which tender he soon takes fire and swears you are the man his hopes shot at, and one of them shall be yours!

In the same play, Clare warns Scarborrow, who offers her a romantic marriage, 'You stray from the steps of gentility; the fashion among them is to marry first, and love after by leisure.'[1]

If this seems a caricature of the 'arranged' marriage, it was not a wholly distorted picture. Prudent parents, then, as in a later age, might make judicious arrangements for the material welfare, as well as the romantic bliss, of their married children. The cautious estimate by a Tudor father of the estates of a suitor for his daughter's hand was not so very far removed from the more decorous inquiry by a Victorian parent as to his future son-in-law's prospects.

If the literature of the time enables us to form some picture of the contemporary attitude to marriage, there is also other evidence at our disposal. 'Body of our Lord!', cried young Henry Kingston when he heard that a wealthy, middle-aged widow had appeared on the marriage market, 'I will go marry this old widow and pay my debts. Then when I have buried her will I marry a young wench and get children!' Marry her he did; but she held him in thrall for thirty-eight years and it was his, not her, death which parted them. But it was not a fruitless match, as Kingston had expected it would be. Their grandson was the famous antiquary Gervase Holles, and it is to him that we owe this story.[2]

This may be an extreme case; but it was the custom to look at marriage with at least as much realism as romance. It was customary also for children to be more ready to acquiesce in their parents' choice than has since been regarded as normal. Mary Darrell once wrote a charming letter to a Mr. Gorge, a kinsman of Burghley's, declining an offer of marriage because it would be

---

[1] G. Wilkins, *The Miseries of Enforced Marriage* (1607), Act 1.
[2] G. Holles, *Memorials of the Holles Family, 1493–1656*, ed. A. C. Wood (Camden Soc. 3rd Ser. lv), p. 215, cited in L. Stone, 'The Anatomy of the Elizabethan Aristocracy' (*Econ. Hist. Rev.*, xviii, 25).

against her parents' wishes. She may have had help in drafting the letter but there is no mistaking her acceptance of the existing order. Lord Stafford wrote to Burghley asking for his help in arranging a match between Stafford's son and the heiress of a rich citizen. Mrs. Frances Cooke, another relative of Burghley's, demanded £1,000 from her son for her consent to his marriage. Long before, in 1521, Lady D'Arcy had told a correspondent that a certain Stapleton had been offered 1,200 marks in cash, and land worth 100 marks, for his son and heir; and 'yet he trusteth to have more'. An uncle of the first Lord Berkeley married four times. On two occasions he sold his marriage for 1,000 marks; on a third for twenty per cent. above that figure.[1]

Indispensable to the marriage settlement was the dowry, which was a great consumer of a father's substance. Lord Willoughby found that the dowries for his three daughters cost him £4,000 and, in addition, he had three grand-daughters to provide for. Lord Sandys tells us that he had to pay £2,000 because, when a ward, he refused a proffered marriage; but later on he had to give £3,000 as a dowry for his daughter—and it was that which severely battered the family fortunes.[2]

But the bride's dowry involved also the widow's dower; and the realism which accompanied the nuptials of the young bride survived right through marriage to protect the welfare of the aged widow.

Of all criticisms, the most severe levelled against feudal marriage is that it led to the marriage of infants: either because their parents married them in haste to avoid a feudal guardianship, should the father die before his heir came of age; or, secondly, because feudal guardians themselves married off their wards at the earliest and most profitable opportunity. Child marriages were undoubtedly all too common and, unless the bride or groom had strength of mind later on to exercise the right to nullify the marriage, they might well be condemned to lifelong unhappiness. Clearly the betrothal normally took little regard of their private wishes.

[1] B.M. Lans. 7, f. 82r; 68, f. 47r; 74, f. 200r; J. Smyth, *The Berkeley MSS*, ii, 80.
[2] H.M.C. *Salis.*, xiv, 189; 94.

Humphrey Winstanley was a ward of Sir Thomas Gerrard 'and the said Humphrey was married, by the constraint of his said guardian, to Alice Worsley, the said Alice then being about the age of seventeen and the said Humphrey under twelve years'; but Winstanley later declined to ratify the marriage. Alexander Osbaldiston was married three or four days before the death of his father to Margaret Hothersall. At that time the boy was under eleven years of age and the girl six or seven; she was 'partly borne in arms and partly led' to the church. Lady Stanhope bought the wardship of John Hotham, had him educated in Cecil's household and married him to her daughter. The marriage proved an unhappy one and he packed the wife off to her relations.[1]

· But were child marriages, and the evils which might accompany them, exclusively the results of feudal tenures? Apparently not. A girl aged four was married to a boy aged seven 'because her friends thought she should have had a living by him'. A girl of eleven was married to a boy of eleven 'because the said Ralph had about forty shillings a year of land', or, as her father put it, 'because she should have had by him a pretty bargain, if they could have loved one the other'. Unfortunately 'the one could not fancy the other', and 'she ever loved other boys'. As a result, she subsequently brought suit for divorce in the Ecclesiastical Court of Chester and, on being asked why she did not bring her suit earlier, her father said 'that she was poor, and had no money; and now she hath gotten somewhat in service, and now spends it in trial of the law'.[2]

Similar reasons operated in other cases. Thomas Fletcher, aged ten, was married to Anne Whitfield, aged nine; 'because the father of Thomas Fletcher was in debt, he married his son to William Whitfield's daughter for a piece of money, for discharge of his said debt with the marriage goods'. In another case it was because 'Richard Bentam, grandfather unto the said Ellen, was a very wealthy man, and [it] was supposed that he would have been good unto them, and bestowed some good farm upon her.' We have

1 *Child Marriages etc.*, pp. 3, 34; *Original Letters*, ed. Ellis (2nd ser.), ii, 320–8.
2 *Child Marriages etc.*, pp. 4, 12.

also the presumably rare case of a boy of eleven, after being married to someone considerably older than himself, declaring to his uncle on the morrow of the wedding 'that the said Anne had enticed him with two apples to go with her to Colne, and to marry her'. The curate was punished by the Archbishop of York 'for marrying at inconvenient times and unlawful persons'; and the bridegroom sued for divorce.[1]

There is a great deal of evidence which shows that many child marriages had nothing whatever to do with feudal tenures; nor did the abolition of feudal tenures in 1660 lead to the disappearance of child marriages. Contemporaries, indeed, did not all feel that a youthful marriage was in itself an evil thing. The circumspect Judge Swinburne, though admitting that the marriage age of fourteen for a boy and twelve for a girl 'may seem over-tender', pointed out also, not for the last time that, in some cases, to delay marriage might lead to immorality. Hence, 'it is better to marry than to burn'. Simonds D'Ewes, the parliamentary diarist, married at the age of twenty-three a girl who was ten years his junior. But he knew that she was an heiress and had made a shrewd assessment of her estate; his account of the negotiation of the marriage contract between the two families reads like the diplomatic transactions of two of the great powers of Europe. William Chaderton, the Elizabethan bishop and scholar, married his daughter at the age of nine to a boy of eleven. The children subsequently ratified the marriage; but it proved an unhappy one and they later parted.[2]

Yet not all such betrothals were necessarily the breeding grounds of unhappiness; and we must end with an example to the contrary. 'We have a saying that marriages are made in heaven', writes Gervase Holles, and he assures us that this was so with his own marriage to Dorothy Kirketon.

Whilst I was yet but a boy and she an infant, I took a passionate inclination to marry her, which every year grew up more and more into a resolution, the goodness of her disposition (with what other

[1] *Ibid.*, pp. 24, 32, 45.

[2] *The Autobiography and Correspondence of Sir Simonds D'Ewes*, ed. Halliwell (1845), i, 306–20; *Child Marriages*, pp. xxii, xliii. For child marriages after 1660 see, e.g., *Notes and Queries*, 6th ser., viii, 176, 524.

perfections of mind or body to be wished in a wife) adding every hour to that resolution. By the sense of which my father likewise was so overcome that (though at first he expressed much regret at it because he knew her father was not able to give her any portion) he not only most entirely loved her, but often pressed me to consummate the marriage.

This Holles delayed to do on account of her youth and poor health. But in due time he honoured his contract and enjoyed a marriage of enduring happiness. It was ended only, as had been his own mother's, by her death in childbed.[1]

Enough has been said, however, to paint a sombre view of the Tudor attitude to feudal marriage. Yet, black as the picture is, we must still be on our guard against taking the contemporary outcry too seriously, or measuring the first Elizabethan age wholly by the standards of the second. Feudal marriage, it is true, resulted not from two young people falling in love, but from bargaining and contract between the elders. But, as we have seen, this was equally true of non-feudal marriages in the Elizabethan period. Romantic love, in medieval literature, was usually extra-marital and adulterous. The taint remained. Romantic marriages in sixteenth-century England were rarities, as they still are in parts of Europe. The overwhelming majority of the marriages were 'arranged'. The change from the 'arranged' to the romantic marriage is, perhaps, a sign of social progress. But to the Elizabethans, the 'arranged' marriage was typical—and permanent.

Royal marriages were, of course, usually 'arranged' and were a long-standing item in international relations. At a critical stage in his diplomacy, Henry VIII pulled off a daring marriage alliance between his sister Mary and Louis XII of France. Louis was a prematurely aged widower of fifty-two, she was seventeen. Before she would agree to go, she extracted from her brother the promise that, if she married this time for her king and country, next time she would follow her heart. A diplomatic courtship was succeeded by a gay marriage, with a wearying husband forced along by the inexhaustible energy of his English princess—the

'Holles, op. cit., pp. 228–9.

'coach horse', as she was politely known in French society. Within three months Louis was dead; and the merry widow was free to choose again.

This time she chose Charles Brandon, Duke of Suffolk, whether her brother liked the idea or not. He did not. But he forgave her at the end, and he came to the wedding. It was not the Duke's first matrimonial exercise, nor was it his last. Before his marriage to Mary Tudor, he had been twice married—in one case a papal bull was first necessary—and after her death he married again within a few months. His first wife had been old enough to be his mother. His fourth wife was less than a third of his age. She had been his ward, for he had bought her wardship for £2,266. 13s. 4d.[1]

Many of the evils, if evils they were, of feudal marriage were the result of the contemporary attitude to marriage, made worse only by the fact that feudal marriages could be bought and sold on the open market. Feudal guardians it is true, in negotiating a marriage, sometimes thought of it in terms of hard cash and the building up of an estate; but so, very often, did parents who, with the best intentions in the world, negotiated marriage contracts on behalf of their children. Nor was a widow expected to stay long in mourning. The turbulent Bess of Hardwick was married four times. So was Katherine of Berain, Welsh grand-daughter of Henry VII. The ascetic and puritanical Lady Margaret Hoby was twice widowed and thrice wedded before she reached the age of twenty-six. [2]

Even more than the Tudors, the Hapsburgs had for centuries treated marriage as an instrument of policy and used it to build up their gigantic estates. So in their quieter way did the English gentry and aristocracy unite their houses and their holdings with results which may be seen in the characteristic pattern of the eighteenth-century shires. His guardian's choice in marriage might or might not be in the interest of the ward; and in resisting a marriage the ward could only claim disparagement or, if that

---

[1] Cecilie Goff, *A Woman of the Tudor Age* (1930), pp. 17, 22–8.
[2] *The Diary of Lady Margaret Hoby*, ed. D. M. Meads (1930), pp. 8–32; A. L. Rowse, *The Expansion of Elizabethan England* (1955), pp. 68–70.

proved impossible, pay his guardian a crippling fine. Yet the sources at the disposal of historians are necessarily those which show the evils of the situation: the lawsuits, the hard bargaining, the intrigue. But for the majority of wards our records have nothing to say. Some may have suffered in silence; but many others seem to have settled down to a contented and fruitful marriage to their guardian's daughters. The fashion amongst the gentility, as Clare told Scarborrow, was 'to marry first and love after by leisure'.[1]

[1] For a charming essay on women and marriage during this period see W. Notestein, 'The English Woman, 1580–1650' in *Studies in Social History: A Tribute to G. M. Trevelyan*, ed. J. H. Plumb (1955).

9

Coming of Age

THE feudal ward was normally married, or contracted in marriage, by the time that he was twenty-one, when he became old enough to claim his inheritance. But this last stage was no empty formality. Indeed, he might first of all be called upon to 'prove his age', for which the official records all too often were sadly lacking.

The would-be registrar of births, deaths and marriages, whom we have met in an earlier chapter seeking to have the office erected on his own behalf, failed completely; and England had to wait until the nineteenth century for such offices to be instituted. It is true that, as the result of Thomas Cromwell's reforms, the keeping of parish registers had been made obligatory throughout the land; but this law of 1538 was honoured as much in the breach as in the observance. In the absence of such sources, how was a man to 'prove his age'?

In ordinary lawsuits, where a feudal inheritance was not the principal point at issue, the procedure for establishing the age of a person was relatively simple. He was called before the judges who, *aspectu corporis*—by his physical appearance—settled his age. If, however, they felt any doubt, they summoned a jury, composed in part of a man's relatives, from whom fuller information was sought. As a rough and ready procedure this may have worked well enough, especially if the question of his exact age was not of primary importance. But in the case of a feudal ward, his age might raise serious questions: his land, his right of marriage, the sale of his wardship might all turn on the exact month and year of his birth, as established by public inquest. Something more specific than *aspectu corporis* was clearly needed and the crown called therefore for as much detailed evidence as could be supplied. But detailed evidence, as any judge or counsel knows, is not necessarily the same thing as accurate evidence; and, as we shall see, the more elaborate system which was evolved brought disadvantages of its own.

The official procedure was for a writ *de etate probanda*—for the proof of age—to be issued to the escheator of the county where the ward was born; and a jury and witnesses would be summoned to testify as to his age. These witnesses came to be known as 'proofs'. In the Middle Ages, and indeed throughout our period, men tried in retrospect to determine the date of a man's birth in much the same way as we do for incidents for which we do not possess official records. We think of memorable events which happened in the same year and which, as it were, help to fix it in its time order. Medieval Englishmen used precisely these methods, though human nature, or the conditions of medieval life, tended to make them use a catastrophe rather than a pleasure as their marker buoy for a significant date. For example, this is what one witness was saying at the end of the thirteenth century about the birth of a certain Philip Paynell: 'He is certain of the time, for one John de Frie of Pyriton married one Emma of Hockday before the said Philip's birth, and the witness met him leading his wife with a great company and struck one William Champeneys, who was very abusive, heavily on the head with a staff, for which he was sore amerced in the hundred [court] of Worth, and made great pecuniary amends.'

A witness in the next century remembered Robert de la Legh's birth date because the witness's sister died on that day (and her death is recorded in the calendar) and also because 'He then saw the said Robert baptised with great solemnity, the priest sprinkling the holy water excessively in his face and in his eyes from the sacred font, wherefore he was angry for a long time with the aforesaid priest; and therefore he well knows that the said Robert has completed the age of 24 years.' The logic does not seem watertight, but colourful details had to serve where more exact proof was not to be had. Another witness, at about this time, says that he remembers a birth date because 'on that Thursday John le Taverner, of Cirencester, came towards his house by the way near the wood of Wetyndon, and met robbers, who killed the said John there, and robbed him of £10'; while someone else remembers the same date because 'on the Friday following, Elizabeth, his sister, fell into a certain marlpit, within her close near Leyecroft, and broke her neck'.

It was, of course, not always a chapter of accidents. One man remembers a birth date because, when he carried the good news to the child's aunt, he was given a silk purse with half a mark in it. Someone else, who informed a man that he had become the father of a daughter, was promised 'the robe in which [the delighted father] was clothed'.[1]

By methods such as these, medieval witnesses brought a touch of verisimilitude to a bald and unconvincing narrative. Yet students of the period have found that, as the Middle Ages advanced, the kind of evidence witnesses brought would have been received with the greatest scepticism by a modern jury. For example, there survive in Essex some of 'the proofs of age' presided over by Richard Baynard, escheator of that county in the early fifteenth century. What impresses one modern investigator was that in 'proving the age' of three quite separate people, witnesses appearing before the escheator testified that

In each case the daughter of a witness died and was buried on the day of baptism.

In each case a witness was playing football and broke his left leg on the day of baptism.

In each case a witness held a burning torch at the baptism.

In each case a witness fell off a cart, laden with hay, and broke his left arm.

In each case a man called John Wargon or John Wareyn or John Warde hanged himself on the day of the baptism and the witness went to see him hanging.

[1] G. G. Coulton, *Social Life in Britain, from the Conquest* . . . (Cambridge 1918), pp. 50–3.

If there is something suspicious in all this, credulity is strained still further in another pair of examples where the same witness, testifying for two different people, one born nearly a year after the other, states on the two separate occasions that he remembers the date because his father died on exactly the same date. Later on in the fifteenth century birth dates, separated by two years and three months, are remembered because, apparently on each occasion, 'the Tyne overflowed and flooded the house of John Raa, and Robert, son of Robert Swynburn, was wounded in the arm by Nicholas Horton'. Moreover the same witnesses appear to have become younger in 1446 than they were in 1444.[1]

More astonishing still is the proof of age of two men in two separate counties: Kent and Essex. One inquisition was held on 24 March 1350, the other on the following 19 May. The escheators were of course different, so were the juries, and so were the witnesses. Yet in both cases a different witness came forward to say that he remembered the birth because he had a son born at about the Feast of the Purification before the date mentioned. A witness in each of the two counties married a wife called Alice on the same day; one witness in Essex and one in Kent set out for Santiago on the date of birth; each county produced a witness who had had his house burnt down on the date in question; and each produced a man who had sent his son Robert to school that day for the first time. What does all this mean? 'History repeats itself, indeed, but not so literally as this', observes one modern commentator on this phenomenon. From what common source was this manufactured evidence being supplied and what did the escheator of the county (if he was not himself the author), and the skilled administrators in London, think of this kind of romance which was apparently being fabricated on their behalf. Perhaps, like their successors in an inland revenue department of today, they shrugged their shoulders and accepted what they could not hope to change.[2]

Custom stood firm against common sense; and if the proving

---

[1] *E.H.R.*, xxii, 101–3, 526–7.
[2] *Ibid.*, xxix, 324; xxii, 527.

of age procedure was showing itself to be no more reliable than the *inquisition post mortem*, like the *inquisition* it possessed remarkable powers of survival. In theory a countercheck existed. For example, it was necessary to have several 'proofs', every one of whom had to be at least forty-two years of age, to testify that the male heir was twenty-one; while in the case of women, the 'proofs' had to be thirty-two because a female heir came out of wardship at the age of sixteen. The proceedings began with the writ *de etate probanda*, directed either to the sheriff or to the escheator, and the heir had to go to his home county and point out the place of his birth. Then the 'proofs' were required to show 'especially circumstances of his age, as the year, the day, and the hour, the the place and other signs of the years, as thunder, earthquake'—a clear invitation to strengthen memory with imagination. A second stage was, however, necessary. A jury of twelve had assembled and they too must declare that the ward had come of age; but they merely had to express their findings in general terms, 'that is to say, of full age, or within age, without any more'. If there was a difference of opinion between the 'proofs' and the jury, the affirmation of the 'proofs' (if they declared him under age) prevailed. If the 'proofs' differed amongst themselves, for two to affirm that he was of age (if they were supported by a jury) was enough.[1]

This system, crude and limited in every respect, was centuries old when Elizabeth I came to the throne and it lasted through and beyond her reign. Amongst the expenses which the unfortunate John Clavell had to meet at the beginning of her reign, when his marriage to Thomasine Horde was being contested, was his charge for proving his age. Here are the

Interrogatories to be ministered to certain witnesses for the trial of the age of John Clavell, gentleman.

1. *Imprimis*, whether did you know John Clavell, gentleman, deceased, father of the said John and how long it is since he died, yea or no?

[1] B.M. Harl. 1323, ff. 196v–198r; Bodley Carte 124, f. 522r.

2. Item, whether do you know the said John Clavell, the son and next heir of the said John Clavell, the elder, yea or no?

3. Item, what age the said John the son was at the day of the death of the said John the elder, his father, and how long before his death the said John the younger was born, and how you know the same?

4. Item, at what parish the said John Clavell the younger was born and baptised and at what time, and how long the same is agone and who was at his birth?

5. Item, whether do you know any other thing concerning the certain time of the birth and age of the said John the younger, yea or no?

The answers given by 'William Hemerford, clerk, parson of Folke and uncle unto the above named John Clavell, gentleman, on the part of the mother, of the age of 46 years or thereabouts', may be taken as typical of some of the straightforward depositions encountered in dealing with 'proofs'. He stated that he knew John Clavell senior and junior both very well, and gave the date of death of the father and birth of the son. This latter date he knew 'by a church book which he hath of the parish of Folke aforesaid, testifying the day of the birth of the said John Clavell'. (Here, at least, Cromwell's law appears to have been in force.) He remembered the birth and baptism, which took place on the same day; a common enough practice in Tudor England, arising from—and perhaps contributing to—the high rate of infantile mortality. To the fifth interrogatory he replied that he knew 'no other thing concerning the certain time of the birth and age of the said John'. William Clavell, also an uncle, was the other 'proof' and his evidence confirmed what Hennenford had stated.[1]

In the same year, the fourth of Elizabeth's reign, an old lady of seventy-two 'proved' the age of a Charles Framlingham of Shelley, Suffolk, by her recollection that it was 'in the same year that the extreme hot summer was in, and this she knoweth to be true by the occasion that she was then servant with the said Francis at the time of the birth of the said Charles, and did within fortnight after his birth bear the said Charles in her arms from Shelley to Crow-

[1] Wards 3.3 (Clavell depositions).

shall in Debenham to be nursed'. The employment of a wet-
nurse was widespread amongst the middle and upper classes in
Tudor England. The rest of her evidence names those present at
the birth, and the godparents. There were six other 'proofs' in this
case but they furnished little in the way of fresh detail. Most of
them seem to have been household servants who recalled their
duties at Shelley Hall in connection with the birth. One of them
adds that she remembers it 'by the occasion that one Robertson,
servant to the said Francis, bought of the husband of this deponent
a calf and a lamb against the churching of the Lady Tylney,
mother of the said Charles, which was fetched away to be killed
about Whitsuntide after'. Another confirms the date because he
came to the place about two years after the heir was born, which
the witness can recall because 'the said Charles, could very well go
[i.e. walk] alone without any help'. On the other hand one witness
frankly says that 'she was not at the christening nor doth remember who were gossips'—godparents—while another says that 'she
was neither at the birth or christening, and more she knoweth
not'.[1]

All this may, of course, be pure fiction. On the other hand there
is nothing inherently improbable in these depositions. But if the
entry existed, the parish register was clearly regarded by contemporaries as a more trustworthy source. 'Whether did this
deponent', a witness is asked, 'ever see or read in the book or
register, kept in the said church for christening and burials, the
certain note of the day and year that the said Humphrey was
christened.' This kind of information was clearly more welcome
than descriptions of climatic conditions, two decades after the
event took place. The summer may have been hot, as one witness
stated, but how could she be sure that the hot summer fell twenty-
one years ago and not at some other time? For one reason or
another we hear little of the more lurid events: the three-legged
calf, the falls from the haycart, the serious accidents at football.
But if the evidence is less of a strain upon the credulity of the
reader, the material provides a puzzle of its own. Why was it, at a

[1] *Ibid.* (Framlingham depositions).

time when possibly a hundred or more minor heirs were coming of age each year, a mere handful of 'provings of age' have survived for every few years of the reign? Loss of the papers, by one means or another, at some later period is not a likely explanation. Even the vicissitudes of the Court of Wards records between the seventeenth and nineteenth centuries could not explain a holocaust of such dimensions, in view of the survival of comparable and related records. Destruction is not the cause and the explanation must be sought elsewhere.[1]

In certain cases the customary procedure did not require proof of age. For example, an heir who had reached his majority before his father's death needed no confirmation, other than the return to the *inquisition post mortem* which, amongst other things, stated that he was over twenty-one years of age (or fourteen in the case of a girl).[2] At other times, even the heir who was a minor at his father's death might receive special treatment when he came of age. For example, in Henry VIII's reign, Robert Asshefeld of Suffolk was granted by patent 'licence of entry without proof of age' to all his possessions. In 1559 Gregory Fiennes, Lord Dacres of the South, was declared by decree of the Court of Wards to have reached full age, 'contingent on the birthday of Edward VI' —though it is odd that the decree should have antedated Edward VI's birth by one year.[3]

In one other way, proof of age, even in the medieval period, could be rendered unnecessary. Early in our history, the conferring of a knighthood meant exactly what it said. The man became a military follower of a king or some great lord, fit to serve him in battle. But the centuries sometimes enhance, sometimes debase, the currency of a title. A Tudor knighthood, as in our own day, recognised a man's achievements rather than his military prowess. Men were still knighted on the field for feats of valour, and the Earl of Essex in Ireland was more prodigal in these honours than the queen had ever been. But these were exceptions to the general

---

1 *Ibid.* (Jenetts depositions).
2 Cf. p. 137 above.
3 *L.P.*, v, 80; *Cal. S.P.D.*, 1547–80, p. 142. For a medieval example, see Tout, *Chapters*, iii, 27.

rule. By now the country gentlemen were recognising that a knighthood set the seal upon their rising power and fortunes in the shires; though it still carried the sound and splendour of a chivalric past, it was primarily an emblem of their social prestige. But it also had its other uses. For a knighthood terminated wardship. By definition, a ward was one unable to render the military service appropriate to his land. By definition also, a knight was a man called to the military service of his lord. The latter state cancelled the former. 'When the king, who is the sovereign and supreme judge of chivalry, hath dubbed him a knight, he hath by this adjudged him able to do him knight service—and all men are concluded to say the contrary to it.'[1]

That was all very well; but an antiquarian lawyer did not have far to seek for ambiguities and exceptions. Supposing, as was common enough, some of the land were not held of the crown but of another overlord: could a knighthood by the crown extinguish the common law rights of another lord? All this had been fought over as long ago as the thirteenth century when the barons, by means of Magna Carta, struck back at King John who, by knighting their wards, was depriving the barons of their feudal rights. It was then established that, after the knighting of a minor heir, the lord kept the *land* of the heir in wardship and retained the 'value of the marriage'. He lost the custody of the ward but that, at least in theory, was all. If, on the other hand, the heir apparent were knighted while his father was still alive (Sir Edward Coke tells us), then the crown and lord alike lost any future claim to both the ward and his land. But now another question is asked. What if the heir, though under age, were knighted not in England but in Paris, and by the king of France? The questioner did not find the answer. Nor, so far as we can tell, did anybody else.[2]

These were not mere abstract inquiries. Whether knighthood extinguished wardship was one of the burning questions of the day; and, in the sixth year of Elizabeth's reign, Ratcliff's case

---

1 B.M. Harl. 738, f. 139r.
2 *Ibid., loc. cit.*; Coke, *Second Inst.*, c. 3.

was fought out on this very issue in the Court of Wards. 'The case had come in question many times before', a law report tells us, 'but they had all compounded with the king or queen for the time being', in other words, though knighted they paid a sum of money to be exempt from feudal wardship. But Sir John Ratcliff was a sturdy fellow: he ' would not compound, but required law and justice'. And justice he got. 'The Court took great deliberation and the rather because the rule of it would be a precedent to others who were in like case.' For three years the matter was before the Court but, at last, 'they came to a full resolution' and announced their verdict in Ratcliff's favour. His victory served Essex well a generation later when, still a queen's ward, he was knighted and so was released from wardship. The certificate which the Earl of Leicester sent to the Court of Wards stating that he had knighted Essex, as well as the young earl's petition for the delivery of his estates, have strayed from the Court of Wards records—as has so much else. Copies only are to be found and they are in the Bodleian Library in Oxford.[1]

Essex was knighted in the Netherlands. Later on, during the brief term of his greatness, he in turn conferred many knighthoods upon men serving under him in France and Ireland. Did these, as in his own case earlier, cancel a royal wardship or two? We have no evidence of it; but his indiscriminate grant of knighthoods undoubtedly brought him into collision with the political and feudal interests of the crown. Burghley protested against it. Later on, at the trial of Essex, Sir Edward Coke, as Attorney-General, attacked him for it. Greater issues than wardship were to break the power of the restless earl. But the general problem of the effect of knighthood upon wardship had by no means been laid to rest.[2]

It was reopened in a case before the Court of Wards in the Easter term of 1607. Sir Drue Drury the younger, after refusing a marriage proposed to him by his namesake and guardian, was knighted by King James I. In virtue of this, and also his alleged

[1] Plowden, *Reports* (1779), pp. 267–8; Bodley Ashmol. 862, ff. 85r–87r.
[2] D.N.B., *sub*. Devereux.

exemption from feudal marriage because of King Edward I's charter to the town of Yarmouth, where he held lands, the youth considered himself free to marry whom he pleased. He married accordingly. But the guardian denied this right and brought action against him for loss of the marriage. The case came before the Court of Wards with Chief Justices Coke and Popham sitting as judges assistant to the Master.

The first plea, based upon the Yarmouth charter, was dismissed on various grounds, notably that the feudal tenure had, as far as Drury was concerned, arisen from the purchase of dissolved monastic lands: a fourteenth-century charter could not, as it stood, operate against a tenure created in the sixteenth century.

The court then turned to the 'great question', namely 'whether, by the making the defendant knight, he was discharged in law of the value of his marriage?' A lengthy debate followed and the judges carefully weighed the argument that knighthood terminated a minority and therefore the feudal right of marriage. After investigating previous cases, and Magna Carta itself, they declared that they must consider not only antecedents but also the consequences of their decision. They concluded that a knighthood conferred upon an heir in the father's lifetime ruled out a wardship if the father subsequently died and the heir was under age. But the same could not apply where the knighthood was granted after the father's death to the heir when he was still under twenty-one. Otherwise, 'surely great prejudice [they said] would ensue to the king'. He might lose heavily as the result of knighthoods either conferred by himself or 'by his lieutenants in Ireland and elsewhere'. He could lose revenue also in that 'none would buy any wardship of the king, when notwithstanding they have paid the value thereof to the king' a knighthood would cancel the grant of the marriage. So 'a man would give little or nothing for a thing which depends upon such an incertainty'. 'It would also be very prejudicial to the subjects', who had bought the wardship, they continued; and here they put their finger on the real grievance.

So, after appearing to favour first one side and then the other, the judges found that the cases of the Earl of Essex and of Ratcliff could not be regarded as precedents since they were determined 'without argument or any resolution of any of the judges of the law' and there were other precedents to the contrary. So it was laid down again, as at the time of Magna Carta but in a different context, that a king could not nullify the profitable rights of his subjects. Coke is said to have been a better politician than judge. He may have shrewdly detected that, had the case been settled the other way, the king might have tried, at least for a time, to have had two conflicting supplies of revenue from the same source: from the sale of a wardship to a guardian and the sale of a knighthood to the ward, thereby setting him free from his guardian. If this were the king's intention it would, in the long run, have been self-defeating for it would have devalued wardships. But a Stuart king was not normally concerned with long-term prospects and, meanwhile, financial needs were pressing. In blocking the king, in Drury's case, Coke may have been looking beyond feudal doctrine to the larger issue of revenue. His allies in the House of Commons had only the year before made inflammatory speeches about the crown revenues, and in 1610 they were to come into open collision with the king. It is perhaps not without significance that Coke's report ends with a high tribute to his colleague in this case, Chief Justice Popham, whose last decision it was. He was a man, Coke tells us, of 'profound judgement, most excellent understanding in the true reason of the law, and of universal and admirable experience and knowledge of all business which concerned the commonwealth'.[1]

The conferment of a knighthood, or special grants by the crown absolving the heir from the elaborate process of suing livery, were exceptions to the normal procedure: most wards reached maturity by a more traditional route. Yet the problem remains: why did they not 'prove their age'? It is here that administration supplies the answer and we must, therefore, first consider how livery— the release of a ward's lands—was obtained.

The long-established procedure, under which an heir came of

[1] Coke, *Reports* (1738), vi, 73-5.

age and assumed possession of his lands, displayed all the outward signs of medieval chivalry. First, he established that he was twenty-one years old and therefore fit for knight service. Then he went to his overlord and, placing his hands in those of his lord, swore an oath of fealty and did homage to him, that is, he ceremoniously announced that he had become his lord's man. In the words of Sir Thomas Smith, he was bound 'in trust and confidence that he shall be true to the lord of whom he holdeth it [the land], pay such rents, do such service and observe such conditions as was annexed to the first donation'. In ceremonial at least, the feudal contract held firm.[1]

In suing livery the heir sought the release of the lands temporarily resumed by the crown after the death of the last tenant—the 'ancestor' of the heir. Since the land might be scattered throughout several counties, the same process would have to be conducted with a whole series of officials, local and central. Here is a summary account, by a seventeenth-century writer, of the procedure to be followed—or, at least, as he thought it was followed in the happy past:

> Every person that held land by homage was to prove his full age, by a writ of *etate probanda*, and ought to return the same into Chancery.
> The Chancellor was to certify the Lord Privy Seal that he was of full age.
> The Lord Privy Seal was to certify the Great Chamberlain thereof, requiring him to receive his homage.
> The Great Chamberlain ought to receive the homage and to certify the Lord Chancellor that the party had done his homage, whereupon the party had livery of his land.

The whole procedure seems disarmingly simple. But he ends with a brief note of the great officers of state who are to receive fees from the heir, namely the Lord Chancellor, the Master of the Rolls, the Lord Great Chamberlain, the king's Secretaries, and the Master of the Wards. He concludes 'and divers other persons

---

[1] *De Republica Anglorum*, p. 135.

have fees also out of every livery upon the recording thereof'. His 'divers other persons' is a polite understatement about the garrison of bureaucrats who stood general guard over the Court of Wards and charged their fees, as the suppliant penetrated deeply into the fortress.[1]

But, as is so often the case, the writer is describing a state of affairs which is passing away. For there were two methods of suing livery: the one which (in a much simplified form) he is here recounting and which was known as a *general* livery; and an alternative and more popular procedure, known as a *special* livery. The general livery, as the term implies, covered the whole field of the heir's possessions. It therefore involved a thorough survey in each county by the feodary as well as the full procedure of proof of age. If we recall our guide of an earlier chapter, who signposted the route for a suitor who wished for the grant of wardship, we find, from his description of the heir's path, that it is as twisted and stony as that followed by his guardian some years before. Here and there we must ignore his directions and take a short cut; but even so the road is still long, and in places perilous. We must also remember that this applied to all heirs holding in chief, whether by knight service or socage (except for land held by socage in chief in the City of London).[2]

On the day that the heir comes of age, or even a day or two earlier, he must present what is called a 'tender' for livery; otherwise he will get none of the profits from the lands between his coming of age and the day of his tender. Then he must supply a copy of the *inquisition post mortem*, held upon the lands of his father or the appropriate ancestor, to whom the young man is heir. If no copy is at hand there he must repair to the Pettibag Office of Chancery which will supply him with one (at the appropriate fee). He must now go to the Clerk of the Liveries in the Court of Wards and carry with him the necessary documents. He must also provide a copy of the survey of land values, supplied by the feodaries, which must be recorded in the office of the

1 *S.P.D.*, Jas. I, xxiv, no. 59.
2 B.M. Harl. 1323, ff. 205r–207r.

Auditor of the Court of Wards. From there he must pass to the Clerk of the Liveries and then back again to the Auditor, who will settle how much should be paid as 'mean rates'—the profit of the lands between his coming of age and his tender for livery. Now he must make payment for this sum to the Receiver-General, and with a receipt and schedule go to the Surveyor of Liveries, who will settle the dates when the payment for livery shall be made. There follow a further visit to the Clerk of the Liveries, to the auditors and the senior officers of the court, including the Master, and a second visit to the Clerk of the Pettibag in order to have the livery prepared for issue under the Great Seal of Chancery. He must now sign an indenture in which he declares that his statement as to his lands is complete and correct, and that he will declare any further information that may come to light. He accordingly enters into two bonds, one that he will perform the undertaking given in the indenture, the other that he will enroll his livery within six months. Finally, he must take the oaths of supremacy and allegiance to the crown, get his indenture sealed, obtain his livery, have it enrolled first in the Auditor's office and then in the Exchequer, do his homage and claim his lands from the escheators of the counties.

There were a minimum of twenty stages in the general livery and it is not surprising that most heirs were reluctant to join so wearisome a procession. There were two serious objections to it, Sir Edward Coke tells us. In the first place it was 'full of charge to the heir', with its inquisitions, surveys in every county, proof of age, and the rest. Secondly, it was 'full of danger'. Once the heir in his suit of livery had acknowledged the tenures, he could never deny them on a later occasion; and he and his heirs were therefore saddled with them for ever. More serious than that, if it were subsequently found that even a fraction of his inheritance were inaccurately described in his suit, then the whole thing became void, the crown resumed possession of the entire estate and enjoyed the full profits, while the new application for livery went again from one end to the other of the feudal process. The same was true if the inquisition were 'insufficient, or the process whereof the livery was made be insufficient, or the like'. In effect the traditional system was not only slow and expensive but was full also of all sorts of hidden traps which might at any time be sprung on the unfortunate heir. If he were unversed in livery procedure, or did not obtain the best technical advice, he might find himself in the position of Robert Browning's luckless monk, faced with the famous text in Galatians—

> Once you trip on it, entails
> Twenty-nine distinct damnations,
> One sure, if another fails.

It was not surprising then that 'for the ease of the heir, and for avoiding of such danger' the majority of heirs did not sue out a general, but a special, livery (which they could do if the lands were worth £20 a year). Amongst its advantages was that it did not need the detailed surveys; indeed the grant of livery included a 'beneficial pardon', which absolved the heir in advance from the errors which beset him on every side. In this context two further points arise. A special livery was an act of grace on the part of the crown. It was therefore not bound by standardised routine, and in one particular this could be extremely important: livery could be granted without the traditional machinery of proof of age. That was an immense advantage. But on the debit side it had to be reckoned that, if an act of grace was not governed by the normal procedure, it was also not governed by the normal costs. A special livery carried a higher fee to the crown than a general livery. In the case of a minor suing a general livery when he came of age, the charge was the equivalent of half the annual value of all his lands. If he were already of full age when his father died, and had none of the expenses of wardship, then he had to pay the equivalent of the full annual value of the lands of which he took possession, and half the annual value of those of which he had only the reversion. For special livery, Coke reminds us, the charge was higher 'but ever with such moderation as the heir may cheerfully go through therewith'. So the crown escaped from an antiquated and utterly untrustworthy method of proving age, and at the same time raised its charges to the wards.[1]

These were, of course, the official payments to the crown for the actual re-grant, or livery, of the lands. They did not include the administrative charges which had to be met at each stopping place on the journey. The act of 1542, which made the Court of Wards responsible for liveries as well as wardship, tried to establish firm control over these official fees; but inflation and officialdom combined to push them up. A descriptive account alone cannot adequately convey the scene of the heir constantly digging deeply into his pockets as he goes from room to room. Here, then, is a list of *official* charges for a special livery, where the land in the survey was worth £22. 7s. 4d. a year[2]:

	£	s.	d.
Item. For a copy of the office [inquisition p.m.] . .	0	4	4
For a search the officers had for the office . . .	0	3	4
For the survey	0	10	0
For the fees in the clerk of liveries' office . . .	6	0	0
For drawing the schedule	1	5	0
For the oath of supremacy	0	7	0
For the indenture and bond in the clerk of liveries' office	1	16	8
For the clerk there	0	3	0
For enrolling the decree, whereby found in the office at £22 now abated to £12	0	13	4
For the casting up the rates at full age	1	9	2
For engrossment for 4 years	0	8	0
For the account.	0	10	0
For the rates within age	0	3	4
For entering the rates.	0	1	0
For expedition	0	3	4
For the king's fine	11	8	8
An acquittance for the payment of the fine . . .	0	1	4
For the warrant	0	1	6
For a note from the clerk of the liveries to the auditors, testifying no rates to be lost of full age . . .	0	1	0
For passing the Great Seal	15	0	0

1 Coke, *First Inst.* Sect. 103.
2 B.M. Harl. 1323, ff. 208r-209r.

Enrolling it in the auditor's office	1 0 0
For enrolling it in the Exchequer	1 4 0
For a docquet to carry to the barons [of the Exchequer]	0 1 0
To the barons for rating the homage	0 2 0
For the homage paying in	0 9 8
To the clerk there	0 3 4
Taking in the bond out of the Court of Wards . .	0 12 0

Sum is £45. 6s. 6d.

The largest items here are the 'fine', that is the payment for the special livery in the Court of Wards, which came to £11. 8s. 8d. and the further sum of £15 payable into Chancery for the placing of the Great Seal upon the grant of livery. On top of this there were the purely administrative fees, which accounted for a further £18. 17s. 10d. Nor, as far as the heir was concerned, did these complete his commitments. He still had to pay his own solicitor's fees, and his expenses in coming to London and going on the administrative rounds. One notices that he paid 3s. 4d. for 'expedition'; but it is unlikely that that is all he paid unofficially to speed his application on its way.

The fees then were substantial and, before leaving them, we may consider the position from the point of view of the senior administrator concerned, the Surveyor of the Liveries. These were his official fees, late in Elizabeth's reign[1]:

For a special livery with pardon, which the clerk of the liveries receiveth of him	23s. 4d.
To his own clerk	0 0
For a general livery, where the land exceed £5 per annum, which the clerk of the liveries also receiveth, for him	20s.
To his own clerk	[Blank]
For liveries under the value of £5 per annum, being two parts of three which pass his hand, no fee at all	
For every tender and every continuance of a livery .	6s. 8d.
To his clerk	3s. 4d.

[1] Bodley Tanner 287, f. 11v.

For an estallment of a fine of a livery, or mean rates, if the
party desire it, which happen seldom, there having but
two passed this last term .   .   .   .   .   .   20s.
To his clerk   .   .   .   .   3s. 4d.
For every order with his hand   .   .   .   .   .   10s.
To his clerk for writing and entering .   .   .   .   3s. 4d.

The note ends with a disclaimer: *Memorandum*, that the surveyor
confines his fees to liveries only and takes none at all upon any
wardship.

These fees seem modest enough at first sight, but they amount to
£4. 10s. 0d.; and this sum merely covered the fees paid in one
office. The burden upon the heir was heavy and it was constantly
growing weightier under the Tudors and the early Stuarts. Coke,
who in one of his works provided a factual account of these
administrative processes, had elsewhere some very sharp things to
say about livery fees and charges 'so great, and the bonds and
covenants etc. so many, so intricate and dangerous, as it were
worthy to be redressed, for the ease and quiet of the fatherless and
widow'. He knew also what lay at the root of the trouble. Officials
were paid by the length of the documents. 'Special liveries were of
ancient times as short as the charges thereof.' Now their growth to
inordinate length was 'no benefit to the king but to fill the purses
of clerks and officers'. The abuse had reached serious proportions
and he felt that it should be dealt with by parliamentary action.[1]
Whatever it may have cost him, the heir did at least, by special
livery, free himself from the necessity of 'proving his age'. He
was also liberated from another antique ceremonial, the swearing
of homage which, if it had been kept up, could have been nothing
but a time-consuming nuisance to the landed classes of England.
To seek out the Lord Chamberlain in order to perform the act of
homage, and pay the fees appropriate to so important a personage,
could hardly have appealed to an heir already heavily occupied
with the minutiae of governmental routine. As a result, the overwhelming majority of Englishmen never swore homage to

[1] *Fourth Inst.*, c. 35.

Elizabeth I. Homage was respited—put off, in fact put off indefinitely. As usual, exemption from a formality could only be obtained by payment of an indemnity to the crown. Respite of homage, perhaps more strikingly than any other item in the feudal apparatus of Tudor England, reveals in all its nakedness exactly what it is: a system of land taxation, bolstered up with archaic doctrine but owing its survival and revival only to its value as a source of land revenue beyond parliamentary control. What was true of respite of homage was true throughout and beyond the whole feudal sector of the royal income; but nothing was done quite so openly as this. A vassal's oath to his overlord, the king, had become simply a payment into the royal exchequer. 'To avoid costs', one commentator explains, 'the use is to purchase a privy seal directed to the Chancellor for respite of his homage, and of that shall be sent a transcript into the Exchequer, after which precept shall be awarded yearly out of the Exchequer against him for to do his homage.' The economic shape of respite of homage is clear enough. It converted what had been a ritual into a periodic tax payable to the crown.[1]

The closest parallel to this, outside of feudalism, was distraint of knighthood. We are familiar enough with the outcry against the practice of the early Stuarts of distraining upon people—fining them—for not taking up the duties of knighthood; but the Stuarts were not alone in using it. One of the first acts of Elizabeth I· after her accession was to instruct commissioners to summon all those holding land to the annual value of £40 'that they appear at a certain day and place . . . to receive the order of knighthood according to the form of the statute'. But the summons was not meant to be taken seriously. The commissioners were given plenary powers to compound with all those who preferred to pay a fine rather than assume the unspecified duties of a knight. But we notice that the order of knighthood, so ambiguously offered in this context, could do nothing towards lightening the feudal dues. Nor could payment for distraint of knighthood bring escape from

[1] Bodley Carte 124, f. 522v.

the revived knight-service in chief with which this book is concerned. Distraint of knighthood was clearly and deliberately kept separate from the whole question of tenure.[1]

If the crown benefited by respite of homage, who was the loser? The payment for the respite was, as we have seen, organised by the officials of Chancery and the Exchequer. Hence 'The Lord Great Chamberlain is now a suitor that homage may be done as in time past it hath been and no more respited, but in certain cases of necessity; and that he may take such fees for the receiving of homage as by the ancient statutes of this realm hath been allowed.' Clearly the Lord Chamberlain regretted the new fashion. But it was not simply the revenues which were at issue. The total official revenue from these respites cannot have exceeded a few hundred pounds a year (the act of 1542 tried to keep the charge down to one shilling for the poorer tenants); but the net was sufficiently widely spread to irritate and disturb a large section of the community. The desire for its abolition was equally widespread, for reasons which had nothing to do with those given by the Lord Chamberlain. The author of *The Discourse of the Common Weal* sought to make his revolutionary tax on sheep more palatable to the victims by proposing that it be accompanied by the abolition of the homage tax. In the House of Commons of 1563 and again in 1571, 'the griefs [which] proceeded by respites of homage' were incorporated into bills for redress, but they were effectively resisted, perhaps on direction from the queen. The abortive 'Great Contract' of 1610, under which the Commons hoped to end the feudal tenures in return for an annual payment to the king, also proposed the abolition of respite of homage. The negotiations with the king broke down and English landowners went on respiting their homage until the outbreak of the Civil War.[2]

The pattern which has so far emerged from our survey of the

---

1 G. W. Prothero, *Select Statutes . . .* (4th ed.), pp. 133–4.

2 *S.P.D.* Jas. I, xxiv, no. 59; *Discourse*, ed. Lamond (Cambridge 1893), p. xliv; *C.J.*, i, 65, 83–4; J. E. Neale, *Elizabeth I and her Parliaments, 1559–81* (1953), pp. 224–5.

livery process is that there was a considerable body of civil servants who were financially interested in the performance (as well
as the non-performance) of the feudal rites. The individual fees
were not always high but the total charges could be quite substantial. Hence, an estate already burdened with debt, and threatened with a heavy repairs bill, might receive a quite staggering
blow as the livery charges were thrust upon it. If, moreover, the
heir died fairly soon after succeeding to his inheritance, and a new
heir faced with a fresh series of livery and other charges took
possession, the outlook was indeed black. To pay death duties
twice over in the space of a few years was a savage blow for any
estate to bear.

For example, Thomas, Lord Berkeley died in September 1534,
less than two years after succeeding to the title, with the instalments upon his livery not yet fully paid. His widow was now
faced with a demand from the Court of Wards to finish the payments for the livery of her dead husband, opposition to the release
of her jointure, and the threat of a lawsuit. Occasionally the costs
might be brought down a little by special direction of the crown,
as when Queen Mary reduced the livery charge upon the Earl of
Sussex by £230; or a debt might be cancelled altogether, as in the
case of a certain Katherine Poulet who owed about £11. In
another case, the government showed its recognition that the
charges might be burdensome by reducing, not the livery charge,
but a man's contribution to the official loan of 1570. On the other
hand, certain lands of the late Duchess of Suffolk were leased out by
the crown to various people 'for lack of livery'. In this case the
crown had clearly taken possession. The lands of John Rossindall,
Lord Mountfenill were seized by authority of the Court of Wards
because of a livery debt and so held for two and a half years. In
one case the Privy Council itself, when directing that a Mr.
Brideman should be exempted from arrest during the three
following months, explicitly declared that he was not exempted
from answering 'to the process issued out of the Court of Wards
by the suing of his livery'. But one man deliberately omitted to sue
livery for years so as to evade a pending demand upon his lands,

which would become payable once they passed fully into his possession.[1]

Apart then from the income of its officials which, as we have seen, was substantial, the crown itself derived a considerable revenue from liveries. In the first year of Elizabeth's reign they came to £5,761, in the third year to as much as £9,247, fifty per cent. above the income from the sale of wardships. In the thirty-ninth year of her reign they were as low as £2,716; but even that was a little higher than the profits from wardship sales. They normally came to about a third or a quarter of the net revenues from the Court of Wards as a whole. That was the position from the crown's point of view. We may select one instance, from amongst many, of how it appeared to a subject. John Salusbury, of Merionethshire, found himself at the end of Edward VI's reign in debt to the Court of Wards to the tune of £300, part of it perhaps arising from the concealment of his wardship. By the middle of Mary's reign he had paid £200 towards the debt but he was nearly three years late in suing his livery. These were not his only troubles. A good deal of his land was held of him by copyhold, that is to say—in part at least—by old, uneconomic and often fixed rents; part of the rest of his land had already been seized by the crown to meet his father's debt of £128, due in the Exchequer; he himself had frequently been obliged to appear before the President of the Council in Wales, and, to cap it all, he had been completely unaware of what would happen if he failed to sue livery. It was a harrowing tale and, in this case, the Court of Wards showed clemency. It exonerated him from his dues accruing since he turned twenty-one, that is to say, from the sums owed by him in not suing livery, but not, of course, from the livery charge itself. How he met his other debts was not the concern of the Clerk of the Court and we are not told.[2]

But the crown was not always clement nor could it afford to be. Like John Salusbury of Merionethshire it had heavy commitments,

---

[1] *L.P.*, vii, 516; viii, 242; ix, 12; xi, 98; Wards 9.103, ff. 229r, 221r; *Acts of P.C.*, 1570, p. 166; H.M.C. *Salis.*, xiii, 189; xiv, 280. *Acts of P.C.*, 1591-2, 473; H.M.C. *Salis.*, xi, 212.

[2] Wards 9.396 fol.; Wards 9.103, ff. 82v-83r.

for which it could expect neither postponement nor exoneration. For the survival of England might depend upon how far the Treasury could meet the ineluctable demands of war, or the preparation for war. The crown was not seriously concerned with the fictitious recollections of a few rustics by which a ward could prove his age, nor with the feudal homage of some hundreds of Tudor country gentlemen. But failure to sue livery was doubly harmful to the crown: revenue was lost but also—and in the long run this was more important—the feudal tenure was concealed and future revenues might go the way of current ones.

Few people in Elizabethan England either proved their age or rendered homage: they replaced an early medieval formality with a thoroughly modern payment. But with livery itself they could not tamper for it had already taken shape as a significant revenue source. Had the crown been willing to let these sources go (which was most unlikely without substantial alternative revenues), the civil service would still have wanted to stand firm upon its rights, or refurbish some that were obsolescent. The Lord Chamberlain was not alone in lamenting the passing glories of the military tenures. The crown and its servants received between them the feudal payments of the landed classes; and it is fundamental to our story to discover who obtained the lion's share. That will be considered in the appropriate place but clearly much would depend upon whether the queen and her subjects were faithfully or corruptly served. It is therefore to the question of corruption that we must first turn.

IO

Corruption

CONTEMPORARIES regarded the Court of Wards as a corrupt institution, and its Master, Lord Burghley, as a corrupt man. For this reason two chapters have been set aside to consider this assertion and to test, as far as possible, whether the charge was justified. But we cannot do so without first attempting to define what corruption means—as well as what it does not mean.

Corruption does not mean ruthlessness, cruelty, or selfishness. It does not mean the exploitation of marriage for mercenary ends. If it meant these things, then the evidence which has already emerged would overwhelmingly support the opinion held by Englishman and foreigner alike. The historian of the Court is indeed plentifully supplied with evidence which shows that the trade in wardships was an evil thing. But if it was an evil thing it was also a perfectly lawful one, upheld by long-standing custom, statutes of the realm, and an institution established on the authority of Parliament itself. The selling of wards for as high a price as possible was a perfectly legal business and, as such, not inherently corrupt. Corruption is the distortion and delay of justice in return for bribes. It is the misuse of public institutions and the sacrifice of public interests for private gains. It is the abuse of power. It is also well to remember that men may grow corrupt without the giving or taking of bribes.

One of the severest handicaps in considering the moral issues of another age is that the writer finds it almost impossible to set himself free from the basic assumptions of his own generation. Nor indeed is it right that he should wholly divest himself of the conceptions of political conduct which govern the public life of his own experience. To dismiss the practices of another century or another continent with a shrug—*autres temps, autres mœurs*— deprives him of both the opportunity and the capacity to write of the historic past in fundamental terms. The historian is, of course, not a judge: it is not for him to reward, in laudatory or patronising terms, the virtuous conduct of a 'good' king or use the downfall of some crafty and brutal politician as an occasion for demonstrating that evil in the end gets the punishment it deserves. If he does use history in this way, he will come upon a good many examples which will make his thesis difficult to sustain. Nowhere are the historian's difficulties more clearly brought out than in the complex problem of corruption. We hold it as a binding doctrine that no public servant should receive in connection with his work any payment other than his official salary. On the other hand everyone in contact with the Eliza- bethan government knew that no statesman or civil servant could hope to live solely on his official salary: he perforce took gifts. What, then, did the queen have in mind when, in her famous charge to Burghley, she required him not to be 'corrupted by any manner of gift'?

The Elizabethans tried, with diminishing success, to draw a distinction between a bribe and a gift to a public servant. Sir Edward Dyer, whose objectionable and notorious patent for concealment we have already considered, tells us in his famous poem:

> My wealth is health and perfect ease;
> My conscience clear my chief defence:
> I neither seek by bribes to please
> Nor by deceit to breed offence;
> Thus do I live; thus will I die;
> Would all did so well as I!

He was, admittedly, writing under poetic licence and most of his contemporaries would, no doubt, have considered the last line ambiguous. Yet the modern reader cannot fail to ponder the circumstances which enabled the same man to be both a great extortioner and a great poet. Dyer's famous contemporary, Francis Bacon, provides an even better practical illustration of the ambiguity of the position.[1]

In the spring of 1621 Francis Bacon, now Viscount St. Albans, had, after a distinguished career in law and politics, been Lord Chancellor for three years. During his tenure of that office he had taken gifts from various suitors. Yet—so his biographer tells us— Bacon at no stage considered himself liable to charges of bribery: 'if anybody had told him, the day before, that he stood in danger of a charge of taking bribes, he would have received the suggestion with unaffected incredulity'. That he had taken gifts he was ready to admit; but these he considered to be within the framework of existing convention and could surely not be distorted and expanded into a charge against his honour. Otherwise, he wrote, 'if this be to be a Chancellor, I think if the great seal lay upon Hounslow Heath, nobody would take it up'. But as the days passed and his enemies collected the evidence against him—some of it extremely dubious—a pattern of corruption began to take shape. For the time being at least, a gift and a bribe were taken to mean the same thing. But Bacon vigorously denied that they were the same. He divided gifts to judges into three kinds. There were first, those taken on the understanding that justice would be perverted in the interest of the donor: here Bacon stoutly affirmed —'I take myself to be as innocent as any born upon St. Innocent's Day, in my heart.' There were secondly, gifts received when the judge understood that the case was ended but had not taken enough care to see whether the whole business was over. Here he admitted that he might be in some degree at fault. There were thirdly, payments made when the matter was really settled and which could have no possible effect upon the issue. In this case, he argued, corruption could not arise.

Bacon had indeed been greedy, short-sighted and indiscreet;

---

1 The material for Bacon's case in the paragraphs which follow is taken from J. Spedding, *The Letters and the Life of Francis Bacon* (1874), vii, ch. vi and S. R. Gardiner, *History of England, 1603–1642* (1883), iv, ch. xxxiv.

he had taken gifts from litigants, borrowed money from them, allowed his servants to mulct them, either for his benefit or their own: but the judgments he gave—when they are examined in detail—turn out to be those which an honest and independent judge would have given, had he been trying the cases on their merits alone. He pleaded guilty, made a grovelling submission to his peers, was deprived of office, imprisoned and heavily fined; but even in his most abject contrition, though he admitted that to take gifts in the circumstances in which he took them was an offence and technically corruption, he showed item by item that money never corrupted the justice he administered. With the surviving evidence before us we are inclined to take him at his word.

'A corrupt judge', said Coke, fierce opponent that he was of Bacon, 'was the grievance of grievances.'[1] Posterity has upheld this doctrine; and to subvert justice for money has generally been regarded as the most heinous of social crimes. However innocent Bacon himself may have been, he undoubtedly brought the law into disrepute and, as he admitted, fully merited the condemnation of his peers. But the law courts represented only one sector, albeit the most important one, of the public jurisdiction of the crown. At Westminster and in the provinces there were, in Elizabeth's reign, a considerable and growing number of officials handling the unwieldy mass of executive and administrative functions of a modern state. Almost without exception the salary that the crown paid them was hopelessly small as compared with the functions that they performed, and the position and way of life that they maintained. Somehow the gap between official income and private expenditure had to be bridged and, as all England knew, this was achieved in two ways: partly by administrative fees for issuing writs, recording grants, preparing schedules, affixing seals and the whole paraphernalia of elaborate and obsolescent procedures; and partly by rewards from suitors, known variously as gifts, presents, gratuities or bribes, according to the mood of the donor, recipient and outside observer. The

[1] Cited in Gardiner, *op. cit.*, iv, 78.

terms have a strongly subjective quality and do not easily submit
to exact definition.

Macaulay, who had some harsh things to say of Bacon for
taking gifts, had in 1835 been brought face to face with the
fundamental issue in his own age, when presiding over the commission for composing a criminal code for India. He investigated
the whole question of the taking of presents by public officials
and stressed the difficulty of drawing up a hard and fast rule
universally applicable throughout the state. But on one point he
remained as immovable as when he castigated Bacon: 'We propose that a judge who accepts any valuable thing by way of gift
from one whom he knows to be a plaintiff or a defendant in any
cause pending in his Court shall be severely punished. . . . The
rule is clear and definite.' But in the case of other public officials
he urged greater flexibility. A lot depended upon the kind of gift
offered, the circumstances, the relationship between the giver and
receiver. For example, the taking of refreshments—even in the
case of a judge—was in his view permissible. Here he was reaching
back to a medieval tradition (based on a statute of the twentieth
year of Edward III), as well as forward to conventions governing
the British civil service of today. After considering the complexity
and delicacy of the position he concluded: 'It appears to us, therefore, that the taking of presents where a corrupt motive cannot be
proved, ought not in general to be a crime cognizable by the
Courts.' We may perhaps use this measuring rod, 'where a corrupt
motive cannot be proved', to examine the habits of Elizabeth's
officials in the Court of Wards.[1]

If by corruption we mean the abuse of power or public office,
then the Elizabethan official had two spheres in which he might
exploit his opportunities. The first concerned the private citizen
who for one reason or another found himself involved with the
administrative business of Tudor government. The second involved the queen herself, the exploitation and sacrifice of the
wealth and authority of government for personal gain. In the

[1] Macaulay, *Works*, ed. Trevelyan (1866), vii, 472–4.

matter of wardship, needless to say, the prospects were rich and the opportunities many.

We have already seen something, in an earlier chapter, of the elaborate and expensive procedures which a mother seeking the wardship of her son had to follow. Her hand was often in her purse and she was paying over and over again for services which, from her point of view, must have seemed both superfluous and incomprehensible. Yet it would be an error to include these costs and charges amongst the evils of corruption and the abuses of the times. Most of them were the normal administrative charges, which of course vary from age to age. They were a perfectly legal and inherent part of the existing governmental system. They were no more objectionable than, for example, the legal and stamp charges which become payable by the purchaser of property today. So long as feudal wardship survived, departmental officials were merely doing what their colleagues were doing throughout the whole range of the government service. But they also held powers in reserve which, by a stretch of the legal imagination, could be employed with devastating effect upon the ignorant and the unprotected. It was the abuse of these powers which constituted corruption.

In its extreme form this kind of corruption was sheer blackmail. Of this the government was fully aware. A patent for searching out concealments was by its very character a twin-headed weapon. It could be turned against the tax evader in defence of the government or it could, for an illegal charge, be turned against the government on behalf of the briber. What was true of the patentee was every bit as true of the feodaries and other wardship officials, in whom the powers to uncover concealments were normally vested. The whole system worked by fits and starts, erratically and capriciously. The evils of informers were notorious: they were the price paid by government and people alike for the large gaps in the executive civil service, made more serious by the inherent difficulties of establishing a tenure by knight-service in chief.

The government used the system of informers; but it did not

like it. At the end of the session of the 1566 Parliament, Burghley drew up a long schedule of evils unreformed and of dangers which threatened. Amongst the unredressed abuses he recorded: 'The oppression of the informers not amended; the commission of inquisitions to unmeet persons.' The judiciary did not like it either. For example, a Mr. Body (whose surname alone we know) was tried in 1596 in the Star Chamber for perjury, subornation and misdemeanour as an informer. He 'was condemned by all, and his misdemeanour as informer and abuser of the laws was judged a good and apt matter to be sentenced in this Court'.[1]

Early in the next reign, an informer was 'greatly blamed by the Court that being so worthy a gentleman, so honourably descended, and otherwise so well deserving in himself, that he would stoop to so base an office as to be an informer, who albeit they be necessary in every well-governed state, yet for the most part they are of the meaner and worst kind of people'. This was the crux of the matter: the belief that informers were essential to every well-governed state. But if the judges had said either an over-governed or inefficiently-governed state, they might have come nearer the mark.[2]

The courts were in a dilemma. The evidence of corrupt and bullying practices by informers piled up before them and cried out for redress. But to take severe measures where informers themselves broke the law might deprive the courts of their apparently essential services. The judges perforce used them and abused them at one and the same time. In essence they saw no escape from an inherently evil system and recognised that the time had not yet come to bring it to an end. The common informer did not finally disappear from our law courts until the present century.

Penal statutes frequently laid down the official rewards to be paid to informers for their work, and the courts could not avoid using the evidence they supplied. How widely they were used it

---

[1] C. Read, *Mr Secretary Cecil and Queen Elizabeth* (1955), p. 370; *Les Reportes del Cases in Camera Stellata*, ed. Baildon, pp. 63, 234–5.

[2] *Ibid.*, pp. 242, 331–2.

is not possible to say, but in the case of the Court of Wards they were not merely useful but indispensable. None the less, informing yielded little when operated by the professional informer, not employed by the court itself.

Much more came by means of the 'argus-eyed' feodary, who lived and worked in the shire for which he was responsible. This was not corruption; the feodary was merely doing what he was authorised and instructed to do. But the temptation to conceal a tenure and reap a larger profit from the tenant than from the crown must always have been great. In the case of a number of the feodaries the temptation proved irresistible. Here was corruption in the full sense of the word: threats, blackmail, exactions. They shared these qualities with their colleagues. In 1566, 'upon a complaint made by Mr. Grafton against Phylpott, a pursuivant in the Court of Wards, touching two promoters for extortion, the pursuivant is sent for'. What happened to him we do not know. We know, however, that for another half century there was a growing outcry against the pressure, legal and illegal, to which tenants in chief were submitted. For example, it was a common practice for an escheator or a feodary to set in motion the machinery for holding an *inquisition post mortem*, even for very poor tenants, although there was no direct evidence that they held by knight-service of the crown. The implication was clear enough. Some landholder of very modest means died. The wretched widow in due course was approached by the local official and told that an inquisition was pending. If she was wise she took the hint, paid privately what she was asked and that might be the first and last that she would hear about inquisitions. Even where it was unlikely that any land was held in chief of the crown, the threat of a feudal inquest might be enough to bring her to terms.[1]

The shadow of inquiries, fees, expenses, delay could be cast over and beyond the purely feudal sector of society. At last in 1612 it was announced that 'His Majesty hath taken into his princely care the unnecessary vexations of his people by feodaries, and other inferior ministers of like nature, by colour of his tenures.' It

[1] *C.J.*, i, 74; Spedding, *op. cit.*, iv. 286–8.

was recognised that these inquisitors '(upon no substantial ground of record) vex the country with inquisitions and other extortions'. Henceforth one day at the end of each law term was to be set aside to examine abuses by these officials, and the Master was to 'take special care to receive private information from gentlemen of quality and conscience in every shire touching the same'. An overdue reform was promised; but it was a sorry business—redress was to be achieved by informers delating against informers. It looks as though the government had begun to run out of ideas.[1]

Manifest bribery and blackmail could on occasion be brought to light, or some general remedy introduced where the abuse had grown to intolerable proportions. But some evils were at the same time too subtle and too much bound up with the existing fabric of administration to be obliterated either by statute or by pious declarations of the Master of the Court of Wards.

Of these abuses the most outstanding arose in connection with the fees charged by officials. The act of 1540 which established the Court of Wards sought to impose a standstill order upon fees—they were to be no more than those payable into the old Office of Wards, now superseded. In the act of 1542, under which the Court of Wards widened its responsibility to take in liveries, the same emphasis was laid upon restricting fees—'such fees as hath been accustomed'. For those whose land did not exceed £5 a year, the cost of the seal attached to the inquisition was to be sixpence 'and for the writing sixpence, and not above'. These seem modest enough but they were by no means the end of the business. The fees of the Lord Privy Seal, the Lord Great Chamberlain, the king's 'Chief and Principal Secretaries', the Master of the Rolls, the king's Clerks of the Signet and the Privy Seal, the Clerk of the Pettibag were safeguarded—along with those of 'all and every other offices and officers and clerks in the Chancery or elsewhere in any other Courts where such liveries shall pass'. Beyond these lay the charges in the shires. For example, lands not exceeding £5 a year involved an escheator's fee of 6s. 8d., a writing charge of 3s., and a jury fee of 3s. 4d. But the escheator was not to raise his

1 *Ibid.*

charge. If he did, he faced a fine of £5 for every offence. It was unfortunate that these well-meaning clauses came precisely at that period when England was entering upon a bout of inflation, hitherto unparalleled in her history. It would have been quite unrealistic to expect civil servants, or any other section of the community, to stand meekly by while their standard of living was washed away by the advancing inflationary tide. The so-called 'covetousness' of Tudor officials sometimes meant little more than a prudent adjustment of their charges to the general price spiral.

For taking such remedial steps as these some defence may be offered. Less defensible, and it raised the greatest outcry, was (what seemed) the multiplication of unnecessary offices and the imposition of unnecessary charges. What has been described in modern times as Parkinson's Law, the growth of administration by what it feeds upon, was familiar enough to Tudor England. The time-honoured processes of the Exchequer tried the patience of king and subject alike: and a practical businessman like Henry VII soon grew weary of its habits and tried to build up new financial institutions, less hamstrung by tradition and less enmeshed with a greedy army of bureaucrats. The reason why there were so many 'reforms' of the Exchequer was because the Exchequer could never be reformed. It always outlasted its reformers. Here and there its processes were modified, though to only a limited extent. The introduction of an overdue reform was normally accompanied by safeguards for the vested interests of established officials. They went on cutting Exchequer tallies to the year 1826, centuries after they had ceased to be relevant to revenue practices; soon after, the decision to burn the tallies led to a disastrous fire, and the House of Commons went up in flames with them. Antique processes might have attractions for their own sake but each one of them meant the employment of an official and the payment of a fee.

What was true of the Exchequer was true of Chancery. It soon became true of the Court of Wards. 'The abuse of the Court of Wards [was] great', cried an early seventeenth century M.P. He had 'known the Clerk of the Wards sit there in a rug gown:

now twenty clerks. And where clerks increase the grievance of the subject groweth'. In 1612 Bacon himself was calling for a 'strait examination concerning the raising and multiplication of fees in that court, which is much scandalized with opinion thereof'.[1]

The evil continued. But justice did on occasion overtake a greedy feodary; and when one of them met his deserts in the Star Chamber, the other feodaries lamented, in a petition to Charles I, that they found it difficult to collect their legitimate fees, especially from 'those whom they have, for your Majesty's profit, in anything opposed'. The king accordingly ordered a departmental inquiry by the Master and his senior colleagues into the official fees of the feodaries. The issue was: should the feodary receive, as hitherto, a fee of 40s. from the tenants for every inquisition, whether the return showed a feudal tenure or not? The Master in his report made the rather odd recommendation that the fee should be paid by the tenant, even though no feudal tenure whatsoever had been found: in other words the tenant should have to pay for an official error. The reason for this, he frankly remarked, was that 'Your Majesty's revenue be not burdened therewith which, if it should, would grow to be a very great diminution of Your Majesty's profit'. Some modest redress, however, was promised to the long-suffering, fee-paying subject: 'We are of opinion that no allowance should be given to him [the feodary] or taken by him, of the subject, more than two shillings for his dinner'; while the jurymen were to be satisfied with 1s. 6d. per head for theirs. In an appendix to the report, the Attorney-General, William Noy, defended these recommendations, and in the process shed light on existing practices. Some feodaries, he said, had asked to be paid for victual and horsemeat. This, Noy said, was wrong. The cost of the feodary's dinner only should be allowed—'otherwise they will grow burdensome with their many attendants'—an interesting footnote to the sharp comment of the Member of Parliament who spoke a generation before of the proliferation of officials. On the other hand, he agreed that the tenant should pay the inquisition fee, whether he

[1] C.J., i, 484; Spedding, op. cit., iv, 288.

proved to be a feudal tenant or not. Otherwise, 'it may make the feodary, who after long being in his office groweth to be powerful with common jurors, to press too much upon the people'. There followed the specious argument that the tenant would gladly pay a fee if the result proved that he did not have to pay the feudal dues.[1]

Each age produces certain practices which lie uneasily between the just and the unjust, the legal and the illegal. The taking of official fees was not corrupt. Nor was the increase of these fees. Nor was the expansion of office staff, all of them taking fees. But when one adds all these together and then includes the unofficial fees of the middlemen holding no established position in the Court of Wards, and in a good many cases doing no useful service whatsoever, then the whole business adds up to extortion and corruption on a national scale. In essence, a considerable body of the landed classes of England were each year held to ransom. They must pay substantial fees for services which they did not want, or pay even larger sums privately to escape them. If a justifiable and logical feudal practice of the eleventh century can be exploited five centuries later for an entirely perverted use, then a logical system has become a corrupt one. This process can, of course, be explained historically and, indeed, defended in terms of government and politics, as will be shown elsewhere. But in the eyes of contemporaries these charges were corrupt charges—the Court of Wards was 'much scandalized'. Good government was running to seed.

There was another way in which mothers, guardians, wards, and others could be mulcted of considerable sums—and this too was a scandal throughout the whole Tudor legal organisation. The sheer cost of litigation itself could be a threat to an innocent man's purse or an insuperable barrier to his hopes of justice. For a lawsuit, or even the threat of one, might involve not only lawyers' fees, journeys to court, time lost in various ways, but also the mounting cost of the legal documents, pleadings, rejoinders, interrogations, rebuttals which grew to intolerable length as the

1 B.M. Add. MS. 26,729, ff, 244r–245r.

century wore on. The defendant had to pay for the overwhelming mass of verbiage which passed back and forth between the lawyers, their clients and the court. A rich man could be made bankrupt by an indiscriminate indulgence in litigation; a poor man might be harried beyond endurance by the alarming costs of a single lawsuit. Here again, the threat of legal action might serve the plaintiff's purpose even where no further step was intended. Defendants might be arrested but when they 'are brought forth to answer to such actions and suits as should be objected against them, then many times there is no declaration or matter laid against the parties so arrested or attached . . . and so the party arrested is very maliciously put to great charges and expenses, without any just or reasonable cause'. Partial redress was sought, in 1566, by an 'Act whereby the defendant may recover his costs, being wrongfully vexed', and in some cases the instigator could be sent to prison. But this reform could only deal with manifest examples of such abuses. Where a crudely malicious motive could not be clearly established, the defendant might seek in vain for escape from an enveloping lawsuit. In 1601 there were two more acts, this time 'to avoid perjury . . . and unnecessary expenses in suits of law', and to avoid 'trifling and frivolous suits in law in Her Majesty's Courts in Westminster'. But again it could only be a limited reform. The judges themselves, meanwhile, took alarm as documents of outrageous length were opened before them.[1]

Of all the departments of state, the Court of Wards can have had no equal in the elaborate ritual of its legal processes; and the fraction of its records which has survived gives some hint of the agonies through which litigants must have passed. For they were concerned not only with the problems of guardianship as such, but with the countless and subtle variations upon land tenure, overgrown and choked with a bountiful foliage of obsolete custom. 'So much more safe is it', said Burghley's secretary, John Clapham, as he surveyed the legal situation as a whole, 'for a man to sit down with a certain loss of a part of his estate, being questionable by law, than with disquiet mind, waste of time,

1 8 Eliz., c.2; 43 Eliz., cc. 5 and 6.

expense of money, long and unfruitful attendance, to make ship-wreck of the whole, as many men, abused by mis-informations, or transported with wilful malice, have oftimes done.' Few were in a better position to judge than Clapham, who must have seen among Burghley's papers the many letters entreating a speedy decision in the suppliants' causes.[1]

But a ward might well prolong his wardship while some unyielding lawsuit dragged on to its appointed term. 'The gentle-man in whose behalf I write', wrote Lord Sheffield to Sir Robert Cecil in 1601, 'having sound grounds whereupon to sue the other for certain lands, he [the defendant] out of a cunning humour holds himself as a ward in the Court for want of paying his livery'—an old trick, this. A ward—of whatever age—who had not yet sued livery was not out of wardship and, therefore, not yet subject to the ordinary legal processes. Whoever brought suit against him must act through the wealth-consuming, time-consuming machinery of the Court of Wards. A ruse of this sort imposed, therefore, what seemed interminable delays upon the plaintiff 'so that he cannot have further trial of the laws of this realm for the recovery of his own'. What gave a quaint flavour to the whole business was the fact that 'the ward is so young that he is grey headed with age, and yet under this pretext debars him that sues him of all lawful proceedings'. Meanwhile the case had dragged on for two years without a hearing. So, continued Sheffield, 'I earnestly entreat you that, for justice' sake, knowing that I cannot move you with anything more forcible, your nature and virtue considered, you will be pleased to bestow the hearing of the cause yourself' at the earliest opportunity. This dubious tribute to Cecil's honour could not be extended to his colleague, the Attorney of the Wards who, 'I know is very partial—a thing God knows, too ordinary in this time.'[2]

Sir Francis Hastings, another correspondent of Cecil's, dispensed with high sounding circumlocution and came to the point at once: 'I am also to ask you to favour my wife's son, the queen's ward,

[1] J. Clapham, *Elizabeth of England*, ed. Read (1951), p. 66.
[2] H.M.C. *Salis.*, xi, 241–2; cf. *ibid.*, p. 212.

in a suit triable before you.' This was the more usual style of approach and Cecil can have set little store by the specious moralising of a favour-hunting suitor. How seriously he took such words we can see from his own answer to Lord Sheffield a year later in which he feels obliged most carefully to defend his uprightness and impartiality in a suit which has just concluded—unsatisfactorily from Sheffield's point of view. Cecil has been apparently accused of distorting justice for family reasons, so he reminds Sheffield that the case was openly heard in the Court of Wards, then referred to the two Chief Justices of England—'persons without exception, if ever any judges of this land were so'—and argued out before them at Serjeaunt's Inn. From them it came back into open court, again to be argued before him and the judges assistant to him. Now, Cecil says, he had no choice but to take his decision. All this, at first sight, seems fair enough; but could justice be impartial while the Master was constantly being bombarded by *ex parte* statements from relatives, friends, officials, courtiers, and anyone with an axe to grind? These letters incidentally are not, and never were, amongst the official records of the Court of Wards, but amongst the private papers at Hatfield House. 'I would ask you to write two lines', wrote a correspondent to the Countess of Warwick, 'or speak to Mr. Secretary [Cecil] on a matter depending in the Court of Wards between my nephew and Mr. Wildgoose and others.' Even a final decision by the Court of Wards was not irrevocable. 'I trust you will find such order taken in the Court of Wards next term as that you will be discharged from the fine, which was set upon you for my occasions', wrote the Earl of Shrewsbury to his uncle, John Manners, High Sheriff of Derbyshire in 1599. If this did not turn out to be the case, 'let him who was your under-sheriff speak to my man Hamon, who, I hope, will give you satisfaction.' Perhaps the best epilogue to these procedures was spoken by Thomas Knyvett at the end of James I's reign. He and his brother had tried in vain to settle out of court a dispute between them over wardship. Now he fears that he has no alternative but to act on his counsel's opinion that the case must go before the Court of Wards. He ends with a despairing prayer: 'God of Heaven keep us from a suit in law!'[1]

Lawyers, officials, litigants could between them drain away the time, patience and money of anyone who took the first bewildered step, either voluntarily or otherwise, into the Court of Wards. But if the drain upon the queen's subjects was substantial, the greatest losses were imposed upon the queen herself. For her there was no effective or lasting escape from the tricks and turns by which her officials diverted the flow of revenue into their private purses. The first essential for successful government, in any age, is that it should be kept fully informed. But in this more than anything else the achievements of Tudor departments of state fell desperately short of their ambitions. They were always trying to leap across the gaps in their knowledge. They were always pressing their officials for information. They were always striving to erect out of a ramshackle collection of incomplete statistics, filled out with half-truths and guesswork, some material upon which a modern administration could base its decisions. It is the fashion to pour scorn upon the questionnaires, duplicate forms and statistical hunger of modern officialdom; but anyone who has sat for a week in a government department cannot fail to recognise the creative thought, patience and judgement which go into their planning, sifting and assimilation. Without all this rich detail, modern government would shortly flounder into darkness and despair, and with it would go all hopes of recognising—let alone solving—the clamorous issues of the day. The Elizabethan governments were ambitious: their passion for 'control' was every whit as bold as any wartime government of modern England. They reached deeply into the private lives of the queen's subjects: they told them what to wear, what to eat, where to live, whom to marry. The so-called liberty of Elizabethan Englishmen is a myth. But the reach of Elizabethan governments exceeded their grasp. They achieved much, outstandingly in defence of the realm and in the maintenance of

---

[1] *Ibid.*, x, 26–7; xii, 474–5, 484; H.M.C. *Rutland*, i, 351; *The Knyvett Letters, 1620–44*, ed. B. Schofield (Norfolk Rec. Soc. 1949), p. 80.

internal peace. But so much else is a record of failure; and one of the principal causes of failure is that the government could not get at the facts. Its own documentary sources invariably let it down.

The records of the Exchequer, says one contemporary report, were 'so ill looked to that they have been utterly perished with pigeon dung; and also I have seen within this three years hangings made of those records and dyed into other colours'.—the early equivalent of converting maps into lampshades. On one occasion the usher took away half a cart-load of the official records and sold them in St. Paul's Churchyard: and still he kept his job. What was true of the Exchequer was true throughout the whole field of royal administration (not least in the Court of Wards): while the subsequent misadventures of the wardship records, including an unhealthy sojourn in a fishmonger's shop, has to be read in its full incredible detail, in the official reports of the House of Lords, to explain the state in which the modern researcher finds them. The historian labours under severe handicaps in trying to penetrate through to the fundamental economic facts. He shares these handicaps with the Tudor governments themselves.[1]

The originating statute of the Court of Wards in 1540 had as one of its objects the provision of more trustworthy information than the old Office of Wards had usually been able to obtain. In the same year the heads of the various financial departments, including the Court of Wards, were asked by the Privy Council to supply 'an abbreviate of all the offices and fees with the names of them that have them at this present'. Five years later, in December 1545, the crown was seeking to make an even more ambitious survey. It appointed a special commission to analyse all the royal revenues and to take drastic steps to recover the king's debts. Six months later there was a new commission of inquiry and, just over a year later, one more. So it went on, from the last year of Henry VIII's reign, through Edward VI's and Mary's and on into the reign of Elizabeth. The great number of these commissions is,

[1] B.M. Lans. 106, f. 10r. For references to reports on the official records see F. S Thomas, *Notes of Materials for the History of Public Departments* (1846).

of course, not a sign of strength but of weakness, of the vain efforts of the government to get through to the facts of the case. Even in the days of their origin the Court of Wards records, like the comparable volumes in other departments, must have seemed a choked-up labyrinth of manuscripts with serious gaps in one series, confusing duplication in another.[1]

But the ravages of time, and official incompetence in drawing up and preserving the records, were not the principal causes of the trouble in the Court of Wards. The root of these lay deeper in the very character of Tudor financial methods. That these methods were elaborate there can be no doubt: what is equally certain is that, even to contemporaries, they could be confusing, vexatious and misleading. As far as the crown itself was concerned they could be the cause of very grave losses of revenue.

The middle years of the sixteenth century display a lamentable picture of the crown trying in vain to come to grips with the financial situation. Inflation, war, a mounting burden of debt cried aloud for the provision of trustworthy and up-to-date information. There are in these years some intelligent and careful reports of royal commissions, inspired perhaps by the reforming Lord Treasurer, Paulet; but, if they stimulated the pious resolves of the government, they did not leave much mark upon the administrators themselves. The whole wardship system showed glaring faults from its origin. For example, the act which erected the Court of Wards in 1540 laid down that the accounts should be audited annually by the Master, Attorney and one or both of the Auditors of the Court. In other words, the audit was an internal one only. Here was a defect which existed from the start. As a check upon the dangers which might arise from it, a further provision was made that the Receiver-General should pay over to the crown, within a month of the annual audit, all the money left in his hands. Had this been done by the Receiver-Generals, they might still have defrauded the crown because of the defective

[1] *Acts of P.C.*, 1540–2, p. 59; *L.P.*, xx, pt. 2, g. 1068 (28); *ibid.*, xxi, pt. 1, g. 1166 (71); *C.P.R.*, Ed. VI, i, 93.

audit system. But at least they would have handed over the cash in hand. Even that was not done.

A statute of 1543 had, in its preamble, put its finger on this long-standing and widespread abuse. Various collectors, it said, were not paying the king the sums collected but had 'retained, occupied and converted the same to their own singular profit and commodity, as in loaning or laying out the same for gains, in purchasing lands of great value and in buying of wools and other merchandise, whereby the King's Majesty hath oft times lost great part of his debts and duties [dues], and sometime forborne the same by a long season'. A decade later another statute observed of the royal treasurers that they 'have not so justly, speedily, neither duly made yearly payments of such sum and sums of money as hath been by them and every of them received'. It was a very modest euphem-ism for the malpractices of Edward VI's ministers.[1]

It so happens that we have, for the decade preceding the accession of Queen Elizabeth, a very important collection of papers which shed a somewhat lurid light upon the financial administration of the Court of Wards. They concern the career of John Beaumont, Receiver-General of the Court of Wards from January 1545 to December 1550. He belonged to the expanding class of Tudor civil servant, the lawyer-financier, who might hope for some of the senior appointments, including a judgeship. He might even, on occasion, like Henry VII's minister, Dudley, or Eliza-beth's minister, Burghley, aspire to the highest political office and, in due course, found a noble family. Beaumont did not belong to this last group but he climbed into distinguished appointments until his over-confidence and greed combined to produce his downfall.

John Beaumont was a Leicestershire country gentleman who, after his legal training at the Inner Temple, turned to administra-tion and the law for his career. By the end of Henry VIII's reign he was already *custos rotulorum*—presiding magistrate—of the quarter sessions for Leicestershire and Receiver-General of the Court of Wards. In Leicestershire, in 1546, he had an unfortunate

1 34 and 35 Hen. VIII, c. 2; 7 Ed. VI, c. 1.

brush with Henry Grey, Marquis of Dorset, over a matter of taxation. Dorset appears to have made threats against Beaumont, who was offered protection by a Sir William Turvil, a local magnate. This might well have degenerated into a bitter faction struggle in the county had not the Privy Council itself felt it necessary to intervene. Both sides were called up to London, Beaumont to justify his allegations, Dorset to refute them. Dorset was ordered not to trouble Beaumont. But, for one reason or another, Beaumont failed to convince the councillors of the misconduct of so eminent a man as Dorset, and for his pains was told not to complain against a nobleman without cause. He departed with 'a lesson to know in better sort his superiors'. This was indeed a setback; but it does not seem to have affected his career. He stayed on as Receiver-General until 27 December 1550; but a fortnight before that he had been promoted to a judgeship as Master of the Rolls. Pluralism was common enough in Tudor England but such a combination was clearly impracticable and Beaumont, naturally enough, relinquished the junior for the senior post. He did not hold the new office for long. Suddenly in June 1552 he resigned and, in the patent of appointment of his successor, we read that Beaumont had in fact been forced to forfeit his office because of his offences against the crown. Soon after we learn that the sheriff of Leicestershire was ordered to levy upon the lands and chattels of Beaumont the sum of £12,000 due to the king. By now Beaumont was already a prisoner in the Fleet.[1]

Of what was Beaumont guilty? There were two quite separate charges against him. The first concerned his conduct of affairs as Master of the Rolls and judge, in which capacity, apparently, he had descended to forgery; had induced, or compelled, members of a jury to perjure themselves; and had concealed a felony by one of his servants. The forgery has an especial interest in that he copied the signature of the Duke of Suffolk, father-in-law of Lord Dorset whom we have already met in the Leicestershire

[1] *Acts of P.C.*, 1542–7, pp. 473, 464–5; *C.P.R.*, Ed. VI, ii, 152; iii, 329; iv, 305; v. 95.

quarrel. This bogus evidence had, in fact, been used in court against Dorset. That he was guilty there seems to be no reason to doubt; and his performance is of course a commentary on the type of man who was coming to power in mid-Tudor England. With that part of his career, however, we are not in this context concerned; but only with his six years' service as Receiver-General of the Court of Wards. And here even the case-hardened judges of the Star Chamber professed themselves shocked with 'so many foul matters, as we think have seldom appeared in any one man'; while Edward VI recorded in his journal that 'he had bought land with my money, had lent it, and kept it from me to the [sum of] £9,000 and above, more than this twelvemonth, and £11,000 in obligations'. This elliptic summary hardly does justice to several years of large-scale peculation so, for fuller details, we must turn to the two confessions of Beaumont, and to the official records of the Court of Wards.[1]

As we read on through his confession and the accompanying mass of evidence, the scheme he operated, as it finally emerges, becomes incredibly simple. But first we must consider the word 'arrearages' or 'arrears' as it appears over and over again in the records. This apparently straightforward expression is used with widely different meanings in the same period, and indeed in the same record. It may mean quite simply arrears owing to the Court of Wards which have not yet been paid. It may on the other hand be lists of arrears which have been collected during the current year—a very different thing. But it may also mean the money which the Receiver-General is holding and has not yet paid into the possession of the crown. These are the arrears with which 'the Receiver-General chargeth himself'—his cash in hand. Here was an intractable problem: the crown repeatedly tried to force its treasurers to hand over, every six months or year, the full revenue they collected. For a short time the laws and directions would work; but soon the old custom would reassert itself and

<hr>

[1] *Illustrations of British History*, ed. Lodge (1838), i, 175; *Ecclesiastical Memorials*, ed. Strype (1822), ii, pt. 2, 498–9; Wards 9.365, ff. 166r–236r; *Literary Remains of Edward VI* (Roxburghe Club, 1857), ii, 422.

a mounting list of arrearages would show that once again the treasurer was piling up the official income under his personal control. From time to time, of course, lump sums were paid over to the crown; but in the interval treasurers felt free to employ the money as they pleased. They regarded it as a perquisite of office. That is what Edward VI was referring to in his surprised comment: 'he had bought land with my money, had lent it, and kept it from me to the [sum of] £9,000'. Beaumont was speculating with the king's money, on the assumption that he would return the capital—but not the interest—when called upon to do so. In this Beaumont was no worse than other royal treasurers and, in fairness to him, we must add that these 'arrearages' are fully set out in his official records, without any attempt at concealment. But there were other sums involved; and that makes a rather different story.

It is, however, also a simple story. When guardians or lessees of lands agreed to pay sums of money to the Court of Wards, they entered into what were called 'obligations', bonds to pay to the Receiver-General what they owed, usually by instalments. When the payments came in, the Receiver-General recorded them in his account book and returned the obligations, duly cancelled, to the debtor or his guarantors. It was this system which Beaumont modified in his own interests. When the debtors brought in their money he handed them their cancelled obligations, as the procedure required. What he deliberately omitted to do was to enter these payments upon his official records: they therefore remained as unpaid debts, and he was accordingly not liable for them to the crown. His position is comparable to that of a business man who keeps two records of his income: one for his own benefit and one for the benefit—if that is the appropriate word—of the inland revenue authorities.

Beaumont's official accounts were bogus; and in the space of five or six years he robbed the crown to the tune of £11,823. What led to the discovery of these defalcations it is impossible with any certainty to say. It may be that Sir William Paulet, Master of the Court of Wards, and now Lord Treasurer also, lighted upon them himself when he embarked upon a complete survey of the revenue. More probably, when Beaumont was promoted to a judgeship and Sir William Damsell took over from him, the new Receiver-General may have decided to wipe out the heavy list of unpaid debts by calling upon the 'debtors' for the money. If he did so, he of course failed to get what he wanted. Instead the 'debtors' must have sent to him a wonderful collection of cancelled obligations. At any rate, from that day to this they survive, pinned to John Beaumont's confession amongst the official records of the Court of Wards, a lengthy collection of cancelled obligations, testifying to the sums which Beaumont received from the crown's debtors but did not acknowledge to the crown.[1]

There may, however, be an additional explanation of these events which has little to do with the financial procedures of the Court of Wards. The year 1552, when Beaumont's crimes were at last brought out into the open, was also the year when the squalid intrigues amongst Edward VI's ministers ended in the final split between the Duke of Somerset, the former Protector, and the Duke of Northumberland who had ousted him from the post. This year also, which saw the execution of Somerset, saw financial charges not only against Beaumont but against a whole group of men including Lord Paget, Richard Whalley, Sir Thomas Holcroft, Sir John Thynne, Sir William Arundel and others. All of them belonged to the entourage of the fallen Protector; and they paid at the same time for their political errors as for their official abuses.

But one of the former followers of Somerset was not included amongst them. Henry Grey, Duke of Suffolk (whom, as the Marquis of Dorset, we have already met in the Leicestershire *fracas* with Beaumont in 1546) had in 1548 switched his allegiance from Somerset to the rising star, Dudley, Earl of Warwick, now Duke of Northumberland and at the height of his power. In 1552 Beaumont, the corrupt treasurer, was also the man who, six years earlier, had accused Suffolk before

1 Wards 9.365, ff. 235v–236r.

the Privy Council. The charge failed, but the memory of an up-
start who challenged the nobleman can hardly have died with it.
So finance and politics worked together to bring vengeance for
an old wound. But it was a short-lived triumph. Suffolk united his
family and fortunes with Northumberland in the ill-starred union
between Lady Jane Grey and Guilford Dudley, Northumberland's
son. They and he ended on the scaffold in 1553 for their plot to
forestall Mary on the throne of England. Suffolk deserted again
and earned the royal pardon. But he only bought a year's life.
In 1554 he joined a rising against the queen and was executed for
high treason.[1]

There is no reason to believe that the followers of the Protector
Somerset had a monopoly of dishonest practices during the period
of minority rule, notorious for its weakness and corruption.
Political loyalty to the new chief minister could easily cast a veil
over the financial disorders of those who were not brought to
book. But the independent evidence which exists in the Court of
Wards destroys any possible suggestion that Beaumont was the
innocent martyr for a vanquished cause. His loss of office and the
confiscation of his property were richly deserved. What is also
certain is that men like Beaumont could flourish in the enveloping
fog which obscured the financial realities of government departments.

So minister after minister struggled on with a heap of un-
correlated financial statements, half factual, half imaginary,
set out in ancient and traditional forms, without regard to either
the needs of common sense or of the crown. On crucial issues
the government was often either misinformed or uninformed.
Again one should not hasten to condemn these practices as unmistakable proof that Tudor institutions were crude and primitive. Statistical divisions always have been the Cinderella of
government departments. 'When I was called upon to clothe the
army', said Lord Woolton as he looked back from 1945 to the
early days of the Second World War, 'the War Office had no
statistical evidence to assist me. Here there could be no doubt

[1] *Literary Remains of Edward VI*, ii, 422–3.

that to guess was to endanger the chance of victory and the
security of the state. I had the greatest difficulty in arriving at any
figures that would show how many suits of uniform and how
many boots were involved.' Tudor governments, like their
successors, advanced into battle with only the haziest ideas about
the state of their supplies.[1]

Beaumont's immediate predecessor, Philip Parris, went out of
office in 1546 owing the crown more than £2,000. He agreed to
pay it at the rate of £80 a year, which seems a miserable return
from an erring civil servant; but that rate was cut by half to £40
in 1554, because of his 'great charges sustained in service to Edward VI' and to permit him also to 'maintain his state according
to the trade and furniture of our commonweal, wherein he is of
late preferred to the place and degree of a knight'. The last payment was expected to come in, half a century later, at the end of
1603! William Damsell, Beaumont's immediate successor, was
accused soon after he took over the Receiver-Generalship, of
financial misdemeanours in Flanders. Nevertheless, we find him
going overseas shortly afterwards on the king's business.[2]

The royal commission of the fifth year of Edward VI's reign
had some frank observations to make about the current practices
of royal treasurers in general, and some well-chosen remarks about
the Court of Wards in particular. The commissioners lamented
the rise in the salaries and allowances of the officials, though in
fairness to them it should be said that the pound bought less under
Edward VI than it did under Henry VIII and it bought less still
under Mary. It was regretted also that the practice of paying
Court of Wards revenues to the Treasurer of the Chamber had
lapsed since the death of Henry VIII, and the alternative method of
payment by warrant, that is, by direct instruction from the Privy
Council for *ad hoc* payments, had come in its place, 'and, as it
appeareth now, upon the view of Beaumont's account, a great
part thereof [the revenues] detained from the king in his hands'.

1 Cited in my *Control of Raw Materials* (1953), p. 84.
2 *C.P.R.*, Mary, i, 135–6; *Acts of P.C.*, 1552–4, 9 and 40.

In any case, it was pointedly remarked, there seemed to be too many officials and too few official records. The annual financial statement had not been completed for the last six or seven years 'which is a great unsurety for the king and meet to be reformed'. The authority of the feodaries was too extensive, the commission went on, in that they estimated the lands of the wards (with all the opportunities for corruption which that involved); it was also wrong that they should act as accountants for the revenues of wards' lands—'which is dangerous for the king and for the ward'. Junior officers in the Court of Wards in London also enjoyed far more power than was in the national interest: 'the clerks need to have over them some controlment to see that they deliver all the bonds that they receive'. Nor had the Receiver-General himself entered into any sureties to pay his receipts to the crown; such an undertaking was clearly necessary 'as experience especially in this office hath of late plainly declared'—one more reference to the habits of John Beaumont. Many other detailed points of reform were brought up and, along with them, the very large issue as to whether economy might not be best achieved by the abolition of a separate Court of Wards and the assumption of its power by another body. About that more will be said elsewhere.[1]

Serious attempts by commission and enactments were made under Mary to set bounds to the cupidity and dishonesty of crown revenue officials, and there were unmistakable signs of a new broom (in the person of Paulet) at work. But it was an intractable problem. Slackness, inadequate information, and vested interest combined to set bounds to the reforming zeal of a handful of ministers. Under Elizabeth I the same consumption ate away at her substance, though there was no shortage of enactments to point out the straight and narrow path for a successful and conservative financial policy. In 1563 we have an important statute which seemed to give a firm direction to the official treasurers. A total

[1] B.M. Harl. 7383, ff. 55r, 58r–59v. For a full report of the important commission of Edward VI and some of its acid comments on the existing system of the Court of Wards, as well as of other departments of state, see B.M. Harl. 7383, ff. 1–72 (reproduced also in ADD. MS. 30198). I am indebted to Prof. W. C. Richardson for the reference.

sum of money was sanctioned for the queen's household each year, some £40,000 in all. In this the Court of Wards was made responsible for the largest contribution: £10,000. This at least looked like one method of forestalling the accumulation of government revenues in the private pocket of the Receiver-General. Secondly, it was laid down that the Lord Treasurer and the barons of the Exchequer could call upon all receivers twice annually to render account, and with it went the power to claim from them all ready money in their possession.[1]

This looked a workmanlike affair. The £10,000 were indeed paid annually to the household but the treasurers did not by any means live up to the high standards which the 1563 act set before them. Three years later there was a bill before the Commons 'for answering the Queen's Majesty's revenues in the hands of receivers'. Five years after that, in the Parliament of 1571, an M.P. laid the financial embarrassment of the government at the door of the 'treasurers of the crown, who have in their hands great masses of money, with the which either they themselves, or some friends of theirs, do purchase lands to their own use, and after become bankrupt'. He exaggerated; but clearly the treasurers were not seriously handicapped by the statute. So another statute became necessary: 'An act to make the lands, tenements, goods and chattels of tellers, receivers, etc. liable to the payment of their debts'. In 1572, the government struck again, this time 'against the deceits of under-collectors of the tenths and subsidies of the clergy'; and in 1585 a new act was required for 'explanation of the statute made anno XIII of the Queen's Majesty's reign [i.e. 1571]', making receivers liable in their goods and chattels for their debts to the crown. In 1597 we have yet one more act 'for the more speedy payment of the Queen's Majesty's debts' and for the better explanation of the 1571 act. At the end of 1601 there was a bill before the Commons 'for reformation of deceits and frauds in certain auditors and their clerks in making deceitful and untrue

---

[1] 5 Eliz., c. 32. Thirty years later Burghley was incorporating the plan of 1563 in draft instructions drawn up by himself (H.M.C. *Salis.*, iv, 528).

particulars'; but it did not reach the statute book. If it had, it could hardly have made any difference.[1]

The best commentary on these procedures is George Goring's tenure of the office of Receiver-General from 1584 until 1594. He was a Sussex country gentleman, well-connected and with all the outward signs of prosperity. Yet he contrived on his death to be in debt to the crown to the tune of £19,777. These were the arrears officially recorded on the wardship records—that is, his cash in hand—but there was no trace of the money. At once the hunt was up and rumour kept pace with it. For example, it was said that there were £12,000 in his house a few days before Goring died, that he 'bought land.in other men's names and he secretly conveyed away his lands to defeat Her Majesty'. What was not mere gossip was that he owned manors in various places in Sussex, that he had a house built of brick at a cost of £4,000 and another of stone costing £2,000. No wonder the sheriff entered and seized his lands and goods, and the queen was 'hardly incensed' against Goring's son when he told a tale full of lamentation. Now there followed a stream of offers, starting with £1,000 down and the rest by instalments—a disgraceful proposal—rising later to an initial offer of £10,000, interspersed with new-year gifts, 'country provisions', the offer also of a house at Chelsea to Burghley, and the indication of other gifts to be had. Against such a background the son had the effrontery to ask for the vacant Receiver-Generalship, as well as for a wardship on behalf of a neighbour and kinsman. Whether the full arrears were ever settled we do not know. Burghley died, the queen died, Goring's son died. In 1604 Goring's daughter-in-law was still negotiating with Robert Cecil about the debt, to the accompaniment of further presents. So much for the harsh treatment which Elizabeth meted out to her faithful servants. Men seeking office do not seem to have been as much troubled by this 'tough' Elizabethan policy as have some historians: when Goring died

[1] *C.J.*, i, 73; J. E. Neale, *Elizabeth I and her Parliaments, 1559–81*, p. 219; 13 Eliz., c. 4; 14 Eliz., c. 7; 27 Eliz., c. 3; 39 Eliz., c. 7; Towshend's *Journal*, p. 146.

there were at least four candidates for his vacant office of Receiver-General.[1]

Any study of corruption is bound to dwell at some length upon the finance officers of the crown, since their opportunities for peculation were both numerous and manifest. But they were merely one group out of many who funnelled royal profits into their private coffers. For the holding of public office throughout Tudor England implied the right to augment a nominal official salary with larger unofficial perquisites. At which stage a perquisite becomes a gift and a gift becomes a bribe is, as we have seen in the case of Bacon, difficult to establish. But when it comes to the actual withdrawing of royal revenues we are faced not with bribery but with pure theft. Two Receiver-Generals did it in forty years—or perhaps we should say two were *caught* doing it. What they did in London could be done, on a smaller scale, in the provinces. Hence the very grave doubts expressed by the commission of Edward VI as to the considerable powers—and limited probity—of the feodaries in the shires. Michael Hickes was a feodary and of him an earlier chapter has shown how he thought fit to conduct his business. The feodary, perhaps more than the Receiver-General, stood at a vantage point half-way between the queen and her subject—and could levy a toll upon both.

John Eveleigh, feodary of Devon, apparently made a common practice of undervaluing the inheritance of wards, with the object of buying up the wardships for himself at bargain prices. Richard Hurlestone, feodary of Cheshire, concealed wardships instead of discovering them, and collected appropriate sums from the grateful wards or their relatives. John Budden, feodary of Dorset, was accused of dubious dealings in crown lands, but we do not know whether the charge was proved. What we do know is that, in 1595, he was telling Robert Cecil of a valuable wardship which, by a subterfuge, might be bought up well below its real value (and therefore secure for the purchaser an unearned increment at the expense of the queen). But Cecil had to be cautious, for the ward's father was not yet dead: 'I beseech you', said Budden, 'to

[1] Wards 9.108, ff. 509v–510v; H.M.C. *Salis.*, iv, ff.

be careful presently, and what shall appertain to your best good shall, by Mr. Escheator and myself, be carefully looked into.' But the utmost secrecy was essential, 'I beseech you', the feodary repeated, 'be careful!'[1]

Marmaduke Willson, feodary of the North Riding of Yorkshire, was said to have dealt dishonestly with crown money but Thomas, Lord Burghley, son of the late Master, spoke vigorously on his behalf and added, 'You know, sir, how easily in these days men, that have to deal in many causes (as by reason of that office he hath), are often unjustly accused and drawn in question.' On the other hand, Richard Shute, feodary of Lincolnshire, was dismissed and called 'shameless fellow' in court for asking for his post back. He tried to drag Sherard, the deputy feodary—'a base fellow who could both whine and bite'—down with him. Peter Palmer, feodary of Bucks, died leaving unpaid his heavy 'arrearages' to the queen. John Killigrew, feodary of Cornwall, died in debt to the crown for £300, a sum 'unlikely ever to be recovered by reason of Killigrew's decayed estate and present imprisonment'. Peter Osborne, a civil servant himself, once sighed that the wardship revenues would be greatly increased, 'if only the feodaries of the court will be true and honest'; but Osborne himself proved no innocent in the shady practices of Tudor finance.[2]

What feodaries could do Clerks of the Court of Wards could do; and Ralph Bosseville and Henry Bosseville, father and son, each in their turn diverted royal funds to their private use. The Attorney, Hesketh, was held to be 'very partial'. He and the surveyor took gifts from the Countess of Rutland. And so it went on. Offices were multiplied, fees were multiplied, opportunities for backstairs dealings increased. Offices were bought and sold, in spite of an act of 1551 aimed precisely against an abuse of this sort, and in spite of the crown's dislike of such practices. Clearly the purchase of an office could have nothing to do with the public interest; the very sale implied that it was freehold property and a

<hr>

1 *Ibid.*, xiii, 124–5, 114; x, 85; v. 217–8.
2 *Ibid.*, xi, 233; [86.98]; ix, 233 [71.31]; Wards 9.389, ff. 276v–277r; H.M.C. *Salis.*, ii, 171.

source of income to the purchaser. Of that income the official salary formed an insignificant share, the rest came unofficially— sometimes corruptly—from either the crown or the community.[1]

While the system lasted it blocked the way to a modern revenue system; but the sixteenth century did not see the end of it. Not until the fundamental recasting of the administrative structure in the nineteenth century did the emergence of a conception of *public* service, in the fullest sense, at last come into view. The Victorian standards of public administration have so deeply written themselves into our memory that we sometimes forget that they are no older than that.

Administration has an unlimited capacity to expand; and the eternal problem of reducing the government service—and therefore the opportunities for corruption—proved insoluble as far as the six- teenth century was concerned. But the position was not always hopeless. In the years immediately preceding the accession of Eliza- beth a major operation was undertaken. One of the economic consequences of the Reformation under Henry VIII had been the establishment of special financial courts for dealing with the accre- tion of royal income, received and anticipated. They may have served a useful purpose at the time in side-stepping the Exchequer as it dragged along in its accustomed ways. But under the reforms of Paulet and his colleagues the Exchequer was in part renovated and, as a means of centralisation and economy, the new financial courts were absorbed into it. The royal commission of Edward VI's reign reported that the 'Surveyor of the Liveries is thought to be a superfluous office' which could reasonably be suppressed, and inquired also whether the Courts of Wards itself might be abolished and absorbed into the Exchequer. The statutes of both Edward VI's reign and Mary's, authorising the amalgamation or abolition of the financial courts, gave permission to extend this plan to the Court of Wards. Yet in spite of these powers held in reserve, and in spite also of the urgent need for retrenchment, the Court of Wards escaped this process of centralisation. Why it did

1 *Ibid.*, xiii, 59; *S.P.D.*, Eliz., xix, no. 65; H.M.C. *Twelfth*, pt. 4, p. 279; 5 and 6 Ed. VI, c. 16; Holdsworth, *op. cit.*, i, 262–4; iv, 520.

so we cannot know for certain because, so far as I am aware, no records of the discussion have survived.[1]

There is, however, some circumstantial evidence which may perhaps yield clues to the motives which induced Mary to shield the Court of Wards from this centralising policy. In Sir William Damsell's new patent of appointment, issued by Mary on 17 January 1554, we find a special provision that, should the Court be abolished, Damsell would retain his office and revenues. But when Sir Francis Englefield was appointed Master on 1 May 1554 there was no reference in his patent to the possible dissolution of the Court of Wards, and no provision whatsoever for his compensation should that take place. If a dissolution were still in prospect it is most unlikely that the queen would have made no provision for the Master, a man senior in office to the Receiver-General and, in the person of Englefield, much closer to her counsels and favour. It looks, therefore, as though some time between 17 January and 1 May 1554 it was decided not to terminate the independent existence of the Court of Wards; and this perhaps provides a clue to one of the causes, though not the most important, which gave it a new lease of life.[2]

The queen trusted Englefield, bound as he was to her in the close ties of religion, a religion which in a few years would cost him his post and send him into his long exile for the rest of his life. She had confidence in Englefield, she had confidence also in Paulet, with the experience of wardship behind him, and now her Lord Treasurer. With two such men in control it was reasonable to hope that the Court of Wards would recover from the blow to its reputation dealt by John Beaumont. If such hopes played any part in influencing Mary's decision, its good administration during the rest of her reign proved her decision to be right.

Whether or not these personal considerations influenced Mary's mind, there were weightier causes which must also have intervened. There had grown up within the Court of Wards special techniques for dealing with the complex and delicate issues in-

---

1 B.M. Harl. 7383, ff. 63r and v; 7 Ed. VI, c.2; 1 Mary, st. 2, c. 10.
2 Pat. Roll, 1 Mary, pt. ii, m. 15; *ibid.*, pt. x, m. 7.

separable from wardship. The Courts of Augmentation and First Fruits and Tenths, which had not survived the new centralising policy were, after all, concerned with the same kind of land and revenue questions as the officials of the Exchequer had been dealing with for centuries. The merging of the departments had, then, a good deal to recommend it and it could be expected that the transfer would be reasonably smooth.

The Court of Wards, it is true, was also a financial department dealing with land and revenue questions; but these formed only a part of its work. It had also to deal with grants of wardships, marriages, abuses of guardianship, licences to widows to re-marry, the suing of livery, and the administration of the affairs of idiots and lunatics. Some of these functions the Court of Wards had taken over from Chancery, others from the Master of Wards and the Master of Liveries, who had been doing this kind of work before the establishment of the Court of Wards in 1540.

Since 1540 these administrative segments had been welded into one homogeneous department and little would be gained in the future from bundling them into the Exchequer, where they would have no reason to feel at home. To try to dovetail them into the already elaborate Exchequer machine would threaten also all the dangers of over-centralisation. It would be far better to leave all the wardship *expertise* in the department where it had grown up, especially if the crown was hoping to increase its revenues—as indeed it succeeded in doing—to meet a financial crisis. Apart from all this, the Court of Wards was a court of law with a tradition and experience peculiarly its own for dealing with the bewildering ramifications of feudal law. Again, prudence would seem to dictate a policy of leave well alone. Perhaps these, and other, considerations had been suggested to Edward VI's mind when, in the last year of his life, he referred to the proposal to bring Augmentations and First Fruits into the Exchequer but said nothing about the Court of Wards, other than that something should be done about reducing its 'superfluous fees'.[1]

So it came about, for one reason or another, that the Court of

---

[1] *Literary Remains of Edward VI*, ii, 544.

Wards survived the first threat to its existence, coming from the government itself. Thereafter there was to be no more talk of its abolition throughout the long reign of Queen Elizabeth—at least as far as the government was concerned. Her subjects thought differently and, by the end of the century, there was a considerable volume of bitter criticism of the Court of Wards and its officers, and the publicly expressed hope that at last they might be sent packing. That, of course, is another question and is not part of the efforts of the queen and her ministers to economise in its administration and purify it of its corrupt practices. These practices survived and soon the number of officials—and their fees—started their upward climb again. Nothing that the queen or Burghley did could force her officials to abandon their accustomed and expensive ways. But not every payment made to an official was a corrupt one: the adjective can only be applied where her officials abused their authority over the people, misrepresented the facts to the queen, or misappropriated the funds in their care. A good many of the fees and perquisites, which to us are tainted with corruption, are capable of an entirely different interpretation if considered within the context of the economic and political structure of Tudor England. To that question we shall revert in our final chapter.

It is time now to return to the question with which this chapter began: was the Court of Wards a corrupt institution? Clearly, a verdict of guilty must be returned. The queen's subjects, as we have seen, were blackmailed and bullied into paying sums of money to escape from the anti-social consequences of feudal wardship. The queen herself was robbed of a good part of her revenues by her own officials, whom she paid to uphold her cause. By whichever moral standards we adopt, Tudor or our own, these practices can be designated by no other term than corruption. Yet, even after we have confirmed what contemporaries said about wardship, the last word has not been spoken. For there are two considerations which must be recognised before final judgement is given.

The first concerns the quality of Tudor society as a whole. Public servants in every walk of life were venal, from the Lord Treasurer to the humblest messenger. No official service was obtained without private payment from the subject; few services were rendered on behalf of the queen which did not at the same time operate in such a way as to deprive her of some of her dues. If we think in terms of administration the evidence is abundant. In this place, one example must suffice. We have seen something of the intractable problem facing the government when it tried to discover what exactly were the Court of Wards revenues. Precisely the same problem faced Elizabeth when she tried to discover what was happening to the men and money that she was pouring into the war in the Netherlands during the years 1586-7. 'Without accounts the queen was helpless', writes Sir John Neale. 'She could only know that her money invariably disappeared long before it ought to have done and listen for explanation to one official blaming the other. . . . But, demand as she would and threaten as she could, months passed and the accounts did not arrive.'[1]

What was true of the army was true of the navy; of the customs and of land management. It was true of the justices of the peace in quarter sessions, those 'basket justices' that 'for half a dozen of chickens will dispense with a whole dozen of penal statutes'. Yet a good deal of administrative corruption, if it cannot be justified, can at least be understood if we recognise that official fees were nominal fees, and that private gifts were written into the whole framework of government. A great many of these gifts—though by no means all—were unofficial payments of unofficial fees. These were not inherently corrupt. They were justified alike by the custom and the conditions of government service.[2]

But does that mean that justice was bought and sold? Some judges were undoubtedly corrupt: Beaumont was one of them. Early in the next century Sir Walter Raleigh, as he prepared himself for death, turned a scathing glance at the judicial system

---

[1] J. E. Neale, 'Elizabeth and the Netherlands, 1586-7' (*E.H.R.*, xlv, 389-90).
[2] *Tudor Economic Documents*, ed. Tawney and Power (1924), ii, 235.

of the world he was leaving. (The angels of the last line represented not only heavenly companions but a common coin of the day.)

> From thence to Heaven's bribeless hall
> Where no corrupted voices brawl,
> No conscience moulten into gold,
> Nor forged accusers bought and sold,
> No cause deferred, nor vain spent journey,
> For there Christ is the King's attorney,
> Who pleads for all without degrees,
> And he hath angels but no fees.

'Attribute this thing to the corruption of the time', said the Duke of Buckingham when referring to the downfall of Bacon. Yet, as the wardship records show, justice was *not* up for sale to the highest bidder. 'The benefit of His Majesty's laws', Lord Dacres of the North was once told after he had seized possession of a ward, 'shall be denied to none.' Lord Burghley was a careful and patient judge and more than one poor ward had cause to be grateful for the shelter of the Court he ruled. There were, of course, miscarriages of justice as well as distortion of the facts; and all men took gifts. But the detailed sifting of the evidence and the cautiously weighed decrees, given often only after advice from the High Court judges present in Court, show that these judicial responsibilities were not taken lightly. Having regard to the existing financial situation, it is remarkable not that some men were corrupt but that, in so many cases, justice was done.[1]

The second consideration we must have in mind is that no age has the monopoly of virtue or vice. And to dismiss any period as corrupt is to ignore certain basic qualities of the human temperament which seem to be a permanent attribute of civilised man. Patronage and favouritism were there for all men to see; and they flourished amid graft and gifts. But it is difficult to see how, in the absence of modern techniques of government recruitment, any other method of appointment could have been employed. We

---

1 *The Poems of Sir Walter Raleigh*, ed. A. M. C. Latham (1951), pp. 50–1; *Acts of P.C.*, 1550–2, 123.

should remember also that the current methods did not always breed corruption. Nor was the system peculiar to the Elizabethan age. Eminent men, in every age, by the very quality of their minds attract a following, who share a little in the lustre of their master. He is their patron and his commendation justly earns them opportunities and offices in which they too may exercise their skills. These are the familiar qualities of patronage.

But where does patronage end and favouritism begin? And at which stage does corruption take a share in the proceedings? It seems an unhistorical approach to speak of the sixteenth and eighteenth centuries as times of corruption and the nineteenth and twentieth centuries as times when the Augean stables were cleansed, once for all. For linked with patronage, in every generation, are the complex qualities of prestige, pride, clientage, and the rest. No money changes hands during these processes. That would be unthinkable. It would be also a corrupt practice and therefore illegal. The Tudor attitude to office and administration was more flexible and more frank than our own. One may go farther and say that without these apparently corrupt practices the Elizabethan civil service would have gone inadequately paid and have ultimately collapsed through shortage of men and money.

We should remember also that if it was a corrupt age it was also an age which rated honour and heroism very highly indeed. And to match every John Beaumont there was a Hugh Latimer, for every Edward Dyer a Philip Sidney, and a hundred others unknown to history. Sometimes the contradictory qualities were combined in one and the same man, as in the case of the Earl of Essex. With all its corruption, the Elizabethan government service stood, then as now, second to none in Europe.

IV

THE RULE OF THE CECILS

. . . This judgement I have of you: that you will not be corrupted by any manner of gift and that you will be faithful to the state; and that, without respect of my private will, you will give me that counsel which you think best. . . .

Queen Elizabeth I to Sir William Cecil, later Lord Burghley,
Her Majesty's Secretary of State, 1558–72,
Lord High Treasurer of England, 1572–98 and
Master of the Queen's Wards, 1561–98.

II

Offices and Office Holders

THE firm distinction which the nineteenth century was to draw between politics and administration did not yet exist under Elizabeth I. The minister in charge of a government department was also its administrative head, its principal accountant, its chief establishment officer. Below him were all the divisions and classes of government officials; but the manner of their appointment bore a closer resemblance to the so-called 'spoils' system of the United States than to our own conception of a permanent, administrative staff. If Elizabeth introduced some change in her council or her ministers, it might be followed at once by a thorough overhaul of the appointments in the department concerned; and, even in quieter times, there was a continual manoeuvring for position throughout the upper and lower ranks of the ministry. Outside, there was a thrusting queue of candidates for any vacancies which might arise; while Lord Burghley's postbags were crammed with the petitions of job hunters, including those who recommended the erection of new posts for the sole reason that they hoped to be invited to fill them.

In this, as in so much else, the Court of Wards conformed to the pattern of Tudor politics and administration. At its head from almost the beginning of Elizabeth's reign was Lord Burghley, already well versed in the devious ways of Tudor rule, and he held on to the reins until almost the end of the age. As a result he enjoyed, as we shall see, enormous powers of patronage, of which a part consisted of the appointment to office within the Court of Wards. This did not, of course, apply to the whole department, for there was a fundamental division within the organisation. At

the top were officials in London, appointed directly by the crown
—although the queen would undoubtedly have consulted Lord
Burghley in making her choice. Also in London were the junior
officials, clerks, messengers and ushers, and these too were royal
nominees. Finally, the senior officers themselves had their following of clerks and personal assistants, not on the official payroll, but
keen partakers of the privileges and perquisites of the departments.
The link between London and the provinces was formed by the
key offices of county feodary, appointed by the Master in virtue
of the authority vested in him by statute.

For the formal analysis of these offices we must go back beyond
the reign of Elizabeth to the originating statutes of Henry VIII.
The first of these, passed in 1540, was concerned with wardship
and marriage only—not the livery of lands—and set out five
principal officers in order of seniority. At the head was of course
the Master, and immediately below him the king's Attorney of
the Court of Wards, who was to safeguard the legal rights of the
crown. There followed the treasurer, or Receiver-General as he
was officially described, and, after him, two Auditors who were
to examine the accounts annually. Next came the two Clerks of
the Court, as well as a messenger and an usher. The five senior
officers (Master, Attorney, Receiver-General, and two Auditors)
had corporate responsibility for the grant of wardships, at least in
theory, but the work could be done by three of them, of whom
the Master had to be one. The Master, with the advice of the
Attorney and Receiver-General, or one of them, could also make
leases of wards' lands; but he alone made the appointments of
feodaries. In essence the main power was concentrated in the
hands of the Master, as was the trial of lawsuits, though the senior
officials advised him here also; and he was able, later on, to call
upon the aid of two common law judges.[1]

So far liveries were outside the jurisdiction of the Court, but
the unnatural division between the two aspects of feudal succession, wardship and livery, was, from the administrative point of
view, clearly unsatisfactory. Within two years, the Master of

[1] 32 Hen. VIII, c. 46.

Liveries had his functions annexed to the Court of Wards, with himself appointed as its second officer, which put him above the Attorney and gave him the new title of Surveyor of Liveries. To help him the crown might appoint a Clerk of Liveries.[1]

It was a powerful and articulated organisation, which possessed all the refinements of Tudor administrative technique. What kind of men were attracted to its service? For the time being we shall omit the Master, for his dominant position calls for more detailed treatment than can be given to his colleagues; and we shall begin with his second-in-command, the Surveyor.

There had been masters—or overseers—of liveries since at least the beginning of the Tudor period, but the expression appears sometimes to have been used loosely by contemporaries of the Master of Wards himself. To this office, held jointly, Thomas Neville and Sir Robert Norwich were appointed in 1529, and on the death of Norwich he was succeeded by Sir Richard Rich in April 1535. These men already ranked high in the royal service. Neville had been a Speaker of the House of Commons; Norwich, Chief Justice of England. Rich was to become Lord Chancellor and to earn himself a second reputation for betraying every master he served. John Hynde took over from Rich in March 1537. The sole tenant of the office when Neville died in 1542, he too rose to a judgeship. As events turned out, however, his tenure was an insecure one and, in the last months of Henry VIII's reign, a certain Robert Keilway was conducting a profitable intrigue with Hertford, the future Protector Somerset, to establish that Hynde's patent was void, as the result of the annexation of his office to the Court of Wards by the act of 1542. This fault was not of course in the office itself but probably arose from a technical lapse on the part of Hynde, who had failed to renew his patent of appointment. Paulet, as Master of the Wards, was approached in the matter, but hesitated to take any drastic action until he was certain in his own mind that Hynde could have

1 33 Hen. VIII, c. 22. For a full discussion of these developments see W. C. Richardson, *Tudor Chamber Administration, 1485-1547* (Baton Rouge, 1952), pp. 296-304.

blundered in this way. However, the ruse worked and the Surveyor was evicted on a technicality—to be replaced by Robert
Keilway. Hynde fought back and the matter came before the Privy
Council shortly before his death. Keilway kept what he had gained
by such dubious means (but—by a curious kind of justice—had to
pay his predecessor £50 a year) and remained in office until 1579.[1]

Robert Keilway's career typifies the middle-grade Tudor civil
servant who rose to power in the Court of Wards and similar
institutions. He was a justice of the peace and *custos rotulorum* for
Berkshire, a sergeant-at-law, a commissioner for the sale of
chantry lands in 1548 and for the sale of crown lands in 1563, and
a 'double reader' of the Inner Temple. In short he was a distinguished lawyer, an experienced land administrator and a senior
officer of the crown. Similar in training and experience, but with
an ecclesiastical rather than economic bent, was Thomas Seckford
who succeeded Keilway in 1579. He was in office for just over
ten years and was followed by Richard Kingsmill in 1590, and by
Cuthbert Pepper in 1600. Neither Kingsmill nor Pepper reached
the same eminence as the other Elizabethan surveyors.[2]

Men of distinction were to be found also in the key office of
Attorney of the Wards. But here we must be careful to differen-
tiate the Attorneys of the Wards—the crown officials—from the
attorneys in the wards, lawyers acting in wardship cases on behalf
of their clients. Thomas Polsted, who was the first Attorney after
the establishment of the Court of Wards, held his office for a few
months only, after which John Sewster succeeded him in February
1541. Of these officials we know little other than that they were
experienced lawyers and that Sewster, having obtained three
wardships himself, died leaving his own son a ward of the crown.
Feudal wardship was a double-edged sword and it more than once
struck back at those who wielded it. After Sewster's death in 1546
came Richard Goodrich—but it was a short tenure for he left it

---

[1] *L.P.*, viii, g. 632 (34); xii, pt. 1, g. 795 (27); *L.P. Add.*, i, pt. 2, no. 1755; xxi, pt. 1,
no. 1165 (44); *Acts of P.C.*, 1547–50, pp. 386–8.
[2] *C.P.R.*, Ed. VI, ii, 225, 57; *C.P.R.*, Eliz., ii, 623–4; *Original Letters*, ed. Ellis (3rd
Ser.), iv, 59.

after eight months to become Attorney of the Court of Augmentations. It was at this point that the Court of Wards drew to its service one of the ablest men of the day, destined in time to become the famous father of an even more famous son. Sir Nicholas Bacon served all the Tudor monarchs, with the exception of the first of them, in a variety of offices, culminating in that of Lord Keeper of the Great Seal. He was Attorney for a significant period, from 1547 to 1561, before being called to higher office. What he saw of wardship in action sickened him; and when he thought that his own young children lay in its shadows, his distress must have deepened. Behind his gross and sensual face there was a conscience and, when he had ceased to be Attorney, he wrote a blunt letter to his brother-in-law, Burghley, who had become Master of the Wards, reminded him of the evils of the system, and put forward some major projects for reform.[1]

Bacon was advanced to the Lord Keepership in 1558, and in 1561 he was succeeded as Attorney by his deputy, Robert Nowell, a member of the Burghley circle and of a family of scholars. Like Bacon, Nowell was a public spirited man; *The Spending of the Money of Robert Nowell* is a contemporary story of his pious bequest. After him there were the short spells of Richard Onslow, subsequently Speaker of the House of Commons, and Thomas Wilbraham. Then in 1573 came Richard Kingsmill, who had tried for the post once before and had to wait many years before at last it was his. He stayed in office for seventeen years until his promotion to the Surveyorship, which he enjoyed for another decade. Into his place as Attorney was appointed the colourful James Morrice, whose puritan fervour as a Member of Parliament earned him dismissal from office and a period of restraint. His career reminds us that, in those days, membership of the government service did not automatically silence a man's voice in politics; but it carried other—and graver—risks. Finally,

---

[1] *L.P.*, xv, g. 1027 (15); xix, pt. 1, g. 80 (31); xviii, pt. 2, g. 449 (66, 67); xix, pt. 2, g. 166 (13); xxi, pt. 2, g. 771 (32); xxi, pt. 1, g. 963 (21), g. 970 (23).

in 1597, came Thomas Hesketh, who continued to serve until the end of the reign.[1]

The Attorneyship was a profitable post. It was also a training ground for higher office. A sixteenth-century Attorney, Bacon, became Lord Keeper; a seventeenth-century one, James Ley, later Earl of Marlborough, became in succession Lord Chief Justice and Lord Treasurer. Another, John Winthrop, sailed away to America, became Governor of Massachusetts and our principal source for the early history of New England.

The chief official, for liveries, under the Master, was the Surveyor; and for legal processes it was the Attorney. For finance it was the Receiver-General, who ranked fourth in the hierarchy. In some ways his office was more attractive than the Surveyorship for by firmly established convention—but not by law—the Receivers kept the official funds in their private possession until called upon to make payments to the crown or its agents. In such a happy climate, as we have seen, George Goring flourished, and left his heirs and the crown to negotiate a long-drawn-out settlement of his debts. It was a clumsy trick which merely postponed the day of reckoning; and the same could be said of John Beaumont's antics some forty years earlier. But there were also more sophisticated techniques by which the revenues of the crown could be used, where opportunity served, for speculation in the money market or in trade.[2]

The Receivership was an office of profit and power: it could arouse competition amongst rising men. Philip Paris and Richard Lee, who held the appointment in succession under Henry VIII, were experienced financiers: and Lee had won his spurs as a tough commissioner for the dissolution of the monasteries. John Beaumont, who succeeded Lee in 1545, was a man of ability, an experienced lawyer and a judge, who might have risen still higher but for his failure to recognise that there was a limit to peculation, even in the Tudor age. What he did, as our examination of corrup-

---

[1] *C.P.R.*, Eliz., ii, 6; *The Townley Hall MSS: The Spending* . . ., ed. A. B. Grosart (Manchester, 1877); *S.P.D.*, Eliz., i, no. 43; J. E. Neale, *Elizabeth I and her Parliaments, 1584–1601* (1957), pp. 267–79; Wards 9.109, ff. 145v–146r.

[2] For Beaumont and Goring, see above pp. 199–204 and 208–9.

tion has shown, would have been considered frankly dishonest by the standards of any age. William Damsell, who succeeded Beaumont in 1550, after experience as a royal financial agent in Flanders, held his post for over three decades, to be succeeded by John Battisforde, who was in office for only two years. There followed the disastrous Receivership of George Goring from 1584 to 1594, after which the office passed to William Fleetwood, whose family had been—and was to remain—distinguished in the public service of Elizabeth and the early Stuarts.

The Receiver's junior colleague on the financial side was the Auditor, and his origin can be traced back to at least the year 1509, when Thomas Roberts was appointed Auditor of all lands in England in the king's wardship. From about 1521 he seems to have held the Auditorship jointly with John Perient; and the latter remained in office up to and beyond the establishment of the Court of Wards in 1540. To this post William Tooke succeeded in 1551, though he had held it in survivorship with Perient since 1544. Tooke's tenure of office lasted exactly as long as Burghley's, thirty-seven years; and by the time of his death in 1588 the Tooke family had well and truly dug themselves into the business, both as private dealers in wardships and in the work of administration. With them the Auditorship stayed until the Court of Wards ceased to exist: a remarkable dynasty. But they did not have a total monopoly for, though Walter Tooke succeeded William, from 1590 onwards the records show once again two Auditors in office, with William Curle as the joint Auditor.[1]

Why were there two Auditors? It may be that increase of work —and the inveterate Tudor disease of multiplication of offices— called for this expansion. It may be that Burghley was anxious to tighten the supervision over the work of the Receiver-General. If that was his intention, it failed: a junior officer, the Auditor, could not control his senior, the Receiver-General. This serious administrative weakness of the Court of Wards Burghley never solved. One Auditor in Edward VI's reign failed to prevent John Beaumont robbing the crown of some £12,000. Two Auditors

[1] *L.P.*, i, pt. 1, g. 190 (43); xv, g. 1027 (9); xix, pt. 1, g. 80 (37); xix, pt. 2, g. 340 (19).

towards the end of Elizabeth's reign failed to arrest the activities of George Goring, whose career ended with a deficit of nearly £20,000.

Of the principal central officers of the Court, the last in order of precedence was the Clerk, although in view of the complexity of the procedure and records his influence was considerable. But in some respects the position is obscure. The act of 1540, establishing the Court of Wards, declared that there should be two Clerks; the act of 1542, which annexed the work of liveries to the court, gave authority for the institution of a third. Yet the Receiver-Generals' accounts establish that, in fact, only one Clerk was paid. We know that Thomas Anton was the first Clerk of the Court of Wards but we find him in 1544 described as 'one of the clerks' of the Court. Then, in October 1551 we find a George Paulet appointed Clerk of the Liveries and after him came William Cooke in October 1561. Meanwhile, to confuse the issue we have the declaration by Queen Mary, of an uncertain date, but belonging to the beginning of the reign, stating that Thomas Anton had acted satisfactorily as *sole* Clerk for thirteen years, and his patent was accordingly modified to ensure the continuance of the practice into the future.[1]

Were there one, two or three Clerks? The work was almost certainly too specialised for one man to handle alone. Liveries had to be treated separately. But, as it happened, the notorious charges for suing liveries provided enough in fees to the Liveries Clerk for him to be excluded from the official payroll. However, even excluding liveries, there was still too much for one Clerk of the Wards to do. Ralph Bosseville who became Clerk at the end of Mary's reign, exercised the office jointly with his son Henry, from the thirteenth year of Elizabeth until her twenty-second year. Then Henry became sole Clerk for a decade, after which John and Hugh Hare held the office jointly until about the end of the reign, when John served alone. It was John, who, as Mr. Bell has shown,

1 *L.P.*, xix, pt. 2, g. 527 (2); *C.P.R.*, Ed. VI, iv, 195; *C.P.R.*, Eliz., ii, 250; *Cal. S.P.D.*, Addenda, 1547–65, pp. 432–3.

strove heroically to bring order into the uncharted papers of his department.[1]

We come finally to the Usher and Messenger—who were not such humble officers as they sound. The Usher was responsible for the maintenance and equipment of the room in which the Court of Wards met, in Westminster Palace, adjacent to the White Hall; the Messenger, or Pursuivant, was in charge of the inter-departmental correspondence, the carrying of writs and the like. Thomas Bate, Quintin Sneynton and William Pratt were in succession ushers in the earlier part of Elizabeth's reign but, from about 1579 until the end of her reign, the appropriately named Marmaduke Servant was in office. He was not as menial as his name, for he was a burgess of Westminster and, in certain negotiations with Sir Robert Cecil, acted as a spokesman for his fellow burgesses. He combined pleasure with business and thanked Cecil for the gift of some venison. For this benevolence there was, no doubt, good reason: it appears that Servant was employed by Cecil not simply in the Court of Wards but as a carrier of secret-service correspondence.[2]

Stephen Claybrooke was Messenger for the first twenty-four years of the court's existence but, by some accident, he was not appointed by patent under the Great Seal; and that had to be rectified at the beginning of Mary's reign. It is from this patent that we learn that his fee was at that time fourpence a day and that he was allowed a further twenty-six shillings and eightpence to purchase cloth for the queen's livery that he wore. He was succeeded by Leonard Taylor in 1564 and by Christopher Goodwin thirty years later. This Goodwin was again no mere transmitter of official files. He was an experienced lawyer who served Thomas Skinner, sometime Lord Mayor of London, in legal matters and was steward of several manors belonging to his master.[3]

The heart of the Court of Wards beat, with some irregularity, in London but its limbs reached out into the whole realm. Upon

1 *C.P.R.*, Mary, iv, 428; H. E. Bell, *op. cit.*, pp. 26–8.
2 Ibid., p. 167; H.M.C. *Salis.*, ix, 333; xiii, 456.
3 *C.P.R.*, Mary, i, 10–11; C.2, Eliz., G.5/15a.d.1600; I am indebted to Mr. W. J. Jones for the chancery reference to Goodwin.

their strength and grasp the crown depended for its feudal revenue. Since early times the provincial feudal administration had been the responsibility of the escheator, who concerned himself not simply with escheats—the lapse of an heir and the consequential recovery of the land by the crown—but with wardship and the related incidents of feudalism. It was an annual appointment and it was held by amateurs: two serious handicaps to efficient administration. But it also carried other, and more serious, defects in its nature.

Throughout the Middle Ages the whole provincial administration had been torn by the conflict inherent in the system. Were these officials—and the same problem manifested itself in the sheriffs, justices, and the rest—answerable to the crown or to the local community? In theory it was undoubtedly the crown, but in practice the official had to weigh up the orders and threats of a distant monarch as against the more intimate pressure of local interests, or the heavy arm of a neighbouring lord. In such cases, his parish or his county might well blot out the distant view of the capital, especially where his private interests moved in harmony with those of the men amongst whom he lived. Hence, as the leading authority on medieval administration tells us, there was an 'endless struggle of the central authority to exercise control over its local representatives, a struggle the more interminable since the state neither abandoned its pretensions nor possessed the executive force to give effect to them'.[1]

In the Elizabethan age the struggle continued, with the county all too often resisting the crown. The early Tudor policy against enclosures and evictions was subverted by the slack and hostile responses of the men in the shire. The Elizabethan thunderbolts against recusant Catholics landed harmlessly in some counties, such as Lancashire, where local magistrates sheltered their neighbours. The Elizabethan Poor Law fell short of its objectives, not because the laws were defective, but because many justices of the peace stubbornly resisted the advancing claims of the welfare state. Men did not mind how many statutes were passed, it was

[1] T. F. Tout, Chapters . . ., iv, 43.

said, so long as they were not enforced. What was true of agriculture, religion, and the Poor Law was true of the feudal revenues.

Our whole story so far has shown that the government's systematic efforts to secure its dues were almost as systematically sabotaged by the gentry and their friends. The escheator was clearly unequal to the task; and the crown, still determined not to abandon its claims, judged him at his worth. It is not in the nature of English administration to destroy a traditional institution and replace it by untried methods. It tends to cling to the old while introducing the new and, for a long time, they may keep each other's uneasy company. So the sixteenth century saw the continuing decline of the escheator as the crown turned increasingly to its permanent official, the feodary. But throughout our period, amateur and professional were joined in the feudal task.

Yet, if the sixteenth century saw the long twilight of the escheator before his sun finally set in the seventeenth, his office was still, under the Tudors, a significant one with its fees, perquisites and opportunities for unofficial rewards. In the holding of inquisitions he was the junior partner, but not without influence upon its proceedings. There was good statutory authority for arguing that the office was an annual one, and Fitzherbert, the contemporary expert on the subject, reveals that severe penalties followed if an escheator outstayed his term of office. No man may be *compelled* to hold office as escheator for more than one year, he goes on. Nor may he be *compelled* to resume office within three years of resignation. We have, however, a good deal of evidence to show that some men were eager for the job. The appointment in theory was made by the Lord Treasurer, on the advice of the justices of assize; in practice, during the second half of Elizabeth's reign, the real channel of appointment was Vincent Skinner, a teller of the Exchequer and a member of Burghley's secretariat. From Skinner the work passed, in the last decade of the sixteenth century, to the egregious Michael Hickes.[1]

---

[1] A. Fitzherbert, *The Office of Sheriffs* . . . etc. (*c.* 1535), sect. ev and fv; B.M. Lans. 77, f. 178r; 108, f. 127r.

William Lambarde, who knew more about local government
than any man alive, wrote in 1593 to Michael Hickes a recommendation on behalf of his servant, a Mr. Mitchell, for the
escheatorship of Kent and Middlesex. If Hickes would help, he
said, 'I will add it to the heap of your manifold favours towards
me, for all which I must be debtor, and leave payment till God
vouchsafe ability'. Lambarde rated highly his candidate's qualifi-
cations: 'touching his skill and sufficiency of living, I know the one
and the other to be answerable, the first by long education and
practice, and the latter by his marriage with a landed wife'. Sir
John Fortescue, Chancellor of the Exchequer, wrote in the same
year to Hickes about a Mr. Griffith Payne for the escheatorship of
Oxfordshire and Berkshire. He had already written to Burghley
on the subject but 'my letters ever since, as I am informed, have
remained with you'. So a broad hint was necessary, in the shape
of a postscript: 'in this doing I will think myself beholding unto
you and requite it where I may any ways'.[1]

A similar hint came from the Earl of Essex in 1596 in recommending his candidate. 'I would be loath to importune his Lordship in suits of this nature', he told Hickes, 'but if he shall be pleased
the rather for my sake to make choice of him for the said office, I
will take myself very much beholding unto his lordship. And for
yourself', he went on, 'what kindness you shall afford him for my
respect, I will be ready thankfully to acknowledge.' In like vein
George Carew wrote to Hickes, with a recommendation of his
kinsman, promising 'not to omit that which others do, in such
cases, according to the saying *hoc fac et illud non omittas*'. The
sensitive pen of Carew found it easier to offer a bribe in Latin than
in English! 'And I will promise you', Sergeant Glanville said on
behalf of his brother-in-law, 'he shall content you with your
kindness in such reasonable sort as I hope you shall be pleased.
What this bearer doth promise, I will see performed . . . what
pleasure you do him herein, I will to the uttermost deserve myself.'
What clearly emerges from this and other material at our disposal

[1] B.M. Lans. 75, ff. 134r, 138r.

is that, in some cases at least, the appointments were neither insignificant nor without reward.[1]

None the less, power was passing to the feodary. In important inquisitions, the escheator was not to sit without the feodary; and it was the latter's survey which was officially accepted as the value of the heir's estate. He, not the escheator, was the collector of the feudal profits gathered in the shires. 'His office', Coke tells us, 'consisteth principally in three things:

1. And principally to be skilful in the knowledge of the king's tenures within his office, out of records and authentical books.
2. At the finding of offices to do his uttermost endeavour to manifest the truth concerning the king's tenures.
3. After the office found, to survey the wards' lands, and rate it.'

The *office* was the inquisition, the first stage in the *post mortem* inquiry. The survey came later in the proceedings and frequently set a much higher value to the estate. Both fell far short of 'the truth concerning the king's tenures', as Coke conceived of it; but without the feodary the official return would have been a mockery of the facts. At this stage we need the reminder of only two examples. The value of some wardship lands of the Earl of Essex in 1576 was forced up by the feodary from £203. 11d. 4d. a year (given at the inquisition) to £381. 7s., a rise of nearly 90 per cent. The lands of the late Thomas Leigh were, in 1598, valued by inquisition at £9. 6s. 8d. and, subsequently, by feodary's survey at £50.[2]

The feodaries were the indispensable agents of the Court of Wards; but their office was older than the Court and has a long and obscure history. During the fourteenth century, if not before, the bailiff of fees, or feodary, was already in his place in the great seigneurial estate, and was charged mainly with the collection of feudal incidents. In the Duchy of Lancaster his powers extended beyond these matters into general financial and legal spheres; and in some duties he is scarcely distinguishable from the medieval

---

[1] B.M. Lans. 82, f. 42r; 77, ff. 168r, 164r.
[2] Coke, *Fourth Inst.*, c. 35; B.M. Lans. 25, f. 113r.

steward. Late in the fifteenth century, when Edward IV set about forcing up the feudal income from his Lancastrian estates—one more hint of the Tudor shape of things to come—he turned to his feodaries, sadly wanting though he knew them to be. It is worth recording also that, in the searching out of these ancient—and conveniently forgotten—tenures, Richard Empson, as feodary, exercised his prentice hand. One day, under Henry VII, he would employ these skills in the king's service, throughout the whole realm.[1]

The Duchy of Lancaster employed different feodaries from those used by the Court of Wards. The only exception, in the Elizabethan period, was Sir Walter Cope, feodary of Oxfordshire for both the Court and the Duchy. But he was an exceptional man; and he ended up by becoming Master of the Court of Wards. We owe to him, also, the skilful defence of the policy of one of his predecessors, Sir Robert Cecil. Nor were feodaries to be found only in the Duchy and in the Court of Wards. The term became increasingly used in the fifteenth and sixteenth centuries and may be taken as a sign of the extending reach of fiscal feudalism: thus we find the office of feodary of the Earldom of Devon granted in 1511 to Thomas Greve, yeoman porter of the gate. But the employment of the term leads also to confusion. Sometimes the title was held by one highly placed person but clearly exercised by another; for example, the queen's jointure in Henry VII's reign included the offices of feodary in Essex, Suffolk and Norfolk. The same applied to the feodaryship of Norfolk, held by Princess Mary in the reign of Edward VI; while during her own reign we find Richard, Lord Rich granted the office of chief seneschal of the feodary of the honor of Raleigh for life, but what precisely that involved it is hard to discover.[2]

The beginnings of the wardship feodary, as such, may probably be seen in 1513 with the grant of the office, usually for two counties, '. . . with authority in the king's name to take the persons

---

[1] N. Denholm-Young, *Seignorial Administration in England* (1937), pp. 33-4; R. Somerville, *History of the Duchy of Lancaster* (1953), i, 98, 112, 243-4.

[2] *Ibid.*, p. 627; *Collectanea Curiosa*, ed. J. Gutch (1781), i, 119-33; *L.P.*, i, pt. 1, g. 749 (37); 11 Hen. VII, c. 32; *C.P.R.*, Ed. VI, ii, 22; *C.S.P.D.*, Addenda, 1547-65, p. 447.

of heirs under age, and deliver them to Sir Thomas Lovell, Treasurer of the King's Household'. From now on we have a continuous series of feodaries, with each one usually made responsible for two counties. But later in the reign we see the practice growing of limiting them to a single county, one more sign of an increasing volume of work. By the reign of Elizabeth the practice of putting more than one county under a feodary had been abandoned, with the exception of Rutland and Northamptonshire which, for this purpose, remained combined. In many cases also feodaries were employing deputies.[1]

Usually the feodaries were men of modest social status and means, who acted as the maids-of-all-work for the Court of Wards in each county. They inaugurated the proceedings at the inquisition, followed it up with the survey, collected whatever fees were payable at each stage, kept full accounts, and a watchful eye upon the wards' lands leased out, and, in between, scoured the shire for concealed wardships. These were routine matters but they must have consumed a great deal of time. As the Court of Wards agent, the feodary might expect any kind of query to come his way. For example, Avery Mitchell, feodary of Sussex under Edward VI, was told that the lands of Lord Dacre, a ward, had been assessed at a hundred marks by the commissioners of sewers. The feodary was instructed by the Master to check the assessment, and, if it were correct, to pay the sum due. The variety of the work, and the scope it gave to play a not insignificant part in the life of the county, meant that it could attract an ambitious, hard-working man who did not mind the strain and the unpopularity of his task.[2]

Such a man was Michael Hickes, secretary to Burghley, friend —for a time—of Robert Cecil, and brother of the more famous Baptist Hickes, the first Lord Camden. Michael Hickes we have already met, as one well versed in the marginal, and corrupt, practices of the Court of Wards; but he was also feodary of Essex for three years at the end of Elizabeth's reign. His surviving accounts show him immersed in the full routine of a county

[1] *L.P.*, i, pt. 2, g. 2222 (12).
[2] *C.S.P.D. Addenda*, 1547–65, p. 422.

representative of the Court of Wards. In his first year he collected
£289 as rent from wards' lands, let out on lease during the
minority; but he gave out in exhibitions for ten wards the sum
of £45. Of the remainder he paid £208 to the Receiver-General,
retained £33 as cash in hand, officially described as 'arrears', and
claimed forty-one shillings for himself as carriage allowance, that
is to say, £1 for every £100 he brought to London. He was also
entitled to £9 a year, as salary. What he claimed from the tenants
in chief, or the heirs, in Essex—apart from the official charges—
we do not know; but he was a man to ride his authority for all
that it was worth. A year later the revenue from land had climbed
sharply to £491, and we notice that he is paying exhibition money
to three more wards than in the previous year. A new Master,
Robert Cecil, at the centre, and a new feodary in the county,
were beginning to ascertain how far they could go.[1]

Hickes, like Cope, was exceptional. So was Walter Tooke,
feodary of Hertfordshire, who was promoted to be Auditor of
the Court of Wards, but in this he succeeded the long reign of his
father. Ralph Bosseville, feodary of Surrey, became Clerk of the
Court of Wards. Fulke Greville, feodary of Warwickshire and
Gloucestershire under Henry VIII, was the father of the Elizabethan statesman and poet of that name. John Budden, feodary of
Dorset under Elizabeth, was father of his more famous namesake,
Professor of Civil Law at Oxford, a distinguished translator and an
eloquent philosopher and lawyer. But the majority did not carry
such famous names. They tended to belong to the lesser gentry.
Sometimes they were lawyers, like George Raymond, described in
a Star Chamber bill of James I's reign as gentleman, attorney, clerk
of the peace and feodary of Gloucestershire. (Clearly, the latter
office did not preclude the holding of other appointments.) Edward
Drew, feodary of Devonshire, was a serjeant-at-law and recorder,
successively, of Exeter and London. He was also, like at least
fifteen other feodaries in Elizabeth's reign, a Member of Parliament. Sometimes they prospered and extended their estates, as
was to be expected of men who knew their county better than

[1] B.M. Lans. 86, f. 160r–162r; 87, ff. 124r–126v and 128v.

most men. Often some of the royal profits for wardship stuck to their fingers. And sometimes they fell into debt. What is quite clear is that the office of feodary was eagerly sought after, and well worth the seeking.[1]

Perhaps Richard Hurlestone, feodary of Cheshire, who wrote an autobiographical letter in his own defence to Burghley in 1584, provides some notion of the class of men drawn to the work. He was, he told the Master, 'servant first to Sir Thomas Seymour (he who afterwards was Lord Admiral of England), serving him in the place of a gentleman during his life; and accounted one of the best sort of his gentleman'. After Seymour's execution, Hurlestone passed to Sir William Herbert, later Earl of Pembroke, 'with whom, during King Edward's time, he gave often attendance, and was often used in matters of importance; and associated with the best sort of his servants'. So he was, he modestly remarks, 'without his desire or thinking of it, made a justice of peace in his country; in which place he continued'. In short, Hurlestone, under his patron, was a rising man in the county.

He was also a puritan; and, when Elizabeth ascended the throne, he considered it his task 'to repair Abraham's wells, that were digged in King Edward's time, and stopped up in Queen Mary's'. So, as a J.P., and with the help of some of the country gentlemen of Cheshire, he raised funds to bring pious preachers into the county. 'By their diligent travail the said power [of Rome] in that place declined.' So he continued in his godly and patriotic duties, without neglecting his professional career, for he was appointed by Burghley to the feodaryship of Cheshire. Unfortunately, his high moral outlook did not extend to financial probity, with the result that he was dismissed from office and charged in the Star Chamber with corruption. Hence this letter. Hurlestone flatly denied the charge. He had made no undue profits from the feodaryship. The exercise of his office 'was a yearly charge unto him, and never any way profitable':—a familiar refrain amongst the great and small in the land. As 'for deceiving the queen, he answered, that to his knowledge he never, by colour of that office,

[1] P.R.O. MS. Index, Star Chamber Proceedings, ii, B.C., p. 81.

did willingly deceive her of the value of one penny'. But his defence has a lame ending. 'It might be, that ignorantly, and by negligence, he might commit something which in duty he ought to have answered more certainly; but that he was never thereof any way accused.' He was, as we have seen, not the only feodary who 'ignorantly and by negligence' committed 'something which in duty he ought to have answered more certainly'.[1]

In the reign of Elizabeth there were seven principal officials at the centre and forty-five feodaries in the shires. But these were simply the named officials for whom provision had been made in the founding statutes. Many of them could not have operated without their deputies and clerks, while Burghley himself carried on his back an army of administrative assistants. Only intermittently do we see these people at work and, more often, in unofficial rather than formal records. But someone had to pay them for the work they did. Were they paid by their seniors: surveyor, auditor, attorney or feodary? Sometimes they were. But clearly that was not enough: for the official salaries in this, as in every other field of Tudor administration, were scant payment for hard and intelligent work by so able a group of men. We may take as an example a salary list of fees and expenses (diet) for the second half of Elizabeth's reign:

Master of the Wards, Sir William Cecil, Kt., Baron of Burghley, Lord High Treasurer	Fee 200 marks. Diet £100. Hire of a horse for him and recorder ... £242. 6s.
Receiver-General	Fee 100 marks. Diet £50. Allowance £6. 13s. 4d.
Attorney	Fee £40, Diet £50
Surveyor	Fee £100.
Auditor	Fee £26. 13s. 4d. Diet £50. 10s. Increase of fee in consideration of livery £20. Other allowances and ordinary expenses £49. 10s. 8d.

[1] J. Strype, *Annals* (1824), iii, pt. 1, pp. 396-9.

Clerk of the Wards	Fee £10. Diet £6. 13s. 4d. Allowances 66s. 4d.
Clerk of the Liveries	No fee or allowance of the Queen.
Messenger	Fee £6. 1s. 8d. Livery 20s. Riding costs by discretion of the court.
Usher	Fee 100s. Livery 20s.
Feodaries in number 45	Fee to every of them £9. Porterage to every of them 20s. upon every £100 delivered to the cofferers: esteemed at £200. Allowance for charges among them: esteemed at £50.
Sum total of all fees and allowances to the officers of the Court of Wards and Liveries	£937. 2s. 4d.

The total unfortunately does not tally with the individual items; and, in various copies of this manuscript, whatever the particular salaries, the summation is given as £937. 2s. 4d. Custom had hardened the original total into a fixed amount; but the office holders had somehow managed to move their salaries upward in the wake of inflation. We shall not be very far from the mark if we raise the scribe's total to about £1,400.[1]

Did the queen maintain her whole wardship establishment for so relatively small a sum? Did some of the most experienced men in England undertake a very difficult assignment for about £200 a year, or less? Manifestly not. We have already seen, in an earlier chapter, that the administrative processes in claiming a wardship or suing livery put fees in the pockets of a whole regiment of officials. These undoubtedly augmented the salary paid by the queen. Yet it is hardly likely that these two sources of income, taken together, could have attracted to the service of wardship so much energy and skill, or stimulated the fierce competition for a

[1] B.M. Harl. 2078, f. 13v. Other copies are to be found in Sloan 1520, Harl. 240 and Add. MS. 12508.

place in the feudal sun. There was a third source of income for these men; and it was the most important. Beneath the whole system of wardship lay a wonderful network of patronage, which was of immense importance in the finance and politics of the time. And at the centre of the network was the Master of the Wards himself.

12

Lord Burghley as Guardian

THE post of Master of the Court of Wards was one which, throughout its history, attracted to its service the greatest men in England. It was often combined with, or led to, the Lord Treasurership and it tended to go to a privy councillor who enjoyed the special confidence of the monarch, for the Master played a dual part in the life and government of Elizabethan society. In the intimate business of appointing a guardian, his decisions, given out on the queen's behalf, would be taken as a measure of Tudor paternalism and show to the world how seriously the queen took her duties towards the orphans whom the accidents of land tenure had confided to her care. A failure on the Master's part to fulfil his obligations would confirm the judgement of the critics that the Court of Wards was a squalid organ for profiting from the misfortunes of the helpless.

But the Mastership was also an office of power, which bestowed upon its holder immense reserves of patronage—and therefore political influence—throughout the realm. It was also an office of profit, potentially vast profit, to a Master who knew how to exploit the opportunities at his disposal. It was no wonder that men like the Marquess of Winchester, Lord Burghley and Sir Robert Cecil were glad to accept the appointment; that the Earl of Essex in 1599, in the bitter hour of his failure to obtain it, burnt his boats and blundered into the Irish adventure which destroyed him.

Before we consider Burghley as a guardian we must say a word about his predecessors. The origins of the Mastership are to be found in the early years of the sixteenth century, when he was described as 'our principal, immediate officer charged with the supervision, government and sale' of all wardships which are, or shall be or ought to be, in the royal custody. That was in 1503 and the post went to John Hussey, an administrator of great ability who gave the crown several decades of service until, playing an ambiguous role in the Pilgrimage of Grace of 1536, he ended his days on the block for treason. But all that lay in the distant future and, when he gave up his control of wardships in either 1511 or soon after to Sir Robert Southwell and Bartholomew Westby, Hussey had many years of service ahead of him. Parallel with this development we find, in 1508, Sir Edward Bellknap appointed Surveyor of the King's Prerogative, whose functions included the grants of marriage licences to widows of tenants in chief: an aspect of feudalism which was to be joined later to royal wardship. For some time, however, the business of wardship was run on a makeshift basis, although Hussey began to be known as Master of the Wards from about 1510. In 1513, under Southwell and Westby, the process of turning personal supervision into administrative control was carried a stage farther when the Masters were granted the Prince's Council Chamber in the palace of Westminster in which to do their work, and a clerk at a salary of £10 a year. It is from this date that we may speak of an 'Office of Wards' which was to mature, a generation later, into a full Court of Wards.[1]

But, for the present, the Masters of the Wards still carried other responsibilities in their office: for example, the control of attainted lands. It is not until 1518 that we find the new, and more specialised, appointment of Sir Thomas Lovell and Richard Weston 'to be masters and chief officers for surveying, custody and selling of the king's wards and their possessions', for which they were each to get a salary of £100 a year. Lovell was Treasurer of the Household, key office in royal finance, and his appointment to the joint Mastership is a sign of the importance that Henry VIII attached to the post. But he was an old man and the burden of his

---

[1] Pat. Roll 19 Hen VII, pt. 1, m.8 (33); *L.P.*, i, 217, 563–4; *C.P.R.*, Hen. VII, ii, 591; W. C. Richardson, *op. cit.*, pp. 169–75.

other responsibilities was very heavy. He accordingly gave up the wards to the experienced Sir Edward Bellknap, administrator and financier, who had already served Henry VII in the related work of the King's Prerogative. But in a little over three months Bellknap was dead, and had bequeathed to his heirs a sordid dispute with the surveyors of crown lands as to the payments due to him.[1]

Weston remained sole Master although he could hardly have found his work as profitable as did some of his successors: he offered in 1525 to throw the post up in return for the Stewardship of the Duchy of Lancaster, an inconceivable proposal in the days of the Cecils. In 1526 he was abroad, so in May of that year Sir Thomas Englefield was brought in, to be joined in the following November by Sir William Paulet. Although this was officially a condominium, it may be that Paulet, in fact, was the dominant partner. He was the financier, Englefield was the lawyer; and in 1534 Englefield went off to concentrate upon his work as a judge. Before that, in 1531, Paulet alone had been appointed Surveyor-General of wards' lands and of the king's widows, and governor of all idiots and natural fools: an office not hitherto held by a Master of Wards but by a separate official, the Surveyor and Receiver-General. In short, we are witnessing a concentration of power as an outstanding minister takes over the reins. The post of Master was never again to be shared; and with the re-appointment of Paulet in 1540, when the Court of Wards was erected, the groundwork had been laid for turning the Mastership into one of the most influential offices of Tudor England.[2]

Now, at last, we see a front-rank administrator directing his mind to the prospects of fiscal feudalism; and one would give a good deal to know about the impact of his views upon Thomas Cromwell while the latter was doing his fundamental work on the structure of Tudor government. His tenure of the Mastership of the Wards lasted twenty-eight years, second in length only to

---

[1] *L.P.*, ii, pt. 2, p. 1217; iii, pt. 1, g. 1121 (10), p. 453.
[2] *Ibid.*, iv, pt. 1, p. 738, g. 2218 (22), pt. 2, g. 2673 (3); vii., g. 1601 (29); v, g. 80 (11); xv, g. 942 (112).

that of Burghley; and, when he resigned in 1554, it was not a retirement but a sign that having finally reached the top of the financial tree four years earlier, as Lord Treasurer of England, he felt the need for more time and energy to carry through a considerable programme of financial reform. Paulet became a rich man and died, at a ripe old age, as Marquess of Winchester, and with a reputation for knowing exactly how to bend before a veering political wind. He had been born in the year of Bosworth, which brought the first Tudor to the throne, and died in 1572 when the last of them was secure in its possession. It is too early to assess him as an administrator; but it may be, when the evidence is forthcoming, that his will not appear as an original or creative mind, but part of the conservative tradition of which Burghley was the outstanding exponent. From what we know of him, Paulet appears as the archetype of the 'safe' man of English politics.

Sir Francis Englefield, who succeeded him in 1554, lacked the stature and fame of Paulet; and contrasted with him also as a man. There was nothing of the trimmer in Englefield. A Catholic zealot and a close counsellor of Mary—which may also account for Paulet's giving up the Mastership to him early in her reign— Englefield held office for too short a time to leave his mark upon it. His religious views were well known and, soon after the accession of Elizabeth, he was summoned before the Privy Council and ordered to hand over the seal of his office, although he was to continue to enjoy 'the fees, commodities and advantages to his said office belonging'. Englefield obeyed, but with a strong protest which he asked to have entered upon the Council records. The Privy Council found it hard to see the basis of Englefield's objection, and so does the modern historian. For Englefield's patent of appointment lapsed with the death of the monarch, Queen Mary, as was the case with all other crown offices. The same thing had happened to his predecessor under Edward VI. The new queen was free either to renew his appointment or to replace him. The lords of the Council agreed to register his opposition but reminded him that, 'in like cases, always betwixt the prince and the subject, where the cause had any manner doubt, the

Sir William Paulet, Marquess of Winchester
Master of the Wards, 1526-1554

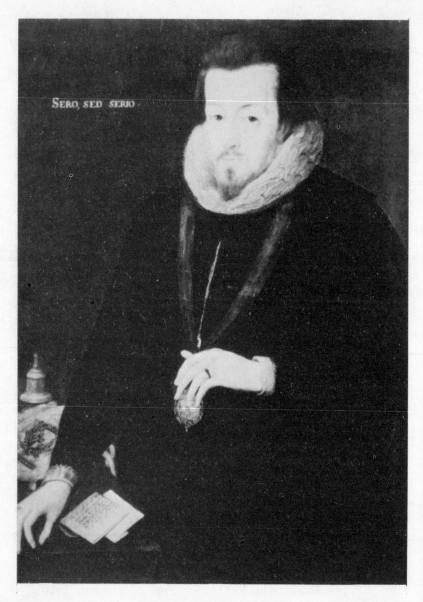

SERO, SED SERIO

Robert Cecil, Earl of Salisbury
Master of the Wards, 1599-1612

prince's cause was preferred—as meet was'. And, they added, 'in this appeared no manner of doubt'. A month later, in January 1559, he was ordered to hand over all his official books and records. In April he left England, under licence, to take the waters abroad for two years; and with him went eight servants, eight horses, six hundred ounces of plate, a hundred marks in money and other necessities. The only condition imposed was that he should not join the queen's enemies and should come back when called upon.[1]

There was no place for Englefield in the changing order; and perhaps the queen guessed that he would never return. He did indeed join the queen's enemies and his voluntary exile in Spain lasted for nearly forty years, until his death. Meanwhile he had been attainted of treason and his property declared forfeit to the crown; but the shrewd man had so conveyed his lands that it required a special act of Parliament, more than thirty years after his departure, to bring his possessions within the grasp of the queen. His personal views on wardship we do not know; but it is not unreasonable to assume that the plan for the abolition of feudal wardship, attributed to Cardinal Allen and Count Olivares, which was to be brought to England by a victorious Spanish Armada in 1588, shows something of the draftsmanship of the aged exile in Spain, sometime Master of the Court of Wards. If that is so, then he is the second official of the Marian Court of Wards—Sir Nicholas Bacon was the other—who in retrospect felt bound to condemn the institution they had once served.[2]

If Mary turned to her confidential adviser for a Master of Wards, Elizabeth did the same thing, after the dismissal of Englefield. She chose Sir Thomas Parry, the Controller of her Household, who entered upon his work early in 1559. There are in fact two patents under the Great Seal making the appointment, one dated 12 January 1559 and the other 26 April. It is clear that the former patent was issued prematurely, when the government had not fully overcome Englefield's resistance, for his patent could not, in fact, be cancelled until 12 April. Then the second patent

[1] C.P.R. Mary, i, 249; Acts of P.C., 1558–70, pp. 29–30, 47; C.P.R. Eliz., i, 54.
[2] 35 Eliz. c. 5.

had to be issued to regularise the position. Certainly, from the point of view of the Court of Wards, it was the later date which mattered, for the salary did not become payable until 25 March. From either date, the new Master's appointment was tragically brief. Before the end of 1560 he was dead, with his heir a ward of the queen.[1]

Parry died on 15 December 1560; and once again the queen turned to a minister in whom she had already confided her trust. William Cecil, later Lord Burghley, was a man whose period of public service was unequalled in English history until the careers of Gladstone in the nineteenth century and of Winston Churchill in the twentieth. When Elizabeth summoned him to the Mastership, on 10 January 1561, he already held the office of Secretary of State, which he would give up ten years later to become Lord Treasurer; but the Mastership he yielded up only with his death in 1598; and by then he had been in charge of the wards for thirty-seven years. The Court of Wards remained in existence, in spite of an increasing volume of criticism, until the Civil War, when it was formally abolished by the Long Parliament in 1646. Thus, for more than a third of its life of one hundred and six years Burghley was its Master; and since, after an interregnum of nine months, he was succeeded by his son, Robert, the Cecil family in effect controlled its destinies for more than half a century. *Regnum Cecilianum!*—the hand of the Cecils indeed lies heavily upon the history of the Court of Wards as well as upon the history of the epoch.[2]

If Burghley would have to face many emergencies, few would be graver than that which inaugurated his Mastership. In 1561, the currency crisis was entering its most crucial stage. The war with Scotland had just ended but, at any moment, the country might be involved in a life-and-death struggle with France, Spain or, if the nightmare should materialise, Catholic Europe as a whole. Money for arms, for men, for allies would be needed in growing volume. What help could Burghley bring in the gathering crisis of his age?

[1] *C.P.R.*, Eliz., i, 60, 102; Wards 9.59, ff. 174v–175v.
[2] *C.P.R.*, Eliz., ii, 44–5.

He had just been appointed Master of Wards; but it was not a hand inexperienced in wardships which took over the controls. As long ago as 1549, when he was secretary to the Protector Somerset, he was approached to use his good offices in obtaining a wardship. In 1552, when Secretary of State, he proved himself a skilful suitor for a wardship on his own behalf, for in the summer of that year Arthur Hall of Grantham became a ward of the crown. Burghley at once staked a claim, in competition with a certain Mr. Sharington. The latter had the powerful backing of the Earl of Pembroke, who made a strong plea on behalf of his candidate especially as 'at the request of my very friend Mr. Sharington, I was a mean to my Lord Treasurer [Paulet, who was also Master of the Wards] for the same in Hall his lifetime, whose grant and promise thereof I had'. Hence, Pembroke suggested that Burghley should withdraw his claim, or, if it was already granted, should let Sharington obtain the wardship from him. Pembroke promised to make good the loss. But already Burghley's influence was considerable. It was not he but Pembroke who withdrew. Once it had been made clear to Pembroke, through William Thomas, Clerk of the Council, that Burghley was set upon having the wardship for himself—or for his sister, as was said on this occasion—Pembroke hastened to say that had he known the full story 'he would for nothing have troubled you with so unfriendly a request'. Mr. Sharington was not the only competitor in the market. Hall's own father, after long service to the crown, had transmitted to Edward VI, through the Privy Council, the request that in the event of his death 'it may please His Highness to give the wardship, marriage and relief of my said son to my wife'. The widow was believed to be heartbroken at the thought of losing husband and son in rapid succession; but against that, too, Burghley proved adamant.[1]

But his troubles were not yet over. In October the *inquisition post mortem* was held at Grantham, to which came Edmund Hall, a relative of the ward, claiming that some of the land was on lease to him. If that were proved, then the wardship of the lands would

[1] *C.S.P.D.*, 1547–80, pp. 19, 43 (*S.P.*, Ed. VI, xiv, ff. 131r, 135r); H. G. Wright, *The Life and Works of Arthur Hall of Grantham* (1919), pp. 24–30.

lose some of its value; so, under instruction from Burghley, George Williams (his agent) proceeded to resist this interpretation in the draft he prepared for the inquisition. There followed a wearing dispute by counsel in front of the jury, and the meeting dragged on late into the evening. The jury asked for an adjournment to another day, but, wrote Burghley's agent, 'Mr. Escheator showing himself to be your assured friend would not grant to that'—if the Earl of Pembroke had given in, how could a mere country jury offer resistance, functioning as it did on Burghley's native heath? So 'with his persuasion they [the jury] returned to counsel again and, debating the matter a great time, gave up their verdict'. It was total victory: their report agreed 'in every point as we put it in'. But, added Williams, writing on 12 October, the full return of the inquisition, written on parchment, might not reach London until Christmas: would that suit Burghley? We do not possess Burghley's answer, but it is easy to guess it from William's next letter, of 23 October. He states that, on receipt of Burghley's reply, he wrote immediately to the escheator for a speedy return, which should already have reached London. So Burghley got his first wardship, at the bargain price of £20, and took Arthur Hall into his household. Hall grew up to be a man of letters, a parliamentarian and a pamphleteer: energetic, cantankerous, quarrelsome and a bore, one of the most unpopular men in the House of Commons.[1]

The formal record of the sale of Hall's wardship to Burghley is to be found amongst the official documents of the Court of Wards, and it is to these records that we first turn for further evidence of such grants. If he tried so zealously, when he was not Master, for a wardship, how much better placed was he nine years later, holding the senior office in the Court of Wards, to gain direct access to its bounty, subject only to the over-riding authority of the queen? It would indeed hardly have been surprising if Burghley had felt that, in seeking to appoint good guardians, he need not look beyond Cecil House in the Strand. Yet from two

[1] *C.S.P.D.*, 1547–80, pp. 45–6 (*S.P.*, Ed. VI, xv, ff. 43r–46r, 68r); J. E. Neale, *Elizabeth I and her Parliaments, 1559–81* (1953), *passim*.

different sources we have evidence which appears to demonstrate that Burghley refused to take advantage of the rare opportunity now at hand. The first is the work of an unknown contemporary biographer, who was a member of Burghley's household, knew him well in his later years and wrote a vigorous defence of the statesman shortly after his death. Burghley would grant away up to eighty wardships in one year but, the author asserts, 'in all the time he was Master of the Wards, he reserved to his own use but three'. One might be tempted to dilute, or entirely reject, the eulogy of a servant for his late employer, were it not that a careful search of the official records confirms the modest demands which the biographer attributes to the Master. One of his wards we have already met—Arthur Hall—but Burghley received this wardship before he became Master. Another, that of Thomas Strickland, he purchased in 1570 for £220. Of no other wardship grant to Burghley has it been possible to discover a single trace. Here, for once, official and unofficial records appear to tell the same story.[1]

But not the whole story. If we turn away from the neat and careful entries of the Clerk of the Wards and call in some of the unofficial and informal materials of family papers, Burghley's role in the business of wardship changes profoundly. It is from these sources that we can build up a significant list of wards to whom he stood guardian. It will include Lord Wharton, the seventeenth Earl of Oxford, Philip Howard, Earl of Surrey, the third and the fifth Earls of Rutland, the Earl of Essex, and the Earl of Southampton. To these we may add Lord Zouche, purchased in the name of Thomas Cecil, the elder son of Burghley, but brought up in Burghley's household. In all, he gained the wardships of eight noblemen, an unique achievement in Tudor England. But it is still significant that, in his thirty-seven years as Master, he took for himself only nine wards. In short, Burghley was interested in quality—not quantity.[2]

[1] Wards 9.369, f. 171v; *Desiderata Curiosa*, ed. Peck (1732), i, 27; Wards 9.373, Receipts for wards, 12 Eliz. and Wards 9.380, ff. 33v, 106r (Strickland).

[2] *Acts of P.C.*, 1571-5, pp. 282-3 (Wharton); *D.N.B. sub.* Vere, 17th Earl of Oxford, Manners, Earls of Rutland, Devereux, Earls of Essex; Wriothesley, Earls of Southampton; *S.P.D.*, Eliz., xci, no. 22 (Howard); Wards 9.273, 12 Eliz. (Zouche).

Two questions at once rise to the mind: how did he obtain them, and how did he use them? In attempting to answer these questions, however, one must consider the peculiar relationship that existed between Burghley and the queen. He was her principal minister, her most trusted confidant and in continuous service of the queen for forty years. As Master of the Wards he worked in an especially intimate association with her. So it came about that, when a great wardship was at issue, the formal processes of a grant need not arise. The wards were the queen's wards and the Master was her personal representative as guardian if the wardship were not sold. No payment for the wardships was called for; no letters patent were issued. An exhaustive search through the surviving records of the Court of Wards has yielded not the slightest evidence of either payment or patent, in the name of Burghley, for the wards.

What we have is evidence of payment by some of these noble wards for their *own* marriages, for example by the Earls of Rutland and of Oxford, shortly before they came of age. In effect their wardships remained unsold, and almost throughout the whole period of their minority Burghley was therefore their guardian. The wardship of the fifth Earl of Rutland was indeed promised to the Earl of Leicester. Leicester died, the project fell through, and we find Burghley acting as guardian. The wardship of the third Earl of Bedford was granted to Leicester and his brother the Earl of Warwick. Both were dead before Bedford came of age; but what happened to the wardship we cannot trace. Warwick, who outlived his brother, made no mention of it in his will. It may be that, in the case of Bedford also, Burghley was guardian. In 1591, shortly after the death of Warwick, a match was under consideration between Bedford and Lady de Vere, Burghley's granddaughter; but nothing came of it. In the absence of fuller evidence, however, it is safer to omit Bedford from the noble retinue to whom Burghley stood guardian.[1]

Although he was Master of the Wards, he would never have

1 Wards 9.159, f. 43v; 380, f. 28v; 118, f. 234v–235v; H.M.C. *Rutland*, i, 260 and *passim*; C.S.P.D., 1581–90, pp. 259, 264, 271; Addenda, 1580–1625, pp. 152–3.

dared retain such important wardships without authority of the queen, probably given by word of mouth. As such, they were substantial gifts and afford us another insight into the Tudor system of payment of royal servants. Each of them could have been sold for a sum running into several thousand pounds. That was their potential value. But what did Burghley gain from them? We have already met the allegation that Burghley had offered one of his grandchildren as a wife to the Earl of Southampton, his ward, that the Earl had declined the match, and that the affront to Burghley had cost Southampton £5,000. There are only two things to be said about this story. The first is that it comes from an untrustworthy source and is confirmed by no other record. The second is that it is the only story in circulation alleging that Burghley tried to extract money from any of his wards.[1]

If we reject the notion that Burghley's interest in his noble wards was primarily for financial gain, what other explanation of his policy can we offer? The answer is to be found, in part, in an interesting quirk in Burghley's character: his yearning somehow to identify himself and his family with the aristocratic estate into which he was climbing. For Burghley, it must be admitted, was a snob, although the word so inadequately conveys that amalgam of emotions and ambitions, more widely diffused than any other amongst civilised mankind. He failed, it is true, to erect an authentic aristocratic past for himself, but there can be no doubt about the nobility of his descendants. Elizabeth conferred upon him the barony of Burghley in 1571. His two surviving sons became earls under James I. An incomplete list of his living descendants, drawn up in the year 1904, covers sixteen folio pages and is a prodigious display of every rank and honour; for he is the father of the English aristocracy.[2] And by the match between his granddaughter Elizabeth de Vere and the Earl of Derby, descended from Henry VII's daughter, Mary, the Cecils joined with the Tudors; a friendship, made before Bosworth, was now confirmed in

[1] *Records of the English Province of the Society of Jesus*, ed. H. Foley (1878), iv. 49.
[2] *William Cecil, Lord Burghley* (Historical Monograph ser., ed. F. P. Barnard, 1904), pp. 126–42.

marriage. So in two generations the Cecils climbed from border yeomanry to aristocracy, in the person of Burghley; and in two more generations his blood would be joined with the blood royal. Tudor society was fluid indeed.

This aristocratic progeny derives in part from the marriage between Burghley's daughter, Anne and Edward Vere, seventeenth Earl of Oxford; and Oxford was Burghley's ward. Was this what Burghley hoped for from his wards: marriages for his children into the established nobility of Elizabethan England? Sir Thomas Cecil, Burghley's son, once received from his father the suggestion that he should purchase the wardship of Lord Sheffield, with a view to marrying him to his daughter. In reply Thomas Cecil, ever in debt, reminded his father of his penury and deeply regretted that he could not take up the offer at the stated price—£2,000. 'And yet I must confess', he added, 'the house being noble . . . I would be loath to overship a match that might be hereafter a strengthening of your posterity.' This may be the clue to Burghley's policy in retaining the wardship of men like the Earl of Oxford. But Burghley himself denied it, and claimed indeed that the proposed marriage to Oxford came as a complete surprise to him: 'I could not well imagine what to think, considering I never meant to seek it nor hoped of it.' He had thought of other eligible young men, including Philip Sidney, but not of Oxford. He did not, of course, attempt to hide his gratification. 'Now that the matter is determined betwixt my Lord of Oxford and me', he told Lord Rutland, 'I confess to your Lordship I do honour him as much as I can any subject, and I love him so dearly from my heart as I do mine own son; and in any case that may touch him for his honour and weal, I shall think mine own interest therein.' It was probably strictly true that Burghley was not the author of the marriage but, with so distinguished a ward in his household, he provided at least the occasion. Perhaps an unkind correspondent of the Earl of Rutland came nearest to the mark: 'The Earl of Oxford hath gotten him a wife —or at the least a wife hath caught him!' The queen gave her consent, but the young ladies of her court felt no joy in the proceedings: 'there was great weeping, wailing and sorrowful cheer of those that hoped to have had that golden day'.[1]

It was an ill-starred match. Burghley, for once, allowed his uncanny ability for judging character to be blinded by social ambition. The Earl of Oxford was mercurial, eccentric, extravagant, and violent. He took an extreme dislike to both his wife and his father-in-law and remained a thorn in the flesh of the older man all his lifetime. Burghley had hoped that his son-in-law would mature into a worthy representative of the ancient aristocracy. Oxford had hoped for office and power far in excess of his deserts, or what Burghley as a responsible statesman could offer. Both were disappointed; but the fault lay in Oxford. Many years after he had come of age, he wrote to Burghley a bitter and insolent letter with a pointed reference to his former status. 'I mean not to be your ward nor your child. I serve Her Majesty and I am that I am!' But Burghley had the last word in this respect. Years before, the Earl had entered into obligations to purchase his marriage from the Court of Wards, a necessary procedure before he could be free to marry Anne Cecil. The full price of his marriage had never been paid and this, and other debts, had long hung over him in the Court of Wards. Then, early in 1589, shortly after the death of Anne, Burghley instituted proceedings against the earl for his debt, and some of his lands were seized and held for payment. Thus Burghley, in some small degree, struck back at his son-in-law for a whole series of humiliations inflicted upon the Cecil family.[2]

None of the other noble wards of Burghley married into his family; and in the case of the only two in which the question of marriage arose, Southampton and Oxford, it is at least doubtful whether he was the instigator. If, then, neither money nor marriage seems to have been his principal concern in these wardships, what other explanation is possible?

An answer, at least in part, may perhaps be found in the pattern of Elizabethan politics. For the main divisions, inside and outside

[1] H.M.C. *Salis.*, ii, 200; H.M.C. *Rutland*, i, 94–5.
[2] B.M. Lans. 42, f. 97r; Wards 9.118, f. 234v–235r.

Parliament, were not formulated on party lines, although the rise of Puritanism gave some indication of the future structure of political life. In the Elizabethan period, when men divided, they broke up into factions not parties. An eminent statesman was not the leader of a party committed to certain coherent principles, but the patron of a group of men who, if they looked to him for guidance, looked more often for reward. The sweets of office, in any age, are very delectable; and a man's survival as a leader would depend upon his capacity to rally behind him, and reward, both in Westminster and in the counties, the men who would supply him with the reserves of power in council and court. Ultimate power, of course, lay with the queen; and her political genius consisted in recognising these factions, balancing them and preventing any single one from becoming dominant.[1]

Within this system political leadership functioned, whether it was held by Thomas Cromwell or Norfolk, Somerset or Northumberland, Burghley or Leicester, Robert Cecil or Essex. They knew the rules of the game—as dangerous as it could be rewarding. But the system is inherent to a society in which party politics either do not exist or have been suppressed. In any age, with politics in abeyance, the contortions in policy are to be explained not in sudden changes of theory but in the rise and fall of faction. No man understood the terms of political trade better than did Burghley. Nor was he the kind of man who would seek to alter them. But he would try to operate the existing system thoroughly and in the national interest. Hence his interest in the rising young men of his age. The Southamptons, the Oxfords, and the Essexes, were not simply the *jeunesse dorée* of Elizabethan England. They might also be the statesmen of the new age. In taking them under his wing, and in giving them the best in contemporary education under his personal supervision, Burghley could reasonably hope, not simply to perpetuate his following, perhaps into the next generation, but to mould the principles of politics of the later reigns.

[1] The best brief account of the structure of politics in the late Elizabethan period will be found in J. E. Neale, *The Elizabethan Political Scene* (Brit. Acad. Raleigh Lecture, 1948), reprinted in *Elizabethan Essays* (1958).

There can be no doubt that, at Cecil House in the Strand, there existed the best school for statesmen in Elizabethan England, perhaps in all Europe. Sir Nicholas Bacon's proposal for a school for wards, which he sent to Burghley, came to nothing. Sir Humphrey Gilbert's proposal met with a like fate. The pragmatic mind of Burghley could no doubt see the difficulties in the way.

But the school for young men—not simply wards—which he set up in his own household surpassed anything that had gone before. Hence the competition for admission. The Duke of Norfolk, when preparing himself for the scaffold, bequeathed the upbringing of his sons to Burghley, his political enemy. The first Earl of Essex, when he lay dying in Ireland in 1576, asked—not for the first time—that his son should be brought up in Burghley's care. Lady Russell, his sister-in-law, asked him to admit her troublesome son, Edward Hoby, to his household, in the hope that he would there learn to mend his ways. The Countess of Lennox seems to have had exactly the same difficulties and therefore asked Burghley to take her son into his home, 'to be brought up and instructed as the wards be, so long time as shall be needful'. The Bishop of Ely asked the same thing on behalf of his own son.[1]

It was a highly selective school to which only very fortunate young men gained admission. 'Most of the principal gentlemen in England', his domestic biographer tells us, 'sought to prefer their sons and heirs to his service, in so much as I have numbered in his house, attending on the table, twenty gentlemen', each worth at least £1,000 a year in lands. Parents were well aware that entry into Cecil House meant not simply unique educational opportunities, but attractive prospects of advancement in later life. The quality of the education—cultural and political—was beyond dispute.[2]

On the purely academic side the education was intensive and, within the limits set by the age, conventional. Lord Oxford's day began before seven in the morning and, after exercise and dancing,

---

1 *State Papers*, ed. Murdin (1759), pp. 167, 301–2; see also *Original Letters*, ed. Ellis (2nd Ser.), iii, 31–3; B.M. Lans. 10, ff. 136r–137r; *S.P.D.*, Eliz., lxxxiii, no. 5; Lans. 25, f. 61r.
2 *Desiderata Curiosa*, ed. Peck, p. 32.

there was an interval of half an hour for breakfast, from seven-thirty until eight o'clock. There followed French, Latin, writing, drawing, common prayers, and dinner. The afternoon was devoted to cosmography, more Latin and French, then 'exercises with the pen', common prayers, and supper. Sunday was spent in prayer, reading the gospel, and 'riding, shooting, dancing, walking and other commendable exercises'. If Cecil House could attract the flower of English youth, it could also attract some of the best scholars of the day. Lawrence Nowell, Dean of Lichfield, was a tutor there; so was Robert Ramsden, Archdeacon of York and chaplain to Burghley; the scholar Sylvius Frisius likewise joined the staff. John Harte, the Chester Herald, one of the earliest spelling reformers and a pioneer of shorthand in this country, exercised a general supervision of the wards. Roger Ascham came and stayed with Cecil. But if the wards learned a good deal from their formal instructors, much more must have been learned about the art of politics from Burghley's guests, the greatest men in the land—and from Burghley himself, the scholar-statesman, whose high promise as an undergraduate at Cambridge, Ascham long remembered: 'In the fairest spring that ever was there of learning', he was 'one of the forwardest young plants in all that worthy College of St. John's.'[1]

Before passing from Burghley's work in this field we should perhaps let him express his own educational creed, which he included in his advice to his son, Robert Cecil:

Bring thy children up in learning and obedience, yet without outward austerity.

Praise them openly, reprehend them secretly.

Give them good countenance and convenient maintenance [a reasonable income] according to thy ability. Otherwise thy life will seem their bondage, and what portion thou shalt leave them at thy death, they will thank death for it and not thee.

And I am persuaded that the foolish cockering [pampering] of

[1] B. M. Ward, op. cit., p.20; H. M. C. Salis., xiv, 78; S.P.D., Eliz., Add., xix, nos. 29—42; B. Danielsson, John Harte's Works, pt. 1 (Stockholm, 1955); R. Ascham, The Scholemaster, ed. J. E. B. Mayor (1863), p.294.

some parents, and the over-stern carriage of others, causeth more men and women to take ill courses than their own vicious inclinations.

Marry thy daughters in time lest they marry themselves.

And suffer not thy sons to pass the Alps, for they shall learn nothing there but pride, blasphemy and atheism.

And if by travel they get a few broken languages, that shall profit them nothing more than to have one meat served in divers dishes. Neither, by my consent, shalt thou train them up in wars. For he that sets up his rest to live by that profession can hardly be an honest man or a good Christian. Besides it is a science no longer in request than use. For soldiers in peace are like chimneys in summer.[1]

And here is his advice for professional advancement:

Be sure to keep some great man thy friend, but trouble him not for trifles.

Compliment him often with many, yet small, gifts and of little charge. And if thou hast cause to bestow any great gratuity, let it be something which may be daily in sight.

Otherwise, in this ambitious age, thou shalt remain like a hop without a pole, live in obscurity and be made a football for every insulting companion to spurn at.

Towards thy superiors be humble yet generous; with thine equals familiar yet respective; towards thine inferiors show much humanity and some familiarity, as to bow the body, stretch forth the hand and uncover the head, with such like popular compliments. The first prepares thy way to advancement. The second makes thee known for a man well bred. The third gains a good report which, once got, is easily kept. For right humanity takes such deep root in the minds of the multitude, as they are easilier gained by unprofitable courtesies than by churlish benefits.

Yet I advise thee not to affect, or neglect, popularity too much. Seek not to be Essex: shun to be Raleigh.

It is the authentic voice of Polonius.[2]

Burghley's greatest pleasure lay in books and in scholarly intercourse with a few chosen friends. He had no love for sport: his sole exercise was ambling on his mule in his lovely gardens—but

[1] *Desiderata Curiosa*, ed. Peck, i, 64-5.
[2] *Ibid.*, p. 66.

still book in hand. When a high-spirited youth, like the fifth Earl of Rutland, came under his care, he would direct to his ward, even on his travels, a stream of good counsel. In response to a request from Rutland for leave to visit his mother in the country, Burghley agreed but added the wish—in other words, the command—'that both your tutor and some books might accompany you thither'. Amongst his other 'honourable pastimes' his learning should be maintained, for it would serve him 'in all ages, in all places and fortunes'. But it must be accompanied with a knowledge and fear of God: otherwise it was all vanity. 'My Lord,' Burghley concluded, 'take my writing to proceed of very Christian love that I bear you, and of a desire that I have to procure you to be an ornament hereafter to your country, when I shall be in my grave.' Here was a clear declaration of what the old statesman hoped to achieve through all the care that he lavished upon his wards. Burghley's next letter was succinct and very much to the point. 'I like very well if you do change your place and follow your tutor, where he shall be master, having before been in a place to be commander.' He agreed also that Rutland should join the Belvoir Hunt, famous still in our day, but again with an admonition that 'you will, when you are weary of hunting, recontinue some exercise of hunting in your book'.[1]

Crabbed age and youth. . . . Two generations separated the correspondents: the one, senior statesman, Chancellor of the University of Cambridge, the most experienced student of men and affairs; the other young, vigorous, impatient, 'magnificently unprepared' for the tortuous ways of Elizabethan life and politics. As we read the letters we can sense Burghley's feelings that, in this case, his task was hopeless.

Was his policy in general a success? The letters from the mothers of the wards, or the wards themselves, with the solitary exception of the Earl of Oxford, confirm the high estimate generally placed on his guardianship. The Earl of Arundel, Norfolk's son, expressed to Burghley his gratitude for 'your fatherly and careful proceeding in all my causes'. Though he suffered long for his religion,

[1] H.M.C. *Rutland*, i, 274–5, 283.

Arundel—so his Catholic biographer tells us—always esteemed
Burghley as his special friend. The Earl of Essex once received
a rebuke from Burghley for extravagance, but replied in the most
docile terms: 'My very good Lord, I hope your Lordship in
courtesy will pardon my youth if I have, through want of
experience, in some sort passed the bonds of frugality. I cannot
but embrace with duty your Lordship's good counsel, whose love
I have effectually proved and of whose care of my well doing I am
thoroughly well persuaded.' On another occasion, also, he wrote
to his guardian in sober and affectionate terms. The earl's mother
thanked Burghley for caring for her son, 'who may say he hath
happily met with a second father instead of a guardian'. Burghley
could be a stern master. But he won the respect, if not the love,
of his charges.[1]

Yet, when all is said, his policy was a failure. Of all his wards,
Lord Zouche had a modest success in his career as a diplomat and
administrator. The third Earl of Rutland showed the highest
promise of a legal career, but died before its fruition. With the
rest it was another story. Thomas Strickland and Lord Wharton
were of no political significance. Arthur Hall was a political mis-
fit. The Earl of Arundel turned Catholic and died in the Tower.
The Earl of Oxford left his mark as a patron of literature but
otherwise brought disaster upon his family and himself. The Earl
of Essex staked all in a clumsy bid for the highest political power,
paid for his failure with his life, and dragged with him, almost to
the block, the Earl of Southampton and the fifth Earl of Rutland,
two more *alumni* of Burghley's school for wards. This happened
three years after he was dead; yet the rebellion was, in effect, an
attack upon his system, *regnum Cecilianum*, the rule of the Cecils,
father and son. But it symbolised more than this. An older pattern
of government, which Burghley had conserved, and which he
had sought to instil in the minds of his political pupils, was passing
away.

1 *S.P.D.*, Eliz., xci, no. 22; *Life and Death of Earl of Arundel . . .*, ed. Duke of Norfolk
(1857), p. 150; *Original Letters*, ed. Ellis (2nd Ser.), iii, 77, 80; B.M. Lans. 24, f. 28r.

13

Lord Burghley as Master

IF Lord Burghley may be acquitted of any charge of misusing his position as guardian for personal gain, he must still face the more searching test of how he conducted himself as Master of the Court of Wards. His office carried with it, as we have seen, heavy responsibilities. He was the queen's principal adviser in determining to whom the wardship of the child and his lands should pass: in most cases, therefore, the decision rested with him. He also made the appointment to the key position of feodary. He had to keep a watchful eye over the welfare of all the wards and step in against an unsatisfactory guardian. At the same time he had to guide the financial policy of his department, augment its profits, and eliminate corruption in its officials. Finally he was its judge, vested with very considerable legal powers to settle, with the advice of his colleagues and judges from other courts, a great mass of lawsuits, some trivial, all complex, and many involving important issues of social welfare and the prestige of the crown itself.

It is not easy to see how such diverse—and conflicting—duties could be performed by one man. Could he, for example, raise the revenue of the crown without sacrificing the interests of the wards? For many of the wardships were ultimately resold, at a profit, to the mothers of the wards, to some other relative or to the wards themselves. If the initial price paid to the crown was high, the final price to the last purchaser should be higher still. In other words, must he impoverish the wards to enrich the Treasury?

How Burghley faced this dilemma we shall consider in the

course of these pages. There was, however, another way of increasing the revenue without having to increase the burden upon the individual ward. That was by raising the total number of wards known to the crown and therefore at its disposal for sale. Indeed, if that could be achieved, it might be possible to *reduce* the load which the individual ward had to bear. To increase the number of wards we know to have been the policy of Burghley, as an earlier chapter, on the searching out of wardships, has already shown. How successful he was in this field it is, unfortunately, impossible to say with any exactitude. All our collections of documents on sales are broken series; nor does any single volume give us a complete list of the numbers sold in any one year. We might alternatively try to calculate the totals from the grants of letters patent, the final stage in the application for a wardship; but, by checking the material with other sources, it becomes clear that not every purchaser had a copy of his patent entered upon the official roll. At each stage one is reminded that the surviving documents were not contrived for the benefit of posterity but for immediate and administrative purposes. Since every record involved a fee, the suitor would take a somewhat utilitarian view as to the number of records he was prepared to pay for. In a search for a complete answer, one is thwarted at every turn.

There is, however, one source which makes possible, not a precise answer, but at least a useful estimate of the annual sales. The Receiver-General, when he drew up his annual accounts, set out in one section the sums he had received from the purchasers of wards. For this purpose we must assume that he was honest—a large assumption, but we must make it (except in those cases where we have evidence to the contrary). On rare occasions guardians received their wardships for nothing and therefore do not appear at all in the accounts. A few others paid in a lump sum. Some ran into debt and did not complete their payments until long afterwards, if at all. But the majority paid for their wardships by instalments over two or three years. On a rough basis we may say that the average period was the equivalent of two and a half years. With this as our guide we may proceed to a broad calculation of the average number sold each year.[1]

Towards the end of Edward VI's reign about fifty wardships were sold. In Mary's reign a little more. In the second year of Elizabeth's reign, the last year before Burghley became Master, the numbers were up to seventy-two. Five years later they had dropped to forty-six; but a decade later they had risen to seventy-eight and stayed there for another decade. Five years after this they rose to eighty-three; and in the thirty-seventh year, towards the end of Burghley's Mastership, they had risen to ninety-two. It is possible to say that, after a poor start, Burghley succeeded in carrying through a modest rise in the numbers sold. It is in keeping with his own statements of policy.

There were more wardships at the end of Elizabeth's reign than at the beginning: in fact, nearly thirty per cent. more. In spite of growing resistance, Burghley and his officials had broken through the barriers of silence, concealment and fraud to uncover, by the end of the reign, more than ninety wardships in a year. This was progress. But it is still necessary to test Burghley's work by means of another source. Each year the Receiver-General reported his total income from the sales of wards; and it is not unreasonable to expect that his figures would, more or less, join in the upward climb of the numbers sold. If more wardships were sold, then more money should have come in to the crown.

Yet here is a paradox. The royal profits from the sales of wardships came to £6,296 in 1560-1, the year in which Burghley became Master. These profits never again reached even £6,000, and only once were they as high as £4,000, during the whole of Burghley's long Mastership. It is worth observing that, within four years of Burghley's death, the profits had soared above his own highest level and had reached £8,525. It would seem that the more wardships Burghley sold, the less profit the queen derived from them.

We may apply another test to this apparent contradiction. The total net revenues of the Court of Wards stood at £29,552 in the year that Burghley became Master. They never stood there again while he was alive. In the year after his appointment they were down to £18,317. The following year saw a drop of another £3,000. There was no significant recovery until the last years of his Mastership, when Robert Cecil, his son and successor, was already doing a great deal of the work. The average annual profits during Burghley's tenure of office were two-thirds of what they were under his predecessor, Sir Thomas Parry, and less than half of what they were in the year of Burghley's appointment. What kind of policy was Lord Burghley, as Master of the Wards and Lord High Treasurer of England, pursuing on behalf of his queen, if the total result of his labour and enterprise was to push her revenue in a downward direction?

The easiest way to resolve this paradox is to acknowledge, as contemporaries believed, that Burghley was a corrupt man. There were plenty of allegations to that effect. His domestic biographer tells us that 'it was imagined he made infinite gain by the wards'. John Clapham, one of Burghley's secretaries, wrote of him after his death, 'he was made Master of the Wards and Liveries by means whereof he grew rich and oft-times gratified his friends and servants that depended and waited on him'. This cannot be dismissed as idle talk: the manuscript was being sent to an expert, Thomas Hesketh, Attorney of the Wards. Thomas Wilson, nephew of Elizabeth's Secretary of State, estimated that wardship brought in yearly between £20,000 and £30,000 to the queen, about twice as much to Burghley and even more subsequently to Sir Robert Cecil. The Earl of Essex, as he sat counting his chickens in the belief that he would succeed Burghley as Master, examined the oath to be taken on appointment and let it be known that he wondered 'how the late Lord Treasurer could dispense so easily and so largely with it and his conscience'.[1]

These may all have been subjective opinions: hearsay nurtured on jealousy and inflated into conviction. We may perhaps

---

[1] *Desiderata Curiosa*, ed. Peck, i, 27; *Elizabeth of England*, ed. Read (1951), p. 75; *The State of England, 1600*, ed. F. J. Fisher (Camden Misc. xvi), p. 28; *The Letters of John Chamberlain*, ed. McClure (Philadelphia, 1939), i, 48.

approach one degree closer to fact by examining some of the correspondence addressed to Burghley and to those in his service. That Michael Hickes, his secretary, was taking gifts for the dubious services he rendered suitors for wardships, we have already seen in an earlier chapter.[1] That Robert Cecil was equally involved during his father's lifetime is also perfectly clear. 'You shall have £1,000', wrote one candidate for a post in the Court of Wards, 'and my Lady Dixie, my brother's wife, will with many thanks send unto my good lady your wife £100 to buy her four coach horses.'[2]

George Goring, the son of a dishonest Receiver-General of the same name, asked for the grant of a wardship with the suggestion that Cecil should get it cheaply in his own name or his wife's to cover up the deal. 'If the ward prove well', he concluded, 'I would be glad to buy him at the full value, of your Honour, for one of my daughters.' 'I understand through my good friend, Mr. Maynard,' Mrs. Elizabeth Hampden, a widow, once wrote to Cecil, 'that I shall have the wardship of the body and lands of my son for eight hundred pounds. The sum is very much more than my estate (without the help of my good friends) is able to perform, yet I will satisfy your Honour of the said sum.' The official price payable to the crown was £153 while the premium for the lease of the lands came to £90. And the remainder of the money? 'I would know to whom the five hundred pounds shall be paid', she wrote a few weeks later. We can guess.[3]

The son and the servant were each heavily committed to the backstairs trade in wardships. What about Burghley himself? Amongst his correspondence there are plenty of offers of gifts to him in anticipation of services to be rendered. 'If I may have your lordship's honourable favour and furtherance,' wrote Sir Drue Drury, 'besides that my money shall be ready, I myself will be as ready at all times to deserve your lordship's favour with all good offices that I can.' Penelope Rich, sister of the Earl of Essex, in

---

1 Above, pp. 68–70.
2 H.M.C. *Salis.*, iv, 531.
3 *Ibid.*, vi, 363; vii, 231, 278; Wards 9.159, f. 50v; 252, f. 31r.

asking Burghley's help, gave an undertaking which was deliberately couched in vague terms but in a familiar euphemism. She promised 'both to deserve it and to show all thankfulness for so great a benefit'. A certain George Reynell was rather more explicit in a letter to Hickes. Burghley had told Reynell 'how much my wife was beholding unto him in suffering her son's office to be found at so low a rate'. Reynell saw the point: it was 'a testimony of his meaning more than I durst remember in my letter'.[1]

A nod is as good as a wink. People do not write to a great statesman, or his secretary, in this way if they have no good reason to believe that he will find such gifts acceptable. But there is a very great gap between promise and performance; hints and offers are no proof that a bribe was given or received. An ambiguously worded suggestion is not the same as an audited statement. It so happens, however, that we possess an auditor's statement upon this very issue. Thomas Fermor, of Somerton in Oxfordshire, died in 1580 and left a son and heir who was about five years of age. He was therefore a ward of the crown; and his wardship was in due course purchased by George Shirley, one of the executors of the father's will, possibly acting on behalf of the mother. Included in the audited account of these executors we have a list of sums paid to agents who mediated with various officials in pressing their suit. The expenditure was as follows:

Item.	Given to Sir Christopher Hatton's man for writing a letter to my lord treasurer	10s.
Item.	Given to Mr Bradshawe, which first moved my lady to deal in it.	£10.
Item.	Promised Mr Medlie £5, and paid him £3, given to Mr Barnard, one of my lord's secretaries, £3 . .	£6.
Item.	Given to speed my lady's chamberlain . . .	£3.
Item.	For writing two letters to my Lady Burghley. .	12d.

[1] B.M. Lans. 107, f. 142r; 57, f. 108r; 108, f. 41r.

So far six people had claimed perquisites of one kind or another for transmitting the suit to 'my lady'. Who was my lady? The answer is provided in the next line of the account:

Item.   Given to my Lady Burghley for obtaining the ward-
               ship   .   .   .   . £250.

Lady Burghley was paid £250 by a suitor for obtaining the ward-ship. From whom? She could obtain it from no other source but her husband: Lord Treasurer Burghley, Master of the Queen's Wards. It is worth recording at this stage that the official price paid to the queen for the same wardship was £233. 6s. 8d. Lady Burghley's profits exceeded the queen's by £16. 13s. 4d.[1]

The servant, the son, the wife: all were involved. Finally we come to the Master himself. Here the position becomes obscure and complex. Official receipts for unofficial payments, needless to say, we are unlikely ever to find. Hints, circumlocutions and the rest convey the atmosphere of the time but fall short of direct evidence. Only occasionally do we come upon something so concrete and specific as to eliminate all doubt. One such record we have already examined in an earlier chapter, where a quarrel between two guardians over the Cholmeley wardship threw up some startling evidence about Burghley's handling of the business.[2] Here, one of the purchasers stated that he had offered Burghley £400 as a gift for the grant of a wardship. Burghley, with a characteristic gesture, had returned £50 and kept the remainder. The queen's fee was £80.

More significant still is a list of eleven recipients of wardships, which has survived in the Public Record Office and dates almost certainly from the time, after Burghley's death, when the Earl of Essex was making discreet inquiries about the Master's profits from wardships.[3] It is worth setting it out in full:

1 *Arch. J.*, viii, 180 (I am indebted to Mr. Lawrence Stone for the reference); Wards 9.221, f. 101r; 384, f. 226r.
2 Above, pp. 82–3.
3 *S.P.D.*, Eliz., cclviii, no. 41.

Ab 1° die Januar: 1596 ad 4 Aug: 1598

Lord Buckhurst	Haughton 1	166–13–4	in plate
Attorney General	Aston	1000	
Sir John Stanhope	Haughton 2	100	
Sir H. Constable	Applegarth	100	
Twisden	Ashburnham	100	
Mr Surveyor of the Liveries	Gifford	200	
Attorney of the Wards	Laborn	20 (£100 sent but £80 returned)	
Receiver of the Wards	Hewett	200	
Hunnings of the Revels	Archdale	150	
Sir Edward Wotton	Barneham	1000	
Mr Bowyer	Henly	66–13–4	
		3103– 6–8	

This note to be burned.

What does this mean and to whom does it refer? There can be no doubt that the recipient of these gifts was Lord Burghley; and the account ends appropriately with the fourth day of August 1598, the day he died. Clearly it was drawn up by someone who knew the work intimately: who knew what came in cash and what in plate and—again the typical reaction—that Burghley gave back to one suitor some of the money that he sent. Three of the men on this list were officials of the Court of Wards: to whom else would they have sent their gifts than to the head of their department, the man who was responsible, under the queen, for making these grants? We possess also a letter from Coke, the Attorney-General, to Burghley written at about this time, in which he refers to a sum that he is about to pay Burghley for his help.[1] Finally, we have in this connection one other significant piece of information. Of the eleven wardships which are here named, it has been possible, through the official records of the Court of Wards, to trace the payments made to the crown for nine of them, (all, that is, except Henly and Laborn). The *official* charge to the purchasers, arranged by Burghley for these nine wardships, was

[1] B.M. Lans. 84, f. 137r.

£906. 13s. 4d.; the unofficial charge, recorded in the paragraph above, was £3,016 13s. 4d. Burghley obtained more than three times as much as the queen. In the space of two and a half years he received about £3,000 from private suitors, at a time when his official salary throughout the period came to less than £400.

The son, the servant, the wife, and now the Master himself. Have we at last the explanation why the total profits from wardships, payable to the queen, *declined* during his Mastership? Was he simply diverting the largest proportion of the total profit into his own pockets? It might seem obvious that we must accept the verdict of some of his contemporaries that he was a corrupt man. Yet, as so often happens, the most obvious explanation is not necessarily the correct one. That Burghley took gifts is beyond dispute. But it is also true that every official in Tudor England, great and small, took gifts. The queen herself knew it and, in a sense, confirmed by her own actions the system of New Year's gifts to which she subscribed. The giving and taking of gifts was an inherent part of Tudor society and government. Without them officialdom would have withered and died away, for the salaries (not perquisites) of even the men in the upper ranks of government were small. The Lord Chancellor was the highest paid at about £1,000 a year. The Lord Chief Justice of England received about £230, the Lord Treasurer £368, the Lord High Admiral £200, and the Master of the Wards £133. 6s. 8d. (and £100 for expenses). At the other end of the scale, the Clerk of the Privy Seal received £5 a year, the Solicitor to the Council in Wales and the Marches, £10, the feodaries of the Court of Wards, £9 and one per cent. of all the money they collected. Every one of these officials and their hundreds of colleagues received gifts. Must we, on these grounds, indict the whole Tudor ministry of corruption?[1]

To prove Burghley guilty of corruption, it is still necessary to show that he corrupted administration and justice for private gain and, secondly, that he robbed the queen of her revenues. A

[1] These figures are taken from *Desiderata Curiosa*, ii, 1–10. There were, of course, administrative fees as well.

consideration of the exact significance of these gifts—or bribes—
we must therefore postpone for a little while to look first at his
general policy in the Court of Wards.

That he was an honest and patient judge we have no reason to
doubt; and there is abundant evidence amongst the official records
to show that he was actively concerned with protecting the interests of the wards against their guardians and others. On one
occasion, although the heiress was already of age, he seized upon
the fact that she had not yet sued livery to protect her with the full
authority of the court against the seizure of her person and lands.
His own grandson was fined £1,500 during Burghley's Mastership
for marrying a ward without authority; but the queen subsequently reduced the fine to £600. On one occasion he rebuked
his own son, Thomas Cecil, for asking too high a price in re-
selling a ward to the ward's mother; and Thomas was obliged to
bring the price down. In 1592 Burghley was trying, as on other
occasions, to safeguard wards against the spoiling of their parks.
Had contemporaries, who criticised him so much, been able to
allege that he was also a corrupt judge, they would have hastened
to do so. But on that subject his enemies were completely silent.

> In cases of justice [wrote his biographer] none could ever do him
> greater despite than to offer him anything, as myself can witness.
> For I have seen him refuse a buck, and many pieces of plate, at New
> Year's tide. And to offer him money was to offend him so as they
> fared the worse, ever saying: 'I will take nothing of you, having a
> cause depending before me'. And I dare avow it, there was never
> any man living could procure him take a penny, in any cause de-
> pending before him, in any court of justice . . . stopping his eyes and
> ears and closing his hands.[1]

In administration, as in justice, there are many signs of the firm
hand of Burghley. His interest in the economic control of government departments can indeed be traced back to a time long before
he came to the highest office. In September 1552 we find amongst
his memoranda, presumably for consideration by the Council, 'The

1 J. Strype, *Annals* (1824), iii, pt. 1, pp. 399–402; Wards 9.388, f. 198r; 86, f. 62v;
H.M.C. *Salis.*, ii, 200–1; Wards 9.109, f. 14v; *Desiderata Curiosa*, i, 25.

discharge of excessive charges in the courts of the revenues.' In 1561, the year that he became Master, he was a member of the royal commission to inquire into revenues. In 1570, even before he became Lord Treasurer, he was engaged in various schemes to augment the royal income. From about this time also there came before Parliament various measures against concealments and other kinds of fraud, by both officials and the general public, which have been discussed in an earlier chapter. Stafford's patent for concealments was carefully re-cast so that the drive for more revenue should not be pressed on at too rapid, and too selfish, a pace. From the late 1580s, as Lord Treasurer, he was working hard, with some measure of success, to overhaul the whole revenue machine and make it respond to the very heavy demands of war. In 1594, after the scandal of George Goring, the Receiver-General of the Court of Wards who had spirited away many thousands of pounds belonging to the queen, he instituted measures for closer control of its finances. So far as he was able, Burghley wrestled to make his department run along orderly and economic lines and, where he could, struck at those who tried to operate the system against the interest of either the queen or her subjects.[1]

How are we to resolve the apparent contradiction between Burghley's care and uprightness as an administrator, and his acceptance of substantial sums as gifts? John Clapham who, as we have seen, bluntly said that Burghley 'grew rich' out of wardships, paints an utterly different picture of him as a judge. 'In the courts of justice', he writes, 'his presence was so grateful to suitors as they desired to have their causes heard only before him', even if, because Burghley was ill or busy, it meant delay, and therefore additional expense. If anyone lost his case he attributed it rather to ' the badness of the matter itself' than to any error in the judgment. A corrupt practice he would openly reprove. 'Condemners of justice he did always punish with great severity for public example, in affairs of meaner nature using lenity, as the case re-

---

1 S.P.D., Ed. VI, xv, f. 19r (see also f. 31r); C.P.R., Eliz., ii, 92–3; F. C. Dietz, English Public Finance, 1558–1641 (1932), pp. 45, 63; H.M.C. Salis., iv, 528.

quired.' The honest judge; yet he was the recipient of secret gifts.
Either there is some coherence in his policy or his whole way of life
becomes a mass of contradictions. It is at this point that we must
consider him within the context of Tudor statesmanship as a
whole.[1]

Burghley held three of the major offices of government under
Elizabeth. He was Secretary of State from her accession until
1572; Master of the Court of Wards from 1561 until his death in
1598; and, most important of all, Lord Treasurer from 1572, also
until the end of his life. In the first of these offices he handled both
the domestic and foreign correspondence of the queen. He was
not a modern Prime Minister since he was neither head of a
Cabinet nor answerable to Parliament; nor was he a civil servant
concerned purely with administration. His work partook of both
functions, and his power and influence extended into all departments. As Master of the Wards he again had a dual task to perform: to protect the feudal revenues of the queen and to shelter
the wards in her care. On top of that he had to share out amongst
her courtiers, officials and others the private profits which feudalism could be made to yield.

It was a political tightrope, and no one could have walked it
better than Burghley. But it was the office of Lord Treasurer which
taxed him to the uttermost. In spite of various projects for reform,
of which the most significant was carried through by Cecil's predecessor, William Paulet, Marquess of Winchester, the whole
financial structure was medieval, though the economic problems of
government cried aloud for a modern system to match them.
Medieval it remained; and Cunningham's view that Burghley's
was the master mind, formulating a planned policy of economic
nationalism looks strange in the context of contemporary economic practices.[2]

It was a government more planned against than planning.
Burghley was indeed a man of ideas who hoped to make

---

[1] J. Clapham, *op. cit.*, pp. 81–2.
[2] W. R. Cunningham, *Growth of English Industry and Commerce: Modern Times*
(Cambridge 1903), i, 53.

England strong, self-sufficing and stable; but every statute with this in mind carried a long tail of exceptions and exemptions, forced out of an impecunious government by groups of vested interests inside and outside of Parliament. Elizabeth needed money sometimes desperately. Though they distorted her objectives, she must in time of need sell exemptions and licences to those who could afford to buy. The Merchant Adventurers, for example, could drive a horse and cart through the trading policies of Burghley; though he hated to let them do it. To have formulated and carried through a truly national economic policy would have required a man of more heroic mould; and it would have meant a recasting of the whole governmental system. It would have amounted also to an economic and constitutional revolution; and he may have rightly judged that the time for it had not yet come. Here and there he struck hard at abuses and tried, where he could, to raise the standard of probity in administration. But under him the Treasury kept largely to its accustomed ways.

If this was Burghley's policy, it was also the queen's. For, with the accession of Elizabeth I in 1558, there began the longest partnership in English history between monarch and minister; and it was only broken, after forty years, by the death of the minister. It was a *mariage de convenance*. Mutual respect, a common attitude to politics and religion, a cool realism: these things bound them, but there was no real warmth, affection or generosity. Behind her back Burghley grumbled about her. She for her part stormed at him and, in 1587, during the crisis after the execution of Mary, Queen of Scots, he did not dare show his face at court. Yet, at the end, they who had grown old together, and shared so many of the hazards of the time, came to understand one another. She was not her father: she did not allow the plots of intriguers to destroy her greatest minister. And, finally, to trust and respect she added affection. He could never act in disregard of her will; and she could sometimes intervene—in matters of high policy or trivial detail—with devastating effect. But on many occasions, both as Master of Wards and a minister of state, Burghley could speak as the *alter ego* of the queen.

It was a conservative partnership in both state and church. The text-book comments about Sir Robert Walpole could, perhaps with better effect, be applied to Burghley. He was only too conscious of what might follow if he aroused the sleeping dogs of Tudor England. So in religion, politics, and finance, once the early formative years of the reign were over, he sought to conserve and improve, not to change or destroy. His foreign policy was unadventurous—his enemies considered it pusillanimous—but in this, too, he stood nearer to Walpole than to Walsingham. Like his mistress, he preferred the tortuous ways of diplomacy to the shining armour of war. He and his queen believed with an unshakable conviction that, with Europe in ferment and with grave threats at home, this was no time for experiment or bold programmes of change. *Après moi le deluge?* There was none of the cynical indifference of Louis XV in the English queen. Rather, if she could buy time by delay, if she could preserve internal peace by holding fast to tradition, she would be happy to leave the fundamental solution of her problems to a new generation and a new dynasty. In this Burghley was the ideal instrument for Elizabeth's policy.

But the traditions which Burghley inherited were a mixed collection; and it is a serious criticism of him that he conserved the bad with the good. The taking of gifts by officials was a practice which he inherited, and under him it showed no sign of abating. On the contrary, it appears to have grown. Inflation was causing relatively stable official salaries to shrink still further in their purchasing power. At the same time, the number of officials employed in government departments and the Household grew apace, as Elizabeth knew only too well, to her cost. On occasion she would utter a sharp protest against the inflation of public offices; but, for most of the time, she and Burghley looked on in dismay as administration manifested its well-known capacity for multiplying itself. As numbers grew, the opportunities for dubious practices multiplied with them. 'The queen's own household corrupt', runs a sad little note in Burghley's handwriting amongst his memoranda for the year 1580. In 1592 he observed that men

were saying of England: 'all causes governed by bribes. Conscience
least accounted'. He was in the best position to know whether
these charges were true and, if they were, he more than any man
could make a bid to alter them. But he knew his limits.[1]

He, more than any man, knew also at whose expense these
profits were being made. We can easily observe how the whole
business was conducted by taking some samples from Burghley's
own correspondence. He was, as we have seen, constantly being
approached by suitors to give them favourable treatment in the
Court of Wards. Sometimes they asked for help against competitors, which meant, in effect, the grant of the wardship *below* the
competitive price. Sometimes they bluntly asked for their grants
at favourable terms, that is, below what we should today call the
market price. Lady Sidney, soliciting Burghley for the lease of
some ward's lands, asked that they be rented 'for such fine
reasonable'—that is, price—'as Your Honour favourably may'.
Hickes was asked by the Earl of Nottingham to show favour to
Nottingham's daughter by setting 'easy values' upon her lands.
The Earl of Essex obtained a wardship from Burghley and thanked
him for the consideration shown him 'in the rating of the fines'.
Here, then, we find clear gaps between the price the queen was
entitled to receive and the price which the Master actually determined on her behalf. The difference between these two sums was,
in effect, subtracted from the queen's revenues and pocketed by
her subjects.[2]

Having obtained the wards cheaply, what did the recipients do
with them? Very often they transferred them to someone else at
a higher price. After receiving consideration 'in the rating of the
fine', Essex promptly sold the wardship for what he was pleased
to call 'a competent sum of money'. Coke, who appears earlier
in this chapter in our list of eleven benefactors of Burghley,
paid him £1,000 and the queen £300 for the wardship of Walter
Aston: £1,300 in all. In other words, the queen received less than
a quarter of the total purchase price. Having completed this stage

[1] B.M. Lans. 102, f. 175r; 103, no. 77.
[2] B.M. Lans. 17, f. 41r; 87, f. 41r; 60, f. 203r.

of the transaction, Coke sold the wardship to the ward himself—for £4,000, three times as high as the price Coke paid and thirteen times as high as the price the queen received. When the Court of Wards sold the wardship of Elizabeth Long to Thomas Cecil, the price was fixed at £250. Before he had paid a penny of this sum, he had sold the wardship to John Manners for more than five times the price, at £1,350. Manners sold it some years later to a certain Charles Morison for £2,450. The queen in effect received only one-tenth of the price the wardship reached on the open market. We must, at this stage, deliberately refrain from commenting on the morality of these practices, for our story is incomplete. It must suffice, here, to draw attention to the wide disparity between the official price paid to the queen and the ultimate price paid by the last purchaser—if he was the last in the series. We must record also that Burghley did nothing to augment the queen's share.[1]

This was conservatism; and for the moment we need not qualify the term. Instead, we may look at the same conservatism as it is reflected in the general price policy for wards. When Masters sold wardships, they tended to fix the price as a ratio of the annual value of the wards' lands. Other things, of course, had to be taken into consideration, such as the age of the heir; the number of brothers who might succeed him if he died young; if the heirs were female, how many there were; what lands might subsequently descend by 'reversion'. The health of the ward, in so far as it could be judged, had, no doubt, also to be taken into consideration. Yet, though no two human beings are alike, the surprising fact emerges that the range of prices, under Burghley, was extremely narrow. For example, if the lands were valued at £10 a year, the wardship would probably be sold by Burghley at either £10, £15, £20 or, occasionally, at £30. Throughout his period the majority were sold at no more than the annual value of the lands or less, or at 50 per cent. above the annual value. Thus, at the beginning of his Mastership, well over four-fifths of the wardships were disposed of in this way; at the end, just under

[1] J. E. Neale, *The Elizabethan Political Scene*, p. 7; Wards 9.107, ff. 9r–10r, 100r, 307r–308r.

four-fifths. In all, there was a drop of only a few per cent. in the wardships sold at exceedingly low rates.

These conclusions, which are based upon a survey of the statistical records of the court, are confirmed by the opinions of two contemporaries. The prices charged for wardships, wrote an official at the end of Burghley's Mastership, were 'after the rate of one year and a half or two years, and seldom more'. Burghley's domestic biographer sets the figure for males at 'a year and a half'. (There were far fewer female wards and they were dearer.) The consistency of the system throughout the thirty-seven years of Burghley's Mastership is impressive. Under Robert Cecil, his son and successor, the whole thing was taken to pieces.[1]

Burghley kept prices down, either that he might make a handsome profit for himself and his friends, or for some other reason that we have not yet explored. It is time, therefore, to revert to the crucial question: was Burghley a corrupt man?

In 1585 there occurred a curious incident, in which Burghley himself took up the challenge made against him by contemporaries that he *was* corrupt. In a celebrated letter to William Herrle, a minor official, he struck back against 'the vile, false devilish exclamations and execrations made by such as I know not'. Amidst pious quotations from the Psalms he declared, 'if my conscience did not ascertain me of God's favour and protection against these satanical and fanatical spirits, I should think myself in a most wretched state'. Burghley begged his correspondent to call upon his traducers to prefer a charge against him so that in open trial he could prove himself totally innocent 'of falsehood, injustice, bribery, discrimination, of double dealing in advice, in counsel either with Her Majesty or with the counsellors'. People envied him his three houses but, he insisted, they were modest affairs. In his house at Theobalds he had enlarged a room, but that was because the queen on her visits had found the room somewhat too small for her taste. His house in the Strand was old and negligible. His house at Burghley, he continued, really belonged to his mother and he had carried out a certain amount of renovation to it.

1 Wards 13.3 20.2, f. 34r; *Desiderata Curiosa*, i, 26.

In a postscript, he went on to refute the charge that he was holding a tight grasp on the public offices, and that those who wanted them had to make suit to him. This was a 'notable, absurd, manifest lie'. On the contrary, the queen used him as a buffer against suitors—and as a whipping boy. 'Her Majesty throweth upon me a burthen to deal in all ungrateful actions: to give answers unpleasant to all who miss.' Other courtiers were used where favourable answers could be given to suitors. So 'if the party obtain, I am not thanked; if not, the fault (though falsely) is imputed to me'. Finally he returned to the question of his income. 'My fee for the treasureship is no more than it hath been these thirty years.' (The same, we might add, was true of his official salary from the Court of Wards: £133. 6s. 8d. and £100 allowance, for expenses, together with his not very substantial revenues from the use of the court seal.) 'And', he went on, in a famous passage, 'this I do affirm: that my fees of my treasureship do not answer to my charge of my stable.' He was anxious there should be no misunderstanding—'I mean not my *table*.'[1]

The whole letter is replete with hypocrisy. We may consider, for example, his remarks about his three houses. Cecil House, dismissed as 'so old as it should not stir any', was probably the most famous town house in England. Theobalds, which he tells us he had reluctantly extended, was in the next reign so to arouse the admiration of James I that he asked Robert Cecil for it in exchange for Hatfield Palace. Of Burghley House, he expostulated that he had 'made the rough stone walls to be square', simply using the old foundations; and 'there are in that shire a dozen larger of men under my degree'. *Qui s'excuse, s'accuse*! Anyone who has seen Burghley House—substantially as he left it—cannot take his protestation at more than its face value. There is a comic element to the whole business, and a final incident which is in keeping with it. Burghley sent this full and elaborate defence to so insignificant a man as Herrle, but clearly he would not have wasted his time upon Herrle alone. The document was designed

---

1 *S.P.D.*, Eliz., clxxxi, nos. 42, 60, 61 (printed in J. Strype, *Annals*, iii, pt. 1, pp. 502–3, pt. 2, pp. 379–83).

for other eyes, as the early paragraphs suggest: and the recipient
acted upon the hint. Ten days later he received a sharp rebuke
from Burghley for circulating his private letters in the city. Poor
Herrle! No wonder he replied—on the same day—saying that he
had always dreaded that, in doing good offices, he would be
crushed between the hammer and the anvil! He swore his innocence, announced that he was ill and took refuge in a bath of
herbs to strengthen and revive him. It required an abler man than
Herrle to understand the complex psychology of Burghley.

But we cannot dismiss Burghley's own defence as mere hypocrisy and no more, for in our final estimate of him we lack, in our
present state of knowledge, certain indispensable information as
to the sources of his wealth. We know that he built lustily. He also
entertained on a lavish scale—not because he loved ostentation but
because he was the most eminent statesman of the day and his
door had always to be open to the great of the land, including the
queen herself. One state visit from the queen could play havoc with
the finances of a great lord: and Burghley had several such visits.
Where did the money come from? Contemporaries believed it
came from the unofficial profits of public office. 'My fee for the
treasureship', retorted Burghley, 'is no more than it hath been
these thirty years.'

That might be; but we must be on our guard against his disin-
genuous use of technical terms. The *fees*, indeed did not significantly rise; that can be clearly shown, in the case of wardships,
from the official records. Can the same be said about perquisites,
gifts, rewards, bribes and the whole collection of *douceurs* which
oiled the wheels of Tudor administration? All men took them.
Since, however, both donor and recipient hid the gift in a maze
of euphemism and ambiguity, since such evidence as existed was
often destroyed as quickly as possible, what numerical value is the
historian to set upon rumour, hearsay, and slander? If, in the case
of Burghley, we knew the extent of the private fortune he inherited, and his income from his estates, we should know how far
his high cost of living was met from these legitimate sources.
Burghley, in fact, argued that it was from these revenues—not from

public office—that he sustained his three houses, his family, and
the way of life of a great courtier and statesman. His father left
him lands. Edward VI, he tells us, augmented them. Not so
Elizabeth: 'In my whole time I have not for these twenty six
years been beneficed from Her Majesty so much as I was within
four years of King Edward'—those indeed were the days when
members of the court and official circle grew fat at the expense of
the boy king. They never came again until the reign of James I.
Yet Elizabeth was not as curmudgeonly as Burghley would have
us believe; she did make grants of land to him. But he says that
he spent as much in her service as she gave him. Unfortunately,
until his private and estate accounts have been scrutinised and
assessed, we shall not know how near Burghley's defence comes
to the facts of the case.[1]

We must here revert to one piece of evidence which establishes
beyond doubt that he was taking unofficial gifts. We have already
seen, in the case of eleven wardships, that Burghley received just
over £3,000 in less than three years of his service in the Court of
Wards: roughly four wards brought in £1,200 a year. What proportion of his *total* unofficial income from this source does £1,200
a year represent? One is tempted to argue that, if four wardships
brought in that sum each year, then the ninety wardships of an
average year must have brought to Burghley £27,000: a tremendous sum.

But for such a conclusion we have no warrant whatsoever, and
a good deal which points to the contrary. The statement about the
eleven wardships is most careful and detailed, obviously drawn up
by someone working inside the Court of Wards: he knew how
much was sent in plate, how much returned to the Attorney. If
this memorandum was prepared, as it appears to have been, in
answer to the questionnaire sent by the Earl of Essex about the
private profits from wardship, then clearly his correspondent
would not omit other large sums which he knew to have been
paid to the Master. A good deal may have passed without his

[1] *Ibid.*, p. 383; *C.P.R.*, Eliz., ii, 165-6; see also C. Read, 'Lord Burghley's Household
Accounts' (*Econ. Hist. Rev.*, 2nd ser., ix, 343-8).

knowledge; but one cannot escape noticing that this statement of Burghley's private profit from four wardships each year appears also in a totally different source. 'I dare be sworn,' writes the domestic biographer, 'because I knew it and saw it, he never took benefit but of two or three, or perhaps four in a year.' This is, of course, part of an *apologia* for Burghley but the other statement was nothing of the sort: yet they march together. Information about the sum of £3,000 clearly comes from a reliable source. Could many large sums have changed hands without leaving a trace to someone well placed in the Court of Wards? That seems hardly likely. It is difficult to argue from negative evidence, but there is no positive evidence of any sort which points in the opposite direction.

In other words, the materials from inside and outside the Court of Wards tell the same story. Let us try—though we must here pass from the known facts to speculation—to state a rough figure which does not quarrel with such evidence as we possess. We must abandon hope of even speculating what Burghley's family, friends, and staff made privately from suitors for wards, and think only of the Master himself. It would be harsh, as well as quite indefensible —on the existing data—to say that there were many more wardships for which Burghley received payment but which somehow escaped the notice of a well-informed official. On the other hand, it would be generous to Burghley to say that these eleven wards *alone* brought him profits during the period. It is a reasonable compromise to argue that the official knew of half the wardships which proved remunerative to the Master. On this estimate Burghley would be receiving about £2,500 a year, unofficially, from the sale of wardships, during the last period of his office.[1]

Occasional windfalls might also drop at Burghley's feet when a high office—such as that of Receiver-General—fell vacant. We know that these posts were keenly sought after and that gifts were offered to obtain them; but we have no fragment of evidence to show that Burghley received a penny in this connection. Even so, £2,500 a year is a substantial sum: over ten times

[1] *Desiderata Curiosa*, i, 28.

more than his official fees and allowances for the year as Master. But it was not a prodigious amount of money in terms of his heavy commitments, or the heavy burden of public service which he carried. It is nothing like the many thousands of pounds which his enemies attributed to him without a single supporting fact. To get his wardship profits into perspective, we should remember that his rentals alone sometimes reached £4,000 a year.[1]

A jury does not condemn a man on the basis of hearsay as evidence; and the historian who searches the wardship records, inside and outside of the Court of Wards, likewise finds no evidence beyond the stale slanders of a past age to condemn a great statesman for corruption. The multitude judged him, his biographers tell us, by what he might have gained rather than by what he did gain. To take £2,500 a year—unofficially—is certainly a diversion of public revenues into the pocket of a minister; and in this Burghley was no better and no worse than his contemporaries. In short, Burghley found the Tudor system of perquisites and gifts at hand when he took over office, and he did not change it throughout his long period of service. We have deliberately avoided the use of the word 'bribes', because our last chapter will be intimately concerned with this whole question. But gifts Burghley took, though probably in not more than five per cent. of the wardships he sold. He operated the system as he found it, but with moderation and conservatism. If this is our verdict, then it is also confirmed by what we know about him from other sources.

After the decease of Sir Thomas Parry [wrote Camden], she [the queen] gave him the office of Master of the Wards, in the third year of her reign; which place he executed, as he did all other, providently for the benefit of his prince and the wards, for his own profits moderately, and for the benefits of his followers bountifully, yet without offence; and in all things with great commendations for his integrity, in so much as the queen, admiring his wisdom, committed in a manner the managing of the whole state to him.

Once again: moderation and conservatism. Camden was an

[1] *Ibid.*, i, 35.

historian, but he was also a friend of Burghley; and we might on that ground be tempted to diminish or wholly reject this estimate. His opinion we have, in fact, hitherto disregarded. But, as it happens, the independent sources which we have at hand have forced us to reach the same conclusion.[1]

Yet, when all this has been considered, we are still left with the fact that, at the time of Burghley's death, there was much in the activities and traditions of the Court of Wards urgently in need of reform. Wardships were still being competed for and granted while the father of the heir was alive. Mothers were still without any special title to be the guardians of their children and could merely take their place in the wild scramble for a profitable wardship. His domestic biographer's claim that he 'preferred natural mothers, before all others, to the custody of their children' is not substantiated in the official records. The situation was not redressed until 1611, when mothers obtained one month's pre-emption over other suitors. The tradition remained, at the end of his Mastership, that applications for wardships went through courtiers, with all the costs that were often involved; the tradition was not ended until 1617, if indeed it ended then. And corruption within the court, from the Receiver-General downwards, continued to diminish the income of the queen and to prey upon the welfare of her subjects.[2]

'This judgement I have of you, that you will not be corrupted by any manner of gift. . . .' Our interim verdict is that he was not corrupted, although the institution he inherited and sustained had a good deal in it gravely at fault. But our verdict is interim for two reasons. In the first place, we do not yet know the full sources of Burghley's wealth, how, in fact, he grew rich. The answer to this may not be known until many years after this book is in print. It is interim also because Burghley's policy was fundamentally changed by his son and successor, Sir Robert Cecil; and for that reason we shall have to consider the work of Cecil, before we look back to make a concluding judgement on the Master of the Wards as a servant of the queen.

[1] W. Camden, *Annales* (1630 ed.), iv, 128.
[2] *Desiderata Curiosa*, i, 26; *S.P.D.*, Jas. I, lxi, no. 6; clxxxvii, no. 51A.

14

The Vacant Mastership

WHEN he was in his late seventies, Lord Burghley could only work sporadically in the Court of Wards and spent much of his time at Theobalds, his country house in Hertfordshire. Gout and other infirmities made movement difficult for him; but the mind was alert to the last. He continued to have a stream of callers, many of them officials, and he went on, as in his early days, to pour out his directions and counsel. But he was bound to relax his hold upon the daily business of the departments of which he remained head; and, as far as wardships were concerned, Thomas Hesketh, the Attorney of the Court of Wards, and Matthew Ewens, a baron of the Exchequer, were called in for legal matters, while Robert Cecil, Burghley's younger son, handled the other correspondence and, in effect, acted as his father's deputy, though without any formal grant of powers.

But Burghley, to the last, did not divest himself of his authority and, whenever his health permitted it, he came up to London to do his work. 'This morning', he wrote to his son in April 1594, 'I have been in the Court of Wards, with small ease and much pain.' He was in his seventy-fourth year. 'I live in pain', he went on 'and yet spare not to occupy myself for Her Majesty's causes.' At the beginning of 1597, in a burst of energy, he called for the facts and figures of the wardship revenues. John Clapham, his secretary, tried to hand him the statement, drawn up by the Receiver-General, but in the crush of people wanting to see Burghley, it was impossible to get near him. Two days later, Clapham managed to give it to him. Burghley read it, liked it, asked for a note of further details, and 'put it in his purse'. The brain was still active in the tired old body. In June 1598, two months before his death, he was reading and annotating documents arising from wardship litigation. But the work was piling up, as Burghley well knew, and he could only on occasion spur himself on to deal with the administrative arrears. 'Here dined today', Michael Hickes told Cecil in July 1597, 'Sir Jerome Bowes, Mr. Francis Bacon and Mr. Hare, Clerk of the Court of Wards. Their errands were nothing else but to do their duties.' Then they had their lunch, packed their files and left. 'And now we be alone, my lord under a tree in the walks with a book in his hand to keep him from sleeping, and we ready to take bowls into our hands but that the weather is somewhat too warm yet.' The old statesman, after a lifetime of service, still clung fast to the discipline of his youth. In this, at least, what he preached he practised : hard work and contempt for ease. As we leave him on that hot July afternoon, rejecting the rest that he had earned after a stiff morning's work, ready as always to learn and to serve, it is hard to accept some versions of him as a time-serving, mealy-mouthed hypocrite. Certainly Queen Elizabeth had no better servant, and she knew it.[1]

When a minister has died after holding the same office for thirty-seven years, he presents his sovereign with an appalling problem in the search for a successor. If, in making her choice, Elizabeth was faced with the unenviable task of sorting out the best man from a group of discordant, jealous and highly sensitive courtiers and statesmen, her problem was made incomparably more difficult by the deepening political crisis whose solution could no longer be postponed. For Burghley had held in his hands a concentration of power unparalleled since the days of Cromwell and Wolsey, half a century before. At the time of his death, there was no one man furnished with the stature, skill, personality, or sense of national interest to be the heir of all the authority which Burghley had for so long wielded. Already the intriguers, the political climbers, the men who trafficked in specu-lation about office, the lesser men greedy for power, were busy

[1] S.P.D., Eliz., ccxlviii, no. 84; Wards 14.3.20.2, ff. 12r–13v; H.M.C. Salis., viii, 244–5; vii, 294.

carving up in their imagination the skin of the dead statesman. And when the spoils had been shared out, these men might well embark upon the quarrels and blood-letting that often follow when the heirs of a powerful minister at last settle down to the feast. If one of these heirs should seek all the power enjoyed by Burghley—and more—without possessing a fraction of his ability or patience, then the queen herself would be faced with a grave threat to her authority, as well as the convulsion of civil war in the twilight of her reign. Of that threat she was aware and, less than three years after Burghley's death and only two years before her own, she was called upon to face its full dangers. Crucial to this central political issue was the vacant office of Master of the Court of Wards.

Her choice of a successor really lay between two men: Sir Robert Cecil and the Earl of Essex, men who were so contrasting in personality and career that it is hard to believe that they lived in the same age, let alone worked within the same governing class. Of the two, Robert Cecil would have appeared as the lesser claimant in the struggle which was now opening; and, even to contemporaries, he must have seemed out of keeping with the vaulting aspirations of the late Elizabethan age.

He was born in 1563, at a time when his father was already entrenched in the councils of the young Queen Elizabeth as Secretary of State and Master of the Wards; but it would have required a prophet to foretell that this sickly, crippled infant would one day succeed to the highest offices in the state. His bent or twisted back may have been, as his doctor thought, the result of a fall while in his nurse's care; but he was in any case very short in stature, and apart from his large and impressive eyes was slight and unattractive in appearance, with high cheekbones, aquiline nose, thin lips, and pointed beard. Fashion and nature combined to wound him. He had the misfortune to grow to manhood at a time when the Elizabethan masculine dress had luxuriated and degenerated into the large, fantastic ruff, the small trunks and the long stockings. An Essex or a Raleigh could shine in the colour and splendour of the courtier. To Robert Cecil the clothes he wore brought the distorted appearance of a dwarf: exaggerated the size of his head, tapered off his legs to absurd proportions. The queen would sometimes address him by 'her sporting name of pigmy'. The expression hurt. Robert Cecil wrote a letter to his cousin—but designed it for her eyes—in which he let it be known that 'I mislike not the name she gives me only because she gives it.' It was the nearest a Cecil ever came to rebuking his sovereign. What he could not hide from the queen he has hidden from us. His surviving portraits, significantly enough, do not usually show him at full length: the artists—or the sitter—withheld from posterity an important aspect of the body and the mind of the statesman.[1]

It often happens that a father will try to compensate his child when birth has not bestowed the health and strength of a normal body. So it was with William Cecil. For his eldest son, Thomas, he had little love and a scarcely veiled contempt. For Robert he had devotion and patience. He gave him complete confidence and guided his early footsteps along the complex ways of Tudor politics. When Robert was twenty-one, a seat was found for him in the Parliament of 1584 as M.P. for Westminster (where he had been born); and in 1588 he was included in a diplomatic mission to the continent. In 1591 he was knighted by the queen. Meanwhile he had married Elizabeth Brooke, a daughter of Lord Cobham, colleague of his father, and by her he had a son and one, or possibly two, daughters. In 1596 she died and her husband was believed to have taken an oath not to marry until three years were past: a long interval in those days. He kept his oath for the rest of his life.

In the last decade of the sixteenth century the political scene, and Cecil's career, were overshadowed by the turbulent and flamboyant personality of Robert Devereux, second Earl of Essex. Cecil was three years older than Essex, but possessed neither the good looks nor fire nor title of the younger man. They knew each other well: one looked to Lord Burghley as a father, the other had been Burghley's ward, for the first earl had died while

[1] J. S. Brewer, *English Studies* (1881), p. 129.

on service in Ireland. Essex, by his exploits at Zutphen (in the company of Sir Philip Sidney), Lisbon, Rouen, and Cadiz had shown himself to possess the courage and imagination desperately needed in the darkening years of war. He was well connected, highly popular, energetic, and a man of ideas. Would the queen choose Cecil or Essex for the vacant Mastership? Sir Francis Bacon, that shrewd calculator of the political chances—his own and other peoples'—believed she would choose Essex, and hastened to leap on to the band-wagon. It proved to be a wagon overloaded with incompetents, bankrupts, and political adolescents; and when Bacon perceived the direction it was going and the company he was keeping, he hastily closed that unfortunate episode in his career. But Robert Cecil could not have foreseen the disintegration of the character and career of Essex, a courtier-statesman of the highest promise; and he must have wondered, when his father was at last laid in his grave, what grim future would open before him in the last, and most bitter, struggle for power of the whole reign.

Burghley died in 1598; but before then Essex had shown that the charm and subtlety of a courtier were poor substitutes for the skill and patient judgement of a statesman. The Tudors—unlike the Stuarts—had a marvellous and unerring capacity to judge character; and the last of the Tudors possessed it *in excelsis*. She admitted Essex to her Privy Council but she would place neither him nor his nominees in high office. 'By God's death', she had once said, 'it was fit that someone or other should take him down and teach him better manners, otherwise there would be no rule with him.' But no one could rule him, save Elizabeth. Patronage, in any age, is a significant ingredient of prestige. But, in the 1590s, he suffered one rebuff after another; as a result, such statesmanship as was in him began to give place to the gambling of the adventurer. In 1590 the office of Secretary of State had been vacant. Essex wanted it, to bestow upon a follower; but Robert Cecil was given the work without the office: a typical Elizabethan manoeuvre. A makeshift arrangement of this sort could not endure for ever and at last, in 1596, when Essex was away at Cadiz, the queen appointed her Secretary of State—Robert Cecil. This could mean nothing but open war between the two men, had not Cecil gone out of his way to be conciliatory to his rival. But two years later the situation repeated itself, for with Burghley dead the offices of Master of the Wards and Lord Treasurer became vacant. For the Lord Treasurership even the ambitious Essex could not hope, but the Mastership was a rich prize which, at this stage, was precisely what was needed to retore his broken pride and fortune.[1]

Here, at last, was a chance for the Master, his colleagues, his friends and a widening circle of the Tudor establishment to make substantial private profits out of the business of wardship. To those who had no access to these sources, and to the country at large, wardship might seem a national scandal which cried aloud for reform. Reform indeed was in the wind, but for the present it was only the lightest of breezes. It seemed unlikely to grow stronger under either candidate for the Mastership.

Robert Cecil, during the last years of his father's life, had been unofficially doing his father's work—again without the title. With Burghley dead, Essex joined in the scramble for the office, was indeed thought by some to have been granted it, and began to make inquiries of the officials as to the profits that could be expected. If he gained the office, then he would be within reach of the reality —not simply the promise—of power. He would gain hold of one of the sources of patronage and wealth; and with the unofficial profits of wardship he would buy solvency for himself and his followers. Already, a hanger-on had written to him: 'I pray that we may hear that you are Master of the Wards, for then I shall hope that you will bestow a male or female upon me.' There would be no more talk of feudal reform. The elastic revenues of wardship would be stretched to breaking point.[2]

The queen must have seriously considered the claims of Essex. Otherwise the rumours could not have grown so strong as to be taken for certainty by no less a person than the Receiver-General of the Court of Wards. It looks, indeed, as though Essex himself

---

[1] R. Naunton, *Fragmenta Regalia* (1808), p. 272.
[2] H.M.C. *Salis.*, viii, 415.

believed that the office was his. 'Latimer,' wrote William Fleet-wood, the Receiver-General, to his clerk, at the beginning of October 1598, 'here I have sent you a note sent unto me by the Lord of Essex concerning the Court of Wards of whom he shall be Master.' This was a positive statement; but neither the new 'Master' nor the Receiver-General felt secure enough to let it be generally known. Meanwhile, Essex was anxious to make himself thoroughly up-to-date about the whole procedure; he requested 'secret and private information of all the particulars specified in this note'. So the clerk was ordered to take 'diligent pains in setting down effectual answers and full satisfactions'. But, he was enjoined again, he must 'keep this and the note secret to yourself only, for that I would not have any man but yourself privy here-unto for a thousand pounds'. The situation was very delicate. For the third time Latimer was urged to 'keep this note safe'.[1]

For a few weeks these rumours continued to circulate. 'The Earl of Essex hath the reversion of the Master of the Wards', wrote Father Garnett to Father Parsons on 19 November 1598. But this retailer of unreliable stories was already getting out of date. Better informed, the man about town, John Chamberlain had told his correspondent, Dudley Carleton, a month before, on 20 October 1598, 'the Earl of Essex be alone in election, yet there is still some rub in his way that he comes not on'. Before the month was out Essex knew that the post was no longer within his grasp, as we shall see from a famous letter of his to be considered shortly. But the queen did not suddenly swing from him to the other candidate. For there was a third possibility open to her and, in so explosive a situation, it had its obvious attractions. She could abolish the office altogether, or so emasculate it that it would not be worth having.[2]

That rumour, also, was in circulation. 'Some say the queen means to dissolve that court', wrote Chamberlain in the letter already cited, 'and instead thereof to raise a yearly contribution

---

1 Wards 14.3.20.2, f. 30r (printed in W. Wheatley, *The History of Edward Latymer and his Foundations* (1953), pp. 59–60).

2 *Records of the English Province of the Society of Jesus*, ed. H. Foley (1878), iv, 49; *The Letters of John Chamberlain*, ed. McClure (Philadelphia, 1939), i, 48.

out of all lands *in capite* or knight service, which would be more for her profit and less grievance to the subject.' The queen, in other words, would extricate herself from an impossible situation by introducing an overdue reform. She would make a virtue of necessity. 'But that', sighed Chamberlain, 'is too good to be true.' Other interpretations, he added, were being put forward—for example, that Essex could have the post if he wanted it but, because it was intended 'to geld or curtail it, he refuseth to accept it unless he may have it whole and unmaimed'. In his parlous financial condition he had no use for the shadow without the substance. Meanwhile, 'the Court of Wards sits not for want of a Master'.

It was a heavy price to pay. The queen had adopted this procedure before, in the case of the Secretaryship of State, vacant from 1590 to 1596. But the work had gone on, with Cecil as Secretary in everything but name. Now it was different. The whole apparatus of the Court of Wards was focused upon the Master; and in his absence the routine procedures might continue, but that was all. This situation had arisen when Sir Thomas Parry died on 15 December 1560, but then the queen had been able to decide quickly, and William Cecil had been appointed within four weeks. But when Cecil died she waited more than nine months. Meanwhile the Court was paralysed. A shocked civil servant drew up a careful—and lugubrious—statement of all the things that the Court could *not* do, for want of a Master:

> No justice can be administered between Her Majesty and the subject, neither between subject and subject without a Master of the Court, for no decree or order can be made but by the Master and Council of the Court.

> No contempt can be punished by fine or commitment to prison without a master.

> No process of privy seal or injunction can be awarded for Her Majesty's possession, or for punishment of any intrusion, or for any other cause whatsoever without a master.

No recognisance can be taken by the Court without a master.

No dower can be assigned to the queen's widows without a master.

Without a master! So the chorus goes on. And, he proceeds to show, this breakdown did not simply produce a whole chain of legal disabilities. It cut down the queen's revenues—and, we may be sure, cut down the revenues of the writer of these lamentations:

No ward can be sold by the officers of the Court without a master.

No fine [price] can be imposed for the ward's marriage without a master.

No lease can be made, nor fine for the same set, without a master.

No composition can be made with the queen's widows for their licence of marriage, nor fine set, without a master.

No wood sales can be made of any ward's lands without a master.

No order can be taken for the queen's debts without a master.

No particular receivers, feodaries or surveyors for wards' lands can be made or appointed, nor their accounts allowed or disallowed, without a master.

And so on.[1]

Once he got down to details, the future seemed even more depressing than the present. 'The revenue of the Court of Wards', he wrote, 'hath been less this Michaelmas term by almost £2,000 than it hath been in former years.' Grants made in the past would, of course, continue to yield some revenue, but no fresh sources could be established, for no new wardships could be granted. Even the existing revenues would decline because there was no formal authority for compelling debtors to come in and meet their obligations or, indeed, to compel sheriffs who had already by authority levied payments for debt to disgorge what they had obtained. Moreover, the writer pointed out, some of the money received into the Court of Wards during the current term consisted of profits accruing from the preceding one, and to that

1 Wards 9.158; Wards 14.3.20.2, f. 41r.

extent masked a more serious deficiency. The real fall was in the nature of £3,000. Clearly, profits would continue to drop as wards came of age but were not replaced by new wardships granted by the Master. In short, by keeping the Mastership vacant, the queen was sacrificing at least £12,000 a year.[1]

But she preferred to lose the money rather than appoint the Earl of Essex. Nor was she the only loser. When one recalls the interlocking system of suitors and patronage which reached right down from the Master through the central officials into the ranks of the county feodaries, escheators and the rest, and when one recalls also the whole series of go-betweens operating both in London and the provinces, then the loss to the queen's dependents seems great indeed.

Meanwhile the wards and their guardians looked on helplessly at a situation over which they had no control. Lady Hastings, a Mrs. Morehouse, and Lady Wentworth had to wait nearly a year after the death of Burghley before his promises to them could be fulfilled. Young Christopher Hatton, heir of Elizabeth's Lord Chancellor, ran into debt with his college at Cambridge, as the machinery of the Court of Wards ground to a standstill. Richard Bancroft, Bishop of London, did not mince his words when he told Cecil of Hatton's plight. Bancroft had earlier transmitted an account of the situation to the queen herself and 'she was pleased to promise other most princely goodness'— 'Since that time nothing hath been done.' In one case, during the vacancy, the queen herself appears to have made the direct grant of a wardship, as she had every right to do. Indeed, she reversed the grant of the late Master. But this was exceptional. Everything else stood in abeyance.[2]

Uncertainty bred fresh rumour: in December Cecil was the strong candidate, but others thought that the office might go to some 'mean man', whose authority and income could be reduced to modest proportions whilst the queen retained greater powers

---

[1] *Ibid.*, f. 42r.

[2] H.M.C. *Salis.*, ix, 207, 213, 215; viii, 463; ix, 178; for Hatton see also above p. 118; H.M.C. *Salis.*, viii, 394.

and greater revenues. These rumours, and the long delays, re-flected the uncertainty in high places; but what is clear is that some time during October, and certainly by 8 November 1598, a fortnight before Father Garnett was passing on his packet of un-sound information to Father Parsons, Essex knew that his own battle for the Mastership had been lost. On 8 November Chamber-lain was telling Carlton: 'it is generally held that the Earl of Essex shall go thither [to Ireland] towards the spring as lieutenant-general'. To confirm this picture of the changed situation, we have a copy of the earl's bitter letter to the queen which, his secretary tells us, was written in October 1598.[1]

In that month it somehow became clear to Essex that his chances were waning, if not extinguished altogether. 'Since I cannot go up to solicit Your Majesty by speech, I must in this paper put Your Majesty in mind that you have denied me an office which one of my fellows so lately and so long enjoyed'—a reference to Burghley's thirty-seven years' tenure of the Mastership. But, Essex also knew, Elizabeth might revert to her old strategy of blunting the edge of rivalry by leaving the office vacant for an indefinite period, a thing which, he said, none of her ancestors had ever done. To him it would be an added humiliation. 'If therefore, your Majesty give it not at all, the world may judge, and I must believe, that you overthrow the office because I should not be the officer.' He trembled at the prospect, and made a final plea: 'Therefore, if Your Majesty value me as you would do any man that had done you half that service, think again of the suit of Your Majesty's humblest servant.'

It was in vain. Early in November, Essex faced the facts of defeat and embarked upon the desperate Irish hazard which was to destroy his career and ultimately himself. For decade after decade, Ireland had sapped the health, wealth, and reputations of the generals sent out by Elizabeth to bring peace and submission to an oppressed and divided people. The father of the earl had himself died of an Irish sickness in that unyielding land. His son who, a generation later, took up his task in a rapidly worsening situation

1 *The Letters of John Chamberlain*, i, 56, 48; H.M.C. *Salis.*, 416–17.

can, in his calmer moments, have hoped for little from the venture. Whether he was wholly of a balanced mind when he took the decision to go, it is impossible to say. Coming so soon after his shattered prospects in the Court of Wards, and after such a letter as we have just considered, it looks like the fevered reflex-action to the experience of total defeat. Perhaps, in the hour of his despair, Essex begged to be released from a royal court which had been the witness of his humiliation; and the queen and her advisers were glad to seize the opportunity to send him on his way. Perhaps, with his last prospect of high office gone, Essex welcomed another title, Governor-General of Ireland, as balm to his wounded pride, though this represented only high office at the perimeter, not at the centre of power. Perhaps, even, he hoped after an Irish triumph to return to London with his reputation at its highest, free to claim his inheritance as a senior minister of state.

If that was his hope, the Irish rains washed it away in despair. This brave man showed himself to be, in Ireland, a demoralised second-rate general who, Elizabeth believed, was making her the laughing-stock of that country and of Europe. Indeterminate struggles were followed by ambiguous negotiations, with the hint of treason never far from the minds of both Essex and his queen. From now onwards, he suffered a complete failure of nerve. He threw up his Irish command without authority, disgraced himself in London, was imprisoned, released and, finally, with 'an all-hail and a kiss to the city' staked everything on rebellion—and lost. On 25 February 1601 he was executed on Tower Hill for high treason.

Viewed historically, there can be no question that when the queen refused to make Essex her Master of the Queen's Wards, the decision was right. Had she appointed him, then with the immense opportunities for patronage and wealth which the post carried he could have placed himself and his followers within reach of the heart of political power. Coming after a period when Burghley had kept his queen's—and his own—demands on fiscal wardship to modest proportions, this bankrupt earl would have been bound to reverse his predecessor's policy, in order to feed himself and his followers. In so doing he would, at one and the same time, have intensified the popular discontent against royal wardship while using his new source of wealth and power to enlarge his political opportunities and ambitions. This young man, in his early thirties, had he destroyed Cecil, Raleigh, and their allies, could have threatened the whole conception of Tudor rule, first as the power behind the throne and then, perhaps, nearer still. No man had ever spoken to a Tudor monarch as he had done to Queen Elizabeth : and the skies alone set limits to his ambitions. All this the queen recognised. Had she made him her Master of the Wards, she would have changed fundamentally the history of the last years of her reign. In the process she might also have profoundly altered the history of the century which was just opening.

We who look back across the intervening centuries can see how sound was the judgement of the old queen—and how faulty that of the young nobleman who made a frontal attack upon her system. But there is also present the element of high tragedy in the break-up of this young man of distinction and promise. Few can have drunk so often and so deeply from the cup of bitterness; but it is impossible, even with the exercise of the historical imagination, to share to the full his feelings in the loss of the Mastership. He had known for years that it must soon fall vacant and he knew also that his own name was being tossed about in the wind of speculation. So he had, unjustifiably, built his own high hopes on the prospect. But in the event, hope had been out-distanced by rumour, and both had been overtaken by despair. And even while he contemplated his fading chances, he savoured the sweet agonies of being addressed as Master by those less well-informed than himself. *Hope deferred maketh the heart sick.* Ill in body and mind, Essex felt that the only thing that he could do now was to leave the court and the capital. He seized the opportunity at hand to set sail for Ireland; and, as he landed on those unwelcoming shores, he opened the last desperate phase of a chronicle of failure.

On 21 May 1599, while Essex was away, the queen at last filled the vacant Mastership of the Wards—with Sir Robert Cecil. What effect the news had upon Essex, bogged down in Ireland, we cannot tell. But his subsequent career proves that he never recovered from the blow.

15

Sir Robert Cecil

THE uncertainty which had hamstrung the Court of Wards during the nine months' vacancy, prevailed until the very moment when the queen's decision was announced. 'Sir Thomas Fortescue', wrote the dowager Countess of Southampton to her son, the earl, 'utterly refuses the wards, whereat most marvel.' The letter was written on 18 May 1599. Yet by 21 May it was known that Cecil was Master. Indeed, on that very day he was already badgered by two suitors, one recommending his candidate for a secretaryship under Cecil, the other for a wardship. To these pressures he was, of course, well used; but far greater problems were crying out for solution. For the whole wardship system was under fire and he must sooner or later advise his monarch as to some drastic measure of reform.[1]

To see more clearly the issues which faced the queen on the eve of Cecil's appointment, we may consider one of the questions which the Earl of Essex put to the Receiver-General during those brief weeks when he thought that the Mastership was within his grasp. 'How may the revenues of the Court increase', he asked, 'without offence to the subject, and the Master of the Wards have the same authority as the last had?' The earl's hopes had come and gone; but the question remained; and now Cecil must face it. England was at war with Spain and she might, when the queen died, face civil war as well. The royal debt was rising, royal revenues were not keeping pace either with inflation or with the inflated structure and costs of government. Every possible source must be made to yield its uttermost—'how may the revenues of

[1] H.M.C. *Salis.*, ix, 173, 176-7.

the Court increase?' That perhaps might still be possible—but 'without offence to the subject'? That was less easy.[1]

The answer which Edward Latimer drafted, and sent to the Receiver-General for transmission to Essex, was the reasonable and guarded answer of a responsible civil servant. First he drew attention to the long-standing faults in administration. Action should be taken to make the discredited *inquisitions post mortem* into something more useful, provided, of course, that nothing extreme were attempted. The escheators and feodaries should 'cause somewhat better values to be found than hath been, where the land will conveniently bear it, and yet not in extremity, for it will cause many tenures to be concealed'. The selling price might also be raised but—we hear the note of caution again—'respect being had as is aforesaid, and that the charge be not otherwise great'. False conveyancing should be attacked; better records should be kept; the searchers out of concealed tenures should be better rewarded. It was an old story: and anyone who had been connected with the Court of Wards had heard it all before.[2]

But it did not touch upon the central issue of the wardship problem, an issue which lay at the root of government policy as a whole. For deeply entrenched in the whole system of national finance was the right of officials to take private profits, in addition to, and much larger than, their official rates of pay. '*How may the revenues of the Court increase?*' One way, as both Essex and Cecil knew, was not by raising the cost to the subject but by cutting the profits to the Master. If, instead of paying part of the price to the queen and the rest to the Master, or some courtier or official—which was the current practice—the guardian paid all to the queen, then the total burden upon the subject would not be increased and the crown would gain at the expense of the officials or the Master. He would then be reduced to the modest rank of the bureaucrat, with appropriate pay and perquisites; and the remainder of the wardship profits would flow, undiverted, to the queen. It was at this prospect that Essex had burked. Hence his question: how

[1] *C.P.D.*, Eliz., 1588–1601, p. 102.
[2] Wards 14.3.20.2, f. 34r.

may the Master of the Wards 'have the same authority as the last had?' Clearly, Essex was not prepared to make the sacrifice.

Nor apparently was Cecil. At least, that is the conclusion we should draw if we judge him by his performance during his father's lifetime. Through him had flowed the gifts, promises, and shady transactions, of which Michael Hickes had been either the author or the agent. During the last years of Burghley's Mastership, there had been plenty of letters of the kind which suitors apparently considered inappropriate for the father but very acceptable to the son. Here is one selection from Cecil's postbag. It is a letter from George Goring, corrupt son of a corrupt father. A neighbour of his, in Sussex, is seriously ill and expected to die shortly. He is a substantial landlord and the wardship of his son will therefore be worth a good deal. Cecil is accordingly urged to buy the wardship but it is suggested that it be put down in Goring's name, with Cecil drawing the profits. Even though the father of the ward is not yet dead, however, it occurs to Goring that he may be too late. 'If my Lord Treasurer have promised it already, then, if your Honour so please, my Lady Cecil may get him of the Queen's Majesty.' Then would come the final stage from which Cecil—and Goring—would derive the hidden profits. 'If the ward prove well, I would be glad to buy him, at the full value, of your Honour for one of my daughters.' Cecil's was an old hand at this complicated business; and, towards the end of the reign, it lost none of its cunning.[1]

But, from 1599 onwards he had authority—not simply influence. He had immense energy, great ambitions. But he was a younger son. His elder brother, Thomas, inherited the title and the great house at Burghley, though Robert was not left penniless. Ahead of him lay the task of building up his fame and family, with money and lands. As Master of the Wards, he was within reach of a great source of wealth, if he applied his energy and skill to this key office in the state. Contemporaries assumed that this is what he would do; and, as the years passed and he displayed all

[1] H.M.C. *Salis.*, vi, 363.

the splendour of a wealthy man, they saw in it a confirmation of their forecast. That forecast, however, has still to be tested.

Before we test it, it is worth considering a somewhat cryptic, but most interesting, observation by Cecil himself at the very beginning of his Mastership. He received his office on 21 May 1599, and on 23 May he was telling the diplomat, Sir Henry Neville, of the appointment. In obtaining it he had had to resign the Chancellorship of the Duchy of Lancaster; but, now, as Master, he found himself 'so restrained by new orders, as in the office I am a ward myself'. Apparently the post was not to be what it had been; 'but seeing it was my father's place, and that Her Majesty hath bestowed it on me, I will undergo it with as much integrity as I can'. But he could hardly look forward to its bounty. 'I vow to you, I have resigned a better place of the duchy for it.' If he was 'restrained by new orders', those orders could come from only one source, the queen herself. Had she, after nine months of vacillation, at last braced herself to give strict instructions to the new Master, under which he must give up his private profits from wardship so that the queen might receive the full sums to which she was entitled? That alone would explain why Cecil found the office less attractive than the Chancellorship of the Duchy; why he lamented: 'I am a ward myself.' That too would explain why Essex sent Fleetwood his pertinent question about the authority of the Master, and why, also, he was refused the post. It might explain finally why Sir Thomas Fortescue declined it. With Cecil as Master, but with his wings clipped, the queen by a brilliant stroke would reduce the Mastership to a minor office, yet obtain a first class administrator to do the work. But success depended upon one thing: whether Cecil kept his word to occupy the office 'with as much integrity as I can'.[1]

Cecil's surviving manuscripts at Hatfield and elsewhere do not, at first glance, encourage one to make a favourable judgement of him. Hickes, for a time at least, remained active. Lesser men also dabbled in the business. For example, Cecil was approached by a certain John Poyntz, who had been beaten in the competition for

[1] Sir Ralph Winwood, *Memorials*, ed. Sawyer (1725), i, 41.

his stepdaughter's wardship by no less a person than Lord Cobham. To compensate himself for the loss, Poyntz accordingly asked for the wardship of the heir of a Mr. Dilland, who was believed to be on his death-bed. But now Poyntz was taking no chances of being outbid in the competition. He offered to bestow £100 on one of Cecil's servants: a euphemism for a gift to Cecil himself. In 1603 we find Cecil advising Hickes to pay that notorious sponger and go-between, Lady Glemmam, daughter of the Lord Treasurer, one hundreds pounds as a bribe. In return Cecil would compensate Hickes with a 'ward to pay for it', or else he would in due course give Hickes double the sum paid to Lady Glemmam. More significant perhaps is the case of Elizabeth Bassett's wardship, which has a lot to teach us about Cecil's methods at this time.[1]

The story begins with a petition to Cecil during 1602 from a certain John Baxter, claiming that he had given legal and other services to the late William Bassett, in Derbyshire, and subsequently to the queen in revealing that Bassett had held his lands by knight-service from the crown. As a result, a wardship had been discovered. Then, with the request for some reward for his efforts, Baxter drops out of the narrative, to make way for more eminent men. The wardship was in fact sold on 18 May 1602 to Henry, Lord Cobham, the Lord Chamberlain, and brother-in-law of Cecil —the same Cobham whom we have already met in the preceding paragraph, standing between Poyntz and the wardship of his stepdaughter. But Cobham kept the wardship for only two days and then sold it to Sir Walter Raleigh 'for and in consideration of a certain sum of money'—not stated—and Cecil himself acted as witness to the agreement. But Cecil's role was by no means simply the passive one of witness. On the very day that Raleigh bought the Bassett wardship at second-hand, he entered into an agreement with Cecil himself, making provision, amongst other things, that in the event of Cecil's death within the ensuing two years, Raleigh would transfer the wardship to the executors of Cecil.

The executors of Cecil? The explanation of this curious arrangement is to be found in the early part of the agreement. After

[1] H.M.C. *Salis.*, xiv, 108; B.M. Lans. 88, f. 105r.

reciting that Raleigh had bought the wardship from Cobham it states: 'the passing of which grant was truly meant and intended by the said Sir Robert Cecil and Henry Lord Cobham to be in trust, and to the only use and behoof of him, the said Sir Robert Cecil and his assigns'. No transfer of wardship could take place without the authority of the Master of the Wards. Cecil clearly wanted the wardship but, for one reason or another, did not dare grant it openly to himself. So Lord Cobham was brought in—does this also explain his part in the Poyntz affair?—and then Sir Walter Raleigh, whose agreement with Cobham would have to be entered on the official records of the Court of Wards. Finally Cecil executed a *private* trust with Raleigh—which, as a trust and not a re-sale, would not have to be recorded amongst the Court of Wards records. So Sir Robert Cecil, as Master, made it possible for Sir Robert Cecil, as a private individual, to reap the profits of a wardship. How many times he did this we cannot tell for we are dependent upon the chance survival of these private papers.[1]

But, it may be asked, is this very different from the policy of his father, who kept some of the greatest wards in England under his care? There was indeed a profound difference. For the wardships of those young noblemen were never sold by Burghley and he laid no claim whatsoever to the profits of feudal guardianship. If the queen did not sell a ward she remained his guardian and Burghley, as Master, was simply acting as *locum tenens* for the queen. When, ultimately, the wardship was sold to the ward himself, so that he might be free to marry whom he chose, as in the case of the Earl of Oxford, the money went to the queen and not to Burghley. All our evidence for these noblemen has shown that, as far as the ordinary profits of a feudal marriage were concerned, Burghley gained nothing. By contrast, Cecil instituted an elaborate tripartite arrangement, in the case of the Bassett wardship, so that he personally would collect the profits from it or, failing that, his heirs would, after his death.

Before we leave this strange incident it is worth considering Cecil's own opinion on the subject, recorded in a personal letter

[1] H.M.C. *Salis.*, xii, 580-1; Hatfield deeds 192.6 and 10.

to his crony, Hickes. He, too, had apparently wanted the wardship but had been refused. 'Mr. Hickes,' Cecil told him, 'your request to me, at this time in this wardship, is not denied out of my indisposition to do you pleasure (for I would be very glad to gratify where I love) but because I know you will, in this particular, see some circumstances which may vary from both our purpose.' He asked Hickes not for one moment to regard his refusal in this case as representative of his general attitude. Competition for the wardship had been very acute; in addition Cecil had been approached by the mother herself for the guardianship of her own child. 'This reason', he said, 'is not the greatest which hath moved me and yet too great (I think in your opinion) for me to deny.' Popular opinion had set too high a value upon the wardship, he added, but it was attractive enough to arouse comment if the Master granted it to so intimate a servant and friend as Hickes. These modest remarks obscure the fact, as no doubt was intended, that Elizabeth Bassett was heir to a substantial fortune. She married, first, Henry Howard, a member of the leading aristocratic family of England and, secondly, William Cavendish who subsequently became first Duke of Newcastle. She is reported to have brought him an income of £2,400 a year and six or seven thousand pounds in cash.[1]

What solution had Cecil adopted? It is here that we strike the purest vein of his hypocrisy. 'I have been driven to some other course', he said, 'to draw some benefit myself and yet not so to appear.' Since he did not feel free to reward Hickes, he was taking the profit himself. But, he said, some eminent man had to be brought into the business, like a suitor acting in the normal way for somebody else—'as if some great person had my grant for the mother'. Hence Cecil's choice of Lord Cobham, since he was not one 'whom they would suspect so much to be (but my figure) as they would do you'. (The thought of the bulky Cobham as but 'a figure'—a man of straw—has a charm of its own.) So, by a

---

[1] B.M. Lans. 88, f. 91r; *Staffordshire Pedigrees* (Harl. Soc. lxiii). p. 20; *G.E.C.*, ix, 525, note (a).

marvellous and roundabout argument, Cecil came to the conclusion that he alone should benefit from the wardship. 'I conclude
that you would not look at one time at me for a gift and that value
(who have so few means for myself).' For a moment we catch
the whine of his father who, as he advanced in wealth and power,
tried to propitiate fate, and his contemporaries, by lamenting over
his poverty. Hickes was urged to be patient, for he would 'be sure
to have in some other manner that benefit clearly which may content your moderate desires'. The letter concludes with a reference
to Cecil's debt to Michael's brother, the notorious Baptist Hickes.

Cecil normally covered his tracks extremely well, as he tried
to do in this case. Time has helped by scattering his evidence to
the four winds. It is only by re-assembling the material from the
manuscripts at Hatfield House, the British Museum, the Public
Record Office, and genealogical sources that we have been able
to piece together an extraordinary transaction. If the pattern of
behaviour which emerges is scandalous, it is what we had come to
expect from Cecil when his father was still Master.

But to meet it in its fullest vigour, when the son had succeeded
to the high office of Master, raises in an acute form fundamental
issues of public policy. It would seem that, with this and similar
evidence before us of Cecil's duplicity, we ought to dismiss him as
an incorrigible exploiter of a public trust for private profit. For if
any state office could claim to be called an office of trust, the Mastership of the Wards had a pre-eminent and peculiar right to the
title. Large numbers of newly-orphaned children came within its
protection each year and many hundreds were under its jurisdiction from previous years. Yet here was the Master himself taking
complicated care to disguise the grant of a guardianship, ignoring
the interest of the mother—'this reason is not the greatest which
hath moved me'—and masking an extremely profitable transaction under a cloud of conveyances. The historian of the Court
of Wards could not be blamed if, at this stage, he added his voice
to the contemporary condemnation of Cecil and concluded that,
under him, wardship was finally prostituted to the greedy and
squalid court circle of the declining Elizabethan state.

Francis Bacon once said of Cecil that he was a man who faced both ways; he was like a boatman rowing his passengers along the Thames, for he 'looketh toward the [London] Bridge when he pulleth towards Westminster'. This, of course, was not a compliment but a warning, included as it was in a letter from Bacon to Essex. Yet the expression perhaps carries with it a more profound concept of Cecil than was intended by a disgruntled philosopher writing to his unsuccessful patron. For, if we judge Cecil simply on the basis of evidence—supplied indeed by Cecil himself as well as others—of his lust for money and his devious ways of getting it, we write off too easily a highly complex personality who, in more senses than one, faced both ways. The evidence is undoubtedly very damaging, but it is incomplete; and we must try somehow to correlate it with a good deal of material which, at first sight surprisingly, faces the other way.[1]

First of all, to counterbalance the shady and ambiguous letters which did no credit to either sender or recipient, we have a good many which pay tribute to his upright and loyal service. The widowed Countess of Essex, a few months after her husband's execution, thanked Cecil for all his efforts to protect her honour and interests in the Star Chamber and elsewhere. She felt that she owed him something more substantial than words of thanks. 'To return only paper and ink for such essential benefits, I confess holds no proportion,' she wrote, 'yet when I look into mine own fortune, I find little therein of better value.' This was no isolated incident. 'I call to my remembrance', she went on, 'how oft you have been pleased to accept of such shadows instead of better substance.'[2]

Lord Sheffield, in entreating Cecil's help in a legal matter, claimed to do so 'for justice' sake, knowing that I cannot move you with anything more forcible, your nature and virtue considered'. Sir Arthur Gorges did try to move Cecil with something more forcible, as a New Year's gift; 'towards the garnishing of your

---

1 *The Letters and the Life of Francis Bacon*, ed. Spedding, i, 262.
2 H.M.C. *Salis.*, xi, 251.

new house', he said, 'I humbly desire leave to add this poor imple-
ment. But for the retaining of your wonted favour', he hastened
to add, 'I present you with nothing but my dutiful affection.' The
gift apparently embarrassed and annoyed Cecil, especially as the
covering letter had been written by a servant and the present
brought by him. So Gorges had to write a second letter, explain-
ing away the modest gift and pointing out that 'my particular
thought varied not from the general opinion of the world, wherein
you exchange gain for glory and servile bribery for free power'.
A New Year's gift, however, was 'the common custom and usual
compliment of the time'. But, he admitted, 'I know your puritan
humour would take offence at the shadow of a gift.' It is perhaps
appropriate, before leaving the question of New Year's gifts, to
recall Francis Bacon to the witness box. Bacon, who never tired
of abusing Cecil behind his back or after his death, wrote as
follows to him on New Year's Day 1608 : ' I do esteem whatsoever
I have, or may have, in the world but as trash in comparison of
having the honour and happiness to be a near and well-accepted
kinsman to so rare and worthy a counsellor, governor and
patriot.'[1]

Bacon who published an essay 'Of Deformity' in the year of
Cecil's death and included in it a scarcely veiled attack on the
statesman, was also the author of an essay 'Of Simulation and Dis-
simulation'. His New Year's tribute is of course the polished in-
sincerity of a climbing courtier and we need not take his estimate
seriously. In short, Bacon, as much as Cecil, looked both ways.
On the issue of Cecil's probity he has shown himself an untrustworthy witness and we may leave his favourable and unfavourable comments to cancel one another out.

But as it happens, we have a letter from a much lesser man who,
if we follow him to the end, may help us better to resolve one problem at least of Cecil's policy. There was a certain Mr. Proby who
sent, on more than one occasion, the present of a book to Cecil.
'When I brought you the book of the state and condition of Ireland',

1 Ibid., xi, 242; xii, 581; The Essays of Francis Bacon, ed. S. H. Reynolds (Oxford, 1890),
p. 310.

wrote Proby, 'you told me that you esteemed books more than gold, as you showed last year when I could not procure you to accept a small token of the good I received by your means.' This, he said, 'astonished me much, until Sir John Stanhope told me it was your practice not to take anything of charge from those you liked best of'.[1]

There are two ways of looking at this conversation. We may be witnessing a charming piece of make-believe, worthy again of Burghley himself, in which Robert Cecil took the opportunity to impress with his high standards of conduct a man who had very little to offer anyway. If that is so, then Stanhope also took part in the game and the whole thing was a wonderful façade behind which Cecil conducted his scandalous business of money-grubbing. But it may be that Cecil, Stanhope, Lord Sheffield, the Countess of Essex, and others meant exactly what they said: namely, that Cecil was not corrupted by presents. If they were right, then we must look more closely at Cecil's policy 'not to take anything of charge from those you liked best of'; of taking gifts from others; of disguising his own purchase of a wardship and yet claiming to be a faithful servant of the crown.

So far we have listened to enemies and friends of Cecil. It is only fair at this stage that we should hear him in his own defence. One place where we may find it is in a letter he wrote to the Earl of Northumberland towards the end of 1600, after he had been Master of the Wards for a year and a half. 'I have received', he wrote, 'a coach and four horses from you, a gift greater than ever I was beholding for to any subject and that I would have refused, whatsoever had come of it, if I could have been present to have argued with you.' He gave three reasons for his attitude. In the first place, 'gifts of value ought not to pass between those whose minds contemn all the knots that utility can fasten'. Secondly, there was a matter pending before the queen in which Cecil had supported Northumberland. To take gifts now would imply that his support of Northumberland was tainted with the desire for profit and not from 'the honour I carry to your person and the

[1] H.M.C. *Salis.*, ix, 8.

knowledge I have of your sincerity and ability to do Her Majesty service'. Finally, it would seem to confirm the mercenary basis of his policy which, Cecil reminded Northumberland, was what his enemies alleged against him. The queen herself might doubt Cecil's integrity. As a result of these anxieties, he very nearly returned the gift, save that he could not bear to hurt Northumberland. 'But what! should I now call back yesterday? For I have accepted your fair present rather than discontent you, and have only reserved an assurance that this was given me out of the vastness of your kindness, not out of any other mistaking my disposition. For requital whereof I can only return this present, that though I have neither gold nor silver, yet I have love and honesty.'[1]

A pretty speech! One courtier writes to another in the understood phrases of polite intercourse, but both giver and recipient know that the system is essential and will go on. That may be. But to some readers, perhaps, the letter carries the ring of sincerity, as though Cecil were trying to break through the accepted traditions of Tudor government and throwing out the first hints of a system that he would like to put in their place. But before deciding whether the letter was born of honesty or hypocrisy or— as sometimes happens—a combination of both, we must consider a little more the system in practice. Gifts, we know, were sent to the Master and others, both before and after Cecil was placed in charge of the Court of Wards. But a lot depended on the kind of gifts and the manner and purpose of the giving. Like his father —and the rest of Tudor England—Cecil was usually prepared to accept New Year gifts. We may look therefore in detail at one list of gifts received by Cecil, in the last New Year of Elizabeth's reign:

> From Lord Burghley: one basin and ewer of silver white, 108½ ounces. 3 plates of silver, 27 ounces.
> From the Company of Merchant Venturers: one great standing bowl in a case.
> From Sir John Roper: one great standing bowl in a case.

[1] *Ibid.*, x, 347.

From My Lord of Hertford: one pair of great Dutch pots, gilt, 162¾ ounces.

From Mr Nicholson,: one fair standing bowl.

From Mr Owen: one other standing bowl, lesser, 8 ounces.

From the Bishop of Winchester: one standing cup.

From Dr Stanhope: one other standing cup, lesser.

From My Lord Norris: one cup of gold in a velvet case.

From Mr Cole of Devonshire: one basin and ewer of fine 'purslen', gilt. Six fair dishes of 'purslen', gilt. Six lesser of fine 'purslen', gilt. One perfuming pot in the form of a cat, of 'purslen'. One fine 'voider' of China, gilt.

From My Lady Digby: one fine cushion, lined with carnation satin.

From Mr Cope: one sweet bag.

From Mr Skinner: one other sweet bag.

From My Lady Layton: one chair embroidered.

From Controller of the Works: a fire shovel, tongs and a lock for the door.

Mr Savage: two barrels of figs.

From Sir Robert Cross: one little casket.

From a ward: one great standing cup of scollop shells: 66 ounces.

From a ward: one great salt set in crystal, 106 ounces.

From Mr Penruddock: one salt, 28 ounces.[1]

It is undoubtedly a lengthy list; and some of the gifts were valuable. For example, his brother, Lord Burghley, sent him plate of considerable worth. Plate was the gilt-edged security of the sixteenth century; and, in the inflated economy of war, it had a considerable attraction as the one stable investment to which men could turn. The gift must have been very welcome; but it was hardly a corrupt one, passing as it did between two brothers who, in spite of their utterly contrasting personalities, were always friendly and loyal colleagues. The cup of gold from Lord Norris, a son-in-law of Burghley, must also have been welcome, as was Lord Hertford's gift. The Merchant Adventurers' standing bowl may have been of some value, and the same was probably true of Sir John Roper's bowl. Cecil did not keep them long. They were both 'sold to Prescott'; and Mr. Nicholson's 'fair standing bowl' went

1 *Ibid.*, xii, 527-8.

the same way. Mr. Owen's 'lesser standing bowl', Cecil either would not or could not sell: he gave it to 'Sir Henry Neville's child'. The ward's 'standing cup with scollop shells' was held only until the christening service of the French ambassador's child, to whom it now passed. Dr. Stanhope's lesser standing cup was wrapped up again and sent off to a Dr. Elvin.

The remainder of the collection is not very impressive and hardly likely to make a great minister of state abandon whatever public policy he intended to pursue. Lady Digby's cushion, combined with Lady Layton's chair, may have given a tired minister a peaceful hour in which to read—or doze over—his dispatches. He may have had on the table beside him Mr. Cope's or Mr. Skinner's sweet bag. The fire shovel, tongs and door lock seem appropriate —and utilitarian—gifts, to be expected from a Comptroller of Works in any age; and Cecil kept them. He also kept Mr. Savage's two barrels of figs. The festive season was just ending and, no doubt, Cecil had a use for them.

Taken as a whole, the list does not read like some massive attempt to corrupt a statesman. But the total value was by no means negligible; and it may have been one of several collections. It is all the more striking, therefore, to see how Cecil began to set his face against these payments in cash and kind.

In 1600, as we have seen, he had told Northumberland about his doubts in accepting gifts. In 1603, in the new reign, he carried the process a stage farther in special instructions to his representatives engaged in the work of wardship. First, he offered to all tenants in chief, in their lifetime, the sale of their heirs' wardships: in other words, to free them from the Court of Wards. Secondly, the sales should be made without any gifts to officials. The purchasers, he declared, must be clearly told in advance 'that they shall not receive their assurance from His Majesty without taking their corporal oath in open court that they have neither promised nor paid, directly or indirectly, any money or other benefit, for obtaining the same other than the sums agreed upon to His Majesty's use, and the ordinary fees of the clerks and officers'. It would have been impossible to make a more explicit declaration.

Was this also part of some elaborate conspiracy to confuse and mislead the crown and the public? Cecil was afraid that that is precisely what would be said 'because the envious minds of men, who judge others commonly by their own affections, will be apt to conceive that I, who am His Majesty's principal officer in the Court of Wards, would not endeavour to further His Majesty's good intention with so great care and such contentment, except some way were open to me by this course to derive to myself some private gain, to countervail the diminution of that power and authority which by this means is taken from me to bind or pleasure any man by virtue of this office during my time'. Cecil, as he feared, failed to convince contemporaries that he was prepared to sacrifice his personal interests for the welfare of the state.[1]

He has also largely failed to convince historians. But we have one advantage over contemporaries in that we can penetrate beyond both his own view of himself and the conflicting views of him by his fellow countrymen; and we can analyse certain statistical material at our disposal. If we assume for the moment that Cecil was sincere and determined in his resolve to abolish gifts to the Master and other officials, what, we must ask, was the object of this revolutionary policy?

In fact, it could be aimed at one of two goals. By abolishing the gifts Cecil could enable the purchaser of the wardship to obtain it far more cheaply—namely, at the official price only and not at the much higher price he had hitherto been paying because he had also to pay a substantial unofficial one. Since few of the purchasers were mothers, the effect of that policy would be to transfer the profits from the go-between and the official to the investor in wardships. This would scarcely be a reform, but the transfer of profits from one class of the community to another. Alternatively Cecil might argue that, since the guardian no longer had to pay substantial *unofficial* sums above the official price to various people, it was reasonable to raise the *official* price to take in these other amounts and thereby to augment the total

1 Edmund Lodge, *Illustrations of British History* (1838), iii, 41–6.

revenue of the government. With these alternatives in mind we may examine Cecil's policy in detail. In order to see it as a whole we must extend the margins of this chapter up to his death in 1612.

In February 1600 the Master and Council of the Court of Wards issued orders to reform its administration. The draft that we possess was corrected by Cecil, and it may serve therefore as a reasonable guide to his frame of mind in the first year of his Mastership. There are thirteen items in the schedule of instructions, which are concerned principally with tightening up the Court's control over the feodary and seeing that he has less opportunity for hiding dues owing to the crown, or robbing the revenues in other ways. But it is the sixth of these directives which is of most significance: 'in all surveys of wards' lands they are not to be passed at under-values, but the rents raised if they will bear it'. That sentence, and the whole body of directions, could have brought small comfort to would-be purchasers. And, as Cecil's policy began to work itself out, it became clear that they, clearly, were not designed to be beneficiaries under his reforms. By the 'rents', Cecil meant the values set upon the wards' lands, since they formed the basis upon which all Masters of Wards calculated the selling price of the wardships. If the 'rents' were raised by the feodary—that is, if his estimates were more realistic—and if Cecil merely followed the same ratio as his father employed in fixing the selling price, then the prices must surely rise.[1]

But Cecil was not content merely to speak with his father's voice. In an earlier chapter we have followed Burghley's technique of keeping the selling price as low as possible, usually at the equivalent of the annual value of the land or at 50 per cent. above it.[2] At once Cecil abandoned this ratio. We may take as an example the first eleven wardships he sold in Kent—and these proved typical of his sales in other counties[3]:

[1] *C.P.D.*, Eliz., 1598–1601, pp. 394–5.
[2] Above p. 275.
[3] Wards 9.160 (Kent).

Sales of Wardships in Kent

Annual Value	Price of Wardship
£38. 2s. 5d.	£130
£34. 0s. 4d.	£66. 13s. 4d.
£1. 13s. 4d.	£6
£4. 18s. 9½d.	£14
£23. 10s. 4d.	£35
£13. 6s. 8d.	£40
£5. 5s. 4d.	£6. 13s. 4d.
£42. 5s. 0d.	£130
£1. 10s. 0d.	£6
£127. 13s. 4d.	£120
£60	£180

It will be seen that in only one case was the wardship sold at less than the annual value, and then only slightly less: a reduction of £7. 13s. 4d. on an annual value of £127. 13s. 4d. Only one wardship was sold at slightly above the annual value, and this was obviously in the case of a ward of very modest means, whose lands were worth no more than £5. 5s. 4d. a year. In one other case the wardship was sold at one and a half times the annual value. Of the remaining eight, one was sold at just under twice the annual value, one at just under three times the annual value, and the remaining six at three times the annual value, or more. Over half the wardships were sold for at least three times the annual value. In only three of the eleven wardships did Cecil's policy bear any resemblance to that of his father. Here was revolution indeed.

If we broaden our interest from the county of Kent to the nation as a whole we find, in the early years of Cecil's Mastership, that more than sixty per cent. of the wardships he sold went at *three* or *four* times the annual value of the lands. In the last full year of Burghley's Mastership the revenues from the sale of wardships reached the total of £2,669. By the last year of Elizabeth's reign, under Cecil, they had leapt to £8,525.[1]

If we bear in mind that Cecil was giving a double crack to the

1 Wards 9.388, f. 363v; 394, f. 259v. See also C. S. Russell, *Notes and Queries*, ccxiv, 33.

whip, that he was raising the estimated land values which formed the basis of the sale, and that he was at the same time forcing up the multiplier for determining the selling price, then it is possible to see what a sudden and profound shock his policy gave to the whole system. Before his day the valuations were, of course, absurd. To bring them nearer to reality was a remarkable step forward, long overdue. Then to sell the wardship at several times above the newly-calculated annual value pressed the royal claim farther still. Contemporaries read the signs well enough. From the time of Henry VIII till Burghley was Master of the Wards, wrote one observer in 1606, 'they [wardships] passed commonly under a year's value, and very seldom raised to the rate of a year'. Burghley, 'to increase Her Majesty's benefit, increased it to a year and a half, and the now Master never under three, sometimes four or five or more'. Meanwhile the Court of Wards grew in power. 'My cousin Garnons told me', wrote the diarist Manningham, 'that the Court of Wards will send a prohibition to any other court to cease from proceeding in any suit, whereof themselves may have colour to hold place in that court: so predominant a court is that now become.'[1]

The pattern of Cecil's policy was already clear when the old queen died. The accession of a new monarch and dynasty presented him with a challenge and an opportunity: a challenge because a worsening economic situation cried aloud for financial reform; an opportunity because with a new occupant of the throne and a growing public outcry against wardships, the climate of opinion seemed more favourable to some major reform in the whole apparatus. As the years passed Cecil grew in prestige and experience. 'All envy of him', wrote the Venetian Ambassador in 1606, 'is now dead; no one seeks aught but to win his favour; it is thought that his power will last, for it is based not so much on the grace of His Majesty, as on an excellent prudence and ability, which secure for him the universal opinion that he is worthy of his great authority and good fortune.' In 1608 he climbed the

[1] *S.P.D.*, Jas. I, xxiv, no. 65 (I am indebted to Professor R. H. Tawney for the reference); *Diary of John Manningham*, ed. J. Bruce (Camden Soc. 1868), p. 19.

last rung of his ambition with his appointment as Lord Treasurer, head of the whole revenue system. To the challenge and the opportunity he was now in a position to respond with boldness and imagination.[1]

The land-owning classes, well represented in the House of Commons, had celebrated the arrival of the new king with a strong demand that the long-standing abuse of wardship should be dealt with once for all. The nine months' vacancy in the Mastership had bred incessant rumours that fiscal feudalism was about to be drastically reformed; and the accession of James I had bred a new rumour—not apparently based on fact—that Robert Cecil had been dismissed from his office. All this served to weaken his position as Master; and the time for decision could clearly not be much longer delayed. He must either act soon or see the initiative pass from him altogether. In 1606 the Commons were pressing harder for some fundamental measure of reform; and when at the end of the year the matter was brought to vigorous debate, some angry wits seized the opportunity of the adjournment to stage a lively scene. The House was being asked, in the usual way, whether the debate should be adjourned until the morrow. 'Yea', called out the more aggressive members, seizing their chance, 'I would it might be tomorrow that wards might be taken away.' 'Yes', echoed others amidst the uproar, 'Tomorrow! tomorrow!' The patience of the House of Commons in this, and in much else, was clearly not inexhaustible.[2]

The overwhelming majority of the Commons wanted nothing less than the abolition of feudal wardship, although some of the best brains amongst them, including Sir Francis Bacon, favoured its retention. But the radicals drew some strength from the belief that they possessed an ally, no longer amongst them but powerful in the counsels of the king: none other than Cecil himself, now Earl of Salisbury. 'It was voiced in the House', a correspondent told him, 'that my Lord of Salisbury is a furtherer of the matter

---

1 *Venet. Cal.*, x, 354.
2 *Ibid.*, p. 33; *The Parliamentary Diary of Robert Bowyer, 1606-7*, ed. D. H. Willson (1931), p. 201, n. 2.

and would be willing, for the glory of your name, that in your time of being Master of the Wards, the wards might be taken away.' In due course Cecil's own acts confirmed the estimate, and he staked his power and fame upon the carrying through of this major reform in society and government.[1]

But no one, least of all Cecil, considered that wardship as a revenue source should be totally swept away without replacement by some new royal income. It was difficult enough for the king to 'live of his own'. If some of 'his own' were taken away without recompense, his position would become intolerable. This, the Commons for their part recognised. But the king hoped for more than this. His responsibilities were far greater than his monetary resources; and his appetites outstripped them both. He wanted not simply a *quid pro quo* for the feudal dues he was asked to renounce. He wanted enough to give him—what no Stuart king ever gained—financial security. So there began the long-drawn-out negotiations over the 'Great Contract', the attempt at a constitutional bargain between James I and his subjects: one of the most interesting experiments in English history.

In 1608 James I appointed Cecil to the office his father had held for so long: Lord High Treasurer of England. Burghley was at the Treasury for twenty-six years: his son for only four, until his death in 1612. Yet the son tried to do more in four years than the father in six times the span. For Cecil recognised at once that the times called for drastic steps and that the highest office carried with it the heaviest burdens of responsibility. The accumulated debt of the crown now stood in the neighbourhood of £1m., of which about a third had been inherited from Queen Elizabeth. The annual deficit was not far short of £100,000. If ever the need for retrenchment and reform was acute, it was in 1608.

But in the matter of retrenchment the minister knew that his monarch was immovable. An extravagant king, married to an even more extravagant queen, and surrounded by a parasitical and insatiable baronage, stood desperately in need of the services of a new broom, though profoundly hostile to its ministrations. Re-

[1] *Ibid., loc. cit.*

trenchment unfortunately had to be ruled out. So Cecil, perforce, gave instructions for pressure to be put upon the available revenue sources to yield, one way or another, whatever financial relief could be hoped for. Taxes due but unpaid were called in; so were outstanding debts. Impositions on trade were forced up. The eldest son of the king was knighted, so an ancient feudal 'aid' was extracted from the king's subjects. Other dubious means were explored, and they too contributed something. It has been estimated that England at peace under James was now paying heavier taxes than in the Armada year under Elizabeth. Still it was not enough. Early in 1610 it became necessary to re-assemble parliament.

The king's necessity was the opportunity for reform; but Cecil must walk warily. To offer at one stroke to abolish fiscal feudalism would at once devalue the reform: in which case the Lord Treasurer might be remembered for his public spirit but hardly for his political acumen or financial skill. So first he set out a detailed statement of the royal finances and called upon the nation, as represented in Parliament, to open its purse: 'And will you see the ship of estate drive so near the port and suffer it to perish, considering that your own fortunes are embarked therein?'

The hard realists who heard the speech easily brushed the plea aside and eagerly got down to debating amongst themselves the terms on which they were prepared to meet some part of the royal needs. More particularly they turned to the king's unprecedented request for 'support'—an annual contribution—and 'supply'—a lump sum to meet the king's debts. If they were to pay, then they demanded 'retribution', by which they meant the grant of reforms by the crown. Their grants would be conditional ones; they would yield nothing without redress of grievances. If they paid the royal piper they would call the parliamentary tune. No Elizabethan parliament had succeeded in writing into the subsidy acts any overt declaration of royal reform; in other words, they had never been able to make their grants conditional grants. But the conditions were often implied. Now, when the new dynasty was only seven years old, they were frankly stated. And, in demanding reform before taxation, the members of the House of Commons were, in fact, making an open bid to control policy. No wonder Cecil's first speech was extremely evasive about 'a general redress of all just grievances'. As the Commons debates were reported back to him, he must have begun to ask himself whether he had opened a door which no man would ever close.[1]

As to the kind of 'retribution' they wanted, members were by no means lacking in ideas. Recusants should be punished, tax-farming should be abolished, purveyance—the purchase by royal agents of farm produce well below the market price—should go with it. But, most important of all, they wanted 'the discharge of tenures and wardships, whereby the subjects should receive a great ease and contentment, and our laws should be more agreeable to the law of God'. Another member, who did not wish to go so far and suggested that they should take the private profits out of wardship and give them to the king, was heard in silence. Half measures were not enough. Upon wardship the issue seemed to turn, and the debate ended with a request to know 'His Majesty's pleasure whether he would be pleased to discharge his tenures'.

At a joint conference between Lords and Commons which followed, Cecil expressed his astonishment that a legitimate demand for money by the crown should be met by the question: *quid mihi dabis?*—'What will the king give to his subjects?' To that question he offered no reply, but went on to state more precisely the king's needs: £600,000 for supply and £200,000 a year for support. Under pressure, he appeared to give way a little and named some reforms which the king 'might haply be persuaded upon good considerations to yield to his subjects'. The word 'consideration' was commonly used to mean a sum of money, paid as the result of a contract, and as such it was here understood. He recited ten possible ways in which the king might lighten the burden upon his subjects; for example, purveyance to be extinguished; 'informers to be taken away (which are all beggars and knaves)'; 'the friends of every ward to have the wardship at

---

[1] *Parliamentary Debates in 1610*, ed. S. R. Gardiner (Camden Soc. lxxxi), from which all further quotations from the 1610 debate are taken.

certain reasonable rates, and the committee [purchaser] to receive no more [from the friend or relation] than he pays'; respite of homage to be made easier. But on the fundamental question of the abolition of feudal wardship, he asked for time for both sides to examine the question. A week later, on 1 March, the Commons made their position clear. For supply, they would work by no other method than the established method of a parliamentary subsidy. For support—that is an annual grant—they could offer no answer until they knew the decision as to wardships.

Cecil had until now continued his elaborate show of reluctance for two reasons. He dared not, as we have seen, cheapen the price of an eagerly sought reform. Nor must he force a hesitant king too quickly down the steep path to change, for at the end of it lay the abandonment of an ancient part of his prerogative. But in face of the Commons' insistent demand he must now come to the central issue of fiscal feudalism. Yet, if bargain there could be, Cecil resolved to drive the hardest one he could. The king, he said, was deeply troubled in his conscience about the abandonment of the royal responsibility for wardships—and here I think we may believe him—and, he went on, the fact that they were now offered the prospect of the end of wardships should not lead them to underestimate the reforms, 'but rather highly to value them because they were never offered before by any king of this realm to his subjects'. Then he made his boldest claim, telling them that they 'must not only consider what the present profit is of the wardships and fines for alienations, *but what may be made of them*'. A promise and a threat! If the bargain fell through, then the profits from fiscal wardship would be forced up to the highest figure which the guardian could pay. Having given his hearers a clear warning that their position was not impregnable, and that the initiative did not lie wholly with them, he offered them sweeter words. 'Let your resolutions sort with these considerations', he said, 'and then you need not despair that you may obtain your desires. And then you may return into your countries and tell your neighbours that you have made a pretty hedge about them.'

So the bargaining went on right through the spring and into the summer. The Commons offered £100,000 a year for the abolition of feudal wardship, purveyance, and certain other abuses. James said it was not enough and asked for £220,000. At last, on 17 July, Cecil could announce that he had persuaded the king to accept £200,000. On 19 July the Commons, for their part, agreed. On 23 July the Lords concurred. Only the details as to how the money would be levied was left for the next session; and on the afternoon of that day James I prorogued Parliament. 'And so', said one observer, 'for this time the king and Commons are like to part in the lovingest terms that ever any subjects of England did rise from Parliament.'[1]

It was a brief honeymoon. Both parties had second thoughts. Courtier-critics of the scheme convinced the impressionable James that his early doubts were justified, that he would lose more than he would gain and, in the process, would betray to the up-start Commons an important and ancient part of the royal prerogative. Parliament re-assembled in the middle of October, but a fortnight passed without any conclusion to the wardship business, for the Commons seemed in doubt as to what precisely the king was prepared to grant. At the end of the month he summoned the Commons to meet him and sharply criticised them for 'slackness and many delays in the great matter of contract, by means whereof his debts did only swell and his wants increase upon him'. He bluntly asked for 'a speedy answer, whether we would proceed with the contract: yea or no?' Either way he would be glad of a decision for, if they abandoned the contract, they would have to find some other means of satisfying his wants. 'He was resolved to cut his coat according to his cloth, which he could not do till he knew what cloth he should have to make it of.'

Still the Commons tarried. On 3 November Sir Roger Owen voiced his doubts and, in doing so, he put his finger on a crucial point. If the substantial annual grant was agreed to then, he urged his listeners, some provision should be made 'that we may

[1] Winwood, *Memorials*, iii, 194.

have parliaments hereafter, though the king's wants be fully supplied'. In other words, if the king were guaranteed an annual revenue, would he ever need to summon Parliament again? These and other doubts were never resolved for, two days later, the king sent a message to the Commons which ended all hope of an agreement. In addition to the £200,000 to be paid annually, he demanded that the Commons should forthwith compensate all the officials of the Court of Wards who would now lose their offices and, on top of that, the Commons should make a grant of half a million pounds to meet his debts. It was an impossible demand and an angry House rejected it unanimously. For another fortnight Parliament remained in session, continuing its fruitless debates. But by now the king had had enough. On 24 November he commanded the Speaker to adjourn the House of Commons. It never met again; for on 9 February 1611 James dissolved Parliament. Of the Great Contract nothing remained.

In its place there survived a deepening bitterness amongst the critics of wardship inside and outside the House of Commons. They had come within an arm's length of ending for ever a social evil which had pressed on them harder with each passing decade. Had victory come, they would indeed, as Cecil had told them, have gone home to their shires and told their neighbours that they and their family had 'a pretty hedge about them', at last security from an oppressive feudal burden. Instead they were sent packing with nothing to show for their pains. They would now have to face the tougher pressures of fiscal feudalism—'*what may be made of them*', as Cecil had told them. For he and his successors at the Treasury had no other choice. Without subsidies, with addled Parliaments, they must use the old, anachronistic devices, contemptible though they were. The very men who refused the royal demands for taxation in Parliament forced the king to employ more intensely these anti-social devices in the country. As a result, when Parliament re-assembled the complaints were louder, agreement between king and Commons grew more remote. Ultimately there came deadlock in government; and then rebellion.

If the failure of the Great Contract was a setback for the reformers in the House of Commons, for Cecil it was total defeat.
His enemies began to gather strength. There was one story in
circulation that an unnamed nobleman, on his death-bed, sent a
special message to James warning him that Cecil's work for the
Contract was a gross betrayal of the royal interests; and that when
James fully realised the implications of the charge, he said the
information was worth £10,000 to him. Thereafter he lost all
confidence in Cecil.[1]

Whether this account had any truth in it we do not know. What
is certain, however, is that the intriguers were at work on this
very issue. We have, for example, a copy of an extraordinary
letter sent to Lord Haddington, a Scottish noble in close friendship with James. The writer of this scurrilous attack on Cecil is
unknown; but Cecil himself read it and bitterly annotated it. It
was addressed to Haddington but it was clearly designed for James.
Yet its message is precisely the opposite to that of the other story,
for Cecil was now blamed, not for inaugurating the Contract, but
for causing its collapse! For, it was said, he and his faction dared
not work for the abolition of the Court of Wards because with its
disappearance would come the end of their wealth and power.
In other words success—or failure—with the Great Contract
meant obloquy for Cecil. Finally his master turned upon him.
'Your greatest error', James told him, 'hath been that ye ever
expected to draw honey out of gall, being a little blinded with the
self-love of your own counsel in holding together of this Parliament, whereof all men were despaired, as I have oft told you, but
yourself alone.'[2]

This daring scheme of Salisbury's[3] is one of the great might-
have-beens of English history; but it is idle to spend long in speculation as to its possible consequences. Yet this much seems certain.
Had the project gone through, the Stuart kings would have

---

[1] G. Goodman, *Court of James I* (1839), i, 40–1.

[2] Hatfield 140.121 [H.M.C. *Salis.*, xviii, 164]; D. H. Willson, 'Summoning and Dissolving Parliament, 1603–1625' (*Am. Hist. Rev.*, xlv, 284).

[3] Sir Robert Cecil was created Baron Cecil in 1603, Viscount Cranborne in 1604,
Earl of Salisbury in 1605.

advanced far towards enjoying a substantial revenue without the need to summon Parliament. Sir Julius Caesar, not the most intelligent of the king's ministers, advised him against accepting the Great Contract for it would cause 'a ready passage to a democracy, which is the deadliest enemy to a monarchy'. He was wide of the mark. Sir Roger Owen, the back-bench Member of Parliament whom we have already cited, understood the position far better when he warned the House that, in fully satisfying the king's needs by this contract, they might free him from his growing dependence upon parliamentary taxation. They might be presiding over the demise of parliamentary institutions. One day the Stuart kings would be overtaken by inflation, or some other cause might oblige them to call back the legislature for supplementary grants. But until then the parliamentary weapon would have rusted in its scabbard and the Pyms and Hampdens and Holleses would have slumbered on in the English shires. In France the Estates-General at about this time went into retirement and did not meet again until 1789. By then it was too late for parleys and legislation and the issue was settled by other means. The English rebellion of 1642 was fought by old parliamentarians, and their sons in 1660 re-built a parliamentary system upon established precedents. But had the Great Contract gone through, a far lengthier interval would have been possible. Then, when Parliament at last re-assembled, with all its skills and traditions gone, and with its differences sharpened, England might have entered upon a bitter and bloody war from which it could have proved impossible to salvage self-government. So, by one of the paradoxes in our history, James, in sabotaging Salisbury's plan, made it impossible for a king to send Parliament on its long holiday and thereby delay, perhaps indefinitely, the coming of self-government in England.[1]

On the morrow of the *débâcle*, Salisbury could hope for nothing from either king or Parliament. He had lost the confidence of both. Prematurely old and sick in body as he was, it would have been natural if he had at last returned his seals to the king whose

1 *Parliamentary Debates in 1610*, pp. 177, 127.

trust he no longer enjoyed. But Salisbury did not yield. He stayed on as minister, trying to paper over the widening cracks in the financial structure. It was a hopeless task. Parliament was dissolved. When it met again, four years later, it was truculent and restless; and James sent the Addled Parliament away without receiving supplies or granting redress. But by then Salisbury was dead, and lesser men stood in his place. In April 1612, with little hope of recovering his health, he had set out for Bath, and on the way back he died. Now the mean, the second-rate and the corrupt were free to give rein to their hatred and imagination, and they sank also to the spreading of slanders about the cause of his death. 'The outrageous speeches against the deceased lord continue still', wrote Chamberlain, 'and there be fresh libels come out every day.' Those who had failed to bring him down in his quarter of a century of public service struck the harder at his memory. It would have been difficult to find a man courageous enough to speak at this hour in his defence.[1]

Difficult: but not impossible. When Salisbury set out on his last journey to Bath, he took with him Sir Walter Cope, his colleague and friend. Cope had worked under him at the Exchequer and, after an interval, succeeded him as Master of Wards. But Cope was not one of those weather-blown courtiers who swing with the wind and defame men abler and more patriotic than themselves. Rather, without regard to his personal interests, he sat down and wrote to James I an *Apology* for his late master. It is easy enough to write a panegyric of a rising statesman. It requires other virtues to defend the policy of a dead and discredited one. What Cope wrote reflects credit on both servant and master. Patiently and in detail he showed James I how Salisbury had followed a disinterested and coherent policy, sacrificing his personal opportunities and rewards to the vision of a solvent Exchequer and a stable financial system. At the same time he tried to maintain probity and honour in the loosening standards of a new age: 'he loved justice as his life and the laws as his inheritance'. But he failed. Cope was quite clear as to the cause of Salisbury's unpopularity. 'He lost the love of your people only for your sake and for your service.' In the end Salisbury gave all that a minister and a man had to give. 'Finding your wants he yielded up [the profits of] his office; and finding he could not relieve them, he yielded up his life.'[1]

[1] J. Gutch, *Collectanea* (1781), i, 120, 132–3.

V

CONCLUSION

I have thought good to put you in mind of our present great payments and of our small means.

Lord Treasurer Buckhurst to Sir Robert Cecil, 1602.

Wardship and the Government of England

EXACTLY half a century after Robert Cecil's battle had been fought and lost, the House of Commons at the Restoration of 1660 presided over the obsequies of the Court of Wards. It had outlived Cecil by more than a generation, its profits stretched to breaking point amidst the mounting fury of the land-owning classes. Yet, during the Civil War, the parliamentarians hesitated for a number of years before carrying out the long-awaited abolition of the Court. For they, like their enemies, found that government cannot go on without funds; and they, too, had to employ whatever means for raising money they found to hand. So, ironically enough, there were for a time *two* Courts of Wards, one functioning in Oxford on behalf of the crown and the other in London in the service of the opposition. But in 1646 the parliamentarians at last closed its doors. And in 1660, when they restored the king, they took good care not to restore his Court of Wards. Instead, with all decorum they proclaimed its demise; and a passage from the ceremony is worth quoting for it may help to explain what went before. The feudal incidents, they said, had been found by experience 'more burdensome, grievous and prejudicial to the kingdom than they had been beneficial to the king'. If this epitaph contains more truth than is customary in such memorials why, we must ask, had the Court of Wards managed to survive for so long? What was its role in the government of Elizabethan England?[1]

---

1 *Acts and Ordinances of the Interregnum*, ed. C. H. Firth and R. S. Rait, i, 833; 12 Car. II, c. 24.

To Blackstone, writing in the eighteenth century, the dissolving statute of 1660 was more momentous in the history of civil property than Magna Carta itself. That the Court of Wards had been 'burdensome, grievous and prejudicial' to a good many of Queen Elizabeth's subjects cannot seriously be denied. Cardinal Allen intended that the victorious Spanish Armada should sweeten defeat for the English by the abolition of feudal wardship. Later on, his fellow exile, an unknown priest, still dreaming of Catholic conquest, remembered the cardinal's scheme and denounced the Court of Wards in language far stronger than was employed by the parliamentary draftsmen of 1660. To him the Court was a 'tyrannical and unchristian office', which 'doth infinitely offend the nobility and gentility generally, as being the ruin of their children both in honour and possessions'. What he said has been confirmed in an earlier chapter, by the evidence of men as different from one another as Hugh Latimer, Sir Nicholas Bacon, Sir Thomas Smith, and Sir Humphrey Gilbert; and each in turn drew attention to a glaring abuse in the decadent feudal customs perpetuated by the Court of Wards. But all these critics were loyal servants of the Protestant church and state, and their angry words were the sincere expostulations of patriotic men. For once, Englishmen at home as well as those in exile held the same views; and they spoke for the generality.[1]

From the opinions of contemporaries, and the material which we have surveyed elsewhere, there would be no difficulty in building up an impressive indictment of the whole wardship system as operated by the government of Elizabeth I. Fiscal wardship undoubtedly fostered grave abuses. For example, it virtually held up widows to ransom—one mother alleged that she was not allowed to see her daughter, a ward of the queen, 'save only at a window into the street where I did see her most rigorously held from my sight and speech'. Others could speak of the hasty marriages rushed through while the father was still alive, the

---

[1] Blackstone, *Commentaries* (5th ed.), ii, 77; *Letters and Memorials of William, Cardinal Allen*, ed. T. F. Knox, p. cvii; B.M. Lans. 512, f. 18v (I am indebted to my former pupil, the Rev. Dr. S. J. Loomie, S.J., for this reference).

imposition of forced marriages for purely mercenary reasons, the development of corrupt practices to evade wardship, and the degradation of marriage to the procedure of an auction mart. The catalogue of abuses is a lengthy one, and we may conclude with an extreme case : the wardship which was reported to have been gambled away between a nobleman and a judge in a game of dice![1]

Feudal guardians, it is also true, while negotiating a marriage tended to think in terms of hard cash and the building up of an estate. But so, very often, did parents who, with the best intentions in the world, negotiated marriage contracts on behalf of their children. The relations of bride and groom would spend long hours, together with their lawyers and estate agents, haggling over the details of the marriage settlement. If parents treated marriage in the light of the contemporary economic outlook and the passion for estate building, so did feudal guardians; but that does not mean that they entered lightly upon marriage or palmed off their children upon wards without regard to their tastes, interests or future happiness.

We must remember also that, disastrous as it might be for a widow to be deprived of her child, there were many cases where it must have proved a welcome release—at least, as far as the child was concerned. More than one mother was found to be 'light and of ill behaviour' ; and, in transferring the care of the child to some more responsible person, the Court of Wards was performing, in a primitive fashion, some of the duties of a twentieth-century magistrates' court. A Tudor widow did not normally mourn her deceased spouse for long. It was very common, before the year was out, for a stepfather to be installed. Thomas Cromwell, amidst his other cares of office, had once asked himself whether legislation could not be introduced to prevent young men marrying aged widows. 'Eve will be Eve', Harrison reminds us, 'though Adam should say nay!'

A lot, of course, depended upon the mother and the stepfather. But some contemporaries seriously asked themselves whether a

---

[1] Inner Temple Petyt MS. 538, 10, f. 16r; *Visitations of Essex* (Harl. Soc. 1878), pt. 1, p. 236. (I owe these references to Miss Helen Miller and Mr. M. J. Crook.)

child might not be better treated by a guardian who had bought the wardship in order to marry the heir to his own child, than by a stepfather who might be much less concerned about the health and welfare of his charge. Some widows, it was said, 'usually upon second marriages, exchange the natural care of their children with the love of their second husbands (for the most part unthrifts or greedy cormorants), that usually make a prey of the children and their estates'. And when we consider the evils attributed to feudal wardship, it is worth recalling that in Jersey, where no Court of Wards existed, it was the custom for guardians 'to be chosen by those who call themselves kin, neighbours and friends of the said infants, which custom is often abused, because the kin, neighbours and friends choose men to serve their base ends, or strive by underhand means to put in other *meneurs* [guardians] at their fancy to the prejudice of the orphans'.[1]

Under a great Master like Burghley, the Court of Wards did concern itself with welfare matters, and more than once intervened decisively to protect the heir against intruders, an oppressive guardian, the waste of his lands, or other abuse. In a lawless age when intrigue, riot, and sudden dispossession were the frequent accompaniment of disputes over land, a minor heir might well benefit, rather than suffer, from being under the shelter of so powerful an institution as the Court of Wards and so eminent a judge as Lord Burghley. And behind him was the supreme executive and judicial authority of the Privy Council, whose thunderbolts upon an erring guardian or a recalcitrant sheriff could, on occasion, be used with devastating results.

The trouble with the Court of Wards, as with other Tudor institutions, was that it was allotted two quite contradictory tasks. One of these, which was social, it inherited from Chancery and, after 1660, to Chancery it would return. The Court spoke, in this context, with the conscience and voice of the queen and, on many occasions, it acted, without charge or favour, in the interests of some young orphan of mean estate. For this it had an honourable reputation and formed part of that Tudor paternalism

[1] S.P., Jas. I, xxiv, no. 65; C.P.R., Eliz., ii, 426–7.

which marked the beginning of the transition from the medieval welfare parish to the modern welfare state. Those who defended the Court of Wards begged James I, when the wardship controversy was at its height, not to yield one jot of its social responsibility and influence. To abolish it, one of its defenders argued, would mean 'the overthrow of an honourable court, by which many orphans have received protection from oppression'. James was urged to turn a deaf ear to 'those who either for pleasing the general fancy of a multitude or supplying any present necessity' carried through such a change; these would-be reformers 'might perhaps in a subsequent age (the nearness whereof is as uncertain as the life of man) be taxed for doing ill-service to the crown or state'. To a conservative, such as the unknown writer of this memorandum, royal wardship was 'a principal flower in the king's diadem, and one of the greatest pillars of his crown'. We have met the expression before. When another ambiguous aspect of the royal prerogative—monopolies—had come under fire in the Parliament of 1597, Lord Keeper Egerton, at the dissolution, had said on behalf of the queen: 'Her Majesty hoped that her dutiful and loving subjects would not take away her prerogative —which is the chiefest flower in her garland and the principal and head pearl in her crown and diadem.'[1]

'*Lilies that fester.* . . .' The undoubted sincerity of some of the Court's defenders cannot obscure the evils arising from its second function, which was purely fiscal. It had to raise money somehow to help run a modern state largely dependent on medieval institutions. And no minister, least of all the Lord Treasurer, could afford for one moment to forget this governing responsibility. A patent of monopoly could be used—and was used—for the laudable object of protecting inventors and investors, just as royal wardship was used for protecting orphans. But both systems underwent organic change and degenerated into social abuses. Like the Star Chamber, in a different context, the Court of Wards had both to serve the people and serve the crown, even when their interests

---

[1] S.P., Jas. I, xxiv, no. 65; J. E. Neale, *Elizabeth I and her Parliaments, 1584–1601* (1957), p. 355.

conflicted : a cruel dilemma, especially for a man like Lord Burghley. But the choice had to be made; the queen's government had to go on. And successive Masters, like the later judges in the Star Chamber, had, if they were to survive at all, to choose the crown's interests.

So, what might have been noble organs for social welfare became perforce crown instruments of oppression; and the Stuart parliamentarians who declared war on the Star Chamber swept the Court of Wards with it into oblivion. Whatever may be argued in defence of royal wardship—and rather more can be said than historians have hitherto recognised—it remains true that its fiscal importance predominated.

Latter-day feudalism, in other words, had nothing to do with the feudal relations which had been the social and economic cement of medieval England. As we have seen, the feudal rights of the crown were already in process of change during the high Middle Ages, and their revival in the early Tudor period was bound up with economic, not military, policy. Progressive land-owners, for example, who had snatched up monastic lands when they first came on the market—and perhaps unwittingly collected a military tenure in the process—would have been more than surprised had they been called upon to serve for forty days in the field. 'The tenure remains', said a parliamentarian in 1606, 'though the use sleeps.' In time of war, said Francis Bacon, 'when it is in question who shall set his foot foremost towards the enemy, it is never asked whether he hold in knight-service or in socage . . . the service and defence of the realm hath in these days little dependancy upon tenures'. '*Vocabula manent*,' he went on—and the epigram repeats what our 1606 parliamentarian said before— '*res fugiunt*.' Fiscal feudalism, in other words, was kept alive for no other reason than to bring in revenue to the government.[1]

If, then, the justification for the revival and survival of royal wardship was—in practice if not in theory—for revenue and not social reasons, then it is in terms of the national revenue that its

---

1 *The Parliamentary Diary of Robert Bowyer*, p. 201, n. 1; *The Letters and the Life of Francis Bacon*, ed. Spedding, iv, 165.

effects must next be considered. For it was here that the Tudor and Stuart monarchy faced its gravest problem. After the death of Henry VII all the rulers of England, from Henry VIII until Oliver Cromwell, ended their terms of office in debt. Henry VIII and James I were extravagant, Mary and Elizabeth were modest and guarded in their expenditure : but the same basic weakness dominated the scene. With growing national ambitions and mounting responsibilities—for war, diplomacy, domestic administration—the government became increasingly unable to live 'of its own', that is, of the traditional income of a great landowner and a medieval king. For additional income, in times of national emergency, it could turn to the House of Commons: for tenths, fifteenths and subsidies, direct taxation dependent upon parliamentary authority. But that kind of bounty brought problems of its own. In the long run, in return for funds, the Commons would seek to confine the royal power to an increasingly narrow sector of the national political life, to bring the royal prerogative within the bounds of parliamentary rule. The conscious beginnings of that process we have already seen in the last chapter. As the crown looked into the future consequences of parliamentary grants, it did not like what it saw.

In any case, such grants as parliament made scarcely touched the wealth of the country. Assessments were notoriously bad. 'If I should tell you', Sir Walter Mildmay, Chancellor of the Exchequer, told the Commons bluntly in 1585, 'how meanly the great possessors in the country, and the best aldermen and citizens of London and the rich men of the realm, are rated, you would marvel at it.' 'Our estates', said Raleigh in the debate of 1601, 'that be thirty pound or forty pound in the queen's books, are not the hundreth part of our wealth.' And even when, at last, the grant had been authorised, the local assessors found, or appeared to find, that the shires were even poorer than their representatives alleged. So the grant shrank. But it shrank still further when the collectors, for as long as possible, sometimes for ever, held on to what they had collected on behalf of the queen. 'Not the sixth part of that which is given'—it is Mildmay again, this time in

1587—'. . . doth come to Her Majesty's coffers.' In spite of these defects the parliamentary sources were indeed important. But no government could lose sight of the fact that the Commons would only yield inadequate sums, reluctantly granted, inefficiently collected—and given on terms.[1]

The administrative resources of the Elizabethan government, like its financial ones, were extremely limited; but its political aims and responsibilities outstripped them both. And from time to time inflation intervened to worsen an already deteriorating situation. 'Her Majesty's great want is such,' Elizabeth's last Chancellor of the Exchequer, Sir John Fortescue, told Sir Robert Cecil, 'as for the present payments, which you are acquainted withal, my Lord your father and myself are so much aggrieved as we know not whither to turn ourselves.' So paternalist rule periodically ran out of cash. If the queen turned to her 'dutiful and loving subjects' she found more than once that their pious loyalty was not accompanied by generosity in taxation. They showed a marked preference for words not deeds. She might meet a crisis by a loan, but loans—other than forced loans—had to be repaid at interest. Alternatively, she could live on her capital by selling crown land, which she did at the beginning, and more especially at the end, of her reign. But that reduced her annual income and stored up trouble for herself and her successors. There remained one last sphere which gave the queen some room to manoeuvre in the endless struggle to secure her prerogative.[2]

This sphere comprised a strange assortment of royal rights from which all, or nearly all, the original character and justification had departed but which were kept artifically alive because, in one way or another, they had developed new uses—namely, for revenue. There were a number of these quasi-legal rights inherent in the crown: monopolies, ship money, the forest laws, distraint of knighthood, and fiscal feudalism. Treated as they were, they were the bastard revenues, neither medieval nor modern, neither legal nor illegal: but in practice—indispensable. Whatever might be

[1] J. E. Neale, *op. cit.* pp. 55, 168; D'Ewes, *Journal* (1868), p. 633.
[2] H.M.C. *Salis.*, viii, 236.

said in their defence, they constituted an affront and a challenge
to the common sense and the interests of the propertied classes.
But the crown had no choice. Hampered at every turn in its
attempts at direct or indirect taxation, it was driven to search for
an income by applying and distorting its constitutional rights,
where opportunity served. Sir Edward Coke, in his examination
of the Court of Wards in his *Institutes*, warned the government
of Charles I, in effect, by quoting a passage from Deuteronomy:
'Cursed be he that perverteth the judgement of the stranger,
fatherless and widow.' But it was the activities of Coke and his
allies which drove the government along the path it was taking.
The parliamentarians could not eat their cake and have it. The
very landed classes who offered so valiant a resistance in the
House of Commons against the government's demands for money,
obliged the government to tax these same landed classes with so
indirect and objectionable a charge as fiscal feudalism. It was an
intolerable situation for any government; and in the end it made
government impossible. The first of the Tudors formulated the
policy, but the time was coming when the Stuarts would have to
pay for it.[1]

That was to be expected; for the last years of Elizabeth heard
the growing rumblings of the approaching storm. But neither
she nor her two successors could afford to alter course. It would
therefore be reasonable to assume that she, and they, derived such
considerable profits from fiscal feudalism that she could not for
one moment contemplate renouncing them. Before making such
an assumption, however, it is important to look at these profits in
some detail.

All estimates of Tudor revenues carry with them two strong
elements of doubt. In the first place the method of accountancy—
and, indeed, of addition—was so rudimentary that receivers, clerks
and auditors could, in all innocence, present unsatisfactory and
untrustworthy statements of their transactions. To these defects,
inherent in the system, there would be added all too often the
human defects of Tudor officials, who, as we have seen, added

1 *Fourth Inst.*, sect. 35.

corruption to inefficiency, with advantage to themselves and to the cost of contemporaries and historians alike. Where we detect either error or dishonesty we can apply a correction factor to the figures at our disposal; but we cannot wholly eliminate all the uncertainties which dog our heels. It is also the case, unfortunately, that a Tudor accountant was by the very nature of his office concerned wholly with his 'charge and discharge', that is, with how much he had received, how much he had paid out and how much he had left. He was not responsible for working out the net revenues for any given year; and, if we wish to discover what they were, we must laboriously go back through his accounts, posing questions which he never thought to ask or answer. Finally we must remember that, under the pressure of inflation, the pound sterling had by the beginning of Elizabeth's reign fallen to a very much lower value than at the beginning of her father's reign, and that by the time she died, it would be worth a good deal less. All these, and other, more technical, difficulties stand between us and an exact estimate of the profits of fiscal feudalism; but by adopting a method which has been fully set out elsewhere, we may go some way towards translating the Tudor figures into a modern statistical language.[1]

In the first full accounting year after the erection of the Court of Wards, September 1541–September 1542, the net revenues came to £4,466, and in the last full year of Henry VIII's reign they had already reached £10,550. This total included the profits from liveries, which do not appear in the earlier figure because the work of liveries had not yet been annexed to the Court of Wards. But the upward movement after the establishment of the Court of Wards is none the less unmistakable. At the beginning of Edward VI's reign the feudal profits were down to £7,638; but towards the end they had nearly doubled, and the average for the whole reign was £11,027. Under Mary the income continued to rise, reaching in the year 1555–6 to as high as £20,020, and averaging

---

[1] An explanation of the method adopted for calculating the revenues, and a statement of the annual profits, will be found in my 'The Profits of Fiscal Feudalism, 1541–1602' (*Econ. Hist. Rev.*, 2nd ser., viii, 53–61).

£15,423 for the reign as a whole. For a while, the rise continued under Elizabeth, but for reasons which we shall shortly examine it was not sustained. The average for her reign as a whole was £14,677, nearly £750 less than for that of Mary. The total net revenues for the whole of Elizabeth's reign, with the exception of the last few months, came to £645,807. If we allow for these months, and add a little for one year for which our information is incomplete, we may put the figure for the reign at £650,000, and the annual average at £14,700.

In other words, there were available in the Court of Wards each year some £15,000 upon which the Elizabethan government could call; and call it did. There were two ways in which it could do so. The first was by special warrants to the Receiver-General, instructing him to pay a certain sum of money to a crown official, a pensioner, or someone charged with a particular duty. The crown, in effect, was treating the Court of Wards as a small Treasury, additional to the Exchequer, and was following a practice dating from an earlier period. For example, late in Henry VIII's reign we find the Receiver-General instructed to make a miscellany of payments: £1,000 for the garrison in the north, £500 for victual for the navy, £600 for the royal household, £1,000 for the labourers at the dockyard at Portsmouth. In Edward VI's reign, there is payment of £21. 19s. 4d. to an armourer for the cleaning of harness; £44. 2s. 8d. for a lawyer and his assistants in going to Cornwall on the king's behalf; £4 to Elizabeth Ryveland 'in respect that she was spoiled upon the borders by certain soldiers strangers, serving the King's Majesty'. And so it goes on under Elizabeth: £1,769. 16s. 9½d. to the queen's goldsmiths towards the total cost of plate and gold chains 'by Her Majesty given away at New Year's tide' in the third year of her reign; £120 to Sir Henry Sidney 'by way of gift for defraying his charges, being presently sent in post to the French king'; £1,000 as a loan to Shane O'Neill in Ireland.[1]

But there was also a second and more orderly way of doing

[1] *Acts of P.C.*, 1542–7, pp. 286, 296, 334, 493–4; 1547–50, pp. 203–5; Wards 9.369, ff. 201r–31r.

things—that is, by the annual assignment of a sum from wardship to a specific purpose. From the beginning of Elizabeth's reign we see the Receiver-General paying round sums of money each year to the Cofferer of the Household. In the first year, seven separate payments amounted to £13,000; in the second year, £9,000 were paid; in the third year, £10,300; and in the fourth year, £8,000. In the fifth year the position was regularised by act of Parliament, under which the Receiver-General was to pay annually £10,000, without further warrant, towards the queen's household, at half-yearly instalments. On top of that, £2,000 went annually to the wardrobe.[1] But this practice of assignments did not supersede the traditional methods of making payment by special warrant. Nor did the two systems, working side by side, account for all the annual income. Receivers continued, as we have seen, to divert some at least of their cash reserves into private financial ventures; and the instructions of Burghley that each year's surplus should be at once transferred to the Exchequer was honoured more in the breach than in the observance.[2] It was very much a hand-to-mouth existence, with the government constantly going through its pockets to see where the money was to be found. And as the reign began so it ended: 'I have thought good to put you in mind', wrote Lord Treasurer Buckhurst to Cecil in 1602, 'of our present great payments and of our small means, and therefore, if possibly you might help us with any convenient sum out of the Wards, it should never come in better time.'[3]

We know, then, that the government set considerable store by its revenues from wardship. But it is still necessary to express in more concrete terms their function in government. Unfortunately, we cannot compare these sources with modern items of national revenue. Neither economists nor historians have so far evolved any method by which Tudor monetary values can be re-cast in terms of our own currency; and, indeed, any estimates of this

[1] Wards 9.369, ff. 49r–50r, 108r, 201r–203r, 267r–270r; 5 Eliz., c. 32.
[2] Above p. 207, n. 1.
[3] H.M.C. Salis., xii, 646.

kind which are made are bound, in the inflationary age in which we live—unparalleled since Tudor times—to lose such little reality as they posssess, even between the writing and the publication of a book. There is, however, another way of looking at these figures, namely as contemporaries were bound to look at them: in terms of other sources of income, and as a contribution towards current commitments. What, in effect, was a total revenue of £650,000 from feudalism—or an annual income of £14,700— worth, in the light of the rising costs of Elizabethan government?

Surprisingly little. Whether we look at the feudal revenues as a part of the national income or as a contribution to the national expenditure, there is very little to show. For example, the 'ordinary'—that is non-parliamentary—income of the crown in the year 1575–6 (with the exception of income from the Duchy of Lancaster and the Court of Wards) came to about £200,000. The Court of Wards during the same year brought in £11,612, one-seventeenth of this figure. If we take 'extraordinary' grants made by Parliament at the end of her reign, from 1588 to 1601, we get a sum of £1,950,000. The total income brought in by feudalism for this period came to £213,354, less than one-ninth of that part of the royal revenue which came through the tight purse-strings of the Elizabethan parliamentarians. On the income side we may make one last—almost ludicrous—comparison. Drake's piratical expedition of 1577–80 brought in over £600,000, of which the queen's share appears to have been more than a quarter of a million pounds: one bold exploit brought in to her as much as fifteen or twenty years' hard work in the Court of Wards.[1]

If we turn to the expenditure side of the balance sheet, the pattern is exactly the same. At the beginning of Elizabeth's reign the interest charges on her foreign debt alone came to £15,000; in other words, this item by itself would have eaten up most of the profits from feudalism for the year. Towards the end of her reign, the queen is alleged to have given to the Earl of Essex gifts to the value of £300,000: nearly half the total income of the Court of Wards went, in a short space, to feed, though not to satisfy, the

1 W. R. Scott, *Joint Stock Companies* (Cambridge 1911), i, 42, 95, 82.

appetite of one minister of the Tudor state. Finally, we must measure these profits against the growing burdens of war. In the decade 1580–90, the queen spent for military and naval purposes over £1½m. In the last third of her reign her wars cost just under £4m., or £267,000 per annum. The profits from feudalism would have kept the military effort going for about three weeks in every year. The question facing historians is not why was Elizabeth I so parsimonious? but how did she manage to find the cash?[1]

With these figures before us we are at once faced with a paradox. Was it for some £15,000 a year that Elizabeth and her government endured the mounting hostility of the landowning classes, the horrified incredulity of foreigners, the evasions, concealments, informers and the rest? Or were Elizabeth and Burghley unaware of, or uninterested in, the evils that accompanied fiscal wardship at every turn? To believe this would hardly fit in with what we know of the shrewd realism of Elizabeth's minister, or her own sensitive appreciation of the mood of her subjects. Alternatively, was it that a government, drowning in its debts, clutched desperately at a feudal straw? Or is there some other explanation? Who, indeed, profited from feudalism?

The answer to this question is only to be found if we look beyond the revenues themselves. For the official records of the Court of Wards conceal as much as they reveal. They tell us only what the queen received, but give no hint of the greater harvests being reaped elsewhere. They reveal nothing of the rewards of the private suitors: the 'solicitors', go-betweens, contact men, petty officials, and informers. Only the accidental survival of other records makes it possible for us to take up this side of the story. Yet such profits were of immense significance. They were an important part of the total market price of the wardship; they provide a major explanation for the survival of the system. It was very rare for a wardship to be sold without the ultimate purchaser paying out to an intermediary a sum or sums of money, apart from the official price. It is this sum of money, where we can

1 *Ibid.*, iii, 496, 508, 503; i, 96.

discover it, which forms the major clue to our understanding of the system.

But the private agents for wardship preferred, naturally enough, to cover their tracks. Yet they left sufficient evidence behind them for us to make a broad estimate of their yield. Earlier chapters in this book have already supplied examples of how much could, on occasion, be made in this way. The wardship of Vincent Randall was bought for £106. 13s. 4d. and re-sold for £400, at a profit of nearly 300 per cent. Elizabeth Long's wardship was bought for £250 and ultimately sold for £2,450, a rise of nearly 900 per cent. The wardship of Hugh Allington was bought for £20 and re-sold for £200, also at a profit of 900 per cent. The wardship of Walter Aston was bought for £300 and subsequently sold for £4,000, an increase of over 1,200 per cent. (and we must remember that Burghley received £1,000 for his services in this connection).[1]

These figures, selected from a larger body of statistics, alone provide evidence of considerable unofficial profits, and begin to suggest a ratio between the official profits of the crown and the unofficial profits of the wardship agents. We may now look at the situation from another viewpoint: that of office holders in the Court of Wards. Hugh Latimer, in the reign of Edward VI, said that candidates were paying between £200 and £2,000 for public offices. But only the very highest posts in the land were worth as much as £200 officially, and none was worth £2,000 or even half that sum. *Officially*—but the private profits of the office holders would easily overtop these figures: hence the competition for posts. At the end of Elizabeth's reign we find that the Clerkship of the Court of Wards was valued at more than £400, but his official salary came to only £10.[2]

There is indeed a famous story about Hugh Audley, the last Clerk of the Court of Wards, who, on being asked the value of his office, replied: 'It might be worth some thousands of pounds

---

1 Above pp. 266–7; 'Lord Burghley as Master of the Court of Wards, 1561–1598 (*T. R. Hist. S.*, 4th ser., xxxi, 110–11).
2 *Sermons of Hugh Latimer*, ed. G. E. Corrie (1844), p. 185; H.M.C. *Salis.*, vii, 531.

to him who, after his death, would instantly go to heaven; twice as much to him who would go to purgatory; and nobody knows what to him who would adventure to go to hell.' Audley's ultimate destination is not known; but a hint of it may perhaps be derived from the fact that, even before his death, he was known as 'rich Audley'. It is a good story but, like all good stories, it has a pedigree. It was in circulation forty years before, and attributed to Viscount Mandeville, later Earl of Manchester, who appears to have described his Lord Treasurership in almost identical terms. He is believed to have paid £20,000 for the office and had to travel to the races at Newmarket to receive the white staff of the Treasury from his sporting king: wood was dear at Newmarket that year—said a contemporary wit. Mandeville became Master of the Wards in 1624 and the story probably went with him into the Court of Wards. There it stayed and—not without justification—it was in due course transferred to Audley.[1]

Yet, when we have cut a way through the exaggerations and slanders, what remains beyond doubt is that every officer in the Court of Wards had access to very considerable profits, well above his official salary. Burghley, as we have seen, was receiving unofficially ten times more than his official salary.

What proportion of the total wardship price went to the queen, and what to her subjects? We have evidence from various sources that up to twelve times as much as the queen's share went into private hands. But clearly, as we do not possess material for the whole field, it would be unsafe to use so high an estimate. On the other hand, we must remember also that there were other profits, apart from those derived from the actual sale of the wardship— for example in the lease of the lands, which Cecil considered were not estimated at one-tenth of their value, thereby giving nine-tenths of the profits to the lessee. But against this, we must allow for the only important item in the Receiver-General's account in which there is not this great margin of difference between official and unofficial receipts, namely the payments for liveries; though in

---

[1] *The Way to be Rich, according to the Practice of the Great Audley* (1662), p. 12; F. C. Dietz, *English Public Finance, 1558-1641*, pp. 182-3.

this case there were still heavy payments to officials as the suit of livery went on its lengthy travels. Assuming a smaller profit in this sector, it would therefore not be unreasonable to argue that the queen's subjects obtained four or five times as much as the queen from the average wardship. Burghley's domestic biographer, in fact, put the ratio at five to one. Bacon, writing in 1612, gave it at three to one. But that was after Cecil had spent a decade cutting away at the private profits from wardship. Clearly the ratio was higher in Elizabeth's reign. Yet, so that we may reach an estimate of only the *minimum* private profits, it is safest to adopt Bacon's figure of three to one, more conservative than anything we have encountered for the Elizabethan period. On this basis, we are now in a position to put the wardship revenues in their national perspective.[1]

The profits of fiscal feudalism were, in essence, ambivalent. One valuation, the royal receipts, we find in the Receiver-Generals' accounts. The other consisted of the perquisites, official and unofficial, and the fees, gifts, profits on re-sales, and other sums which, if they were not bribery or blackmail, belonged to that legal twilight familiar enough to students of the Tudor period. When one considers not simply what the purchaser paid for the wardship as such to the middleman but the gifts, bribes and 'necessary expenses' paid to go-betweens, official and freelance, it is possible to gain a vision of a whole community of men deriving all or part of their incomes from the unofficial profits of feudalism. These profits, on our conservative basis, emerge as three times as high as the queen's. In other words, if the queen received £100 for a grant in the Court of Wards, various of her subjects pocketed £300; the price on the open market, had there been one, would have been £400. If then, we return to our figure of £650,000, which is what the queen received from fiscal feudalism throughout her reign, and restate it in terms of the over-all net profits to queen and subject alike, they rise three times higher, in all to £2,600,000. If the full profits had been paid to the Court of Wards, and none had gone to intermediaries,

1 *Desiderata Curiosa*, ed. Peck, i, 28; Spedding, *op. cit.*, iv, 287.

the queen would have been provided with an unexpended surplus of £2m. In fact, she received one-fourth of the sum, and a group of her subjects were, between them, making about £2m. out of the business. This fact is of immense social and political significance.

Viewed from one aspect it could be used as a massive indictment of both Lord Burghley and the merciless and predatory courtier-class of which he was a member. For it looks as though, as Master of the Court of Wards, he deliberately insulated its official revenues from both the general price movement and the enormous needs of a government at war; and, in so doing, he put into the pockets of those dealing with wardships an unearned increment at the expense of the queen. And all this was going on while Burghley, himself Lord Treasurer, saw before him the clear signs of national bankruptcy. It would also be easy, on this reading of events, to let loose a flood of righteous indignation against the courtier-class and their corrupt hangers-on, who preyed alike upon the queen and her subjects with an equal disregard for the national interest and the private welfare of the wards. In short, Burghley was rapacious for himself and his friends and—as far as wardship was concerned—the queen was blind. Such an approach is readily understandable, for the charge of corruption against Burghley and his colleagues came easily to the lips of his contemporaries. They have usually been echoed by historians.

But when we test this charge in detail, a quite different interpretation emerges. In an earlier chapter we printed a list of seventy recipients of wardships during the last four years of Burghley's Mastership.[1] Amongst them it is true that we find the names of Lady Leighton, Lady Paget, and three other titled ladies. And the rest? The remaining sixty-five names are drawn almost exclusively from the officers of the Elizabethan state. If we simply take them in the order in which they appear, we find Sir John Wolley, Latin Secretary to the queen, privy councillor and member of Parliament; Sir William Waad, diplomat and Clerk of the Privy Council; Sir Arthur Gorges, parliamentarian, traveller and man

[1] Above, pp. 125–7.

of letters; Sir John Fortescue, Chancellor of the Exchequer; Dr. Bull of the Chapel Royal; Mr. Seckford of the Privy Chamber; Mr. Herbert, Master of Requests; names such as these go on to the end. The other lists that we possess tell exactly the same story. The recipients were not in fact court sycophants and parasites extracting their unearned profits from the state. A survey of the names in the Court of Wards records reads like a roll-call of the statesmen and civil servants of Tudor England: Burghley, Cecil, Leicester, Bacon, Knollys, Bedford, Essex, Coke, and the rest. And from them we go to the lesser lights: Hunnings of the Revels, Nixon of the Wardrobe, Carswell of the Guard—to quote our list of names again—the departmental officials, clerks, surveyors, attorneys, receivers, feodaries, escheators. Their official fees, in whichever department they worked, were small and notoriously out of line with their responsibilities, their importance, and their standard of living. Their unofficial fees bridged the gap.

This was an established custom before the reign of Elizabeth; and it was also a time-honoured custom to deny that any such money was being received. Burghley himself persistently denied that he was growing rich at the public expense. Richard Kingsmill, the Surveyor of the Court of Wards, once heard it alleged in the House of Commons that a certain bill would be beneficial to the officers of the Court. He was at once stung to reply: 'I trust I shall be accounted an honest, poor man. For any profit I get in my office, more than the dignity of serving Her Majesty, I would another had it.' Arthur Hall said, in 1591, in a letter to Burghley, 'Her Majesty's servant I have been these twenty-six or twenty-seven years.' But, he added, 'from Her Highness I never received any way the benefit of anything'. His father, half a century earlier, had said almost the same thing of his own service of Henry VIII. The complaint that public service meant private bankruptcy may, in some cases, have been based on fact. But there is another side to the story. If, for example, Leicester emptied his pockets to serve the queen, it was she who had filled them in the first place.[1]

---

[1] J. E. Neale, op. cit., pp. 92–3; H. G. Wright, The Life and Works of Arthur Hall of Grantham (1919), pp. 25, 202–3.

The short answer to those who alleged that they held burdensome and profitless office under the queen is—apart from other evidence—to be seen in the intense competition for these very offices they held. 'I will forbear', said John Clapham, secretary to Burghley, 'to mention the great and unusual fees exacted lately by reason of buying and selling offices, both judicial and ministerial, as also the privileges granted unto private persons, to the great prejudice and grievance of the common people.'[1]

The significance of the feudal revenues in the Tudor period lies not in their direct yield to the state but in their importance as a method of payment, albeit indirectly and capriciously, to ministers and civil servants. In place of any adequate system of direct taxation of the nation, it was a method of informal and unofficial taxation of the landed classes to help meet the heavy cost of government. When Cardinal Allen wrote that, 'The gain in this [feudalism] to the sovereign is very small indeed, compared with the loss to the subjects', he was putting his finger on the great weakness of fiscal feudalism; but he was still only stating a half-truth. The *direct* gain to the sovereign was indeed small: but the indirect return was far from negligible. Sir Robert Naunton comes nearer to the truth when he tells us that 'we have not many precedents of her liberality, or of any large donatives to particular men. . . . Her rewards consisted chiefly in grants of leases of offices, places of judicature.' Naunton was in a good position to comment: he was himself Master of Wards under the early Stuarts.[2]

Burghley, if we are to judge him by his actions, recognised fiscal feudalism for the purposes it served: a traditional method of indirect taxation which, with all its inefficiency, could be made to serve two purposes. It could be employed to bring in an annual income to the crown and, secondly, in lieu of salary, an annual income to the government service. There may not be a great deal to be said in defence of a revenue system such as this, which was as

1 J. Clapham, *Elizabeth of England*, ed. C. Read (1951), p. 66.
2 *Letters and Memorials of William, Cardinal Allen*, p. cvii; R. Naunton, *Fragmenta Regalia*, ed. E. Arber (1870), p. 18.

inefficient as it was time-consuming. But at least it had an ancient tradition, it made possible the powerful exercise of patronage, and it did not need parliamentary consent. We would do well not to underrate the importance of these considerations in the minds of both Burghley and the queen.

But there was always an implied condition in the whole system —namely, that it was not driven too hard. If the official price were forced up, and the intermediaries still claimed the same charge, then the *total* market price was bound to increase, and up with it would go the outcry from the wards' relatives and friends, where they were the ultimate purchasers. If the *total* price were already at its maximum and could not be forced up any farther, then a rise in the official price could only be made at the expense of the intermediaries, the official and ruling class, the 'court party', to which Professor Trevor-Roper has called our attention in another connection. Neither measure was Burghley willing to adopt. He wanted neither the official nor the market price to rise. When he took over the Mastership in 1561, he at once reversed the upward rise in revenues and kept them low throughout his period of office. Only by these means could a decrepit yet essential method of government be made to work. And all this is in keeping with what we know of the insight, caution, and conservatism of the man. Long afterwards, when both Burghley and Robert Cecil were dead, Bacon characteristically damned with faint praise Cecil's reputation in the eyes of James I. 'I do think he was no fit counsellor to make your affairs better,' he said of his late rival, 'but yet he was fit to have kept them from getting worse.' Applied to Robert Cecil, the remark shows an extraordinary misunderstanding; but applied to his father it becomes the briefest and best epitome of his career. For nearly forty years Burghley operated the wardship system in his accustomed fashion and, until almost the end, there was no sign of a change.[1]

But the times were changing. In the last decade of Elizabeth's reign the war with Spain had drifted into a dragging and costly

[1] H. R. Trevor-Roper, *The Gentry, 1540-1640* (*Econ. Hist. Rev.*, Supplt. no. 1); Spedding, *op. cit.*, iv, 278, note.

stalemate. The drain upon the revenues became unbearable. The queen lived on her capital, and her debts accumulated. There was urgent need for a new approach. We have seen that the profits from fiscal feudalism began to rise only during the last years of Burghley's life, at a time when Robert Cecil was half-way in the saddle of the Mastership. In May 1599 he was in full control.

A new Master might, on entering office, do one of three things. He could keep to the ancient ways and let the official revenues remain stationary or even decline, while the unofficial profits continued to flow into private pockets, including his own. Or he might, secondly, try to bring the official revenues into line both with the rising price-level and the rising cost of government, thereby reducing the share of the middleman. He might, as it were, try to gain for the crown a larger slice of the total feudal cake. Or he might, thirdly, given goodwill all round, and if he possessed the necessary authority, completely shut down the Court of Wards and seek to open up a new avenue for national taxation. This would be a tremendous undertaking and a complete break with tradition; but if he succeeded in carrying it through, his achievement would be unchallengeable.

The first of these policies, the maintenance of the *status quo* was, as far as Cecil was concerned, clearly out of the question. In the last years of his father's life he had handled a good deal of the wardship business, on his father's behalf; and he more than any man could form a just assessment of the ancient ways. However much he may have benefited from them as an individual, as a statesman and an administrator he could have had for them nothing but contempt.

Instead, he adopted the second policy, the aggrandisement of the royal share in the feudal profits—and treated it as a stage on the way to the third policy: the total abolition of the Court of Wards. At once, as we have seen, he trebled the official price of wardships, which was in essence an attack on the middleman—the whipping boy of Tudor politicians and reformers. That was the new price-policy and it began at once to pay a dividend. But it was not enough. It was merely the curtain-raiser to a more adventurous

theme: to sell to tenants in chief, in their own lifetime, the wardships of their children. In other words, a parent would pay an
insurance premium to the crown and, in return, his heir would be
protected against fiscal feudalism. But where would the middlemen be in all this? A certain John Willoughby, at the beginning
of James I's reign, approached a correspondent for help in obtaining an escheatorship for his uncle. Back at once came the warning,
'I doubt when yourself and your uncle shall understand of the
course intended to be held for the wards, you will scarcely be
willing to hazard any money in procuring that office.' If the reform went through, he was told, 'I see not wherein the escheator
can benefit himself.' And with the profits of the escheator would
go those of the feodary, the informers, the agents, and the whole
breed of intermediaries.[1]

The aim was to bring the official price nearer to the market
price and cut to the bone the profits that went to the men who
stood between the king and his subjects. In a short space of time,
Robert Cecil turned upside down the established doctrine upon
which the Court of Wards had been operating during the sixty
years since its erection. First he tried to adapt medieval machinery
to modern needs. Then, in 1603, he tried to reform the system so
that feudal wardship would exist only in name, with the crown the
only beneficiary. Finally, in 1610, at the height of his power, he
tried to sweep the whole system of feudalism, lock, stock and
barrel, into limbo and replace it by a fundamentally new revenue
machine. That was the Great Contract: the third and last desperate expedient open to a Master of the Wards.

Here was a progressive and statesmanlike plan. And, if he
could at the same time, sell out the royal right of purveyance and
thus clear out of the way another medieval financial apparatus
which creaked and groaned under the burden of years, *tant mieux*.
More was at stake than the welfare of a few thousand orphans.
The existing revenue system, and with it the whole structure of
government, would have been submitted to a drastic overhaul in

1 *Trevelyan Papers*, ed. Trevelyan (Camden Soc. 105, 1872), pt. iii, pp. 53–4; cf. H.M.C,
Salis., xv, 264–5, 276.

all its aspects. But to the king this move was depicted as a betrayal of his royal prerogative and with the Commons it enjoyed no greater popularity. And time was short.

If Cecil could have looked forward to the long decades of his father's life, then perhaps, moving slowly and surely, he could have negotiated a compromise. The powerful vested interests that stood against him were united in nothing save hatred of Cecil. Given time, he could have waited for the misbegotten unity of his enemies to crack and have won either the king or some of the king's counsellors to his side. But time he did not have; and his attempt to hammer out a new revenue system proved a gallant failure. He frankly confessed himself puzzled by the collapse of the Great Contract. At first the Commons seemed to want it; so did the king. 'Nevertheless, it proceeded not,' he said wearily, 'wherein they could not find the impediment but that God did not bless it.' [1] Not God alone; but all the representatives of entrenched conservatism, within the government and the court circle, stood squarely against it. One day, after revolution and civil war, the chance of government reform would come again. But then it would be carried through at the expense of the Stuarts, and the initiative for reform would have passed for ever from their hands.

[1] *Somers Tracts*, ed. W. Scott (1809), ii, 151. I should like to draw attention to *Sales of Wards in Somerset*, 1603-41, ed. M. J. Hawkins, (*Somerset Rec. Soc.* LXVII) which has appeared since this book was first published.

Index

Note: The names of Wards are preceded by an asterisk and of the Officers of the Court of Wards by a dagger.

Abergavenny, Lord. See Neville, Edward
*Acton, —, 126
Admiral, Lord High, 268
Advowsons, 89, 122–3
Agarde, Arthur, 99
Age, Proof of, 157–64, 168, 170, 172
Alabaster, Thomas, 80
*Alambridge, —, 125
Aldred, John, 48
Alford, Edward, 48
Alienation fines, 39, 319
Allen, Cardinal William, xv, 245, 330, 348
*Allington, Hugh, 343
All's Well That End's Well, xiii, 129
Ambassador, French, 310
Ambassador, Venetian, xv, 314
Anatomy of Abuses (Stubbes), 149
*Andrews, —, 125
†Anton, Thomas, Clerk of Wards, 228
Ap Evan, David Lloyd, 104
Apology, by Sir W. Cope, 324–5
*Applegarth, —, 267
*Archdale, —, 267
Argol, Mr., 62
Armada, the Spanish, xv, 245, 317, 330
*Armorer, William, 86
Arundel, Earl of. See Howard Philip, Earl of Surrey
Arundel, Sir William, 203
Ascham, Roger, 119, 256
*Ashburnham, —, 267
Ashton-under-Lyne (Lancashire), 143
Aspectu corporis, 157
*Asshefeld, Robert, 164
Aston, John, lunatic, 73
*—, Walter, 266, 274–5, 343
Attainders, 39
Attainted lands, 242
Attorney-General, 106. See also Coke, Sir Edward

*Aucher, Anthony, 128
†Audley, Hugh, Clerk of Wards, 343–4
Audley, the Lords, 123
Augmentations, Court of, 213
—, Attorney of, 225

*Babington, —, 126
Babram (? Babraham, Cambridgeshire), 37
Bacon, Sir Francis, 191, 284, 287, 315, 334, 345, 347; corruption of, 183–5, 216; on Irish wardship, 106–7; on Robert Cecil, 305–6, 349
—, James, 26
†—, Sir Nicholas, Attorney, xiii, 25–7, 119, 120, 225, 245, 255, 330
—, Thomas, 26
Bagott, Richard, 50
*Baker, —, 126
Bamford, Isabella, 143
Bancroft, Richard, 292
Baptism, 158–9, 162–3
Barber, John, 65
Barnard, Mr., 82, 265
*Barneham, —, 267
Barnes, William, lunatic, 72
Barrett, Mr., Knight of the Cellar, 126
Barrow, Richard, 77
Barwell (Leicestershire), 59
Basforth, Elizabeth, 9
Bashford, Mr., 81
*Bassett, Elizabeth, 301–4
—, Mrs., 148
—, William, 301
†Bate, Thomas, Usher, 229
Bath, Earl of. See Bourchier, William
*Battesford, John, 115
†Battisford, John, Receiver-General, 227
Baxter, John, 301
Beale, Robert, Clerk of the Council, 125

†Beaumont, John, Receiver-General, 28, 199–206, 212, 215, 217, 226–7.
Beck, Mr., of the Spicery, 125
Becon, Thomas, 149
Bedell, Joan, alleged idiot, 74
Bedford, Earls of. See Russell, Edward and Francis
Bedfordshire, 126–7
Bell, Mr. H. E., 229
Bellingham, Edward, 116
*—, John, 116
†Bellknap, Sir Edward, Master of Wards, 242–3
†Bellot, Robert, feodary, 49
Belvoir Castle, 51
— Hunt, 258
Benett, Mr., 61
Berain, Katherine of, 155
Berke, Margaret, 148
Berkeley, Barons of, 98–100, 151
—, Henry, Lord, 99
—, Lady, 99
—, Thomas, Lord, 178
Berkshire, 224, 232
Bertie, Peregrine, Lord Willoughby de Eresby, 64, 70
*—, Robert, Earl of Lindsey, 70–1
Berwick, Marshal of, 70
*Best, —, 125
†Bethel, Hugh, feodary, 48
Birche, Mr., 147
Blackborow, Peter, 43
Black Death, the, xix
Blackmail, 42
Blackstone, Sir William, 330
Bladwell, Giles, lunatic, 65
Blount, Thomas, 78
*Blunt, —, 126
*Bodleigh, William, 115
Body, Mr., 187
Bondmen, xiv, xxi–xxii, 7, 25
*Booth, —, 122
—, Sir William, 122
†Bosseville, Henry, Clerk, 210, 228
†—, Ralph, Clerk, 39, 49, 210, 228
Bourchier, William, Earl of Bath, 124
Bowes, Sir Jerome, 284
Bowyer, Mr., 267
Boyles, Brian, 115
Brackenbury, Mr., 127
Bracton, Henry de, xvi, 97–8
Bradshawe, Mr., 265
Brandon, Charles, Duke of Suffolk, 155, 200. See also Tudor, Mary
*Branthwayt, —, 125
Breame, Mrs., 147
Bribery, 72, 75, 181–8, 192–3, 210, 274, 281, 345; of informers, 46; of juries, 54

Bridlington (Yorkshire), 135
Brinklow, Henry, xiii, 25
Bristol, Mayor of, xxi
Brooke, Elizabeth. See Cecil, Lady Elizabeth
—, Henry, Lord Cobham, 62, 66, 125, 301–3
—, William, Lord Cobham, 125, 286
—, Sir William, 125, 126
Browne, Sir Humphrey, 33
—, Lady, 83
—, Thomas, 61
Buckhurst, Baron. See Sackville, Thomas
Buckingham, Duke of. See Villiers, George
Buckinghamshire, 115, 125, 127, 210
†Budden, John, feodary, 236
—, John, Professor of Civil Law, 236
Bull, Dr. John, of the Chapel, 125, 347
*Bulstrode, Edward, 115
Burgh, Lady, 127
Burghley House, 276–7, 299
—, Lords. See Cecil, William and Thomas
Burrell, Sergeant, 126–7
Burrow, Mr., the Sewer, 126
*Burton, Ralph, 99
Buskell, Thomas, 82
*Butcher, —, 125

Caesar, Sir Julius, 81, 323
Calverley, Mr., 65
Cambridge, University of, 71, 118–9
Cambridgeshire, 125, 258
Camden, William, 281–2
Canterbury, Archbishop of, 78, 102
Cardiganshire, 104
Carew, Sir Gavin, 115
—, George, 232
Carey, George, 103
Carleton, Dudley, 289, 293
Carr, John, 38
*Carrant, —, 125
Carswell, Mr., of the Guard, 125, 347
Cartebote, 89
*Carter, Charles, 118
*Carvill, —, 125
Catholics, Roman, 119–20, 230, 318
Caustey, Mr., of the Queen's Chapel, 115
*Cavell, —, 125
Cavendish, William, Duke of Newcastle, 303
Cecil, Anne. See De Vere, Anne, Countess of Oxford
Cecil, Lady Elizabeth (wife of Robert Cecil), 286, 299
Cecil House, 248, 255–9, 276–7
—, Jane, 59, 276
—, Mildred, Lady Burghley, 265

Cecil, Philip, 62
†Cecil, Sir Robert, Earl of Salisbury, Master, Chap. 15; 41–2, 49, 55, 73–4, 194, 246, 254, 256–7, 283–4, 304, 307, 347; appearance, 285–6; and vacant mastership, 285–96; appointment as Master, 297–9; petitions to, 61 ff., 77, 79–80, 208, 264, 297; offers wardships, 69, 301–4; his own wards, 78, 80, 102, 301–4; wardship policy, 87, 119, 236, 263, 276, 282, 294–5, 310 ff., 350–2; reforms, 345; servants of, 49, 61–2, 67–70, 229; gifts to, 308–310; corrupt proposals to, 52, 62, 80, 194–5, 208–10; dubious dealings of, 69, 102, 264, 299–304; attacks on, 324; defence of, 195, 234, 300, 305–8, 311; as Lord Treasurer, 69–70, 316–24; relations with Michael Hickes, 68–70, 77, 299–304. See also Elizabeth I and James I
—, Thomas, 2nd Lord Burghley, 49–50, 210, 286, 299, 308–10; and wards, 66, 80, 249, 252, 269, 275
†Cecil, William, Lord Burghley, Master, Chapter 12; 29, 37, 49 ff., 75–6, 151, 166, 187, 208, 210, 232, 238, 347; petitions to, Chapter 4; 26, 34, 35, 37, 40, 42, 58–60, 62, 80, 103, 145, 221, 247, 274; appointment of officials, 38, 221, 237; grants of wardships, 125–7, 249; his own wards, 102, 117–9, 127, 142, 144–5, 247 ff., 286, 302; wardship policy, Chapter 13; 86–7, 119–20, 312–4, 332, 346, 349; reforms, 40, 227, 269–70; views on marriage, 143, 147; on education, 118–9, 127, 152, 255–9; servants of, 60–1, 78, 123, 193–4, 225, 231, 238, 248, 255–6, 263, 265, 280; gifts to 83, 128, 182, 264–8, 271, 279–80, 305–10, 344; dubious dealings of, 264–7; attacks on, 181, 263, 268, 346; defence of, 249, 269, 276–281; last years of, 62, 69, 78–9, 283–4, 299, 346–7; as Lord Treasurer, 270–1, 277, 316, 336; as a judge, 216, 269–71; as a statesman, 271–3, 278. See also Elizabeth I
Cecil, William (grandson of Burghley), 269
Chaderton, William, bishop, 153
Chamberlain, John, 289–90, 324
—, Lord Great, 169, 175, 177, 180, 189
—, Robert, 65
Chamberlayne, John, 133–4, 139
Chancellor, Lord, 33, 169, 176, 183, 268

Chancery, 47, 76, 81, 88, 90–1, 169–71, 173, 177, 189, 190, 213, 245–6, 332
Chantry lands, 20
Charles I, 193, 337
Chaworth, Sir John, 51–2
Cheshire, 19, 44, 122, 126, 209, 237
Chester, Bishop of, 122–3
—, Countess of, 146
—, County Palatine of, 101–2
—, Diocese of, 122
—, Ecclesiastical Court of, 152–3
—, Earls of, 102
★Chevrell, —, 126
Cheyney, Anne, 49
—, Thomas, 48–9
Chief Justice, 195, 226, 268. See also Wray, Sir Christopher; Popham, Sir John
★Child, Agnes, 44
Childwall (Lancashire), 34
Cholmeley, Mary, Lady, 65
★—, Thomas, 82, 266
★—, William, 82, 266
Churches, presentations to, 89
Cinque Ports, 102
Civil Servants, Elizabethan, Chapter 11; 60, 67, 124, 178, 180, 182, 184, 190, 337–8, 346–9; and fees, 210, 215, 273, 277, 298; and gifts, 209, 215–6; and sale of office, 210–11, 348
Civil Servants in Soviet Union, 95; in United States, 94–5, 221
Civil Service, organisation of, in Tudor period, 211, 221–2
Civil War, the, 177, 329
Clapham, John, 67, 193–4, 263, 270, 283, 348
★Clavell, John, 130–3, 142, 161–2
—, William, 162
Clavencurry, Mr., 86, 90
†Claybrooke, Stephen, messenger, 229
Clayton (Yorkshire), 100
Clerke, Margaret, 135–6
★Cleyburne, Thomas, lunatic and ward, 74–5
Clientage, 60, 97, 216–7, 240, 241, 254, 287–8, 292, 349
Clifford, Francis, 4th Earl of Cumberland, 100
—, George, 3rd Earl of Cumberland, 52, 62, 69, 100
—, Henry, 2nd Earl of Cumberland, 127
★Clifton, —, 119
★Cobbe, —, 126
Cobham, Anne, Lady, 65, 145
Cobham, Lord. See Brooke, Henry

Coke, Sir Edward, xiii, 4, 98, 233; and inquisitions, 57; and wardships, 71, 266–7, 274–5, 336, 347; and marriage, 134–5, 138, 140; and knighthood, 166–8; and livery, 171–5; and corruption, 184

Cole, Mr., 309

*Collye, Alice, 86

Comberton (Worcestershire), 100

Commissions, 81–2, 101–6, 176–7; for concealed lands, 39–41; for concealed wardships, 34–6, 39–41, 86, 186; for idiocy and lunacy, 49, 74; for *inquisitions post mortem*, 47 ff.; for land sales, 20–4; to manumit bondmen, xxi; for revenues, 197, 205–6, 211–2; to sell wardships in Ireland, 85–6, 105–6, 182

Commons, House of. *See* Parliament

Commonwealth of England, The. See: De Republica Anglorum

Complaynt of Roderyck Mors (Brinklow), 25

Concealment of lands, 35, 38, 270

— of wardships. *See* Wardships

Conisbie, William, 33

Constable, Sir H., 267

—, Robert, 98

Contract, the Great, 177, 316–24, 351–2

Controller of the Works, 309–10

*Cook, —, 126

Cooke, Sir Anthony, 65

—, Avis, Lady, 65

—, Mrs. Francis, 151

†—, William, Clerk of Liveries, 228

Cooper, Thomas, 58

Cope, Mr, 309–10

†Cope, Sir Walter, feodary (later Master), 234, 236; his defence of Robert Cecil, 324–5

Coppinger, Henry, 123

Cordell, Sir William, 66

Cornwall, County of, 210, 339

—, Duchy of, 102

Corruption, Chapter 10; 10, 23, 181, 210; of commissions, 49, 54; of feodaries, 44–6, 53, 188–91, 206, 209–10, 237–8, 298; of juries, 53–7; of justice, 54, 200–1, 215–6; of officials, 33, 206, 209–10, 273–4, 338, 348

See also Wards and Liveries, Court of

*Cotton, George, 86, 115

—, Philippa, 79

*Covell, —, 126

†Coxe, John, feodary, 81

Cranmer, Mr., of the Jewel House, 126

*Cresacre, Anne, 144

*Crofts, Herbert, 126

—, John, 59

—, Thomas, 59

*—, William, 59

Cromwell, Edward, Lord, 63

—, Oliver, 335

—, Thomas, 15–16, 157, 162, 243, 254, 284, 331

Cross, Sir Robert, 309

Crowshall (Suffolk), 162–3

Cuffe, Hugh, 79

Cumberland, Earls of. *See* Clifford

Cunningham, W. R., 271

†Curle, William, Auditor, 227

*Dacre, Anne, 144–5

*—, Elizabeth, 144

—, Lord of the South. *See* Fiennes, Gregory

*—, Mary, 144

*Dacre of Gilsland, George, Lord, 144

—, Thomas, Lord, 144

—, William, Lord, 216

Dacres of the North. *See* Dacre of Gilsland

Damport, the Queen's footman, 126

†Damsell, Sir William, Receiver-General, 115, 203, 205, 212, 227

Danvers, Sir John, 48

D'Arcy, Lady, 151

Darrell, Mary, 150–1

Davis, Sir John, 147–8

*Deane, Alice, 19

De Clandestinis Nuptiis, 143

De Etate Probanda, writ of, 158, 161, 169

De La Ware, Baron. *See* West, Thomas

De Mandeville, Geoffrey, 146–7

Denbighshire, 49, 121, 126

*Dent, Alice, 81

*—, Mary, 81

*Derby, Earls of. *See* Stanley

Derbyshire, 125–6, 195

De Republica Anglorum (Sir Thomas Smith), xiv–xv, 120

Description of England (Harrison), xiv–xv

Devenerunt, writ of, 46

De Vere, Anne, Countess of Oxford, 50, 144–5, 252–3

—, Anne, 144, 250

*—, Edward, 17th Earl of Oxford, 102, 129, 144–5, 249, 250, 252–3, 255–6, 258–9, 302

—, Elizabeth, 251

—, John, 15th Earl of Oxford, 144

Devereux, Dorothy, 140–1

—, Frances, Countess of Essex, 305, 307

—, Lettice (later Countess of Leicester), 259

*Devereux, Robert, 2nd Earl of Essex, 79–80, 118, 164, 166, 168, 217, 232, 233, 241, 249, 254, 257, 259, 264, 274, 305–6, 341–2, 347; and vacant Mastership, 263, 266, 279, 285–96, 297–9, 300
—, Walter, 1st Earl of Esex, 255, 293
Devon, Earldom of, 234
Devonshire, 47, 115, 126, 209, 236, 309
D'Ewes, Simonds, 153
Diem Clausit Extremum, writ of, 45
Digby, Lady, 125, 309–10
Discourse of the Common Weal, 177
Divorce, 25
Dixie, Lady, 264
Dorset, County of, 77, 82, 125–7, 209, 236
—, John, 132
—, Marquess of. *See* Grey, Henry
Dower, 145–6, 148, 291
*Downes, —, 125
Dowry, 65, 151
Drake, Sir Francis, 341
†Drew, Edward, feodary, 236
*Drew, —, 125
Drury, Sir Drue, 166, 264
—, Sir Drue, the younger, 166–8
Drury's Case, 166–8
Dudley, Ambrose, Earl of Warwick, 250
—, Anne, Countess of Warwick, 78, 195
—, Edmund, 7, 9, 19, 57, 199
—, Guilford, 204
—, John, Earl of Warwick, later Duke of Northumberland, 22, 203–4, 254
—, Robert, Earl of Leicester, 76, 121, 124, 127, 168, 250, 254, 347
—, Robert, Earl of Warwick, 100
Duport, Thomas, 99
Durham, Bishopric of, 101–2
Dyer, Sir Edward, 40–1, 182–3, 217

East Greenwich, Manor of, 19–24
Ecclesiastical lands, sale of, 10–11, 14, 20–4, 26
Edmunds, Dorothy, Lady, 66
Edward IV, 234
Edward VI, 10, 23, 28, 34, 164, 201–2, 247, 279
Egerton, Sir Thomas, 63, 333
Eliot, John, 135–6
Elizabeth I, Queen, 54, 112, 123, 176–7, 215, 252, 335, 337; attitude to wardship, 29, 241, 290, 332, 342, 346, 348; attitude to marriage of maids of honour, 52, 140; interference in care of ward, 63–4; direct grants of

wardships, 70–1, 78, 86, 90, 292; New Year gifts, 268, 339; relations with Burghley, 222, 250–1, 260, 272–3, 277–9, 281–2, 284, 302; relations with Robert Cecil, 286, 300; relations with Earl of Essex, 285–96, 341–2; and vacant mastership, 284–96; alleged harsh dealings with her ministers, 208–9, 347–8
Ellis, Richard, 39
Elvin, Dr., 310
Ely, Bishop of, 255
Empson, Sir Richard, 7, 9, 19, 57, 234
†Englefield, Sir Francis, Master, 25, 27, 28–9, 36, 72–3, 211–2, 244–6
†—, Sir Thomas, Master, 243
Enrolments, Statute of, 12–13
Escheators, 34, 45–57, 73, 81, 92–3, 158–61, 188–90, 230–3, 351; address to jury, 46–7, 56–7; corruption of, 53, 210, 248; inefficiency of, 44, 47, 230–1, 292
Essex, County of, 115, 126, 234–6
—, Earls of. *See* Devereux
Estates-General, 323
Eton, scholars of, 119
Evans, Mr., 68
†Eveleigh, John, feodary, 209–10
Ewens, Matthew, 283
Exchequer, the, 15, 28, 76, 171, 174, 176–7, 179, 190, 197, 213, 324, 340; —, Barons of, 40, 174, 207, 283; —, Chancellor of. *See* Fortescue, Sir John *and* Mildmay, Sir Walter
—, Reform of, 211–2
Exeter, 236
Exhibitions, 83, 89, 105, 114 ff., 236
Expenditure, Government, 339, 341–2

*Farre, —, 126
Fealty, Oath of, 169
Fees. *See* Wards and Liveries
Felton, Mr., 53
Ferdinando, Mr., of the Privy Chamber, 127
Fermor, Thomas, 265
*Fermor, —, 265
*Fetherston, —, 126
Feudal incidents, 17, 21, 35, 36, 39, 89, 103, 176–7; aids, 8, 99, 317; primer seisin, 35, 39; reliefs, 35, 98; ouster le mayne, 39
Feudal Rights, 8, 21; Concealment of, 8, 12–14, 16, 17, 33 ff., 53, 180; Resistance to, Chapter 2; 6–7, 11, 13–14; Revival of, Chapter 1; 18, 238, 334; Extension of, 27, 35

Feudalism, xiv–17
Feudalism, Fiscal, 205–8, 348–50; Profits of, xv, 9, 27–8, 105–7, 226, 231, 260; 297–8, 336–7; Profits of, under Edward IV, 234; Profits of, under Henry VIII, 9, 27–8, 338; Profits of, under Edward VI, 28, 338; Profits of, under Mary, 28, 338–9; Profits of, under Elizabeth I, xv, 179–80, 262–3, 268, 271, 275, 291–2, 312–4, 339–42, 344–6
Fiennes, Gregory, Lord Dacre of the South, 164, 235
First Fruits and Tenths, Court of, 213
Fitzherbert, Anthony, 231
Fitzwilliam, Henry, 79
—, William, 105
*Flatman, —, 126
†Fleetwood, William, Receiver-General, 227, 267, 283, 288–9, 297, 300
Folke (Dorset), Parson of, 162
Folton (Yorkshire), 48
Forest Laws, 336
†Forshawe, William, feodary, 45
Forster, Richard, 145
Fortescue, Sir John, 65, 71, 125, 126, 232, 336, 347
—, Sir Thomas, 297, 300
*Fortescue, —, 126
Framlingham, Charles, 162–3
—, Francis, 162
—, Lady Tylney, 163
Fraudulent Conveyances, 36
Freedom in Tudor England, xiv–xxii, 8
Frisius, Sylvius, 256
Fulstowe, Richard, 64
Fyrebote, 89

Gall, Sir Henry, 48
Garnett, Henry, S.J., 289, 293
Garnons, Mr., 314
Gascoigne, John, 61
Geff, Nicholas, 41
*Gell, —, 125
Gentlemen Pensioners, 54, 67
Gerald, James, 79
Gerrard, Sir Thomas, 80, 152
*Gifford, —, 267
Gilbert, Sir Humphrey, 120, 255, 330
Glanville, Sir John, 232
Glanville, Ranulf, xvi
Glemmam, Lady, 301
Gloucester, Isabel, Countess of, 146–7
Gloucestershire, 125, 127, 236
Glyn, Mr., 68
*Godden, Neville, 145
Goldesborough, John, 99
†Goodrich, Richard, Attorney, 224–5

†Goodwin, Christopher, messenger, 229
Gorge, Mr., 150–1
Gorges, Sir Arthur, 63, 125, 305–6, 346
†Goring, George, Receiver-General, 116–7, 208–9, 226–8, 270
— —, jun., 208–9, 264, 299
Grafton, Richard, 188
Grantham (Lincolnshire), 247
*Gratwicke heirs, 64
*Green, Thomas, 115
†Greene, Thomas, feodary, 44
Greenwich (Kent). See East Greenwich
Gregory, John, 60
Greve, Thomas, 234
†Greville, Fulke, feodary, 236
—, Sir Fulke, 50, 236
Grey, Henry, Marquis of Dorset, 200, 203–4
—, Lady Jane, 204
*Grey, —, 125
Guardians, Chapter 7; 37, 81–3, 89–90, 92–5, 139, 155, 298; —, complaints of, 63–4, 81–2, 114; —, lack of care for wards, 25–6, 74–5, 330–1. See also Wards

Hackett, William, 43
Haddington, Viscount. See Ramsay, John
Haddon, Sir Walter, 66, 77
Haines, Gilbert, 126
*Hales, —, 126
*Hall, Arthur, 247–9, 259, 347
—, Edmund, 247–8
—, Edward, chronicler, 13
—, Francis, 347
*Hamden, —, 127
Hampden, Elizabeth, 264
Hampshire, 89, 126, 130–2
Handen, Mr., 78
†Hanley, Roger, feodary, 45
*Hannam, —, 127
Hardwick, Bess of, 155
Hardy, Mr., 49
†Hare, Hugh, Clerk, 228
†—, John, Clerk, 228–9, 284
—, Sir Nicholas, 33
†—, Mr., Clerk, 82
Harrison, William, xiv, 331
*Harrison, —, 126
Harte, John, 256
*Harteys, —, 126
Hastings, Sir Francis (1558–9), 54
—, Sir Francis (1599), 194
—, George, 4th Earl of Huntingdon, 68, 71, 141
*—, heiresses, 19
—, Henry, 3rd Earl of Huntingdon, 80
*—, John, 90

Hastings, Lady, 292
Hatfield Palace, 277
— House, Records at, 34, 59, 82, 195, 300, 304
Hatton, Sir Christopher, Lord Chancellor, 71, 117, 265
*—, Christopher, 71, 117, 292
—, Elizabeth, Lady, 71
*Haughton, —, 125-6, 266-7
Haverford West (Pembrokeshire), 60
Hawkins, Mr., of the Guard, 126
*Hawtrey, —, 125
Hedgebote, 89
*Hedges, —, 125
Helford (Cornwall), 59
*Henly, —, 267
Hemerford, William, 162
Henry I, 5
Henry II, 5, 146
Henry III, 76
Henry VII, 7, 8, 15, 190, 335
Henry VIII, 8-20, 22, 24, 28, 52, 70, 90, 135, 147, 154-5, 242, 272, 335
Herbert, Henry, Earl of Pembroke, 76
—, Sir John, 68
*—, Lord, of Cherbury, 111-4
—, Mr., Master of Requests, 125, 347
—, William, 237, 247-8
*Heron, Giles, 144
—, Sir John, 144
Herrle, William, 42, 276-9
Hertford, Earl of. See Seymour, Edward
†Hesketh, Thomas, Attorney, 194, 210, 226, 263, 283
*Heveningham, Anthony, 38
*Hewitt, —, 267
Hickes, Baptist, Lord Camden, 235, 304
†Hickes, Sir Michael, feodary, 67-70, 77, 231-2, 235-6, 264-5, 284, 303. See also Cecil, Sir Robert
Hill, Mr., of the Guard, 126
Hoby, Sir Edward, 62, 255
—, Lady Margaret, 155
Holcroft, Sir Thomas, 203
*Hole, —, alias White —, 126
Holles, Gervase, 150, 153-4
Homage, 169, 171, 175
—, Respite of, 176-7, 180, 319
Horde, Agnes, 131
—, Roger, 130-2
—, Thomas, 130-2, 161
Horsley, Cuthbert, 38
*Hotham, John, 152
Hothersall, Margaret, 152
Housebote, 89
Household, Royal, 273, 339; Cofferer of, 340; Controller of, 245; Treasurer of, 235, 242

Howard, Charles, Earl of Nottingham, 68-9, 274
—, Henry, 303
—, Lady Margaret, 144
*—, Philip, Earl of Surrey (later Earl of Arundel), 144-5, 249, 258-9
—, Thomas, 3rd Duke of Norfolk, 254
—, Thomas, 4th Duke of Norfolk, 144-5, 255
*—, Lord Thomas (heir to Audleys), 123
—, Lord Thomas, 144
Howland, Richard, 123
Hudson, James, 41-2
Hunnis (Hunnings), William, of the Revels, 125, 267, 347
*Hunt, Christopher, 77
—, Rowland, 147
Hunte, George Lee, 65
Huntingdon, Countess of, 141
—, Earl of. See Hastings
*Huntley, Stephen, 99
†Hurlestone, Richard, feodary, 44-5, 209, 237
Hussey, Sir John, 7, 242
Hutton, Matthew, 102
†Hynde, John, Surveyor, 223-4

Idiots. See Lunatics and Idiots
Impositions, 317
India, Criminal Code of, 185
Inflation, 19, 173, 190, 273, 336, 338
Informers, 34, 36-43, 45-6, 186-9, 318, 342, 351
Inquisitiones Post Mortem, 44-53, 55-7, 81-5, 92-3, 101-2, 122, 164, 170, 173, 188-9, 231, 233, 235, 247-8; Deficiencies of, 46, 54, 63, 68-9, 84, 87, 161, 171-2, 191-2, 233, 265, 298; Traverse of, 46, 55
Inquisitions for Idiocy and Lunacy. See Lunatics and Idiots, and see also Juries
Institutes, the (Coke), 337
Intermediaries, 60, 192, 341-51
Ireland, 23-4, 164, 166, 293-6, 306
—, Wardship in, 85-6, 91, 105-7
Iveson, Richard, 61

James I, 69-70, 99, 100, 112, 166, 315, 333, 335; his relations with Robert Cecil, 277, 316-25, 349, 352
Jenny, Ambrose, 125
Jennye, Francis, 61
Jersey, 103-4, 332
Jesus College, Cambridge, 118, 292
Jobson, Jane, 79
—, Walter, 48
John, King, 5, 146, 165

Johnson, Sir Robert, 35
Jointure, 178
Judd, Sir Andrew, 73
Judges Assistant, 16
Juries, xviii, 35, 43, 46, 75–6, 81–2, 142,
    158–62, 189; intimidation and
    corruption of, 52–7, 192, 248. See
    also Sheriffs
Justices of the Peace, 230, 237

Keeper, Lord, 226
†Keilway, Robert, Surveyor, 115, 210,
    223–4
Kent, 115, 126, 232, 313
Ket's Rebellion, 25, 96
Ketton (Rutland), 59
Khruschchev, Nikita S., 95
Kildare, Countess of, 78, 127
†Killigrew, John, feodary, 210
Kilmersdon (Somersetshire), Custom of,
    145–6
Kingsmill, Lady, 50
†—, Richard, Attorney, later Surveyor,
    224, 225, 267, 347
Kingston, Henry, 150
Kirketon, Dorothy, 153–4
Kirkham, Edward, of the Revels, 125
Kitchin, Mr., 56
Knight Service. See Tenure
Knighthood, 164–8
—, Distraint of, 176–7, 336–7
Knightley, Sir Richard, 125
Knollys, Sir Francis, 66, 105–6, 124, 347
Knyvett, Thomas, 127
—, Thomas (of Norfolk), 195–6
*Knyvett, —, 125

*Laborn, —, 267
Lacye, Robert, 48
Lambarde, William, 232
Lancashire, 34, 55, 126, 230
Lancaster, County Palatine of, 101–2
—, Duchy of, 233–4, 243, 300, 341
Lane, Sir William, 126
*—, William, 19
Lanman, Mr., of the Guard, 126
Latimer, Edward, 289, 293, 298
—, Hugh, xiii, 25, 26, 120, 217, 330,
    343
Layton, Lady, 309–10
Lee, Sir Henry, xxi
—, Richard, 226
—, Robert, 74
—, Rowland, lunatic, 74
—, Mr., 77
—, Mrs., 80
*Lee, —, 126
Leicester Assizes, 99

Leicester, Earl of. See Dudley
Leicestershire, 125
Leigh, Sir Piers, 66
*—, Thomas, 233
Leighton, Lady, 125, 346
Lennox, County of, 255
*Lental —, 125
Lentall, Philip, 77
L'Estrange, Eleanor, 144
—, John, 144
Letters Patent, 89–90
†Ley, James, Attorney, 226
Leyland, John, the Elder, 73
—, John, the Younger, lunatic, 73
Lincoln College, Oxford, 122–3
Lincolnshire, 51, 126, 210
*Lingwood, —, 126
Littleton, Sir Thomas, 134, 138
Liverpool, 34
Livery, Suing of, 39, 168–80, 194, 213,
    222–3, 228, 269; revenue from,
    27–8, 344–5. See also Wards, Court
    of
Llechewethllwivan, 104
Lloyd, Evan, 121–2
*—, Morgan, 121–2
Loans, 178, 338
London, 52, 88, 92–3, 112, 115, 170, 335
—, Bishop of, 140
—, Lord Mayor of, 62, 73
—, Wards in, 47, 62, 102–3, 125–7
*Long, Elizabeth, 275, 343
Long Parliament, 107, 246
Lord Treasurer's Remembrancer, 38
Lords, House of. See Parliament
Losely, manuscripts at, 113
Louis XII, King of France, 154–5
Louis XV, King of France, 273
Lovell, Sir Thomas, 235, 242–3
*Lovell, —, 126
Lowther, Richard, 74–5
Ludlow (Shropshire) 74
Lunatics and Idiots, 49, 65, 72–6, 140,
    243; Inquisitions for, 49, 73, 75–6

Macaulay, Thomas Babington, Lord, 185
Mackworth, Thomas, 98
Magdalene College, Cambridge, 123
Magna Carta, 6, 139, 146, 165, 167, 330
Maids of Honour, 52, 252–3
Maitland, Frederick William, 76
*Malyns, —, 125
Man, Mr., 147
Manchester, Earl of. See Montagu
Mandamus, writ of, 45–6
Mandeville, Viscount. See Montagu
*Manley, —, 126

Manners, Lady Bridget, 52
*—, Edward, 3rd Earl of Rutland, 51, 249, 250, 252, 259
—, Elizabeth, Countess of Rutland, 51–2
*—, Mr. John, 275
—, John, 4th Earl of Rutland, 51
—, John, Sheriff of Derbyshire, 195
—, John, of Haddon, 51
*—, Roger, 5th Earl of Rutland, 63, 249, 250, 258–9
—, Mr. Roger, 126
Manningham, John, 314
Manwood, Sir Roger, 106
Marcher Lords, 102
Marches of Wales. See Wales
Markham, Mr., 77
Marprelate, Martin, 123
Marquis, Frederick, 1st Earl of Woolton, 204–5
Marriage, Attitude to, xiii–xiv, 149–56, 331; to alleged idiot, 74; Child, 134–5, 151–4; Disparagement in, 139–42; Feudal rights of, Chapter 8; xiv, 3–5, 17, 18, 23, 83–4, 89, 96, 181, 213; Forced, 100, 141, 152, 331; to prevent wardship, 49, 331; Refusal of, 137, 141–3, 155–6; Secret, 65, 143; Value of, 99, 114, 138, 142, 152; of a ward, Chapter 8; 83, 112–4, 120; of widows, 39, 145–8, 213, 242–3; without licence, 130–3, 142, 269. See also Wards, Wards and Liveries, and Wardships
Marshal of Berwick, 70
Marvin, Sir James, 67
Mary I, 28, 70, 178, 204, 228, 234, 335
Mary, Queen of Scots, 272
Massachusetts, Governor of, 226
Mattingley, Mr., 126
Maynard, Henry, 67, 264
Mayne, Joseph, 78
Maynwaringe, Sir George, 63
Mean Rates, 171, 175
Medlie, Mr., 265
Melius Inquirendo, writ of, 46
Melton Mowbray, 98
*Mendham, —, 125
Merchant Adventurers, The, 272, 308–9
Meredith, Mr., 55–6
—, Mrs., 147
Meredith v. Rede, 55–6
Merionethshire, 179
Merton, Statute of, 142
Meryng, Francis, 77
Metals on ward's lands, 123
*Metcalf, —, 126
Middlesex, 115, 232
Mildmay, Sir Walter, 66, 335–6

Miseries of Enforced Marriage, The (Wilkins), xiii, 149–50, 156
†Mitchell, Avery, feodary, 235
Mitchell, Mr., 232
Monasteries, dissolution of, xix, 9–11, 16, 19–20, 167
Monastic Lands, sale of, 10–11, 14, 20–4, 334
Monmouthshire, 53
Monopolies, Patents of, 333, 336
†Montagu, Henry, Earl of Manchester, Master, 344
Montgomery Castle, 112
Moore, Alice, 147
More, Cecily, 144
—, Sir George, of Losely, 113–4
—, John, 144
—, Sir Thomas, 127, 143–4, 147
Morehouse, Mrs., 292
†Moreton, Gilbert, feodary, 34, 72
*Morgan, Henry, 86
Morison, Charles, 275
Morley, Lord. See Parker, Edward
†Morrice, James, Attorney, 225
Moryson, Fynes, 134, 139
Mountfenill. See Rossindall
*Musgrave, —, 125
Myrfyn, Mr., 147

†Naunton, Sir Robert, Master, 348
Neale, Professor Sir John, 215
†Necton, William, feodary, 81
Nedeham, Mr., pensioner, 126
Neile, Dr. Richard, 66
Netherlands, War in the, 215
Neville, Edward, Lord Abergavenny, 44
—, Sir Henry, 300, 310
†—, Thomas, Surveyor, 223
Newcastle, Duke of. See Cavendish
Newport, Sir Francis, 112–3
Newport, Henry, 75–6
Newton, Katherine, Lady, 65
Nicholls, Degory, 123
Nicholson, Mr., 309
Nixon, Mr., of the Wardrobe, 125, 347
Norfolk, 125–6, 234
—, Dukes of. See Howard, Thomas
Norman custom, 104
Norris, Francis, Lord, 309
—, Henry, Lord, 48
—, Sir John, 41
—, Lady, 49
Norroy King-at-Arms, 141
North, Dorothy, Lady, 65
—, Roger, Lord, 37, 127
Northamptonshire, 19, 235
Northumberland, Earl of. See Percy
Norton, Mr., of the Cellar, 125

*Norton, John, 86
Norwich, 41
†Norwich, Sir Robert, Surveyor, 223
Nottingham, Earl of. *See* Howard, Charles
Nowell, Lawrence, 256
†—, Robert, Attorney, 128, 225
Noy, William, 191

Obligations, 88, 202–3
Officials. *See* Civil Servants *and* Wards
Olivares, Count, xv, 245
O'Neill, Shane, 339
†Onslow, Richard, Attorney, 225
Ormskirk (Lancashire), 34
*Osbaldiston, Alexander, 152
Osborne, Peter, 38, 210
Owen, Mr., 309–10
—, Sir Roger, 320, 323
Oxford, Bishop of, 123
—, City of, 329
—, Earls of. *See* de Vere
—, University College, 112
—, University of, 112
Oxfordshire, 65, 126, 232, 265

Paget, Lady, 125, 346
—, William, Lord, 146, 203
†Palmer, Peter, feodary, 210
Pamplyn, Robert, 72
Parker, Edward, Lord Morley, 63
Parliament, 36, 42, 55, 57, 81, 175, 181, 187, 236, 270, 286, 349; Acts of, 8, 12, 14, 15, 20, 21, 24, 36, 42, 57, 116, 135, 189, 193, 199, 207–8, 210, 245, 329, 340; Addled, 324; and Great Contract, 316–24
—, Commons, House of, 5, 8, 10, 13, 41–3, 66, 168, 177, 190–1, 207, 225, 248, 315, 321, 329, 333, 335–7, 352
—, Lords, House of, 197
†Parris, Philip, Receiver-General, 205, 226
Parry, Lady, 124
—, Thomas, 48
†—, Sir Thomas, Master, 29, 245–6, 281, 290
*Parsloe, —, 126
Parsons, Robert, S.J., 289, 293
Patronage. *See* Clientage
Paulet, Sir Anthony, 104
†—, George, Clerk of Liveries, 228
—, Sir Hugh, 82
†—, Sir William, Marquess of Winchester, Master, 28–9, 90, 198, 202–3, 206, 211–2, 223–4, 241, 243–4, 247, 271

*Paulet, —, 126
*Pavet, —, 127
Payne, Griffith, 232
Pembroke, Earls of, 100. *See also* Herbert, Henry
Penkraige, 104
Penruddock, Mr., 309
†Pepper, Cuthbert, Surveyor, 224
Perceval, Richard, 67–8
Percy, Henry, Earl of Northumberland, 307–8
†Perient, John, Auditor, 227
Perquisites, 239, 265–6, 273, 278, 281, 298, 310–11, 345
Perrot, Sir John, 60
—, Sir Thomas, 140–1
Peterborough, Bishop of, 123
Petre, Mr., 76
—, Sir William, 66
Phettiplace, Sir John, 48
†Phylpott, Mr., messenger, 188
Pilgrimage of Grace, 14, 24, 242
Plessington, Humfrey, 64
Ploughbote, 89
Politics, Structure of Elizabethan, 254, 272, 295, 308
†Polsted, Thomas, Attorney, 224
Poor Law, Elizabethan, 230
Popham, Sir John, Chief Justice, 67, 167–8
Portsmouth, dockyard at, 339
Poulet, Katherine, 178
Poyntz, John, 330–1
—, Mr., Clerk of the Kitchen, 126
†Pratt, William, Usher, 229
*Prediaux, Thomas, 19
Prerogativa Regis, by W. Staunford, 26–7
— —, 'Statute' of, 98 ff.
Prerogative wardship. *See* Wardship
Prescot (Lancashire), 34
Prescott, Mr., 309
Presentations to Livings, 89, 122–3
*Prest, —, 126
Privy Council, 36, 43, 54, 70, 104–6, 119–20, 122, 127–8, 178, 200, 203–6, 224, 244–5, 247, 332
Privy Seal, 82
—, Clerk of, 189, 268
—, Lord, 169, 189
Proby, R., 306–7
Purefy, Mr., 99
*Purefy, —, 125
Purveyance, 318, 320
*Pyrry, William, 177

Que plurima, writ of, 46
Quia Emptores, Statute of, 97
*Quiny, —, 125

Radcliffe, Thomas, Earl of Sussex, 178
Radnorshire, 53
Rainsforde, Paul, 38
Raleigh, Honor of, 234
—, Sir Walter, 79, 91, 105, 215–6, 257, 285, 295, 301–2, 335
Ramsay, John, Lord Huddington, 322
Ramsden, Robert, 256
*Randall, Vincent, 343
Ratcliff, Sir John, 165–8
Ratcliff's Case, 165–8
†Ratclyf, Robert, feodary, 45
Rathborne, Aaron, 87
Ravishment of ward. See Wards, Seizure of
*Raylop, —, 125
†Raymond, George, feodary, 236
Raynsford, Miles, 72
Reade, Mr., 50
Rectories, 73
Recusants. See Catholics, Roman
Rede, Mr., 55–6
Reformation, the, xix, 10
Registrar, of births, deaths and marriages, 42; of descents, 42
Rents, arrears of, 39; reserved, 35
Revenues, Royal, xv, 5, 8, 10, 16–17, 168, 176, 178–80, 191, 197–8, 207–8, 213, 215, 270, 297, 316–24, 335–7, 341, 348–52
Reynell, George, 265
Rhydd, 104
Rich, Penelope, Lady, 264–5
—, Richard, Lord, 100–1, 223, 234
Rivet, Lady, 37
—, Sir Thomas, 37
Roberts, Thomas, Auditor, 227
Rolls, Master of the, 169, 189
*Rootes, —, 126
Roper, Sir John, 308–9
Rossindall, John, Lord Mountfenill, 178
*Rossiter, Richard, 115
*Rowse, Nicholas, 86, 115
*Russell, Edward, 3rd Earl of Bedford, 250
—, Francis, 2nd Earl of Bedford, 347
—, Lady Elizabeth, 255
Rutland, County of, 98, 235
—, Earls of. See Manners
— wardships, 100
Ryveland, Elizabeth, 339

Sackville, Thomas, Lord Buckhurst, 126, 266, 301, 340
St. Davids, Bishop of, 78
*St. John, —, 125
St. John's College, Cambridge, 119, 123, 256

Salusbury, John, 179
*Samways, —, 125
Sandys, William, Lord, 151
Savage, Mr., 309–10
Saye, —, of the Privy Chapel, 126
Scotland, 104
Scott, Mr., lunatic, 49
Seckford, H, 125–6, 347
†Seckford, Thomas, Surveyor, 224
*Seckford, —, 126
Secretaries, King's, 169, 189
— of State, 246–7, 271, 287–8, 290
Sefton (Lancashire), 34
Sergeants' Inn, 195
Sermon of the Plough (Latimer), 25
†Servant, Marmaduke, Usher, 117–8, 229
Sewers, Commissioners of, 235
†Sewster, John, Attorney, 27, 224
Seymour, Edward, Duke of Somerset, 27, 76, 203, 223–4, 247, 254
—, Edward, Earl of Hertford, 309
—, Sir Thomas, Lord Admiral, 27, 237
Shakespeare, William, xii, 117, 129, 141
Sharington, Mr., 247
*Sheffield, Edmund, 1st Baron, 144
—, —, 3rd Baron, 194–5, 252, 305, 307
Shelley (Suffolk), 162–3
Shelton, Sir John, 33
†Sherard, Mr., deputy-feodary, 210
Sheriffs, 37, 81, 161, 195, 208, 230, 332, and empanelling of juries, 46, 53–4, 57, 291
—, Under-, 195
Ship Money, 336
Shirley, George, 265
*Short, —, 125
Shrewsbury, Earl of. See Talbot
†Shute, Richard, feodary, 51, 210
*Sibley, —, 127
Sidney, Sir Henry, 66, 339
—, Lady, 274
—, Sir Philip, 217, 252, 287
Signet, Clerk of the, 189
Skinner, Mr., 309–10
—, Thomas, 229
—, Vincent, 67, 231
Smallman, Mr., 75
*Smelt, —, 127
*Smith, John, 86, 115
—, Sir Thomas, ambassador, xiv, xviii, xxi, 120–1, 169, 330
—, Sir Thomas, Clerk of the Council, 126
—, Dr., the Queen's physician, 125
*Smith, —, 126
Smyth, John, of Nibley, 98–100
†Sneynton, Quintin, Usher, 229
Socage tenure. See Tenure
Solicitor-General, 106

Solicitors, 51–2, 55–7, 66, 81, 174. *See also* Wardships
Somerset, County of, 62, 82, 125–6
—, Duke of. *See* Seymour, Edward
—, Edward, 4th Earl of Worcester, 53–4, 69
—, William, 3rd Earl of Worcester, 76
Southampton, Earl of. *See* Wriothesley
Southwell, Lady Elizabeth, 69
—, Sir Robert, 68–9
—, Sir Robert, Supervisor of Wards, 242
Soviet Union, 95
Spelman, Henry, 144
Spending of the Money of Robert Nowell, The, 225
Spousals, A Treatise of (Judge Swinburne), 136
Spousation, 135
Stafford, Edward, Lord, xxi, 151
—, Sir Edward, 39–41, 270
Stamford (Lincolnshire), 59
Stanhope, Anne, Lady, 152
—, Edward, 48, 126
—, John, 48
—, Sir John, 67, 74, 125–7, 267, 307
—, Thomas, 59
—, Dr., 309–10
Stanley, Ferdinando, 5th Earl of Derby, 53
—, William, 6th Earl of Derby, 55, 251
Stapleton, Mr., 151
Star Chamber, 33, 75, 143, 146, 187, 201, 237, 333–4
Starkey, Mr., 126
Staunford, William, 26–7, 98
Stephen, King, 146
Stileman, Mr., 61
Stone, Mr., the Queen's footman, 125–6
*Strickland, Thomas, 249, 259
Stubbes, Philip, 149
Style, William, 78
Subsidies, 335
Suffolk, County of, 61, 125–6, 162, 164, 234
—, Dukes of. *See* Brandon *and* Grey
—, Katherine, Duchess of, 178
Suitors. *See* Wardships and Intermediaries
*Sullyard, —, 126
Supremacy, Oath of, 173
Surrey, County of, 125–6
—, Earl of. *See* Howard, Philip
Survey, Feodary's. *See* Wards and Liveries
—, Manorial, 87
Surveyor of the King's Prerogative, 242–3
— of Idiots, 243
Sussex, County of, 126
—, Earl of *See* Radcliffe
Swinburne, Henry, 136, 153
Symons, John, 61

Talbot, Gilbert, Earl of Shrewsbury, 125, 195
*Talbot, —, 126
Tanning, Patent to dispense with statutes for, 41
†Taylor, Leonard, messenger, 229
—, Mr., 50
Tenths and Fifteenths, 335. *See also* Revenues.
Tenure, xvi–xxii, 20, 34, 138, 170–1; Burgage, 20; Copyhold, xx; by knight service in chief, xviii, xxii, 8, 10, 12, 14, 21–4, 26, 34–5, 42, 44, 46, 53, 97, 102, 104–5, 167, 170, 233, 290, 334; by knight service of a lord, Chapter 6; xviii, 21–4; by knight service of a ward, 44; socage, 20–4, 34, 53, 170, 334.
Theobalds (Hertfordshire), 61, 276–7, 283–4
Thomas, William, Clerk of the Council, 247
*Thornton, Agnes, 115
Thynne, Sir John, 203
Tichborne, Peter, 88
Tomson, Mr., lunatic, 127
†Tooke, Walter, feodary (later Auditor), 82, 227, 236
†—, William, Auditor, 227, 236
Townshend, Henry, 67
—, Henry, Commissioner for Concealed Wardships, 39, 86–7
†Trafford, William, feodary, 45
Treasurer, Lord, 207, 215, 226, 231, 241, 244, 246, 268, 277, 288, 333, 344
Tresham, Sir Thomas, 73
Trevor-Roper, Professor H. R., 349
*Tuckevill, —, 126
Tudor, Mary (later Duchess of Suffolk), 154–5, 251
Tunstall, Cuthbert, 101
Turvil, Sir William, 200
Tutors of Wards. *See* Wards
Twisden, Mr., 267
Tyler, Sir William, 147
Tyrell's Case, 29
*Tyrwhit, Robert, 52

Udale, John, 79
Underhill, John, 122–3
United States, 94–5
Universities, 40. *See also* Oxford *and* Cambridge
Use, the, 13, 29
Uses, Statutes of, 12, 13, 14, 15, 24

*Vaughan, John, 86, 115
*Vaughan, —, 127

*Vaux of Harrowden, Edward, Lord, 80
—, Lady, 73
*Verney, Edward, 121
Villiers, George, Duke of Buckingham, 106, 216
Vizakerly, Mr., of the Guard, 127
Vowell, John, 60

Waad, Sir William, 125, 346
Wakering, Gilbert, 61
Wales, 42, 76, 104, 112
—, Marches of, 104
—, Council in Marches of, 73, 122, 179, 268
*Walgrave, —, 128
Walker, Thomas, 143
Walpole, Sir Robert, 273
Walrond, Robert, 76
Walsingham, Sir Francis, 51–2, 273
Walter, William, 39, 86–7
Walton (Lancashire), 34
Wannesford, Christopher, lunatic, 72
Ward, 'Sir' John, 143
Ward holding (in Scotland), 104
Wards, Administration before 1540, 9, 15, 16, 19, 213, 226–7, 241–3; care of, 25–7, 113 ff., 127–9, 251–9, 260; care of property of, 118, 121, 269; female, 84, 86, 137, 164; education of, 25–7, 116 ff., 127, 143–4, 255–9; tutors of, 118–9, 121–2, 256; seizure of, 25, 36, 99, 122, 143. See also Guardians and Exhibitions
Wards and Liveries, Court of:
Establishment of, 9, 12, 14, 15, 17, 120, 222; at Oxford, 329
Seal of, 93
Site of, 229
Records of, 9, 62, 77–8, 111, 130, 164, 166, 193, 197–8, 201–3, 229, 245, 248–50, 261, 341–2
Procedure of, 9, 70, 83 ff., 140, 222
Relations with juries, 53–4, 55, 75–6
Revenues. See Feudalism, Fiscal
Lawsuits in, 51–2, 55–7, 74, 116, 130–3, 141, 166–8, 192–7, 260, 283, 290, 314
Debts to, 9, 179, 253, 261, 291
Fees and expenses, 78–83, 91, 94, 169–70, 175, 178, 186, 189–92, 197, 205–6, 213, 228, 238–9, 261, 265–6, 268–70, 310–11, 347
Inefficiency of, 205–6, 227
Criticism of, 214, 245, 314–5, 321. See also Wardship, Abuses of
Defence of, 331–4

Reform of, 92, 124, 282, 288, 290, 298–9, 310–11
Proposals to abolish, 211–4, 245, 315–24
Abolition of, 107, 329–34, 350–2
Officers of, Chapter 11; 50, 57, 81–2, 90, 92–4, 169–79, 188, 197–9, 206, 209, 238–9, 310–11, 343–5, 348
Master of, Chapters 12 and 13; 16, 26, 28–9, 36, 69, 71–2, 83–90, 92–4, 117, 119, 124, 142, 171, 189, 191, 198, 212, 238, 297–8, 304. See also Cecil, Englefield, and Paulet
Mastership, Vacancy, Chapter 14; 63, 78, 79, 118
Surveyor of Liveries, 115, 174–5, 210–11, 222–4, 238, 267, 347. See also Hynde, Keilway, Kingsmill, Neville, Pepper, Seckford
Attorney, 16, 25, 27, 47, 48, 81, 92–3, 130–3, 141, 194, 198, 210, 224–6, 238, 267, 279. See also Bacon, Goodrich, Hesketh, Kingsmill, Ley, Morrice, Nowell, Onslow, Polsted, Sewster, Wilbraham, and Winthrop
Receiver-General, 28, 47, 88–9, 93–4, 115–7, 171, 199–209, 211, 226–7, 236, 238, 267, 280, 282, 339–40
Receiver-General's Accounts, 27–8, 198–203, 228, 261–2, 339–40, 344–5. See also Battisforde, Beaumont, Damsell, Fleetwood, Goring, Lee
Auditor, 47, 94, 171, 198, 227–8, 238. See also Curle, Perient, and Tooke
Clerk, 39, 45, 47–9, 66, 77, 82, 91–4, 104, 130, 190–1, 210, 228–9, 239, 260, 343. See also Anton, Bosseville, and Hare
Clerk of Liveries, 92, 170–1, 173–5, 223, 228, 238. See also Cooke and Paulet
Usher, 117–8, 229, 238
Messenger, 229, 238
Feodary, 9, 34, 42, 44–50, 53, 62, 68, 81, 83–5, 89, 93, 104, 116, 121, 186, 188–91, 206–10, 222, 231–9, 237–8, 268, 291–2, 298, 312, 349
Feodary's Survey, 84–5, 87, 121, 170–2, 233, 312
Deputy Feodary, 210
Wardship, Abuses of, 25–6, 66, 74–5, 80, 91, 96, 101, 103, 120–1, 129, 134, 149, 175, 187, 190–1, 213–4, 225, 282, 329–30. See also Corruption and Wards and Liveries, Criticism

Wardship, Decline of royal rights of, 21, 23, 28, 35; exemption from, 9; extension of rights of, 4–17; prerogative, 6, 97–102; of Land, 3, 14, 25, 39, 78, 82, 84–5, 87–9, 93–4, 98, 123–4, 138, 165, 235, 247–8, 269, 274, 291, 344

Wardships, Applications for, Chapter 4; 62–3, 65, 80, 247. See also Wardships, Grants of; cancellation of, 90; competition for, 47, 60, 63, 65, 71, 76–80, 91, 123, 247, 274, 300–4; concealed, 7, 9, 35–41, 45, 61, 105, 235, 262, 298, 301; disputed, 104–5, 122; grants of, Chapter 5; 5, 26, 57, 61, 65, 70, 80–1, 111–2, 115, 124–7, 133, 168, 181, 213, 250, 261–3, 269; price of, 39, 83–7, 90, 94, 105, 114, 124, 127, 260, 274–6, 298, 311–4, 349–51; re-sale, 124, 128, 274–5, 301; unsold, 91, 250

Warwick, Countess of, 146. See also Dudley, Anne

—, Earl of. See Dudley

Warwickshire, 236

★Washburn, —, 125

Webber, Mr., of the Privy Kitchen, 126

Weddean (Denbighshire), 49

Wells, Dean of, 96, 101

Wentworth, Anne, Lady, 65, 71, 292

West, Thomas, Lord de la Ware, 126

★West, —, 126

Westby, Bartholomew, 242

★Westby, —, 126

Westminster, Palace of, 229, 242

Weston, Richard, Master of Wards, 242–3

Whalley, Richard, 203

★Wharton, Philip, Lord, 249

White, Anne, 65

★White, —, alias Hole, —, 126

Whitgift, John, 123

Whyte, John, 61

Wiatt, Captain, 66

Wigan (Lancashire), 34

†Wilbraham, Thomas, Attorney, 225

Wilbram, Mr., 49

Wildgoose, Mr., 195

Wilkins, George, xiii, 149

★Wilkinson, —, 126

Williams, George, 248

Willoughby, John, 351

Willoughby de Eresbie. See Bertie

Willoughby of Parham, Charles, Lord, 62–3

Wills, 55–6, 117, 128, 265

—, Statute of, 12, 14, 116

†Willson, Marmaduke, feodary, 210

Wilson, Thomas, 263

Wiltshire, 43, 82, 125

Winchester, Bishop of, 66, 132, 309

—, City of, 131–3

—, College, 130–2

★Winstanley, Humphrey, 152

†Winthrop, John, Attorney, 226

Wolley, Sir John, 125, 346

Wolsey, Thomas, Cardinal, 127, 147, 284

Woodford, James, 38

★Woodward, —, 127

Woolton, Earl of. See Marquis

Worcester, Earls of. See Somerset

Worcestershire, 100, 125–6

Worsley, Alice, 152

Wotton, Sir Edward (later Lord), 43, 267

Wray, Sir Christopher, 51–2, 106

Wriothesley, Henry, 2nd Earl of Southampton, 117

★—, Henry, 3rd Earl of Southampton, 117, 142, 249, 251, 253, 259

—, Mary, Countess of Southampton, 297

Wroth, Sir Robert, 66

—, Sir Thomas, 66, 115, 128

Wyne, James, 74

Wynne, Mr., gentleman-harbinger, 127

★Wynne, —, 127

Yarmouth (Norfolk), 167

York, Archbishop of, 127–8

— Herald, 140

Yorkshire, 19, 48, 100, 115, 125–7, 135, 210

★Zouche, Edward, Lord La, 73–4, 249, 259